SCIPIO AEMILIANUS

SCIPIO AEMILIANUS

BY

A. E. ASTIN

OXFORD
AT THE CLARENDON PRESS

OXFORD

UNIVERSITY PRESS

Great Clarendon Street, Oxford OX2 6DP

Oxford University Press is a department of the University of Oxford.
It furthers the University's objective of excellence in research, scholarship,
and education by publishing worldwide in

Oxford New York

Auckland Bangkok Buenos Aires Cape Town Chennai
Dar es Salaam Delhi Hong Kong Istanbul Karachi Kolkata
Kuala Lumpur Madrid Melbourne Mexico City Mumbai Nairobi
São Paulo Shanghai Singapore Taipei Tokyo Toronto

and an associated company in Berlin

Oxford is a registered trade mark of Oxford University Press
in the UK and in certain other countries

Published in the United States
by Oxford University Press Inc., New York

© Oxford University Press 1967

British Library Cataloguing in Publication Data

Data available

ISBN 0-19-814257-9

1 3 5 7 9 10 8 6 4 2

Printed in Great Britain
on acid-free paper by
Biddles Ltd.,
Guildford and King's Lynn

TO MY WIFE

PREFACE

THE name of P. Cornelius Scipio Aemilianus, the younger Africanus, is familiar to all who have studied Republican Rome. His military achievements and his cultural interests ensure him a place in numerous writings, both general and specialized. Brief assessments of him are frequent. Yet there have been surprisingly few studies of his career as a whole or of his significance in Roman political life. Undoubtedly the main reason for this comparative neglect is the fragmentary and disjointed nature of the surviving sources, which leave serious gaps in our knowledge and impose considerable, and often frustrating, restrictions upon the kind of study which can be attempted. These peculiarities, which are examined in Chapter I, are such that it might seem unwise to venture upon a coherent account at all; yet the attempt is worth making, partly because Scipio himself was a person of unusual importance, partly because his career leads up to the great crisis of 133 B.C., the political background of which merits more attention than it often receives. The limitations of the evidence have always to be recognized; some pressing questions just cannot be answered; nevertheless enough can be discerned to establish something of the characteristics of Scipio as a man and as a political personality, and also something of the developments and trends in political life which led up to the climactic events of 133 B.C.

The special character of the source material has been responsible also for a kaleidoscopic variety of judgements upon Scipio's career. The way has lain open both for legitimate differences of interpretation and for insecurely based speculation. Consequently he has seemed many things to many men: a noble and chivalrous hero; a quasi-autocrat who, but for his own reluctance, could have been a Princeps a century before Augustus; something of a 'healthy hedonist', delighting in war, though not in its cruelties, lacking the taste and the patience for the game of politics; a saddened pessimist, aware of the ills of the state but seeing no possible cure; an uncritical exponent of aggressive imperialism; a humane advocate of a paternalist imperialism, activated by a sense of responsibility for the governed; a reluctant conqueror, convinced that Rome's outrageous behaviour would bring retribution, or that the empire had already outgrown the capacity of Rome's institutions; a political moderate, trying to strike the balance between entrenched conservatives and headstrong reformers; an anxious guardian of the mixed constitution; or a statesman whose intense preoccupation with Polybius' theory of the central importance of that constitutional balance blinded him to an evident need for reform and for monarchical government.

This book is concerned primarily with Scipio's political career. There is no intention to minimize his merits as a general, or the interest of his campaigns (which, being relatively well recorded, have been examined at length in several distinguished studies), or the intimate interconnexion of the political and military elements in the Roman state. But the principal purpose of the book is to offer a new assessment of Scipio as a political figure, in relation both to contemporary politics and to the more general political development of the Roman Republic.

As far as possible I have relegated to footnotes and appendixes those discussions which are predominantly technical or negative in character; and the bulk of the appendixes is yet further increased by the collection of the *dicta* attributed to Scipio. This collection is included partly to eliminate much repetition in footnotes, partly to provide a convenient body of substantiating evidence, but also in the hope that it will prove a useful tool for the researches of others. The book was effectively completed by the early summer of 1965. I have included in the bibliography, and occasionally mentioned in footnotes, a small number of articles which became available to me in the later months of 1965, but these are essentially addenda; the book was not written in the light of them.

In my work on this subject I have experienced great kindness from many quarters, and the time has come to express my gratitude: to Professor Sir Ronald Syme, for his initial suggestion and his unfailing encouragement; to Professor H. H. Scullard and Professor F. W. Walbank, for helpful discussion and for allowing me to see material which at the time was unpublished; to Professor Kathleen Atkinson and many other friends, in Belfast and elsewhere, for their interest and assistance over the years, and in particular to Dr. Mary Small-wood, Dr. Malcolm Errington, and Dr. David Gooding, who shared the proof-reading and whose diligence led them to suggest many valuable improvements; to the Institute for Advanced Study at Princeton, for its generous hospitality and the use of its magnificent facilities; to The Queen's University, for granting me leave to go to Princeton; and to the Clarendon Press, for its patience, its guidance, its careful efficiency, and especially for the honour it is doing me by publishing this book. Finally, although I have disagreed with a number of eminent scholars, I trust that there is nothing in the manner or content of my arguments to give offence: it will be apparent to all who are acquainted with the field that I am deeply in their debt.

A. E. A.

The Queen's University, Belfast
May 1966

CONTENTS

ABBREVIATIONS

TITLES of periodicals are abbreviated in accordance with the system used in *L'Année Philologique*. Some very short abbreviations for a few standard works of reference are listed below. All other abbreviations are such that the full titles can be identified without difficulty in the Bibliography. In references a single 'f.' is used to indicate either one or several following pages or sections (e.g. pp. 7 f.).

CAH   *Cambridge Ancient History*.

CIL   *Corpus Inscriptionum Latinarum*.

Excerpta *Excerpta historica iussu Imp. Constantini Porphyrogeniti confecta* i–iv, ed. C. de Boor, T. Büttner-Wobst, U. P. Boissevain. Berlin, 1903–10.

HRR   H. W. G. Peter, *Historicorum Romanorum Reliquiae* i². Leipzig, 1914.

ILS   H. Dessau, *Inscriptiones Latinae Selectae*, 3 vols. Berlin, 1892–1916.

MRR   T. R. S. Broughton, *The Magistrates of the Roman Republic*, 2 vols. and suppl. New York, 1951–60.

ORF²   H. Malcovati, *Oratorum Romanorum Fragmenta²*. Turin, 1955.

RE   Pauly–Wissowa–Kroll, *Real-Encyclopädie der classischen Altertums-wissenschaft*.

I

THE SOURCES

1. General Characteristics

THE source material for the study of Scipio Aemilianus and of Roman politics in the years 153 to 129 B.C. has certain marked characteristics, which have an important bearing on the kind of history which it is possible to write. It is convenient to begin by summarizing these characteristics.

(i) There once existed a considerable number of contemporary accounts, none of which has survived in more than a limited number of fragments and most of which have disappeared almost entirely.[1]

(ii) There was also a significant volume of other published material, available to writers later in antiquity but again very largely lost to us.[2]

(iii) Although the surviving literature of subsequent generations preserves much information about this period, extended narratives are concerned only with the Punic and Spanish wars (and thus only incidentally with related political matters) or with the tribunate of Tiberius Gracchus in 133. Other narratives survive only in fragments or in brief epitomes.[3]

---

[1] Influential contemporary historians included Polybius, Cato, L. Cassius Hemina, C. Acilius, Cn. Gellius, L. Calpurnius Piso, C. Fannius, P. Rutilius Rufus, and Sempronius Asellio. Evidence assembled in HRR i².

[2] A substantial number of speeches were published, concerning which see p. 7 and esp n. 2. The satires of Lucilius may have been of some assistance to later writers. Copies of senatus consulta, laws, and other state documents were preserved and to some extent were available for consultation, though evidently the filing system was highly unsatisfactory (Cic. De Leg. 3. 46); on the other hand Cicero knew of a book containing the senatus consulta of 146 (Ad Att. 13. 33. 3) and presumably similar books existed for other years. Publication of the annales maximi in eighty books by P. Mucius Scaevola made available at least a firm factual outline of formal and notable events. Cf. Walsh, Livy, pp. 110 f.

[3] The more important narratives are discussed later in this chapter. At least two biographies of Scipio were composed in antiquity, one by Plutarch (Ti. Grac. 21. 9; C. Grac. 10. 5), the other, mentioned in Gell. 3. 4. 1, possibly by Hyginus: Münzer, RE, s.v. Cornelius, no. 335, col. 1439.

(iv) The remaining material tends to be anecdotal in character, in many instances reporting sayings or witticisms (*dicta*). Thus many incidents, though interesting and revealing, are given without clear indications of context or sometimes even of chronology.

(v) There are enormous contrasts in the amount known about the political personalities of the period. To a limited extent this may reflect relative importance: thus, Scipio Aemilianus, mentioned in well over three hundred and fifty separate passages, far more than any other individual, was certainly the most important single figure; but it is not a true reflection of the importance of Scipio's main rival, Appius Claudius Pulcher, censor and Princeps Senatus, that he is mentioned in only about thirty separate passages; and some men even of consular rank are scarcely known at all.

The essence of all this is that much material is available, yet it is not particularly well suited to the composition of a coherent narrative account either of Scipio's career or of Roman politics. Our picture is essentially episodic: about some years and some episodes there is much to be said, but in between are extensive blanks, and on occasion it is not possible to determine the relative chronology of episodes; the talents and personalities of some men can be at least dimly discerned and to some extent can be linked with their political activities, but in other cases little or nothing can be traced; something can be made out of the political groupings of the period, yet the associations of not a few important personalities remain obscure; some political clashes are essentially personal, others can be seen to involve issues of policy and principle, while in other cases the relative importance of these elements can only be guessed. In such circumstances it might seem unwise to attempt a coherent account; yet the attempt has seemed worth making, for reasons set out in the Preface to this book. As is there stated, provided always that the limitations of the evidence are borne in mind, it is possible to discern enough to recognize something of the characteristics of Scipio as a man and as a political personality, and above all something of the developments and trends in political struggles and political methods which were leading up to the climactic events of 133 B.C.

2. Individual Sources

The remainder of this chapter is devoted to a more detailed survey of the nature and limitations of the main sources. The less specialized reader may prefer to pass over this section.

The only contemporary writer whose work has been preserved in any quantity at all is the Greek Polybius, whose universal history extended to 146 B.C.[1] The continuous text of the later part of the work is lost, but there is a substantial number of fragments. Polybius was one of the Achaean leaders deported to Italy in 167, after the defeat of Perseus of Macedon by L. Aemilius Paullus, and not released until 150; but he fared better than many of his companions. At an early stage he struck up a friendship with Paullus' sons, who arranged that he should be detained in Rome itself, and his friendship with the younger son, Scipio Aemilianus, became particularly intimate. Hence he is an unusually valuable source, both because of his personal knowledge of Scipio and because of his exceptional opportunities for gathering information about Roman affairs, especially in the later years, when Scipio and other acquaintances were becoming more deeply involved in public life. Furthermore, Polybius almost certainly went to Spain with Scipio when he served under L. Licinius Lucullus in 151–150, and quite certainly was present in Scipio's entourage during the siege of Carthage; thus, since he also played a part in the settlement of Achaea after the anti-Roman movement of 146, personal involvement gave him exceptional opportunities to inform himself about many of the events with which he concluded his history. Great though his authority is, however, there is need of caution. Polybius was not only a friend of Scipio and his family, but a client and a fervent admirer. There can be little doubt that at times prejudice overcame impartiality and in particular that he was much inclined to highlight Scipio's activities and to put the best possible construction upon them.[2] The clearest and entirely sufficient demonstration that Polybius can be partisan is his assertion that fear and cowardice were patently the motives behind

---

[1] On Polybius' career and his value as a source see esp. Walbank, *Commentary on Polybius*, i, pp. 1 f. and 26 f.; Ziegler, *RE*, s.v. *Polybios*, no. 1. Cic. *Ad Fam.* 5. 12. 2 shows that he wrote also a separate monograph on the Numantine war, but this is lost entirely.

[2] Cf. Polyb. 31. 30 and 36. 8. 6.

M. Claudius Marcellus' recommendations for peace with the Celtiberians in 152. The absurdity of the accusation is evident from a
glance at the career of Marcellus, one of the ablest generals of the
day, twice a *triumphator*, and in 152 holding his third consulship; but
Scipio was among the many who disapproved of Marcellus' conciliatory policy, so Polybius has reproduced what was doubtless
a standard item of political polemic.[1]

The main narratives which have survived are those of another
Greek writer, Appian, who in the second century A.D. wrote his
accounts of Rome's wars of conquest, arranging them on an ethno-
graphic, or geographic, basis.[2] Leaving aside for separate comment
the problem of the first book of the *Civil Wars* and its relation to
Plutarch's life of Tiberius Gracchus,[3] two of Appian's works are
important for the present subject: the latter part of the *Iberica* and the
latter part of the *Libyca*.

From about 154 to 133 Rome was engaged almost continuously in
warfare in Spain. For these wars Appian is the main source of information. Broadly speaking his survey seems to be reliable and
chronologically accurate, though allowance has to be made for the
partisan estimates of the achievements of Roman commanders which
at times influenced his sources, and also for the comparative brevity
of many parts of his narrative. Significant here is the quite disproportionate amount of space devoted to the campaigns in which Scipio
Aemilianus participated, and particularly to his final campaign against
Numantia in 134–133, which occupies seventeen chapters out of
a total of fifty-seven. It is virtually certain that Appian's account is
authentic and follows closely the work of the contemporary writers
from whom it is ultimately, though not immediately, derived; but
the attempt to identify the sources is largely futile. It is possible, but
by no means certain, that Polybius is one of the influences behind the
version of events to 146; and the very well-informed account of
Scipio's campaign and siege in 134–133 may go back to Rutilius
Rufus, who participated and whose autobiography is mentioned by
Appian.[4]

---

[1] Polyb. 35. 3. 4; 35. 4. 3 and 8; Simon, *Roms Kriege*, p. 39 n. 45.
[2] Schwartz, *RE*, s.v. *Appianus*, no. 2.   [3] Appendix XI.
[4] *Iber.* 88; cf. Cic. *Rep.* 1. 17; Rut. Rufus, fgt. 13. But Rutilius is not the only possibility:
Sempronius Asellio was there also (Gell. 2. 13. 3; cf. 13. 3. 6 = Asell. fgt. 5), and Polybius

With the *Libyca* we are on firmer ground, for there is no doubt that Appian's account of the Third Punic War is very largely derived from and very close to Polybius—so close indeed that it has been argued that Appian used Polybius directly. There are objections to this, and an intermediate source, probably in Latin, must be postulated; but the fact remains that in essence Appian's account is an abbreviated version of that given by Polybius.[1]

A third Greek writer deserving of special mention is Plutarch, who wrote a generation or so before Appian. His *Lives* included a biography of Scipio, unhappily now lost.[2] However, besides the special relevance of the biography of Tiberius Gracchus, several of the other *Lives* have informative passages, and there are a number of others in the *Moralia*. Most important of all is the collection of *Sayings*, or *Apophthegmata*, which includes an exceptionally large number of sayings of Scipio—more than of any other Roman save Cato. The authenticity of the *Apophthegmata* has been much disputed, in the sense that the collection was probably not made by Plutarch himself and, though very similar to a collection from which he drew anecdotes for his *Lives* and other works, it is perhaps not the actual collection which he used;[3] but this scarcely affects its value as a source. Sufficient of the sayings themselves are supported by other testimony or carry circumstantial confirmatory detail to justify regarding the whole collection as generally reliable.

Two other Greeks may be mentioned briefly. A number of fragments survive from the relevant books of the world history of

wrote a monograph on the Numantine war (Cic. *Ad Fam.* 5. 12. 2). In an earlier passage, *Iber.* 67, Appian mentions Fannius the son-in-law of Laelius. One of the two C. Fannii active in this period wrote a history, but in view of the later confusion between the two men there is uncertainty not only about which of them was the historian (not necessarily the son-in-law of Laelius) but also about which was believed by Appian or his source to be the historian (p. 84). Thus Fannius the historian *may* have been one of the sources behind Appian, but equally the mention of Laelius' son-in-law may simply be a passing reference derived from some other writer fairly closely linked with Scipio and his associates—for example Rutilius Rufus.

[1] Gsell, *Hist. anc.* iii, pp. 336 f., argues for direct use of Polybius. Comparison of Appian with the relevant Polybian fragments, esp. 36. 6–8, establishes the close link but shows sufficient small differences, notably of vocabulary, to require the intermediate source posited by Schwartz, *RE*, s.v. *Appianus*, no. 2, col. 220, and Kahrstedt, *Gesch. der Karthager*, pp. 620 and 624 f.

[2] Plut. *Ti. Grac.* 21. 9; *C. Grac.* 10. 5.

[3] Ziegler, *RE*, s.v. *Plutarchos*, no. 2, cols. 863 f.

Diodorus Siculus, who was writing in the time of Caesar and Augustus. Down to 146 he relied heavily on Polybius, whom he used directly; thereafter his main source was Polybius' continuator, the competent Poseidonius of Apamea.[1] Thus Diodorus' work was probably more satisfactory for this period than for some others. However, the fragments are few in number and therefore only of occasional assistance, though they are the chief evidence about the Sicilian slave rebellion of the 130's. Even fewer fragments are preserved of this part of Dio Cassius' history, though we have also the very brief history of the Byzantine Zonaras which is based on Dio's work. It seems probable that Dio was drawing mainly on the work of Latin historians, and it is unlikely that he made any use of contemporary sources.[2] Nevertheless, despite the paucity of the remains and despite the lateness of the work, several of the fragments preserve interesting material.

Among the Latin sources a key figure is Livy, for although his account of these years is lost the two extant epitomes are of fundamental importance in establishing the chronology of events. Livy's methods of work are well known: he is unlikely to have made much use of contemporary writers but rather relied on those of one or two generations later.[3] On the other hand, the contemporary sources were extensive, so that a considerable volume of material was passed on to Livy.[4] Of the two epitomes, the so-called *Periochae*, though selective and brief, has rather more extended notices but is sometimes chronologically imprecise; the *Oxyrhynchus Epitome* has very brief notices, its text is poor and much mutilated by damage to the papyrus, and it covers only the years 150–137 (effectively only 149–138), but nevertheless it has the great merit of indicating clearly the year under which Livy recorded each item.[5] In addition, various other works are derived from Livy, the most important being the *Historiae adversum Paganos* of Orosius (who for these years was using an epitome of Livy more detailed than those which have survived)

---

[1] Schwartz, *RE*, s.v. *Diodorus*, no. 38, cols. 689 f.

[2] Schwartz, *RE*, s.v. *Cassius*, no. 40, cols. 1696 f.   [3] Walsh, *Livy*, esp. chs. v and vi.

[4] Books 48–58, treating the years 153–133, average slightly under two years per book; even Books 51–55, treating 147–137, average only just over two years per book.

[5] In this book the two epitomes are referred to as 'Livy, *Epit.*' and 'Livy, *Ox. Epit.*' respectively.

and to a lesser extent the biographical notices in the *De Viris Illustribus*, attributed to Aurelius Victor; the *Liber Prodigiorum* of Obsequens is occasionally useful; Eutropius' extremely brief history, though accurate, has little to add and is so little concerned with internal affairs that it fails to mention the Gracchi; and the *Epitome Bellorum* of Florus suffers from inaccuracy and confusion, exacerbated by the rhetorical tone of the writing.

A second Latin writer whose extant works supply a very great quantity of information is Cicero, whose letters, speeches, and rhetorical and philosophical treatises contain numerous references to events and personalities of the period. The reasons for this are various: partly the volume of suitable, especially anecdotal, material available; partly that this was the first period in which large numbers of speeches had been published and thus were available for Cicero to study; partly that Cicero saw in Scipio Aemilianus in particular the great man of public affairs, the political giant, who combined with success in action that enjoyment of learning which Cicero valued so highly. Moreover, Scipio seemed to Cicero to contrast markedly with the successful generals of his own day: seemingly content with a place of honour and leadership, he did not attempt a *dominatio*; in his courage, his *fides*, and his temperate personal life he could be seen as an exemplar of the traditional Roman virtues; and in the last years of his life he took the lead in the struggle against the 'popular' Gracchans. This tendency to idealize Scipio and his times necessitates a cautious attitude to Cicero's generalizations and moral judgements, but it does not seriously vitiate his evidence in other respects. Cicero had access to—and had read a great part of—many contemporary historical accounts,[1] plus a large selection of published speeches of the period,[2] plus later historical

---

[1] He knew the works of at least the following: Polybius, *Rep.* 2. 27, 4. 3, *De Off.* 3. 113, *Ad Att.* 13. 30. 2, *Ad Fam.* 5. 12. 2; Cato, *Pro Planc.* 66, *Brut.* 66, 75, 80, 89, *Rep.* 1. 27, etc.; C. Acilius, *De Off.* 3. 115; Cn. Gellius, *De Divin.* 1. 55; Piso, *Brut.* 106, *De Leg.* 1. 6, *Ad Fam.* 9. 22. 2; C. Fannius, *Brut.* 81, 101, 299, *De Orat.* 2. 270, *Acad.* 2. 15, *Tusc.* 4. 40, *De Leg.* 1. 6, and, for Brutus' epitome, *Ad Att.* 12. 5b; Asellio, *De Leg.* 1. 6.

[2] Badian, *JRS* 46 (1956), p. 219, comments that 'few speeches survived in Cicero's day and fewer were read'; but the word 'few' is relative. Cicero certainly indicates or implies that the speeches of many orators had not survived or had not even been committed to writing (e.g. *Brutus*, 91 f., 108), but the evidence of the *Brutus* leaves no doubt that he had a considerable quantity of material from the hands of many men of the period: e.g. (references

writings,[1] plus the *annales maximi*,[2] plus at least some contemporary public documents;[3] in addition he could and did seek the expert advice of Atticus.[4] The volume of reliable material available to him was therefore substantial; his use of it may be evaluated best by distinguishing between the various categories of his writings.

(i) The letters are relatively unimportant, though a few passages in which Cicero asks Atticus for information or comments upon information are very valuable.

(ii) References in the speeches to events and personalities need to be treated with caution. In the first place, although Cicero had read much, although accurate information could be obtained, and although for other purposes Cicero certainly went to some trouble to check his memory and to secure accurate details, nevertheless in the ancient book-roll it was not always easy to look up details, and his numerous appeals to Atticus for information show that he did not always have immediately available the books he needed for this purpose.[5] Therefore there is a very real possibility that in composing his speeches Cicero often did not trouble to check the accuracy of his historical allusions and illustrations. Moreover, the speeches are usually polemical and the historical allusions almost invariably have a polemical purpose; at the least this could have encouraged negligence in checking; sometimes there may be deliberate distortion.[6] Thus, if taken literally, Cicero twice seems to date Scipio Aemilianus' prosecution of L. Aurelius Cotta after the former's second consulship in 134, whereas it actually occurred in 138, and, seen in

---

to the *Brutus*) Q. Metellus Macedonicus, 81; Ser. Sulpicius Galba, 82, 91 f., 295; C. Laelius, 82, 94, 295; P. Scipio Aemilianus, 82, 295; L. Scribonius Libo, 90; L. Mummius, Sp. Mummius, Sp. Postumius Albinus, L. Aurelius Orestes, C. Aurelius Orestes, 94; M. Aemilius Lepidus Porcina, 95, 295; Tiberius Gracchus and C. Papirius Carbo, 104; M. Fulvius Flaccus, 108; not to mention the great Cato, more than a hundred and fifty of whose speeches were available, 65, 294.

[1] e.g. *De Leg.* 1. 7 shows Cicero knew the work of C. Licinius Macer and also that of a certain Clodius, possibly Q. Claudius Quadrigarius. The Libo of *Ad Att.* 13. 30. 2 and 32. 3 is probably Cicero's contemporary: *HRR* i², p. ccclxxvi.

[2] *De Orat.* 2. 52.

[3] *Ad Att.* 13. 33. 3.   [4] p. 9 n. 3 and n. 4.

[5] Apt examples are in *Ad Att.* 12. 5b.; 13. 30. 2; 16. 13b. 2. In these Cicero asks Atticus to give details or confirm recollections of points about which he, Cicero, has heard or read previously. Cf. also 4. 14. 1, where he seeks access to Atticus' books in the latter's absence.

[6] For a discussion of Cicero's use of historical examples see Rambaud, *Cicéron et l'histoire romaine*, pp. 25 f., and for his misuse of them esp. pp. 46 f.

its context, Cicero's error is readily explicable by the factors just outlined.[1]

(iii) Among the *philosophica* three are in a category by themselves: the dialogues *De Republica* and *Cato Maior* (or *De Senectute*), because in these Scipio is cast as one of the leading interlocutors, and the *Laelius* (or *De Amicitia*), which not only has Scipio's closest friend as its leading character but is represented as having occurred just after Scipio's death. The remaining *philosophica* contain a scatter of passing references and anecdotes of widely varying importance, the general authenticity of which there is no reason to question, even though some allowance must be made for Cicero's readiness to attribute every virtue to the great figures of the age, and especially to Scipio and Laelius. Much the same can be said of the three dialogues set in the 'Scipionic' period; but in addition there is the question of the extent to which Cicero has drawn an authentic picture—apart, that is, from the tendency to idealize his characters. In the first place, it is quite improper to suppose that the philosophical views put into the mouths of the characters in any way represent views actually held by Scipio, Laelius, and the rest. Cicero was concerned to argue and present his own views, and his readers would no more regard this as a historical presentation of Scipio's opinions than they would consider Plato's *Republic* a faithful record of the teaching of Socrates. The point is reinforced by the fact that at one stage Cicero planned to cast himself and his brother as the main characters in the *De Republica*.[2] All that can be inferred, and it is of little value, is that Cicero is unlikely to have attributed to his characters opinions violently and notoriously in contradiction to those held by the persons themselves.[3] On the other hand the background detail used in the dialogues is likely to be reliable, for Cicero's letters show him to have taken a good deal of trouble over even quite minor points.[4] Finally, it has

---

[1] *Pro Mur.* 58; *Div. in Caec.* 69 (and from the latter Ps.-Ascon., p. 204 Stangl). The true date is given in Livy, *Ox. Epit.* 55.   [2] *Ad Quint. Frat.* 3. 5. 1 f.

[3] Some concern about this point is shown in *Rep.* 3. 8 and in his difficulties with the characters of the *Academica*: see esp. *Ad Att.* 13. 13. 1; 13. 19. 5; 13. 32. 3; Reid, edition of *Academica* (London, 1885), pp. 32 f. But the latter case also illustrates the possible licence.

[4] *Ad Quint. Frat.* 3. 5. 1 f. and *Ad Att.* 4. 16. 2 f. show Cicero consciously avoiding anachronism and interested in the appropriateness of his setting. Inquiries and discussion in *Ad Att.* 12. 5b; 12. 20. 2; 12. 22. 2; 12. 23. 2; 12. 24. 2; 13. 4. 1; 13. 5. 1; 13. 6a; 13. 30. 2; 13. 32. 3; 13. 33. 3. Cf. also refs. in previous note and p. 8 n. 5.

to be asked whether Cicero's representation of persons engaged in amicable discussion is in any way evidence of the actual relationship between those persons in real life. Broadly speaking this does seem to be so. In several instances there is independent evidence to attest a friendly or close relationship; and while it is true that in some cases Cicero could have exaggerated the degree of intimacy, and true also that a social relationship may not necessarily indicate frequent and close political association, the probability is that he always had some justification for depicting a social relationship, and equally that such a relationship in practice often was accompanied by political co-operation; and above all it seems highly improbable that he would have represented in this way men who were known to have been politically or personally at loggerheads.

Yet, when all is said, even these dialogues are comparatively unimportant as evidence for Scipio and his contemporaries. They provide a few points of great value, but much of the detail they contain is known also from other sources. The most valuable part of Cicero's evidence lies elsewhere.

(iv) The most valuable portion is in fact the *rhetorica*, and especially the *Brutus* and the *De Oratore*. It is most fortunate that the middle and later years of the second century provided Cicero with so much material of interest to him in a field where he himself was an expert, was concerned to be accurate, and had no motive for misrepresentation. In consequence we are given in great measure helpful personal details, evidently careful and well-founded assessments of the talents of orators, and illustrative quotations and anecdotes. Without this evidence our knowledge of many personalities would be drastically curtailed.

Another Latin writer who merits special mention is Valerius Maximus, in no sense a historian but the author of a large compilation of anecdotal material.[1] His books of 'memorable deeds and sayings', arranged under headings such as *de religione, de disciplina militari, de fortitudine, de severitate*, often with a strong moralizing tendency, were an attempt to provide a handbook of anecdotal examples to save others, presumably chiefly orators, the labour of searching for them. His purpose and his manner of work combine to make him

[1] Helm, *RE*, s.v. *Valerius*, no. 239.

careless and unreliable in some respects. He is guilty of chronological inaccuracies, of occasional confusion of identity, and of other errors arising from failure of memory when he reached the stage of working with excerpts divorced from their context. Above all he was inclined to present his examples in a dramatic and rhetorical manner, consequently at times expanding and distorting his material. Yet, despite these drawbacks, he remains a useful source. If the attempt to identify the particular authors from whom he took his examples must remain largely futile, nevertheless, writing in the reign of Tiberius, he had access to and evidently worked from a great volume of material, including works by Cicero and Varro. Sometimes he records events or sayings unattested elsewhere; and in other cases some of the useful circumstantial details which he adds can scarcely be the product of rhetorical embellishment.

Aulus Gellius, writing more than a century later than Valerius Maximus, contrasts with him in many ways, yet also typifies the fragmentary nature of the evidence. His *Noctes Atticae* is a collection of miscellaneous information on a great variety of topics; but he was both well-read and careful, so that his work is a valuable quarry for the modern scholar and is particularly productive of fragments of speeches.

Many other writers, both Greek and Roman, supply occasional information about Scipio or his contemporaries, but there would be little profit in listing and discussing them one by one. Enough has been said to indicate the character of the main literary sources and the general attitude towards them adopted in this book.[1] The non-literary sources are comparatively unimportant, except for the consular *fasti*, which can be reconstructed completely from the remains of the Capitoline and other epigraphic *fasti*, plus such lists as that of Cassiodorus. Filiations, however, are not always preserved. A few other inscriptions are helpful, but the numismatic evidence is of little value, though there are indications that it might be useful if the series and issues of this period could be dated with greater precision. The contributions of archaeology are mainly in the military sphere, with which this book is not primarily concerned.

---

[1] Plutarch's life of Tiberius Gracchus and the early section of Appian, *B.C.* 1 are considered in Appendix XI.

II

P. CORNELIUS SCIPIO AEMILIANUS

PUBLIUS CORNELIUS SCIPIO AEMILIANUS was born in 185 or
possibly in 184 B.C. He was the second son of L. Aemilius
Paullus, himself the son of the consul who fell at Cannae.[1]
Paullus was aedile in 193, praetor in 191, consul in 182 and again in
168, censor in 164, and an augur from about 192 onwards; in 191–
189, after an initial reverse, he won a military victory in Spain, and in
181 he celebrated a triumph over the Ligurians; but above all it was
he who in 168 brought to a successful conclusion the war against
Perseus, the last king of Macedonia, thereby earning a second and more
splendid triumph.[2] So Scipio not only belonged to an ancient and
famous patrician *gens* but was the son of a man who had achieved
great personal eminence. Through his mother he was descended from
another of the old patrician *gentes*, for she was the daughter of
C. Papirius Maso, consul in 231, subjugator of Corsica, and the first
general to celebrate an unofficial triumph on the Alban Mount.[3]
More brilliant still was the splendour in lineage conferred by adoption into the family of the Cornelii Scipiones. Admittedly Scipio's
adoptive father, P. Cornelius Scipio, although an augur and possessed of considerable learning and rhetorical ability, was prevented
by physical infirmity from pursuing a normal public career, so that
he held no high office;[4] but the grandfather by adoption was none
other than Africanus, the hero of Rome's second epic war against
Carthage, sometimes referred to as Scipio the Great.[5] Of this house
Aemilianus in time became the head.

---

[1] Most of the ancient references to Scipio, including the many which indicate his paternity
and adoption, are collected by Münzer, *RE*, s.v. *Cornelius*, no. 335. For the date of birth see
Appendix I.

[2] Klebs, *RE*, s.v. *Aemilius*, no. 114. The report of another triumph, for his exploits in
Spain, is probably incorrect: Degrassi, *Inscr. Ital.* xiii. 1, p. 553; 3, p. 51.

[3] Plut. *Aem.* 5. 1 and 5; Plin. *Nat. Hist.* 15. 126; Diod. 31. 27. 3 f.; cf. Polyb. 31. 26. 6 f.
and 28. 7; Münzer, *RE*, s.v. *Papirius*, nos. 57 and 78.

[4] Livy, 40. 42. 13; Cic. *Brut.* 77; *De Sen.* 35; *De Off.* 1. 121; cf. Vell. 1. 10. 3.

[5] Polyb. 18. 35. 9; 31. 26. 1; 31. 27. 1; Plut. *Aem.* 2. 5.

His family tree had yet greater complexities. The wife of Africanus, Aemilia, was the sister of Paullus, so Aemilianus' grandmother by adoption was by blood his aunt; and the children of Africanus, by adoption his father and aunts, were by blood his cousins.[1] The elder of these daughters of Africanus married P. Cornelius Scipio Nasica Corculum, and the younger daughter married Ti. Sempronius Gracchus, whose sons were the famous tribunes of 133 and 123 and whose daughter Sempronia married Aemilianus himself.[2] Paullus, too, had daughters, one of whom married M. Porcius Cato, elder son of Cato the Censor, and another married Q. Aelius Tubero.[3] Finally there was a link with another famous patrician house; for Scipio's elder brother had become Q. Fabius Maximus Aemilianus, adopted by a grandson, or possibly a son, of Verrucosus, the Cunctator, five times consul.[4] Yet the brothers were the heirs not only of their respective families of adoption, but also of Paullus, for his two younger sons both died as youths in 167.[5]

Records survive of only a few events in Scipio's earlier life. Within two or three years of his birth, Paullus divorced Papiria and remarried, but Scipio evidently maintained a close relationship with both parents.[6] There is no record of when he and his brother were adopted into their new families, except that in both cases it was before 168 and probably after 179.[7] Equally uncertain is the date of the death of Scipio's adoptive father: all that can be established is that it

[1] Stemmata on p. 357; Polyb. 31. 26. 1 f., thence Diod. 31. 27. 3; Plut. *Aem.* 2. 5; Livy, 38. 57. 6; Val. Max. 6. 7. 1.

[2] The Corneliae: Münzer, *RE*, s.v. *Cornelius*, nos. 406 and 407; see esp. Polyb. 31. 27. 1 f.; Livy, 38. 57. 2. Sempronia: Münzer, *RE*, s.v. *Sempronius*, no. 99; App. *B.C.* 1. 20; Plut. *Ti. Grac.* 4. 5; Livy, *Epit.* 59; Oros. 5. 10. 9 f.; *Schol. Bob. Mil.*, p. 118 Stangl; Val. Max. 3. 8. 6; 6. 2. 3.

[3] There was evidently a third daughter. Klebs, *RE*, s.v. *Aemilius*, nos. 151, 152, and 180; see esp. Plut. *Aem.* 5. 6.

[4] Münzer, *RE*, s.v. *Fabius*, no. 109, cf. no. 105; see esp. Plut. *Aem.* 5. 1 and 5; 15. 4 (= Polyb. 29. 14. 2); Polyb. 31. 23. 5; 31. 24. 3.

[5] Polyb. 31. 28. 2; Livy, 45. 40. 7; Plut. *Aem.* 35. 1 f.; Vell. 1. 10. 3 f.; Val. Max. 5. 10. 2; App. *Maced.* 19; Diod. 31. 11. 1; Cic. *Ad Fam.* 4. 6. 1; *De Amic.* 9.

[6] Polyb. 31. 26. 6 f., thence Diod. 31. 27. 3 f.; Plut. *Aem.* 5. 1 f.; cf. Cic. *De Amic.* 11. The elder son of the second marriage was probably born in 181 (refs. in previous note).

[7] Plut. *Aem.* 5. 5 states, and Livy, 45. 41. 12 implies, that the adoptions were made when Paullus had two sons by his second marriage. Although some looseness of expression is possible, this is likely to be correct. The younger son was probably born in 179 (refs. in n. 5). All references to Fabius and Scipio in 168 or later presuppose that they had already been adopted.

was before 162, when Scipio's activities and responsibilities consequent upon the death of Aemilia prove that he was already head of
the family.[1] Earlier, in 168, he and Fabius accompanied Paullus on his
campaign in Macedonia, probably Scipio's first active military service. At the battle of Pydna he pursued the fleeing enemy with such
zest that for a time he lost contact with the Roman army and was
feared dead.[2] Subsequently he spent a considerable time hunting on
the Macedonian royal preserves, which his father had placed entirely
in his hands. He also accompanied Paullus on his tour of Greece, and
at the end of November 167 he took part in his father's triumph.[3]
When still in Greece, he and Fabius had become friendly with one
of the thousand Achaean leaders now held as political detainees in
Italy; this was Polybius, the future historian. A little later, probably
early in 166, the friendship between Scipio and Polybius became
closer still.[4] When Paullus died in 160, Scipio not only gave to his
less wealthy brother his own share of the inheritance but also contributed a large sum towards the cost of the splendid funeral games
given by Fabius. Shortly afterwards Papiria died, when Scipio was
still in his twenties.[5] He is heard of again in 155, when he was among
the crowd of eager young aristocrats who were fascinated by the
discourses of three distinguished philosophers who had been sent as
Athenian ambassadors.[6] It is reasonable to assume, though no record
has been preserved, that at about this time, or perhaps a little earlier,
he held the quaestorship.[7] By the end of 152 he was a member of the

---

[1] Polyb. 31. 26. 1 f., thence Diod. 31. 27. 3 f. Münzer, *RE*, s.v. *Cornelius*, no. 331, argues
that P. Scipio died after 167, on the ground that he was an augur and his death and re-
placement are not recorded in the extant books of Livy; but the *lacunae* in the text of Livy
are such that these events could have been recorded under 176, 175, or 171, or possibly under
178 or 170.

[2] Livy, 44. 44. 1 f.; Plut. *Aem.* 22. 3 f.; (Victor) *De Vir. Ill.* 58. 1; cf. Diod. 30. 22; Cic.
Rep. 1. 23.

[3] Polyb. 31. 29. 5 f.; Livy, 45. 27. 6; 45. 40. 4; cf. Eutrop. 4. 8. The triumph is dated by
the *Fasti Capitolini*.

[4] Polyb. 31. 23. 3 f.; below, pp. 19 f.

[5] Polyb. 31. 28. 1 f.; Diod. 31. 27. 5 f., cf. 31. 25. 1 and 2; Livy, *Epit.* 46; Plut. *Aem.* 39.
10; Cic. *Parad. Stoic.* 48; *Didasc.* Ter. *Adelphi* and *Hecyra*. Papiria: Polyb. 31. 28. 7 f.; Diod.
31. 27. 7.   [6] Cic. *De Orat.* 2. 154 f.

[7] Fraccaro, 'I "decem stipendia" ', *Opusc.* ii, p. 216, argues that if Scipio had held the
quaestorship there would have been some mention of it; but the sources available are such
that this carries little weight. Although at this date the quaestorship was probably not
a compulsory prerequisite it was certainly the normal preliminary to further advancement:
Astin, *Lex Annalis*, pp. 28 f.

Senate, and from that point on it will be possible to trace his career in greater detail.

A passage in Plutarch's biography of Aemilius Paullus throws some light on Scipio's educational background: 'He brought up his sons in accordance with the traditional native type of education, as he himself had been brought up, but also, and more zealously, on the Greek pattern. For the young men were surrounded not only by Greek teachers, scholars, and rhetoricians but also by Greek sculptors, painters, overseers of horses and hounds, and instructors in hunting.'[1] If Scipio's adoptive father had any share in his upbringing, his influence too will have shown a leaning towards philhellenism, nor is anything else to be expected among the Roman aristocracy at this period. Indeed, the Greek element in Scipio's education is attested independently,[2] and there is no doubt that it endowed him with a considerable knowledge of and interest in Greek literature and learning, a knowledge and interest which not only helped to bring about his long association with Polybius but must surely have been deepened through that association. The evidence for this lies not merely in the generalizations of Roman writers in later periods, but in specific items, such as the permission granted to Scipio and his brother to take what books they liked from the Macedonian royal library, in Scipio's interest in the embassy of philosophers in 155, in his ability to quote from Greek writers, and above all in his close association in later years with the Stoic philosopher Panaetius, who lived with him in Rome for a time and who, about 140–138, accompanied him on his embassy to the countries of the eastern Mediterranean.[3]

Yet Scipio's literary interests were not confined to the Greeks. Like his close friends Laelius and Furius Philus, he was a patron and friend of Terence. Indeed, the dramatist's enemies, besides attacking him for the freedom with which he adapted his Greek originals, alleged that the true authors were Scipio and Laelius, a charge which presumably must have been at least superficially plausible. Later in life he became the patron of the satirist Lucilius, whose work

[1] Plut. *Aem.* 6. 8 f.
[2] Diod. 31. 26. 5. P. Scipio: Cic. *Brut.* 77. In general cf. Kienast, *Cato*, pp. 101 f.
[3] Cic. *De Amic.* 104; *Tusc.* 1. 5; *Brut.* 84; *Verr.* 2. 4. 98; *Rep.* 1. 17; 1. 29; 1. 34; 3. 5; Vell. 1. 12. 3; 1. 13. 3. Library: Plut. *Aem.* 28. 11; cf. Polyb. 31. 23. 4. Embassy: Cic. *De Orat.* 2. 154 f. Greek writers: Appendix II, nos. 1, 9, 48, and 62. Panaetius: Appendix VI. 2.

owed comparatively little to the Greeks.[1] Scipio was no fanatical philhellenist. If he had been, Polybius would not have mocked A. Postumius Albinus for that very fault, nor yet have attributed to Greek influence the growth of luxury, extravagance, and licence at Rome.[2] Nor should Scipio's interest in learning and literature be exaggerated, considerable and serious though it was. The admiring Cicero contrasts him with Q. Aelius Tubero, who devoted his whole time to philosophy for its own sake; and it may not be entirely a projection of Cicero's own attitude when he states that Scipio's interest in learning lay in its practical application.[3] Such was certainly the attitude of Polybius to history;[4] and it is surely significant that a book 'which Scipio always had in his hands' was Xenophon's *Cyropaedeia*, not one of the great literary masterpieces, nor yet characterized by intellectual profundity, but markedly pragmatic in outlook.[5] Moreover, Cicero is not consistent. If in one passage he asserts that Scipio and Laelius spent all their leisure time in study and learning, in another he reveals that when they retired to the country they 'used to become boys again in an astonishing degree', 'descending to every mental relaxation and sport', even to collecting shells or pebbles on the sea-shore. He might have mentioned another quite unintellectual pastime, hunting, to which Scipio was much addicted and devoted a great deal of time.[6]

Speaking of Scipio's personal morality Polybius says:

The first direction taken by Scipio's ambition to lead a noble life was to attain a reputation for temperance and in this to excel all his contemporaries. This is a great prize indeed and difficult to gain, but at this time it was easy to pursue at Rome owing to the moral deterioration of most of the youths. For some had abandoned themselves to amours with boys, others to prostitutes, and many to musical pleasures and drinking-bouts and extravagant spending on these. . . . Scipio, however, setting himself to pursue the opposite course of conduct, combating all his appetites and moulding his life to be in every way coherent and consistent, in about the first five years established a universal reputation for self-discipline and temperance.[7]

[1] Suet. *Ter.* 1; 3; Hor. *Sat.* 2. 1. 71 f. and esp. schol. ad loc.; Cic. *De Fin.* 1. 7 = Lucil. 594 M.; cf. Hor. *Sat.* 2. 1. 16 f.

[2] Polyb. 39. 1. 3 f.; 31. 25. 4. [3] Cic. *De Orat.* 3. 86 f.; cf. *Rep.* 1. 15; 3. 4 f.

[4] Walbank, *Commentary on Polybius*, i, pp. 6 f.

[5] Cic. *Ad Quint. Frat.* 1. 1. 23; *Tusc.* 2. 62.

[6] Cic. *De Amic.* 104; *De Orat.* 2. 22, thence Val. Max. 8. 8. 1; Polyb. 31. 29. 3 f.

[7] Polyb. 31. 25. 2 f.

Admittedly Polybius was a friend and panegyrist, and such a picture was not, as he would have his readers believe, absolutely unchallenged in Scipio's lifetime;[1] but in general it is probably accurate. Certainly it is consistent with what is known of Scipio's public activities and pronouncements as also with his reputation for scrupulously keeping his word, his *fides*, which is several times attested.[2]

On the other hand, like his father Paullus, indeed like most Romans, he had a strong streak of harshness, even of cruelty. This appears time and again: in his evident pleasure at being a spectator at a great battle; in his satisfaction at the final destruction of Carthage; in the relentless, brutal treatment of Numantia, which some ascribed to the fact that he was given to passionate anger and was vindictive towards captives;[3] the games he gave to celebrate his victory at Carthage were enlivened by throwing to wild beasts deserters of allied origin, an idea for which his father Paullus had provided a precedent but which clearly was not ordinary practice; at Lutia in Spain he did not hesitate to cut off the hands of four hundred young men, an act of frightfulness to deter potential rebels which almost certainly involved many who were innocent along with the guilty.[4] On a different plane, but still indicative, is the punishment of a man in 142 for alleged cowardice at the battle of Pydna, twenty-six years before.[5] There is in fact a considerable body of evidence suggesting that throughout his career Scipio believed in the value of harsh punishment as a deterrent.[6] *Fides* and personal abstemiousness would not prevent such a man being ruthless and unscrupulous in politics.

Along with hardness of character went exceptional personal bravery —the display of which was doubtless assisted by Scipio's good health and physique. Polybius' testimony to his outstanding courage, perhaps

[1] There were allegations of immorality with Terence: Suet. *Ter.* 1.

[2] Cf. pp. 116 f.; Appendix II, nos. 20, 53, and 57; cf. Cic. *Verr.* 2. 4. 81. On his famous embassy in 140 (p. 127) his retinue was notable for its modest size: Val. Max. 4. 3. 13; Athen. 6. 273 a = Polyb. fgt. inc. 76 BW = Poseid. fgt. 59 *FGrH*; 'Plut.' *Apophth. Scip. Min.* 14; (Victor) *De Vir. Ill.* 58. 7. *Fides*: Diod. 32. 7; App. *Iber.* 54; *Lib.* 101; Cic. *Pro Mur.* 58. Cic. *De Off.* 1. 108 mentions his *vita tristior*.

[3] App. *Lib.* 71; Polyb. 38. 21. 1; App. *Iber.* 98. On Numantia, cf. also Oros. 5. 7. 12 f.; Florus, 1. 34. 12 f.; App. *Iber.* 95 f.; Livy, *Epit.* 59; Val. Max. 2. 7. 1; Vell. 2. 4. 2.

[4] Livy, *Epit.* 51; cf. *Ox. Epit.* 51; Val. Max. 2. 7. 13; App. *Iber.* 94. For Paullus see also Val. Max. 2. 7. 14. The fact that the fate of the deserters is reported shows that it was not standard practice at this date.

[5] Cic. *De Orat.* 2. 272 = Appendix II, no. 23. [6] p. 331.

not to be trusted implicitly if it stood alone, is amply confirmed by attested deeds. The best known of these were performed in Spain in 151–150. He accepted a challenge to single combat and slew his opponent, and he won the *corona muralis* for being first on the wall of Intercatia. In some battle he saved the life of a certain M. Allienus, and as a military tribune in Africa he won the *corona obsidionalis* for his daring rescue of some cohorts which had been cut off.[1]

Scipio undoubtedly had considerable military talents. The record of his exploits as military tribune in Africa in 149–148 was clearly impressive, even though the surviving accounts have almost certainly been tinged with panegyric and propaganda.[2] As a general he achieved total victory in two wars which had proved extremely troublesome. In each case the chief task was the conduct of a siege, and his tactical abilities were never tested in a full-scale, set-piece battle; but throughout the impression is of firm discipline, skilful manœuvring, and efficient precautions against surprise; both sieges presented formidable physical difficulties, necessitated elaborate construction works and called for a high degree of organizational ability in the handling of man-power and supply.

In Rome, where military and political advancement were so closely interrelated, such talent was a very considerable political asset. Another such asset was skill as an orator, and of this too Scipio had good measure. Expressions such as *eloquens* or *summa eloquentia* are several times applied to him.[3] Some of his speeches were preserved and were examined by the rhetoricians of later ages. Cicero, two generations later, thought highly of his ability, though he rated him below his contemporaries Ser. Sulpicius Galba and C. Laelius. Quintilian thought his style characteristic of the age in that it lacked polish, while Cicero thought similarly characteristic his purity of language— though Gellius believed him to be outstanding in this. That he did not speak with exceptional emphasis or shouting is consistent with the outstanding *gravitas* with which Cicero credits him.[4] But the

---

[1] Polyb. 31. 28. 12 f.; 31. 29. 11 f.; Cic. *Tusc.* 4. 50; below pp. 46 f. and p. 62.

[2] pp. 62 f.

[3] Cic. *Brut.* 82 f.; *De Orat.* 1. 215; *De Off.* 1. 116; *Pro Mur.* 58; Vell. 2. 9. 1; Plin. *Nat. Hist.* 7. 100.

[4] Quint. *Inst.* 12. 10. 10; Cic. *Brut.* 258; Gell. 2. 20. 5; Cic. *De Orat.* 1. 255; 3. 28; cf. *De Amic.* 96.

contents of his speeches could be forceful enough. He could deliver scathing and bitter attacks, often reinforced by devastating witticisms. He excelled, it seems, in irony, but not in that alone. The samples of his *dicta* which have been preserved show that he possessed, and readily employed against many individuals, the ability to produce witty and pungent comments of a most biting, damaging, and insulting nature. This talent too had political significance: it might at times have captivated a crowd and routed ignominiously an opponent, but it was also likely to ensure that opponents really were enemies, to have made it far easier to antagonize than to conciliate.[1]

This propensity towards antagonizing others will have been reinforced by certain further features of Scipio's character. For the understanding of these a helpful passage is Polybius' account of the conversation which established the special bond of friendship between himself and the young Roman noble.[2] This took place in Rome, almost certainly in the early months of 166. Already contact arising from the loan of some books had won for Polybius the friendship of the two sons of Paullus; already they had persuaded the praetor in charge of the detainees to allow their Greek protégé to remain in Rome itself. The three of them were walking together, and when Fabius went off by himself, Scipio asked Polybius why he constantly addressed all conversation to his elder brother and ignored Scipio himself. 'Or is it clear that you too share that opinion of me which I learn the rest of my countrymen have? For, as I hear, everybody considers me quiet and lazy, far removed from the character and ways of a Roman, because I do not choose to plead cases in the law courts. And they say that my family needs a champion not like me but the very opposite. And it is this which especially distresses me.'

Polybius, understandably in some surprise, denied that he had such an opinion, assuring Scipio that the conversation was directed mainly

---

[1] Many examples in Appendix II, e.g. nos. 17, 19, 20, 22, 25, 26, 29. Irony: Cic. *Acad. Pr.* 2. 15 = Fannius, fgt. 7; *De Orat.* 2. 270; *Brut.* 299. See also pp. 89 f.

[2] Polyb. 31. 23. 1 f.; for the date see p. 245. The passage was written many years after the event, but Polybius' recollection of its general tenor, and especially of Scipio's attitude of mind, must have been accurate (admitted even by Friedländer, 'Socrates enters Rome', *AJPh* 66 (1945), pp. 337 f., esp. p. 346, who believes that Polybius consciously reflected the conversation between Socrates and Alcibiades in the Platonic *Greater Alcibiades*).

towards his brother solely because he was the elder. 'Yet I am glad to hear you say now that it distresses you that you are milder than is fitting in members of this family; for it is evident from this that you have a serious mind.[1] I myself would gladly devote myself to helping you speak and act in a manner worthy of your ancestors.' For this task Polybius expressed the opinion that Scipio would find no one more efficient or helpful than himself. Scipio's response was enthusiastic: he looked forward to the day when he would have an undisputed first claim on Polybius' attention: 'for from that moment I shall at once seem to myself worthy both of my house and of my ancestors.' 'After this discussion', Polybius continues, 'the young man was never parted from Polybius, preferring his society to anything else. From that time onward they continually gave each other proof of an affection which came to be like that of father and son or near relations.'

If there really was a streak of laziness underlying Scipio's difficulties, it would seem to have been overcome later in life; so also if as a youth he suffered from shyness, which would be quite compatible with Polybius' account. But whatever the underlying weakness, it is absolutely clear that Scipio was widely regarded as an unworthy representative of his family and ancestors. What is more, the whole episode, together with Scipio's distress and the readiness with which he linked himself to and accepted help from this non-Roman acquaintance,[2] leaves little doubt that this unfavourable opinion was shared by members of the family. In all this, Scipio cannot have been unmindful of his descent from the Aemilii and from Paullus himself, but the family principally in his mind must have been that of which he was to become the head, if he was not so already, the great house of the Scipios; and the ancestor most in his thoughts, and in everybody else's, must have been the most brilliant scion of that house, the great popular hero, the conqueror of Hannibal, the almost legendary Africanus.[3] Of this man he, Scipio Aemilianus, was now the direct

---

[1] δῆλος γὰρ εἶ διὰ τούτων μέγα φρονῶν. Both Shuckburgh and Paton translate 'have a high spirit'; I take it to mean that Scipio is shown to be concerned about matters which are really worth while.

[2] Little is known of the nature of that help. See p. 31 and Additional Note A, p. 339.

[3] See esp. the eulogies in Polyb. 10. 2 f. and 10. 40, which doubtless reflect the family opinion of Africanus. It is at least possible that his *imago* had already been placed in the

heir; and with consciousness of this went both distress at his reputation as an unworthy heir and a great anxiety to confound the general
opinion. The conclusion to be drawn is unmistakable: we may expect
to find Scipio's career marked by intense ambition—ambition to
prove himself worthy of his distinguished ancestry, a worthy grandson of Africanus; ambition for honour and glory, for military success
and consequent fame, ambition to be a great and popular hero, to be
the outstanding man in the state.

The expectation is fulfilled. Cicero mentions ambition as a feature
of his character; another writer, Dio, who otherwise presents eulogistic accounts of Scipio's qualities, reports that his ambition was greater
than was in keeping with his general excellence; and some alleged
that Scipio's treatment of Numantia was inspired by a belief that
great disasters are the foundation of far-famed glory.[1] Moreover,
there is much about Scipio which takes on added significance in relation to this background. It is interesting, for example, that he was so
attached to Xenophon's *Cyropaedeia*. Here is a work which not only
portrays a man who delighted in battle, not only emphasizes the
profits to be gained from personal abstemiousness, from unfailingly
keeping one's word, from liberality, and especially from Scipio's
favourite sport, hunting, but which glorifies a man's ambition for
power, fame, and military renown. There is an even more interesting
feature of Scipio's career. Several times the writers of antiquity observe that Scipio earned by his own merits the same cognomen,
'Africanus', which he had inherited from his grandfather;[2] but it did
not need the literary men of later generations to conceive of this idea.
The cognomen was highly distinctive; the parallel must have been
intentional. Perhaps then it is not merely coincidence that Scipio
found his closest friend in a Laelius, that his achievements as a

temple of Jupiter on the Capitol: Val. Max. 8. 15. 1; App. *Iber.* 23. For the 'Scipionic legend'
in general see Scullard, *Scipio Africanus in the Second Punic War*, pp. 13 f.; Haywood, *Studies
on Scipio Africanus*, pp. 1 f., with Scullard's review in *JRS* 23 (1933), pp. 78 f. The disputed
questions do not affect the present discussion.

[1] Cic. *De Off.* 1. 108; Dio, fgt. 84, cf. 70. 4 f.; App. *Iber.* 98. Cic. *De Off.* 1. 116 is too
artificial to be reliable evidence. Val. Max. 8. 15. 4 states that Scipio was not a *civis ambitiosus*,
but this is a rhetorical elaboration in Valerius' own comment and owes nothing to his
source.

[2] Cic. *Rep.* 6. 11; Val. Max. 2. 7. 1; 2. 10. 4; Eutrop. 4. 12; Zon. 9. 30. Very similar are
Vell. 1. 12. 3 f., Diod. 30. 22, and Flor. 1. 31. 12.

military tribune in 149 inspired talk that he was the only worthy successor of Paullus and the Scipios, that reports circulated that he was
aided by the same deity that had enabled Africanus to foresee the
future,[1] that he achieved the consulship at an unusually early age and
that he attained the command in the struggle against Carthage.

The objects of Scipio's ambition in themselves were not necessarily
radically different from those pursued by many other Roman nobles,
not a few of whom could equally well have spoken Scipio's words:
'From innocence is born dignity, from dignity honour, from honour
the right to command, from the right to command liberty.'[2] But
behind Scipio's ambitions was a distinctive personal background
which gave them a heightened intensity. Similarly, there is no suggestion that this powerful ambition was the sole motive behind Scipio's
political activities or that he did not endeavour to judge issues on their
merits. In the preceding pages attention has been drawn already to
some traits of his character and outlook which may have had some
influence on his opinions, and to them may be added a genuine
patriotism[3]—a trait which perhaps fits well with a passion to be the
greatest man in the state. Nevertheless, it is not always easy for a man
to separate private interest and objective judgement; and underlying
all Scipio's public activities was the consciousness that as a young man
he had been thought unworthy, and, consequent upon that, an
intense, driving ambition.

And when Scipio's ambitions began to be fulfilled, when he
found himself brilliantly successful and a popular hero, it is no surprise that he exhibited a pride which merged into general arrogance.
Admittedly, he showed himself aware of the common Greek doc-
trine that those tempted to over-confidence and presumption should
be mindful of the infirmity and instability of human affairs, of contrasts which a change of fortune might bring. But a man will rarely
admit that he is proud and arrogant: indeed, he may well not be
aware that he is so. It is no cause for astonishment if he is found
echoing or paying lip-service to a common sentiment of this type—
especially if he can repetitiously illustrate it with an ingenious simile
of his own invention.[4] Such notions did not preserve Scipio from

---

[1] App. *Lib.* 101, 104.   [2] Appendix II, no. 57.   [3] p. 78.
[4] Appendix II, nos. 8, 9, and 61.

pride and arrogance. If one source only, and that very late, attests in so many words his pride in his achievements—*ob res gestas superbus*[1]—the cumulative evidence of many words and deeds confirms it. A minor manifestation was a certain affectation, noticeable in his speech and perhaps to be seen also in his novel practice of having himself shaved every day.[2] He was ready to boast that his concern had not been to know many citizens but to be known by all, and that Rome could not fall while Scipio lived.[3] To recall his victory in Spain he added to 'Africanus' a further name, 'Numantinus'; he constructed a temple to Virtus, the implication of which is clear; to his rival for the censorship he issued the irrelevant challenge that they should both go to Spain and let the troops judge the valour of each; when there were complaints at his cautious campaigning, he retorted that he had been born a general, not a mere soldier; when prosecuted in 140 he scorned to appear unshaved or in the conventional soiled garments.[4] When he was censor, a calculated insult to his colleague is expressly said to have earned him a reputation for arrogance; and the same failing is seen in another direct insult to that same colleague, the declaration that 'I would perform all duties in a manner worthy of the majesty of the state, if the citizens had either given me a colleague or had not given me one.' Other of his *dicta* betray a similar spirit, culminating in an outburst in 131 which was full of political significance.[5]

There are a number of passages in the ancient literature, especially in the works of Cicero, which seem to contradict this picture of pride and arrogance. Cicero says that Scipio always showed respect towards Fabius as his elder brother, and that he never affected any superiority over Furius Philus, Rupilius, Sp. Mummius, or friends of lower rank;[6] elsewhere, attacking Cato Uticensis for the *asperitas* which he derived from his Stoicism, he asserts that the effect of the teaching of Panaetius was to render Scipio very mild, *lenissimus*;[7]

---

[1] (Victor) *De Vir. Ill.* 58. 8.

[2] Appendix II, nos. 59 and 60; Plin. *Nat. Hist.* 7. 211.

[3] Appendix II, nos. 13 and 54.

[4] 'Numantinus': p. 231. Temple: Plut. *Fort. Rom.* 5. *Dicta*: Appendix II, nos. 14 and 44. In 140: Gell. 3. 4. 1.

[5] Plut. *Praec. Reip. Ger.* 20; Appendix II, no. 17. For the outburst in 131 see p. 233.

[6] *De Amic.* 69.   [7] *Pro Mur.* 66.

he applies to Scipio the words *politus, humanitas*, and *aequitas*;[1] he
states that Scipio's quarrels with Q. Metellus Macedonicus and
Q. Pompeius were conducted without bitterness, and that he was
endowed with an affable disposition, *moribus facillimis*.[2] Other authors
reflect similar ideas: Dio records Scipio's moderation and reasonable-
ness, 'so that he alone of all men, or at least more than others, escaped
the envy of his peers, as well as of everyone else. For he chose to
make himself the equal of his inferiors, not better than his equals,
and inferior to greater men, and so passed beyond the reach of
jealousy, which is the one thing that injures the noblest men.' This
last sentiment is shared by the elder Pliny, who sees in Scipio one
who enjoyed the same talents as Cato 'but without the widespread
ill-will under which Cato laboured'.[3]

This is not such a formidable body of evidence as it may seem at
first. Some of the passages simply do not reflect the truth. Cicero is
certainly wrong in saying that the quarrels with Metellus and Pompeius were without bitterness.[4] Dio and Pliny are equally wrong in
saying that Scipio escaped jealousy and envy: some enemies alleged
that Laelius was the true author of Scipio's achievements, Scipio
himself being only the principal actor;[5] ill-will is manifest in the
charge of immorality with Terence; and at the end of his life Scipio's
enemies were crying 'Kill the tyrant.'[6] Of the remaining passages
some are probably concerned more with other aspects of his character
—his culture and his liberality[7]—but others may reflect the truth,
even if it has been exaggerated in order to bring out a moral. For the
most proud and arrogant man can show respect towards his brother,
can have a circle of friends towards whom he is easy and affable.
Cicero has a circumstantial story of Scipio affably inviting to dinner
friends and clients in the country, though it tells nothing of whether
or not Scipio was proud.[8] Indeed, it might be held that the very

---

[1] *De Orat.* 2. 154; *Verr.* 2. 2. 86.   [2] *De Amic.* 11; 77; *De Off.* 1. 87.
[3] Dio, fgt. 70. 9; Plin. *Nat. Hist.* 7. 100.   [4] pp. 311 f. and 313 f.
[5] Plut. *Praec. Reip. Ger.* 11; *An Seni Sit Ger.* 27; Julian, *Orationes*, 8. 244 C. Strictly speaking
these passages could refer to the elder Scipio and Laelius, but much more probably refer to
the younger. Similarly it may well have been Aemilianus rather than Africanus who was criticized by his enemies for his readiness to sleep: Plut. *Praec. Reip. Ger.* 4; *Ad Princ. Inerud.* 7.
[6] Suet. *Ter.* 1; 'Plut.' *Apophth. Scip. Min.* 23 (= Appendix II, no. 54).
[7] Clearly so in Cic. *Verr.* 2. 2. 86.
[8] *De Fato*, fgt. 4 = Macrob. *Sat.* 3. 16. 3 f.

course of his subsequent career presupposes in Scipio a certain popular charm; yet it is beyond doubt that he could be bitter and scornful. One passage stands in direct contradiction to the impression of pride and arrogance, namely Dio's portrait of a man personifying modesty and humility; but this, itself part of a more extensive eulogy, must be rejected as fictitious idealization. The evidence to the contrary is extensive and varied—and includes Dio's own statement that Scipio's ambition was greater than was in keeping with his general excellence.[1]

This then was Scipio Aemilianus: a scion of the noblest aristocracy; cultured and serious, yet physically strong and fond of hunting; disciplined and temperate, of high personal morality and integrity, outstandingly brave, yet hard and cruel; talented both as general and as orator; capable of charm, ease, and informality with friends but endowed with a wit that could be biting and scornful; as a youth, depressed by a reputation for idleness and unworthiness, and in consequence intensely ambitious, anxious to prove his worth, so that achievement brought pride and arrogance.

[1] Dio, fgt. 84. 1.

III

POPULARIS

POLYBIUS' narrative of the conversation in which he pledged his assistance to Scipio is intended to explain the origin of the friendship between the two of them, but also it is part of a discussion of 'how it came about that Scipio's fame in Rome advanced so far and became so brilliant unusually rapidly'.[1] The report of the conversation itself is followed by an account of the development of certain aspects of Scipio's character: personal morality and temperance; liberality and integrity in financial matters; and courage.[2] This account is clearly regarded by Polybius as directly relevant to the overall purpose of the passage, to the conversation, and to the fulfilment of Scipio's desire to be looked upon as a worthy representative of his family.

Towards the end of this account, Polybius states that Scipio was assisted in his desire to win a reputation for courage by an opportunity to develop his liking for hunting.[3] After the battle of Pydna in 168 Scipio was given unlimited use of the fine hunting preserves of the Macedonian kings and as a result acquired an enduring passion for the sport. When he returned to Rome this passion was matched and encouraged by the similar enthusiasm of Polybius. In consequence:

all the time which the other young men devoted to legal cases and to greetings, spending their time in the Forum, thereby trying to ingratiate themselves with the populace, Scipio devoted to hunting; and by continually performing great and memorable exploits he won a higher reputation than the others. For they could not win praise except by injuring one of their fellow-citizens, since that is the usual consequence of judicial proceedings; but Scipio, without annoying anyone, won this universal reputation for courage, matching his deeds against their words. And so in a very short time he outstripped his contemporaries more than is recorded of any other Roman, although in his pursuit of fame (ἐν φιλοδοξίᾳ) the path he followed was quite the opposite of that taken by all the rest in accordance with Roman usage and custom.

[1] 31. 23. 2 f.   [2] 31. 25–30.   [3] 31. 29.

Doubtless Polybius has exaggerated both the amount of time Scipio spent hunting and the extent to which his exploits in the chase won him a reputation for courage; on the other hand his account cannot conceivably be without a substantial element of truth. *It must be true that Scipio devoted to hunting a considerable portion of the time that a young Roman aristocrat with political ambitions would normally have spent in legal matters and in formal greetings. It may be that, as Polybius indicates, these activities could be a means to winning some popularity; but what he forgets—or chooses to ignore—is that they played a very great part in the creation and cementing of the elaborate social relationships which were integral to and prominent in Roman public life. They were devices for securing influence, for exercising patronage, for conferring the favours, the *beneficia*, which placed the recipient under a formal and serious obligation. The early-morning greetings, the giving of legal advice, the pleading of cases in the courts were all important means to building up the complex nexus of 'friends', patrons, and clients (*amici, patroni*, and *clientes*), which in turn made possible the manipulation of large blocks of votes, the striking of bargains, and the achievement of considerable power through social connexions.[1] In other words, Scipio neglected some of the most vital means of laying the basis of political influence. That this was a really serious matter is clearly proved by Polybius' own testimony; for not only does he admit that Scipio's behaviour was in defiance of Roman custom and usage, but a little earlier he puts into Scipio's own mouth the statement that the reason why he was regarded as indolent, as un-Roman, and as unworthy of his family was precisely his unwillingness to plead in the law courts.[2]

To this fundamental political weakness may be added the consequences of Scipio's ready and often scathing wit. His sharp tongue, coupled with the self-assertion that came with success, must have made it much easier for him to alienate other politicians than to court their support by diplomacy and tact. There is indeed evidence that later in his career he lost the support of several one-time associates.[3]

---

[1] Gelzer, *Nobilität*, part ii *passim*. Val. Max. 9. 3. 2 (probably with reference to the 120's) illustrates succinctly the importance of clients in consular elections.

[2] 31. 23. 11 f.   [3] pp. 19 and 85 f.; cf. pp. 89 f.

There is, of course, no suggestion that Scipio, a member of the highest aristocracy, heir to the wealth and resources of one of the greatest Roman families, was devoid of clients or *amici*; but it is hard to believe that his neglect of customary methods, reinforced by his temperament, did not result in a comparative weakness in this type of political influence. Yet, despite this weakness, he rapidly outstripped his contemporaries, as Polybius says, and became the most influential figure in political life. It may well be asked how this was achieved.

The concepts of kinship, patronage, and mutual obligation were certainly of great moment in Roman political life; the allegiance of a large *clientela* and the cultivation of formal relationships with persons of all degrees were very important for the pursuit of political advancement and of the magistracies which marked stages in that advancement. Nevertheless, they were not the only factors at work. In the first half of the second century, and probably in all periods, there was a substantial body of voters in the assemblies whose votes were not automatically determined by the wishes of a patron. These people, at least sometimes, would vote according to their own preference, and their preference could be influenced. Thus the element of popular appeal entered in. It is likely that the number of such voters was increasing in the second century, owing to the growth of a large urban population, both rich and poor, less easily controlled by traditional social pressures and less easily held to allegiance to a single house. But however that may be, it is clear that such voters were important at this time, and that the courting of them prompted increased expenditure of wealth and effort. The growing extravagance was certainly made possible by the increasing wealth available to the aristocracy and new opportunities of drawing upon the resources of clients in the provinces.[1] Part of it, no doubt, was sheer ostentation, a perennial desire to outdo those who had gone before. But there were also political motives at work.

'Popular appeal' is a broad and imprecise expression, which may embrace many methods of influencing the voter: the sheer magnetism of a brilliant and powerful personality, or the recommendation of men themselves distinguished in public life. Military ability was

[1] Some examples of this in Badian, *Foreign Clientelae*, pp. 161 f.

likely to count for something,[1] especially in times of crisis, and senior
magistrates were so often employed on campaigns that known
military ineptitude must have been a real handicap. But other things,
less rational and less reputable, also had a great impact, and it is
these which reveal the 'floating vote'. Twice, in 181 and 159, it was
necessary to legislate against electoral corruption—and at least one
of these laws actually made bribery a capital offence. Such laws are
not needed unless bribery is effective; and bribery is only effective if
there are voters sufficiently free to be swayed by it.[2] If these laws
restricted the amount of direct bribery, there were numerous voters
ready to be swayed by various forms of indirect bribery, such as free
entertainment and distributions of oil or food, or by spectacular dis-
plays or dedications which might impress upon their minds the name
of a man or a family.[3]

Thus, even in the early decades of the second century, a man who
sought the kind of influence which would enable him to secure his
own election to office, or to assist the election of others, needed not
only to secure the support of clients and *amici* but also to court
popular favour. These were not alternatives; no one could dispense
entirely with either. But since the possibilities of effectively courting
popular favour were there, ambitious politicians exploited them.
Scipio Aemilianus carried on this development and exploited popular appeal more intensively, more unscrupulously, and with greater
success than any other leader since the Senate had established its
overwhelming ascendancy during the Second Punic War;[4] and in
this way he compensated—in certain fields—for his comparative
neglect of more traditional methods.

The evidence for such an assertion about Scipio rests in part on the
cumulative success of applying it to the interpretation of his career;
but explicit testimony is to be found, most forcefully in the following
passage from Plutarch's biography of Scipio's father, Aemilius Paullus:

[1] For such factors at work see Livy, 35. 10. 1 f. on the consular elections of 193.
[2] Livy, 40. 19. 11; *Epit.* 47; Polyb. 6. 56. 4. Cf. also Obsequ. 12; in 166 the Senate held
a special debate because the elections had been conducted *ambitiosissime*. The attempt of
Q. Fulvius Flaccus to secure election to a suffect praetorship in 184 also demonstrates that
even at that date the exploitation of popular appeal might threaten to overwhelm massive
opposition: Livy, 39. 39.
[3] Additional Note B, p. 339.
[4] Cf. also Earl, *Tiberius Gracchus*, pp. 74 f.

And this too was distinctive and remarkable in Aemilius, that although he was admired and honoured by the people beyond measure, he abode by the aristocratic policy, and neither said nor did anything to win the favour of the multitude, but in political matters always associated himself with the leading and most powerful men. And in later times this was cast in the teeth of Scipio Africanus by Appius. For these men, who were then the greatest in the city, were candidates for the censorship, the one having the support of the Senate and nobles (for this was the traditional policy of the Appii), while the other was great on his own account, but always made use of the good will and enthusiasm of the people towards him. When therefore Appius saw Scipio bursting into the Forum accompanied by men of low birth and former slaves, but who frequented the Forum and were able to gather a crowd and to force all issues by shouting and inciting passions, he called out in a loud voice, 'O Paullus Aemilius, groan beneath the earth when you learn that your son is escorted to the censorship by Aemilius the herald and Licinius Philonicus.' But Scipio had the good will of the people because he supported them in most things, while Aemilius, though he was aristocratic, was loved by the masses no less than he who seemed to play the demagogue most and to associate with the masses to win their favour.[1]

With a different emphasis but similar implications, Appian reports the reaction to Scipio's intervention in the agrarian dispute in 129: 'And thereby Scipio aroused the irritation and hatred of the people against himself, because, though they had loved him to a degree which was the envy of others, and on many issues had opposed the powerful leaders on his behalf, and had twice chosen him consul contrary to the law, they saw him acting against their interests on behalf of the Italians.' Again, it is known that *populares* leaders in the late Republic sometimes named Scipio amongst those whose example they were following, and Cicero, albeit reluctantly, seems to admit that there is some truth in the claim.[2] Finally, there is an anecdote which sums up admirably the contrast between Scipio's methods and the more conventional methods of Appius Claudius: 'When Appius Claudius was his rival for the office of censor and said that he greeted all the Romans by name, whereas Scipio knew scarcely any of them, Scipio said: "You are quite right; for my concern has been not to know many citizens but to be known by all." '[3]

[1] Plut. *Aem.* 38. 2 f.; Appius' *dictum* also in Plut. *Praec. Reip. Ger.* 14. As it appears in Plutarch the story has been given overtones of the characteristically Greek contrast between aristocratic and democratic policies, but this does not affect the significance of the story itself.
[2] App. *B.C.* 1. 19; Cic. *Acad. Pr.* 2. 13; 2. 72.   [3] Appendix II, no. 13.

Scipio, then, pursued his ambition by deliberately seeking and exploiting publicity and popularity, rather than by the customary methods of legal activity and formal greetings. This conclusion is not at all vitiated by the report that 'he observed the precept of Polybius and tried never to leave the Forum before he had in some way made an acquaintance and friend of somebody among those who spoke with him';[1] for much depends upon the frequency with which Scipio visited the Forum, on the success of his attempts to observe the precept, and on the kind of friends he won. The evidence already discussed suggests that the visits were rather infrequent, the new friends neither numerous nor of great social influence, and the attempts perhaps not particularly successful. But the story does draw attention to a further question, namely to what extent Polybius influenced Scipio's approach to the problem. No certain answer can be given, but there is a strong *a priori* probability that the Achaean politician, coming from a background where patronage and obligation were less formal, less highly developed, and less influential in politics, will have considered the key factor to be the attraction of popular attention and favour, and especially so in the early stages, when he was a newcomer to Rome; so that he is likely to have been only too ready to encourage Scipio to pursue the path to which he was naturally inclined. He certainly implies that he encouraged Scipio to indulge his passion for hunting, and it is significant that he writes as though he saw in the legal activities of the young aristocrats only a means of winning favour with the masses.[2] It is impossible to avoid the suspicion that long before he actually wrote this passage Polybius knew perfectly well what other gains were to be had but ignored them because a mention of them would have spoiled his attempt to show how Scipio fared better than his more conventional contemporaries. But whether or not this is so, and whether or not Polybius did influence to any degree Scipio's approach to the matter, the preoccupation with fame and popularity is prominent in Polybius' account of the development of Scipio's character.

In this account Scipio's personal morality and moderation, his liberality and his courage are all discussed, but the emphasis throughout is on the attainment not of the virtues themselves but of the

---

[1] 'Plut.' *Apophth. Scip. Min.* 2; *Quaest. Conviv.* 4. 1.   [2] 31. 29. 8 f.

extensive reputation which they conferred.[1] The first of 'the noble things' which Scipio is said to have sought is not temperance but 'the attainment of a reputation for temperance', and it seems to be the reputation rather than the virtue itself in which he was anxious to excel his contemporaries; and his achievement in the first five years is clearly stated: 'he established a universal reputation for self-discipline and temperance.'

Scipio's next objective was 'to distinguish himself from the rest by magnanimity and uprightness with regard to money'. That the prime concern is again with winning a wide reputation is obvious from what follows. The first example concerns the magnificent personal possessions of Aemilia, Scipio's adoptive grandmother. When she died in 162, Scipio gave them all to his own mother, Papiria, who was comparatively poor, and who proceeded to display them on public occasions. 'In consequence the women who saw what had happened were astounded at Scipio's kindness and generosity. . . . This then was the first origin of his reputation for nobility of character, and it advanced rapidly, for women are fond of talking and once they have started a thing never have too much of it.'

The next example given by Polybius is also a consequence of the death of Aemilia. The two Corneliae, the daughters of Africanus, had been promised dowries of fifty talents each, but only half had been paid on marriage. Scipio was entitled by law to pay the remainder, which was now due, by instalments over three years, but he insisted on paying the whole sum at once, so that the husbands of the Corneliae, Tiberius Gracchus and Scipio Nasica Corculum, are said to have been astounded at his magnanimity. In this instance Polybius is not so explicit about the attainment of a reputation, though this is certainly to be understood in the light of what precedes and follows. Pursuing the same theme of liberality and generosity, Polybius proceeds to the death of Paullus in 160, when Scipio surrendered to his less wealthy brother his own share of the estate. 'This was much talked about', Polybius notes. Furthermore, Scipio also contributed half the cost of the gladiatorial games given by Fabius at Paullus' funeral, and the next item is introduced by: 'When the report of this was still spreading . . . .' The next item itself

[1] Polyb. 31. 25–29.

is that when Papiria died Scipio handed over the whole of her estate, including Aemilia's former possessions, to his sisters: 'and once more Scipio's reputation for liberality and family affection was renewed.'

The discussion so far is summed up in a passage which speaks for itself:

Having laid these foundations from his early years, Scipio progressed in his pursuit of a reputation for temperance and nobility. By expending on this perhaps sixty talents (for that was what he spent out of his own property), he had a generally accepted reputation for nobility, and he achieved his purpose not so much by reason of the amount of money spent as by the seasonableness of the gift and the gracious manner in which it was bestowed. His claim to temperance cost him nothing, but abstention from many kinds of pleasures brought the additional profit of bodily health and fitness.

Finally Polybius turns to Scipio's courage, and it is here that he recounts Scipio's passion for hunting. He says, it will be recalled, that 'by continually performing great and memorable exploits he won a higher reputation than the others. . . . Scipio, without annoying anyone, won this universal reputation for courage.' And so Scipio rapidly outstripped his contemporaries, 'although in his pursuit of fame the path he followed was quite the opposite of that taken by all the rest'.

If 'doxa', fame, and 'philodoxia', the love or pursuit of fame, are constant themes in Polybius' account, this does not mean that he is implying that Scipio was hypocritical. He clearly intended it to be understood that Scipio fully deserved his reputation for the virtues described; indeed, he ends with an explanation that his discussion was intended both as moral encouragement and to secure credence for his account of Scipio's subsequent career, and to ensure that Scipio's achievements should be attributed to his own merits and not to chance.[1] Nevertheless, it is equally clear that in Polybius' eyes it is even more interesting and significant that through these excellent qualities Scipio secured a widespread and favourable reputation. The reputation had political significance, and it is this which makes the discussion relevant to the preceding passage which records Polybius' undertaking to help Scipio become worthy of his family and ancestors. Doubtless Polybius has exaggerated in a number of respects,

[1] 31. 30. 1 f.

but it would be extreme scepticism to deny his assertion that Scipio won public attention and favour in the ways he describes, and little less extreme to doubt that this was politically important. Moreover, Polybius certainly indicates that Scipio himself was consciously seeking this public attention and favour for the sake of his own advancement, and three further considerations support him in this too. First, there is the markedly ostentatious character of several of the events he describes; secondly, such an attitude in Scipio harmonizes extremely well with the other evidence, already noticed, for his exploitation of 'popular appeal' as a political tool; and, finally, precisely the same pragmatic, utilitarian outlook appears in an extract from one of Scipio's speeches: 'From innocence is born dignity, from dignity honour, from honour the right to command, from the right to command liberty.'[1]

In the previous chapter attention was drawn to Scipio's ambition. In this chapter it has been seen that in his pursuit of that ambition Scipio showed a marked tendency to compensate for some weakness of influence in other fields by seeking and exploiting popular favour. Given the nature of that ambition, it is scarcely surprising that his endeavours in this direction tended to be ostentatious and exceptional.

[1] Appendix II, no. 57.

IV

THE CELTIBERIAN WAR

THE public career of Scipio Aemilianus can be traced in reasonable detail only from the year 151. It has been possible to discover something of the personal antecedents to that career, but of the political antecedents there is less to be said, because very little is known about the internal politics of the period from 166 to 152. For the years prior to 166 the surviving books of Livy supply the names of many lesser magistrates and junior officials, as well as much circumstantial detail; for the period following 152 there are the narratives of the Punic and Spanish wars, plus a growing volume of anecdotal material. But there is little assistance of this kind for 166–152, and without it the bare list of consuls and censors does not reveal very much. It is not possible to compare the rate of advance in the careers of leading men, or, in many cases, to distinguish with confidence their allies and their opponents, their allegiances and their feuds, let alone to link these with matters of policy.[1]

The easiest task is to distinguish the really powerful men, of whom five seem to have been outstanding. Pre-eminent was M. Aemilius Lepidus, who had held two consulships and the censorship, had celebrated a triumph, and was a pontifex for forty-seven years, from 199 till his death in 152, Pontifex Maximus since 180, and Princeps Senatus for twenty-seven years, having been nominated first in 179 and reappointed by five subsequent pairs of censors. Then there was the great M. Porcius Cato, a 'new man' but one who had reached the highest ranks, by the 150's almost certainly the senior surviving consular. The other three were of more recent fame: M. Claudius Marcellus, who in 152 held his third consulship—the first man to achieve more than two since his grandfather's fifth in 208—and who celebrated his third triumph in 151; Ti. Sempronius Gracchus, who died in the late 150's or early 140's, twice consul, twice *triumphator*,

---

[1] Cf. Scullard, *Roman Politics*, p. 220.

censor, and an augur for possibly half a century or more; and lastly P. Cornelius Scipio Nasica, nicknamed Corculum for his sagacity, the successor of Lepidus both as Pontifex Maximus and as Princeps Senatus, who achieved the consulship twice, a triumph, and the censorship.[1]

Scipio Aemilianus had family ties with three of these five. Cato's son had married his sister, and Nasica and Gracchus had married the two Corneliae, his adoptive aunts. But even this is not very informative, for there are uncertainties about the relationships of these men towards each other and towards Scipio. Thus a chain of events which in 162 compelled Nasica to resign his first consulship as *vitio creatus* could easily have created considerable tension between him and Gracchus.[2] Equally, Scipio's relations with each of them may have been strained, for Scipio's distress at being considered an unworthy representative of his family and his readiness to accept help from Polybius strongly suggest that the two Corneliae and their husbands did not express great confidence in him. Moreover, the two Corneliae may not have been too pleased at seeing their mother Aemilia's finery and processional equipment pass first to Papiria and then to Scipio's sisters. If there was such family tension, it might have been carried over into politics. And more than one interpretation is possible of Scipio's action in 162, when he paid the dowries of the Corneliae in whole instead of by instalments. It might have been a gesture of genuine generosity, or of reconciliation, or of scornful independence towards those who had despised him.[3] With the family of Gracchus Scipio certainly formed new bonds, for he married his daughter, Sempronia, and in 147 Gracchus' son, the young Tiberius, was serving under him as a *contubernalis*.[4] On the other hand the late 150's saw a new quarrel, political in character and attested beyond

---

[1] Refs. in *RE*: Klebs, s.v. *Aemilius*, no. 68; Gelzer, s.v. *Porcius*, no. 9; Münzer, s.v. *Claudius*, no. 225; s.v. *Cornelius*, no. 353; s.v. *Sempronius*, no. 53. Cf. also entries in *MRR*. Carcopino, *Autour des Gracques*, pp. 77 f., argues that Gracchus died in the first half of 154. The conclusion is perfectly possible but the arguments fall short of proof. Fraccaro, *Athenaeum* 9 (1931), p. 310 n. 19 = *Opusc.* ii, p. 68, puts his death as late as 148 or 147, but this depends on the hypothesis that the younger Tiberius was the immediate successor of his father in the college of augurs. Plut. *Ti. Grac.* 4. 1 does not establish this, though it does make it unlikely that the father died much later than 147.

[2] Cic. *De Nat. Deor.* 2. 10 f.; *De Div.* 1. 33; 2. 74 f.; *Ad Quint. Frat.* 2. 2. 1; Val. Max. 1. 1. 3; (Victor) *De Vir. Ill.* 44. 2; Plut. *Marc.* 5. 1 f.; Gran. Licin. pp. 8 f. Flemisch; Scullard, *Roman Politics*, pp. 226 f.; Astin, 'Leges Aelia et Fufia', *Latomus* 23 (1964), pp. 434 f.

[3] For these matters see pp. 19 f. and 32 f.　　　　[4] p. 13 n. 2; Plut. *Ti. Grac.* 4. 5.

doubt: the dispute between Cato and Nasica about the fate of Carthage.[1] Meanwhile it is possible to begin to trace other events, in which Scipio is first heard of in public life but which also were of great moment in themselves.

In 154, or possibly in 155, serious fighting broke out in both Spanish provinces.[2] By the end of 154 the news reaching Rome was sufficiently serious to cause the beginning of the official year to be advanced from 15 March to 1 January, obviously in order to enable commanders to reach their provinces sooner.[3] In Further Spain (Ulterior), despite initial defeats and losses, the campaigns were conducted by praetors, and in 150 the enemy, the Lusitani, were subdued (though only temporarily) by Ser. Sulpicius Galba, whose methods were both brutal and treacherous. The war in Hither Spain (Citerior), against the Arevaci and their allies, evidently gave rise to much more serious concern at Rome, for it was decided to send out one of the consuls of 153, Q. Fulvius Nobilior. Even if the surviving narrative reflects a hostile tradition, it is certain that Nobilior's campaign was singularly unsuccessful, not to say disastrous. Several severe reverses involving heavy casualties were followed by the loss of the base containing the supplies and money, and culminated in the sufferings of a harsh winter spent in a most unsuitable camp with a serious shortage of supplies. Reports of many of these events, of the exceptional ferocity of the fighting, and especially of the heavy losses suffered on 23 August, will have reached Rome in time to have influenced the consular elections;[4] it is scarcely a coincidence that M. Claudius Marcellus was elected to a third consulship and assumed the command in Citerior for 152.

[1] pp. 52 f.
[2] The date in Ulterior depends on whether the praetors Manilius and Piso were successive or, as is more probable, contemporary, one being governor of Citerior: App. *Iber.* 56; *MRR* i, p. 451 n. 1; Simon, *Roms Kriege*, p. 13. Q. Fulvius Nobilior, cos. 153, is the first known commander in the Celtiberian war, but the fighting must have started in the previous year at latest. The only surviving narrative of these wars is App. *Iber.* 44 f. (Citerior) and 56 f. (Ulterior), supplemented by Polyb. 35. 1 f., Livy, *Epit.* 47 f., Oros. 4. 21. 1 f., and a few brief references in other sources. Sulpicius Galba's atrocities attracted rather more attention: p. 58. In general see De Sanctis, *Storia*, iv. 1, pp. 466 f.; Schulten, *Numantia*, i, pp. 332 f.; *Gesch. von Numantia*, pp. 33 f.; Simon, op. cit., pp. 11 f.
[3] Livy, *Epit.* 47 (linking the change directly with the Spanish wars); Cassiod. *Chron.*; *Fasti Praen.*, *CIL* i². 1, p. 231.
[4] The 'fiery war': Polyb. 35. 1. 1, thence Diod. 31. 40. 23 August: App. *Iber.* 45.

Although in the course of the year Marcellus was to become involved in a dispute about Roman policy in Celtiberia, it is unlikely that this had arisen as yet or that it influenced the outcome of the election. Marcellus is much more likely to have won his consulship on the strength of his military reputation; for he was clearly one of the foremost generals of the day. With the possible exception of Ti. Gracchus, who may still have been alive but would have been nearly seventy, Marcellus was almost certainly the only man living who had celebrated two triumphs, and the second of them was as recent as 155. Moreover he had had some experience in Spain, since as praetor he had governed both provinces together and had engaged in at least some successful warfare.[1] It is probable that no one in Rome seemed more suitable for the command in Celtiberia in 152.

But in Rome a man needed to be not only suitable for an appointment but eligible in law. A considerable variety of conditions of eligibility had been laid down, and among them was the rule that one individual should not hold the consulship twice within ten years;[2] yet Marcellus' second consulship had been in 155, only three years before. If it is easy to understand why many were willing to vote for him, it still remains to be explained how a man who by law was ineligible came to offer himself as a candidate, to be accepted as such by the presiding magistrate, and to be declared elected. Unfortunately the scanty sources give little help in answering these questions. It is conceivable that, like others after him, Marcellus was assisted by special *ad hoc* legislation, but on the whole this does not seem very probable.[3] The recent second consulships of C. Marcius Figulus and Scipio Nasica Corculum are likely to have been much more significant. In 162 a fault in religious procedure at their election had compelled these men to resign their first consulships as *vitio creati*.[4] In 159 Nasica became censor, which accords with the principle that those who resigned as *vitio creati* were nevertheless deemed to have held the office in question; but then Marcius was elected consul for 156,

---

[1] Livy, 43. 15. 3; 45. 4. 1. For his reputation cf. App. *Iber.* 48: ἐπιτυχὴς δὲ τὰ πολέμια ὤν.

[2] Astin, *Lex Annalis*, p. 19 n. 6.

[3] De Sanctis, *Storia*, iv. 1, p. 471, suggests that there may have been a special plebiscite (cf. also Scullard, *Roman Politics*, p. 234), but see Astin, 'Leges Aelia et Fufia', *Latomus* 23 (1964), pp. 438 f., where it is suggested that the form taken by the reaction to Marcellus' election would not have been particularly appropriate if this had been the case.

[4] Refs. p. 36 n. 2.

and Nasica followed suit in the next year, so that both secured second consulships in well under ten years. Since Marcius was the first for more than half a century to breach the ten-year restriction, there can be little doubt that he did so by exploiting the idea that in some sense he had not held the consulship in 162 and by devising some intricate legal arguments; and in the next year Nasica successfully followed the precedent set by Marcius. Their success certainly pointed the way for Marcellus, in the sense of encouraging a search for means to circumvent the law, and thus of breaking down a psychological barrier established by long usage; and in all probability these two second consulships played a more conspicuous role, either as direct precedents or because issues raised in these instances provided a basis for some of the legal arguments which Marcellus and his supporters presumably advanced.[1]

The silence of the sources embraces not only the methods employed but also the vital question of whether Marcellus' election was opposed or facilitated by the majority in the Senate. That there was some opposition may be taken for granted, and among the opponents was Cato. For Cato supported a law, passed at about this time and generally agreed to have been a reaction to Marcellus' third consulship, which prohibited altogether the tenure of even a second consulship.[2]

But, as events were shortly to show, legislation was not an adequate answer to what had happened. Whatever means may have been employed, whether the majority in the Senate opposed or condoned, for the first time for more than half a century, since the great crises of the Hannibalic war, a constitutional law—or at least the clear and hitherto observed intention of the law—had been successfully overridden. Admittedly there had been the recent second consulships of Marcius and Nasica, and the influence and impact of these are not to

[1] Calvert, 'M. Claudius Marcellus cos. II 155 B.C.', *Athenaeum* 39 (1961), p. 23, suggests that the ban on holding office twice (*iterum*) within ten years was felt to apply only to the second tenure, not the third, though he admits that Cicero, *De Leg.* 3. 9, and Livy, 7. 42. 1, did not understand it to be so. It is conceivable that Marcellus advanced some such argument, but that the law had not hitherto been understood in this sense is shown by the long interval during which no one had achieved a third consulship.

[2] *ORF²*, fgts. 185 and 186, pp. 75 f.; Scullard, *Roman Politics*, p. 234; Kienast, *Cato*, p. 92. It is possible also that Cato's speech *Contra Annium, ORF²*, fgt. 109, p. 45, was directed against the consul presiding at Marcellus' election (T. Annius Luscus: his colleague was in Spain), although it is usually assigned to Cato's censorship: *ORF²*, loc. cit.; Scullard, op. cit., pp. 264 f.; but Kienast, op. cit., p. 164, lists it among the speeches of uncertain date.

be ignored. On the other hand there was a real sense in which these men had not held their first consulships, in which they might be held not to have been *iusti consules*; and evidently they had simply taken advantage of ambiguities or uncertainties in the legal provisions, so that what they had done, arising from very unusual circumstances, did little to prejudice the possibility of clarifying the position by new legislation. But Marcellus went significantly further. In the first place, though he too probably exploited legal uncertainties, his consulship in 155 had been quite normal, so that his third consulship openly and obviously violated the intention of the law; and, though these particular uncertainties might be resolved, his success could only encourage others to look for means of overriding or circumventing inconvenient laws. In the second place, it is a safe assumption that he and his supporters urged the necessity of his election and argued on the basis of the expediency of the state, and that, whatever the legal arguments, what happened in practice was that constitutional law was subordinated to immediate expediency. It may well be that Marcellus and his supporters did not fully appreciate the gravity of what they were doing, but grave it was; for once such ideas as these have been successfully translated into action, there is a greater readiness to tolerate them, to accept them, and to imitate them. And in their nature they are ideas against which laws are no defence. It is possible to legislate against second or third consulships, but not against the growth of an attitude of mind which finds it reasonable to seek ways of circumventing the clear intention of the law, nor yet against a growing belief that in special circumstances it is proper to subordinate law to expediency.

Marcellus' campaign in Citerior met with considerable success, with the result that before long he was able to make a truce with the enemy and send their ambassadors to Rome in an attempt to secure a negotiated peace. Their position was that if a fixed penalty were imposed upon them they would accept it, provided that the Romans then re-established the successful arrangements which had endured from 179 until the present war. Marcellus himself sent dispatches recommending the conclusion of peace.[1]

---

[1] On the negotiations and the debate in the Senate see App. *Iber.* 48 f.; Polyb. 35. 2 f.; Simon, *Roms Kriege*, pp. 35 f.

But Marcellus' lenient policy was not acceptable to many senators. There was a strong feeling that the war should be carried on until the Celtiberians made a formal *deditio*, that is, surrendered unconditionally, placing their persons and property at the absolute discretion of the Romans, without prior guarantees. The main considerations behind this policy seem to have been concerned with prestige. In 153 Nobilior had rejected an offer to negotiate and had demanded a *deditio*.[1] It was felt that to moderate this demand would be to create the impression that the Romans could be forced to make concessions and that this would weaken Roman authority throughout Spain. The situation was further complicated by those Spaniards who had remained loyal and who were now pressing for the severe punishment of the rebels; and it was also argued that such punishment would ensure the submission of the whole of Spain.[2] However, the sequel suggests that with many senators these considerations were less important than that of prestige. At the time this harsher policy prevailed, and it was resolved to send L. Licinius Lucullus, one of the consuls of 151, to take over the command from Marcellus; among those who favoured this decision was Scipio Aemilianus, though as a comparatively junior senator he is unlikely to have had any special influence on the discussion.[3]

Traces survive of the polemic which accompanied the debate. Marcellus was accused of 'favouring the enemy more than the allies', and he was alleged to be afraid of continuing the war—an absurd idea

[1] App. *Iber.* 49; Diod. 31. 41, which surely refers to Nobilior; Simon, *Roms Kriege*, p. 27.

[2] Polyb. 35. 2. 6 f.; 35. 3. 9; App. *Iber.* 48. Blázquez, 'La Conquista de Hispania', *Klio* 41 (1963), pp. 168 f., speaks of the Senate's policy of aggression and conquest in these wars; but the Romans more probably regarded them as the punishment of Lusitanian raiders and the suppression of rebels. The war in Citerior started with the fear of potential rebellion and a clumsy attempt to assert Roman authority. App. *Iber.* 44; Diod. 31. 39; Simon, *Roms Kriege*, pp. 11 f. and 15 f.

[3] Polyb. 35. 4. 8: δοκῶν σύμβουλος γεγονέναι. Bilz, *Die Politik*, p. 52 (cf. Scullard, 'Scipio Aemilianus', *JRS* 50 (1960), p. 60 n. 7), rightly rejects the idea of a war party led by Scipio and suggests that the phrase may mean no more than that Scipio voted for continuation of the war. Simon, *Roms Kriege*, p. 38 and n. 44, favours a middle course, that Scipio exercised unusual influence for a *quaestorius*. But even if this is what Polybius implies, he could easily be exaggerating, and in any case, what would such 'unusual influence' amount to in relation to the influence of consulars? Blázquez, 'La Conquista de Hispania', *Klio* 41 (1963), pp. 168 f., esp. pp. 169, 171 f., returns to the view that Scipio was a dominant influence in these wars, in 151 and later, though he does not go as far as Schulten, *Numantia*, i, pp. 273 f. and 278 f.; *Gesch. von Numantia*, pp. 81 f.; *CAH* viii, p. 323.

in the light of his career.[1] But there may be more truth in the charge that he was anxious to end the war himself in the expectation of thereby winning fame and glory. At any rate, before Lucullus arrived the Celtiberians had made a formal *deditio* to Marcellus, who let them go free as soon as he had secured an enormous sum of money and hostages from all their communities. It is not hard to credit the suspicions that Marcellus secured this surrender by private negotiation, that he preserved the outward appearance of a *deditio* but skilfully put into effect his own moderate policy. With Roman prestige upheld by the *deditio*, a majority of the Senate was apparently ready to accept what Marcellus had done, and the war was at an end.[2]

There were, however, unexpected consequences of the original decision to continue the war. Lucullus was to take with him to Spain fresh troops, but when he and his fellow consul, A. Postumius Albinus, commenced the levy serious trouble arose. According to Polybius, reports of the ferocity of the recent fighting produced unprecedented alarm among the younger men, so much so that it proved impossible to enlist not only troops but even military tribunes and *legati*. In this crisis Scipio Aemilianus, who had been going to Macedonia, unexpectedly offered to serve in Spain, an example which had a profound effect. For not only were others shamed into offering themselves as officers, but crowds flocked to the levy.[3] The surviving fragment of Polybius records no more, but other sources reveal a serious dispute concerning the severity of the levy. One source reports that in the course of the dispute the tribunes of the plebs placed the consuls in prison, and another states that in consequence of the dispute the use of the lot was introduced for the first time into the procedure of the levy, evidently to determine which of the men who had been levied were to go to Spain.[4]

Several aspects of these events are significant. In the first place they

[1] Polyb. 35. 3. 2 and 4; 35. 4. 3.

[2] App. *Iber.* 49 f.; cf. Livy, *Epit.* 48. Poseidonius, fgt. 51 *FGrH* = Strabo, 3. 4. 13, states that the sum exacted was 600 talents, an enormous amount, which must have been a crippling blow to the Celtiberian cities. It is very likely that this encouraged the Senate to accept Marcellus' *fait accompli*; so Schulten, *Gesch. von Numantia*, p. 56; Simon, *Roms Kriege*, pp. 44 f.

[3] Polyb. 35. 4; repeated in Livy, *Epit.* 48 and Oros. 4. 21. 1; cf. Val. Max. 3. 2. 6.

[4] Livy, *Epit.* 48; App. *Iber.* 49.

demonstrate that in certain circumstances the difficulty of recruiting sufficient troops could be very considerable and posed a serious problem for the state. It was not a new problem, but it seems now to have become more severe; in 169 Roman failures in the war against Perseus created a similar situation, but this did not generate such tension and was overcome without any concession such as had to be made in 151.[1] The second noteworthy point is that this heightened popular feeling is matched by the readiness of the tribunes to respond to it. This too is in contrast with 169, when there is no hint of tribunician intervention.[2] Whether on this occasion the tribunes were motivated by a genuine desire to redress serious grievances or were exploiting the discontent for political reasons, they did succeed in winning some concession; and in an age when popular favour was a significant political factor it must have been made obvious to many that such situations could be used with great profit for political ends.

But the most revealing item is the incarceration of the consuls. This must mean first that the tribunes exercised their veto, either against the levying of certain individuals or against the whole levy—and that in itself is interesting, for it shows a readiness to thwart the will of the Senate, at least as a means of pressure to achieve other ends; and it must mean further that the consuls took the virtually unprecedented step of attempting to carry on despite the veto, thus technically violating the *sacrosanctitas* of the tribunes.[3] Presumably the consuls felt strongly that the veto was impeding, in a serious and unreasonable manner, action which was of urgent public importance; but to attempt direct defiance was a grave matter.

After the Struggle of the Orders the tribunate had gradually lost

---

[1] Livy, 43. 14. 2 f.; 43. 15. 7 f.

[2] Taylor, 'Forerunners of the Gracchi', *JRS* 52 (1962), pp. 20 f., draws attention to other earlier instances of the tribunes' inactivity or ineffectiveness in such matters. Unfortunately the two situations which seem to offer the best contrasts are not quite certain, since they may have been influenced by exceptional considerations. In 193 there may have been real alarm at the Ligurian invasion which interrupted the tribunes' intervention (Livy, 34. 56. 9 f.), and in 191 an appeal from certain maritime colonies which the tribunes referred to the discretion of the Senate may have been handled in this way because it raised problems about the geographical limits of the tribunes' powers (Livy, 36. 3. 5).

[3] So, rightly, Bleicken, *Volkstribunat*, pp. 102 f.

its original revolutionary character and to a considerable extent had been absorbed into the scheme of the Roman public offices. Hence it had become an instrument of government, especially of government by the Senate; but at the same time its extensive powers made it an excellent tool of political and factional struggle, and by the second century it was being used extensively in this way.[1] What is true of the office as an entity is true also of the power of veto. The tribunician veto had been founded upon awesome religious sanctions and had been used to protect citizens against oppression. Though this purpose no doubt continued to be quoted,[2] in reality the veto had become a political device, looked upon like other political devices, except that its peculiar nature was openly and directly to impede and frustrate. And an exercise of the veto which was claimed to be in defence of citizens or in the interests of the state, in the eyes of those who were impeded might all too easily seem unwarranted abuse of this power in pursuit of factional or personal interests.[3] Hence there developed an attitude of mind which no longer considered it quite so outrageous or unreasonable to attempt to circumvent the veto. The episode in 151 marks an important stage in that development.[4] And it was a development of profound importance. Since the Hannibalic war the Senate had been the effective government of Rome, the wishes of the majority of senators determining virtually all policy and legislation. In theory, however, every magistrate, and especially the tribunes, had the right to lay proposed legislation before the assemblies, whose power was final, without previously consulting the Senate. In the period 200–150 there seem to have been few attempts to do this, and such as there were met with almost no success, but the reason for this was that almost invariably it was possible to find at least one of the

[1] Bleicken, *Volkstribunat, passim*, esp. chs. 3–5; cf. pp. 94 f. and pp. 131 f. for factional uses. De Sanctis, *Storia*, iv. 1, pp. 535 f.

[2] Cf. Taylor, 'Forerunners of the Gracchi', *JRS* 52 (1962), p. 20 and esp. n. 10.

[3] Livy, *Epit.* 48 and App. *Iber.* 49 preserve the rival points of view in 151: on the one hand, that the consuls were conducting the levy without favouritism while the tribunes were seeking exemption for their friends; on the other, that the consuls were conducting the levy inequitably and with favouritism.

[4] An earlier stage is marked by the complicated dispute in 169 between a tribune, P. Rutilius, and the censors, C. Claudius and Ti. Gracchus. It seems that Gracchus did successfully ignore Rutilius' veto, but the issues at stake were essentially personal and the readiness of the assembly to acquit Gracchus suggests that he produced some plausible legal arguments. Livy, 43. 16; Bleicken, *Volkstribunat*, pp. 102 f.

ten tribunes willing to veto such an attempt.[1] The veto was therefore a key element in the maintenance of senatorial authority. At a time when the assemblies could increasingly be swayed by factors other than *clientela* any undermining of the veto would ease the way towards defiance and circumvention of the wishes of the majority of senators. This is why the behaviour of the consuls of 151 is so interesting. Their attempt to defy the veto failed, but it is symptomatic of a trend, and other attempts were to be made before many years had passed.

In comparison with other aspects of the affair the behaviour of Scipio Aemilianus is of relatively minor importance. Yet it is not without interest. While few will doubt that Polybius has exaggerated the impact of his action upon the crisis and its resolution, the basic story must surely be true: Scipio had been invited to Macedonia to assist in settling certain disputes and it had been arranged that he should go; but, probably during a senatorial debate on the recruiting crisis, he announced that he was willing to serve in Spain, either as military tribune or as *legatus*. Very probably this gesture, which in the circumstances must have been sufficiently sensational to make a considerable impression, did lead other young aristocrats to volunteer, and it is certain to have been widely publicized in the attempt to overcome the general reluctance to serve. As for motive, it would be unreasonable scepticism to doubt that Scipio was genuinely shocked by the situation and anxious to assist. On the other hand Polybius himself indicates that there were other motives as well, for he returns to the theme of Scipio's widespread fame: 'Having won an unquestioned reputation for nobility and temperance, but desiring a reputation for bravery . . . he said that it would be both safer and more agreeable to him to go to Macedonia . . . but that the needs of the country were more pressing and summoned to Spain those who truly sought fame. . . . Scipio immediately earned great praise.' Such remarks harmonize with Scipio's character and outlook, and there can be little doubt that it was no accident that Scipio's gesture was dramatic, likely to draw attention to himself and to create an

[1] Cic. *De Leg*. 3. 24. The factors here discussed are illustrated by the unsuccessful attempt of M'. Iuventius Thalna, as praetor in 167, to secure a declaration of war on Rhodes without consulting the Senate. For the two laws which may have been carried in defiance of the Senate see Additional Note C, p. 340.

impression of courage; nor that it offered him an opportunity to serve
with distinction in difficult warfare—an opportunity which he would
scarcely have had otherwise, since Lucullus is most unlikely to have
taken him if he could have avoided it.[1] Moreover, it may be no
coincidence that Africanus himself had achieved early distinction by
volunteering to serve in Spain when others were unwilling—or at
least it could be made out that this was what had happened.[2]

  Scipio did see active service, despite the termination of the war
with the Arevaci and their allies before the new army reached Spain;
for Lucullus campaigned against peoples further to the west. The
surviving account of his activities must be treated with some caution,
since it is almost certainly tendentious. With a most unfavourable
portrayal of Lucullus' motives and character is contrasted a very
favourable presentation of Scipio.[3] This obviously reflects a deep
hostility between the two men and gives us only a hostile interpretation of Lucullus' actions. Nevertheless the outline is clear. In 151,
attacking the Vaccaei and others, he treacherously massacred the
male inhabitants of Cauca, which had negotiated terms of surrender.
Then, when he attempted to take Intercatia by siege he ran into
serious difficulties over supplies, until the besieged eventually made
terms through Scipio. Lucullus next attacked Palantia but was hampered by the enemy's cavalry and by a further shortage of supplies,
and eventually had to make a difficult retreat. After wintering
further south, in Turdetania, he clashed with the Lusitanians and
concluded his operations by co-operating with Ser. Sulpicius Galba
in the final suppression of the rebel bands.

  It is also clear that in the course of these events Scipio several times
achieved prominence, especially at Intercatia,[4] where he accepted the
challenge of an enemy chieftain to single combat and overcame him

---

[1] See below on the probable relationship between them.

[2] Livy, 26. 18 f.; Val. Max. 3. 7. 1; App. Iber. 18; Zon. 9. 7. Scullard, Roman Politics,
p. 66 and n. 2, and Walsh, Livy, p. 96 n. 2, observe that it is improbable that in 210 no one
else dared to volunteer for the important Spanish command. They note the resemblance to
the events of 151. It would be extremely interesting to know who first gave the story this
feature.

[3] App. Iber. 51–55, passim.

[4] App. Iber. 53 f.; Polyb. 35. 5. 1 f., cf. fgts. 6 and 18 BW; Livy, Epit. 48; Vell. 1. 12. 4;
Val. Max. 3. 2. 6; Oros. 4. 21. 2; Plin. Nat. Hist. 37. 9; (Victor) De Vir. Ill. 58. 2 f.; Florus,
1. 33. 11 (wrongly stating that Scipio won the spolia opima); Plut. Praec. Reip. Ger. 10;
Ampel. 22. Scipio's official status is uncertain: see Additional Note D, p. 340.

after a considerable struggle. In an unsuccessful assault on the city he was first on the wall, thereby earning the *corona muralis*. And it was he who conducted the negotiations for the surrender of the city. Our source says that he did so because the Intercatians distrusted Lucullus himself, fearing a repetition of the massacre at Cauca, but accepted Scipio's word on the strength of his reputation for virtue (or possibly 'bravery'). Though this may well be tendentious, it is quite possible that this version of the affair was circulated at Rome. In the autumn or winter Scipio was sent to Africa to obtain elephants from the Numidian king Massinissa. In itself this was not remarkable: Scipio probably inherited from Africanus a patron–client relationship with Massinissa, which would make him the obvious choice for the assignment. But it so happened that he arrived on the eve of the great battle in which Massinissa defeated the Carthaginians. After the battle, the latter, learning of Scipio's presence, asked him to bring them to terms with Massinissa. Scipio therefore presided over a conference, and though it proved abortive, and though he may not have exercised exceptional influence at it, this linked his name closely with events which must have been widely reported and discussed. Though this was a gift of fortune, it was one which he will have found especially congenial.[1]

Thus the impact of the Celtiberian war upon the internal politics of Rome was multiplex. Apart from the immediate issue of policy, it was the occasion for—indeed provoked—several developments which not only revealed but encouraged and advanced certain significant trends, such as a growing readiness to champion and perhaps to exploit popular discontent, likewise to override constitutional restrictions for the sake of immediate expediency, and to seek to overcome the tribunician veto. On a different but still significant plane, it did much for Scipio Aemilianus, not merely in several times bringing him to public notice but in building up the popular image of the courageous military hero—an image which he himself was certainly trying to establish.

[1] App. *Lib.* 71 f.; Val. Max. 2. 10. 4; 5. 2, ext. 4. For the date see pp. 271 f.

V

THE CARTHAGINIAN CRISIS AND THE FIRST
YEAR OF THE WAR

WHILE the Spanish wars were in progress and still the subject of political controversy another and a greater issue was emerging at Rome—policy towards Carthage. There were, of course, other topics as well, some of which have left traces in the sources. Thus in 151, or possibly 150, Scipio Nasica Corculum, evidently genuinely alarmed lest the provision of seating for the populace should undermine Roman hardiness, persuaded the Senate to decree the destruction of the permanent theatre begun by the censors of 154, and further to prohibit altogether the provision of seating at *ludi* within or close to the city of Rome.[1] In 150 there was a sexual scandal in which the conviction of a certain C. Cornelius Cethegus on a charge of *stuprum* was only just prevented from leading on to a public hearing of even more outrageous charges against a young man of senatorial family, P. Decius Subulo.[2] In the east, though the Egyptian question seemed to have been settled and a deceptive calm reigned in Macedonia, Greece, and Asia Minor, a Roman-sponsored campaign was attempting to replace the distrusted Demetrius I Soter of Syria by the young Alexander Balas— a venture which was about to achieve success.[3] All these matters

[1] Livy, *Epit.* 48; Oros. 4. 21. 4 (which makes 151 highly probable); Val. Max. 2. 4. 2; Vell. 1. 15. 3; Aug. *De Civ. Dei*, 1. 31, cf. 32 f.; App. *B.C.* 1. 28 (incorrectly dated). The second part of the decree seems to confirm the genuineness of the motive and to refute the unsupported hypothesis of Altheim, *Römische Religionsgeschichte*, i², p. 280, that Nasica's motive was primarily religious, a concern lest a permanent theatre should 'secularize' the *ludi* by separating them from the temples and rituals with which they were originally associated.

[2] Livy, *Ox. Epit.* 48; Val. Max. 6. 1. 10; cf. Cic. *De Orat.* 2. 253; Cichorius, *Untersuch. zu Lucil.*, pp. 310 f.; Münzer, 'Anm. zur neuen Livius-Epitome', *Klio* 5 (1905), pp. 135 f.; Badian, 'P. Decius P. f. Subulo', *JRS* 46 (1956), p. 91.

[3] Egypt: Scullard, *Roman Politics*, pp. 236 f.; Badian, *Foreign Clientelae*, p. 110; De Sanctis, *Storia*, iv. 3, pp. 99 f. Syria: Bevan, *The House of Seleucus*, ii, pp. 209 f.; De Sanctis, op. cit., pp. 162 f.; McShane, *Foreign Policy of the Attalids*, pp. 189 f.

must have involved political discussion, and at least the internal events must have generated tensions; but inadequate information prevents any assessment of their political impact.

One other topic involved Scipio Aemilianus personally, shortly after his return from Spain, in the late summer or autumn of 150. When the Senate once more debated whether to release the survivors of the thousand Achaeans, among them Polybius, who had been interned in Italy nearly seventeen years before, Scipio obtained the support of Cato, whose pungent intervention in a long debate was regarded by Polybius as a major factor in securing an affirmative vote: 'As though we had nothing else to do, we sit here the whole day debating whether some old Greeks should be buried by Italian or Achaean undertakers.'[1] But although the incident is interesting evidence about the relationship between Cato and Scipio, among the affairs of the Senate it was a comparatively minor item—as Cato so emphatically pointed out—paling into insignificance beside the Carthaginian crisis, which was about to break into open war.

The crisis developed in the context of worsening relationships between Carthage and the Numidian king Massinissa.[2] At the end of the Second Punic War Carthage had been allowed to retain all her territories in Africa, except that Massinissa was to have any territory which at any time had been held by himself or his ancestors. The failure to define these excepted areas more accurately resulted in Massinissa repeatedly encroaching upon Carthaginian possessions. Carthage was prevented by her treaty with Rome from sending an army beyond her borders, and thus from ejecting Massinissa from disputed territory. Time and again Roman arbitrators either favoured Massinissa or did nothing—which in practice left the king in possession. In 161 they quite unjustly approved Massinissa's seizure of a particularly large and prosperous area, and a further example occurred around 158–156.[3] Inevitably feelings of impatience, resentment,

[1] Plut. *Cato Mai.* 9. 2 f. = Polyb. 35. 6; cf. Paus. 7. 10. 12. For the date see p. 245 n. 6.

[2] There are numerous modern discussions. See esp. Kahrstedt, *Gesch. der Karthager*, pp. 606 f., 620 f., 638 f.; Gsell, *Hist. anc.* iii, pp. 312 f.; Scullard, *Roman Politics*, pp. 240 f. and 287 f.; Badian, *Foreign Clientelae*, pp. 125 f.; De Sanctis, *Storia*, iv. 3, pp. 1 f. Some special topics are considered in Appendix III. The main source is App. *Lib.* 68–94, supplemented by Livy *Epit.*, by Plut. *Cato Mai.*, by a few fragments of Polybius and Diodorus, and by lesser writers such as Florus, Orosius, and Zonaras.

[3] Polyb. 31. 21; Livy, *Epit.* 47.

anger, and distrust spread and deepened among the Carthaginians, weakening the pro-Roman and pro-Numidian factions and strengthening the more militant democrats. In 153, while the Romans were preoccupied in Celtiberia and Massinissa was embroiled elsewhere, these feelings found expression in raids on Massinissa's settlers in disputed areas and in inciting rural Africans against the king. The consequent fighting, probably consisting mainly of raids and counterraids, was ended by Roman ambassadors, who nevertheless once more left Massinissa in control of the disputed territory.[1] Soon the king raised a new dispute, again Carthage appealed to Rome, and again, in 152, an embassy was sent out. The ambassadors, among whom was Cato (and probably also Scipio Nasica), offered to arbitrate, while Massinissa staged a withdrawal from some of the disputed territory—doubtless confident that Roman arbitration would favour him at least in part. But the patience of the Carthaginians had been strained too far, their distrust had grown too great: holding that Massinissa was patently in the wrong, and that the task of the embassy was simply to restore to them the land which he had occupied, they refused to submit to arbitration. Cato and his companions, returning to Rome with the quarrel undecided, must have been much perturbed. The rejection of Roman arbitration must have been a most unwelcome manifestation of independence and self-confidence, and they themselves had seen the basis of that confidence in the all-too-evident prosperity and wealth of the city.[2] From that point on tension mounted steadily. Now, or perhaps just before the embassy, Cato began to press for war and the destruction of Carthage, and Scipio Nasica began his equally famous opposition. Thus by the time Scipio Aemilianus set out for Spain early in 151 the crisis was already far advanced.

During Scipio's absence from Rome there were further serious developments. Late in 152 or in 151 Numidian complaints and reports that Carthage was rearming led to a new embassy of investigation. Cato had demanded immediate war, and with others he renewed

---

[1] App. *Lib*. 68; Livy, *Epit*. 47.

[2] App. *Lib*. 68 f.; Livy, *Epit*. 48; Zon. 9. 26; Plut. *Cato Mai*. 26. 1 f. Livy, loc. cit., states that the Carthaginian senate was willing to accept arbitration but that the people were roused to reject it. This is plausible, despite the obvious fiction that the Roman *legati* escaped violence only by flight.

the demand when the embassy reported military activity at Carthage, but more moderate counsels reduced this to a threat of war unless Carthage disarmed.[1] But before this compromise could be tested the Carthaginians committed themselves irrevocably. They expelled the small pro-Numidian faction, refused Massinissa's request for their restoration, and attacked the retinue of his son Gulussa. When Massinissa retaliated they sent out a large army which took the decisive step of pursuing him beyond the recognized frontier (winter 151–150). There followed the great battle witnessed by Scipio Aemilianus, who had arrived the previous day on his mission to fetch elephants from Massinissa. The long and fierce struggle went in favour of the Numidian, and was followed by an attempt to negotiate a settlement. At the conference, which was arranged by Scipio at the request of the Carthaginians, the latter offered large concessions but absolutely refused to hand over Numidian deserters who had joined them. In renewed hostilities the Punic troops were encircled and eventually compelled to surrender—most of them to be treacherously massacred by Massinissa's son Gulussa.[2]

The outcome of this disastrous attempt at self-assertion was far worse than the loss of a field army. Earlier Scipio Nasica had urged that there was not yet a *iusta causa* for war, a plea which was now seriously undermined.[3] By the time Aemilianus returned to Rome a Punic war was certain and military preparations were under way. Desperate and abject Carthaginian ambassadors were rebuffed; war was declared early in 149; the *deditio* of Utica, perhaps a little earlier, made available a suitable base for the disembarkation of the expeditionary force which now set out. There followed the *deditio*, the formal surrender to Roman discretion, of Carthage itself, and the successive demands by which the Romans secured first three hundred hostages and then the Carthaginian stocks of arms, until the final demand for the abandonment of the city and resettlement at least ten miles inland drove a disarmed people to desperate resistance.[4]

[1] Livy, *Epit.* 48.

[2] App. *Lib.* 70–73; Livy, *Epit.* 48, cf. 49; Diod. 32. 1; Zon. 9. 26; Val. Max. 2. 10. 4; 5. 2, ext. 4. For Scipio's mission see p. 47, and for the date Appendix III. 1.

[3] Livy, *Epit.* 48; cf. Polyb. 36. 2; Diod. 32. 5.

[4] App. *Lib.* 74 f.; Livy, *Epit.* 49; Polyb. 36. 3–7; Diod. 32. 3 and 6; Zon. 9. 26; Oros. 4. 22. 1 f.; Florus 1. 31. 3 f.

The agitation for the destruction of Carthage had been inspired and directed by Cato. Whether this final demand of 149 represents all that Cato had wanted we cannot know, but clearly a majority of senators were ultimately induced to support a fairly extreme policy which embodied Cato's main objective. No doubt there lay behind the decision irrational forces of prejudice and hatred, as well as a trend, discernible in this period, towards harsher methods of maintaining Roman power and influence, but the main motive was certainly fear: fear of a Carthage economically resurgent and rearming; fear of a people who had shown themselves restive and impatient, liable to support leaders who advocated a policy of military self-assertion and who sought to crush Numidia; fear of a city which had every reason to hate Rome. The demand of 149 reflects a determination to end that fear once and for all, and at the same time a belief that it could never be ended so long as the Carthaginians occupied a site so politically and strategically advantageous.[1]

As famous as Cato's campaign for the destruction of Carthage is Scipio Nasica's opposition. He argued that if Rome acted without adequate pretext this would have an undesirable effect on foreign opinion, and perhaps also that Rome needed Carthage as 'a counterweight of fear'.[2] In the end his arguments proved vain, but it is a familiar—and just—observation that he succeeded in restraining the Senate for more than two years. While Cato urged war, Nasica at first persuaded the Senate to send commissions of inquiry, then to vote that Rome would not go to war if Carthage disarmed. Polybius reports that 'disputes about the effect on foreign opinion very nearly made them desist from going to war'.[3] The Carthaginian attack on Massinissa made war virtually certain, but Nasica still kept up his struggle. When Carthage made her *deditio* he attempted to secure some moderation in the policy already agreed;[4] and it is quite possible that the Roman demands in 149, accompanied as they were by

---

[1] Appendix III. 2.   [2] Appendix III. 3.
[3] Polyb. 36. 2. 4; Livy, *Epit.* 48; cf. Zon. 9. 26. Diod. 32. 2 and 4, probably from Polybius and associated with the Carthaginian question, may reflect a hint of an answer to Nasica's argument: empires, once won, have to be retained through fear and acts of terrorism; the savage punishment of a people not fully obedient would inspire in others fear and submission.
[4] Livy, *Epit.* 49; Zon. 9. 26.

a promise that Carthage would retain her freedom, autonomy, and territory, were a compromise, representing a policy less harsh than Cato would have wished.[1] The Carthaginian breach of the *deditio* led inevitably to the new decision that the razing of the city should be accompanied by the destruction of the nation and the annexation of its territory; but even at this stage Nasica may have continued some form of opposition.[2]

Such a prolonged and tenaciously fought dispute, shot through with prejudice and fear, must have been a highly significant factor in the internal politics of Rome. Unhappily, few further traces of it can be discerned. Cato was supported by *principes*, but they are not named; of his opponents, other than Nasica, only one is known, L. Cornelius Lentulus Lupus.[3] Beyond that, it is possible to deduce the attitude of one person of more junior rank: Scipio Aemilianus.

It is true that by the time Scipio returned from Spain war was certain and in all probability had already been resolved upon in a secret session of the Senate; but the dispute had already been under way before he left Rome, and when he returned Nasica was still striving to modify Cato's policy. Scipio was in a difficult position. He had family and traditional ties with each of the chief protagonists, who were two of the most important men in the state. Whichever side he supported, he was bound to incur disfavour, was likely to forfeit potential assistance for his own advancement, and might create serious enmities; yet he can scarcely have avoided committing himself, for inevitably the notions of patronage and obligation will have generated great pressure from both sides.

It is virtually certain that Scipio gave his support to Cato.[4] There is no reason to question that his choice was determined primarily by his opinion of the merits of the case—indeed, it accords well with the belief, discernible at various times in his life, in the effectiveness of savage punishment as a deterrent to others.[5] Nevertheless, it

---

[1] Cf. Münzer, *RE*, s.v. *Cornelius*, no. 353, col. 1500; Florus 1. 31. 5: *medium senatus elegit*— at best from Livy, at worst a plausible guess by Florus himself.

[2] Zon. 9. 30, certainly erroneous as it stands but not a straight doublet of 9. 26; it could reflect a real debate in 149.

[3] Livy, *Epit.* 48; Cic. *Tusc.* 3. 51. Cf. Astin, 'Scipio and Cato', *Latomus* 15 (1956), p. 176.

[4] Appendix III. 4; Astin, op. cit., pp. 159 f.

[5] p. 331.

indubitably proved fortunate from the point of view of his later advancement. In the first place, although Nasica's election as Pontifex Maximus shows that he was still powerful at least in the early part of 150,[1] his reputation and influence must have been seriously undermined by the turn of events and especially by the Carthaginian successes in 149 and 148, which must have been widely interpreted as confirmation of Cato's warnings. It was perhaps as well not to have been closely identified with Nasica's opposition. But more than this, the war carried Scipio to an early consulship and thence to magnificent success; yet it is not credible that he would have been elected to the consulship of 147, in the face of tremendous resistance, if his opponents had been able to play upon earlier opposition to the destruction of Carthage. Thus, though in 150 it is unlikely that his standing was sufficient for him to have influenced the outcome of the dispute very much, his choice was highly significant for his own career.

A military expedition against Carthage was something not to be missed, either by aristocratic officers with an eye to prestige and reputation or by the rank and file, who expected quick success and doubtless plentiful booty (for they enlisted before the *deditio*).[2] It so happens that three Scipios are known to have served. Cn. Scipio Hispanus and Nasica Corculum's son (the later Nasica Serapio) were the officers who supervised the surrender of the Carthaginian armaments;[3] and, not surprisingly, Scipio Aemilianus was there, as a military tribune of the Fourth Legion.[4] The attractive character of the command may have had other consequences as well. Thus the very unusual decision to send both the consuls of 149 may well reflect private compromise as much as the seriousness with which the task was regarded; for both this decision and the election of the consuls must have been complicated by an immense amount of private argument and bargaining. And the consuls themselves seem a curiously undistinguished pair to have succeeded in an election at a time when

---

[1] Cic. *De Nat. Deor.*, 3. 5; *De Orat.* 3. 134; dated by *De Sen.* 50; cf. Aug. *De Civ. Dei*, 1. 30.

[2] App. *Lib.* 75.

[3] App. *Lib.* 80. They were probably military tribunes: *MRR* i, p. 459.

[4] Cic. *Rep.* 6. 9; the rank also in App. *Lib.* 98 and 112; (Victor) *De Vir. Ill.* 58. 4; Zon. 9. 27; Plut. *Praec. Reip. Ger.* 10.

everybody must have realized that a Punic war was imminent. They were certainly rivals for office, and it looks very much as if in the struggle for a promising command other candidates, with more distinguished ancestry and perhaps more notable talents, split the vote too widely, letting in two 'second choices'.[1]

L. Marcius Censorinus, who commanded the fleet, admittedly came from a consular *gens* and could point to distant ancestors of great distinction, but for several generations none had attained high office, and his father and grandfather almost certainly failed to reach the praetorship. Other branches of the *gens* with more recent successes may have helped him, but even so the amount of 'transferred prestige' could not have been great since they were only distantly related. Since almost nothing is recorded about his talents, his previous career, or his political ties, it is possible that he possessed some recommendation unknown to us; yet he remains an undistinguished choice.[2]

But what causes surprise is not that one consul should have come from the less eminent senatorial families but that both should. For M'. Manilius, who commanded the land forces, probably had no ancestor even of praetorian status, and his own praetorship had been marred by serious military defeat in Spain. Possibly his reputation as a lawyer was a slight electoral asset, but it was obviously irrelevant to the immediate tasks and can scarcely have outweighed these handicaps. Of his political links all that can be said is that he stood close to Scipio Aemilianus; not only is a close association attested for a later date but in the spring of 149 Manilius summoned Polybius from Greece to give assistance. But at this time Scipio was still comparatively junior, so this association does not reveal much about the forces which carried Manilius to the consulship.[3]

The consuls did not achieve the rapid success anticipated.

---

[1] Although the tradition that one consul should be a patrician had been violated in 172 and several times since, the *fasti* show that it still retained considerable force; thus it is very unlikely that two plebeians stood other than as rivals, especially two with such unpromising backgrounds.

[2] Münzer, *RE*, s.v. *Marcius*, no. 46, with the stemma at cols. 1539 f. No ancestor of Marcius is found among the praetors of 218–166, almost all of whom are known.

[3] Münzer, *RE*, s.v. *Manilius*, no. 12. Spain: App. *Iber.* 56; cf. Livy, *Epit.* 47; Obsequ. 17; Simon, *Roms Kriege*, p. 13. As a lawyer: esp. Cic. *De Orat.* I. 212; *Rep.* I. 20; 3. 17; Just. *Dig.* I. 2. 2. 39. Scipio, in 129: Cic. *Rep.* I. 18. Polybius: Polyb. 36. 11.

Admittedly, Polybius' account, the ultimate origin of most of our information, was written in such a manner as to highlight the qualities and deeds of Scipio Aemilianus, who is portrayed as repeatedly saving the army from desperate situations;[1] but even so the familiar tale of Roman failure in 149 must be in general true. The initial assaults were not only repulsed but were met with energetic and by no means profitless counter-attacks. Endeavours to establish a regular siege suffered various set-backs. After the departure of Censorinus (to hold the elections) Manilius made only limited progress in reducing other Punic strongholds, while the first of his two vain attempts to bring to battle Hasdrubal's field army led to a serious reverse which might easily have become a major disaster. Only at the end of his command, in the spring of 148, did he perhaps have some minor successes.[2] Then his place was taken by one of the new consuls, L. Calpurnius Piso Caesoninus.

Both consuls of 149 had been sent to Africa; they had been provided with an exceptionally large expeditionary force; they enjoyed almost total command of the sea; and, although it is true that Hasdrubal had a substantial rebel army in the field, the city of Carthage had been deprived of all its armaments. A quick victory was expected, and not without good reason. Under such circumstances it is not credible that the Romans were largely content with sanguine reports from Censorinus and Manilius, and that the disappointing lack of success was not an important issue at the consular elections. It is therefore a remarkable comment on the Roman system that the man who succeeded Manilius had evidently been associated with him, as joint commander, in his disastrous defeat in Spain: six thousand Romans are said to have perished. Nor did Piso owe his election to aristocratic birth. Only one previous member of the family had attained the consulship, and Piso himself had evidently been adopted from the exceptionally obscure gens of the Caesonii. The explanation

---

[1] pp. 62 f. For the course of the war and discussion of sources see esp. Kahrstedt, *Gesch. der Karthager*, pp. 620 f. and 645 f.; Kromayer–Veith, *Schlachtfelder*, iii, p. 705 f.; Kromayer, *Schlachten-Atlas*, Röm. Abt., Bl. 11 and cols. 51 f.; Gsell, *Hist. anc.* iii, pp. 336 f. and 355 f.; Hallward, *CAH* viii, pp. 479 f.; De Sanctis, *Storia*, iv. 3, pp. 39 f. Baradez, 'Nouvelles recherches sur les ports antiques de Carthage', *Karthago* 9 (1958), pp. 45 f., is of great importance for the topography. The main source continues to be App. *Lib.* 94 f., supplemented by Livy, *Epit.* 49 f., Zon. 9. 26 f., and brief notices in other sources.

[2] Livy, *Epit.* 50; *Ox. Epit.* 50; Oros. 4. 22. 8; cf. Zon. 9. 27.

is probably that he achieved the consulship as a protégé of his patrician colleague, Sp. Postumius Albinus Magnus, of whom little is known personally but whose ancient and famous family were at this time enjoying a phase of electoral success: Spurius was the third Postumius to reach the consulship in seven years. If this is the case, both the fact itself and the further fact that, whether the decision was by agreement or by sortition, Piso was allowed to go to Africa, carry the implication that Postumius and many other senators saw merit and talent in him (and doubtless he was very ready to blame Manilius for the defeat in Spain).[1]

*Another element which is perhaps relevant to the outcome of the election is that both the new consuls were politically hostile to Scipio Aemilianus. Not that Scipio himself was yet a significant consideration in people's minds, but the close association between him and Manilius suggests that disappointment, and perhaps shock and alarm, induced by the failures of 149 swung opinion away from those who had supported and recommended Manilius to men who were known to be hostile to him and who exploited the situation. In the event the election of Postumius and Piso opened the way for similar exploitation by Scipio: he had no sense of obligation towards Piso—or his reputation.

The Punic war and the consular elections were not the only political preoccupations of 149. Abroad, a disturbance in the client kingdoms of Asia Minor necessitated the dispatch of a special senatorial mission;[2] and when the pretender Andriscus, the 'Pseudo-Philip', invaded Macedonia with the aid of some Thracian chieftains, Scipio Nasica Corculum was sent to organize local resistance—though later it became necessary to send a legion under P. Iuventius Thalna, who suffered a disastrous defeat, probably early in 148.[3] At home the

[1] Spain: App. Iber. 56; Simon, Roms Kriege, p. 13. De Sanctis, Storia, iv. 3, p. 56, infers that at the elections there was no special concern about Africa. Piso and Albinus: Münzer, RE, s.v. Calpurnius, no. 87 and s.v. Postumius, no. 47. On the relations of the Calpurnii and Postumii towards each other and towards Scipio see pp. 91 f. and p. 95.

[2] Nicomedes of Bithynia, backed by Attalus II of Pergamum, rebelled and seized his father's throne: Magie, Roman Rule in Asia Minor, i, pp. 28 and 317, with note; De Sanctis, Storia, iv. 3, pp. 87 f.; McShane, Foreign Policy of the Attalids, p. 190. The composition of the embassy was the subject of one of Cato's witticisms: Polyb. 36. 14; Plut. Cato Mai. 9. 1; Livy, Epit. 50; Ox. Epit. 50; App. Mith. 6.

[3] Wilcken, RE, s.v. Andriskos, no. 4 (add Livy, Ox. Epit. 50); De Sanctis, Storia, iv. 3, pp. 122 f. Nasica: only in Zon. 9. 28, but there is no need to doubt it.

tension and peculiarity of the year were reflected in the first irregularity for more than sixty years in the five-year cycle of the census, which was held in 147 instead of in 149, and also in the postponement of the secular games, due and possibly authorized in 149 but not held until 146.[1] Then, late in the year, death was to remove from the political arena one of its most powerful personalities, M. Porcius Cato.[2] But the best-recorded event, and one full of significance, is the attempt to prosecute Ser. Sulpicius Galba.

In 150 Galba had followed up his victory in Further Spain with the massacre of a large number of surrendered Lusitanians and the sale of others into slavery, all allegedly in violation of his pledged word. In 149 a tribune, L. Scribonius Libo, introduced a bill proposing the release of those enslaved and the setting up of a special court.[3] No doubt Libo and his supporters were genuinely outraged, but the matter quickly took on a political complexion, if only because of the personalities who became involved. Galba was supported by Q. Fulvius Nobilior, Libo not only by L. Cornelius Cethegus but most energetically by Cato, who was an old enemy of both Galba and Nobilior.[4] There was a considerable struggle, in the course of which Galba delivered at least three speeches. One of his arguments, the inadequacy of which was exposed by Cato, was that the Lusitani had been using the respite to plan a new rebellion.[5] Ultimately the bill was rejected, so the enslaved Lusitanians were not freed and Galba did not have to face a formal trial. Yet the affair was not without wider consequences.

In the first place, it is highly probable that Galba's escape gave the

---

[1] Nilsson, *RE*, s.v. *Saeculares ludi*, cols. 1701 f. and 1707, with table at 1699 f. Censorin. *De Die Nat.* 17. 11 shows that the contemporary writers Piso, Gellius, and Cassius Hemina recorded them under 146, but Valerius Antias, Varro, and Livy (cf. *Epit.* 49 and *Ox. Epit.* 49) put them in 149. Nilsson suggests a fiction by Antias, to preserve the interval of precisely a century; but it is surprising that Varro should have been deceived. A *senatus consultum* of 149 might account for the misunderstanding.

[2] Cic. *Brut.* 61; 80; Vell. 1. 13. 1; Plin. *Nat. Hist.* 29. 15; cf. Plut. *Cato Mai.* 27. 5.

[3] Numerous refs. collected by Münzer, *RE*, s.v. *Sulpicius*, no. 58, cols. 762 f.; cf. esp. Livy, *Epit.* 49; Cic. *Brut.* 80; 89 f.; *De Orat.* 1. 227 f.; 2. 263; Val. Max. 8. 1, abs. 2; 9. 6. 2. Several speeches are mentioned and some fragments survive: *ORF*², pp. 79 f., 112 f., 138 f. Simon, *Roms Kriege*, pp. 62 f., attempts a more elaborate reconstruction of the course of the dispute than that offered here, but many of the details he suggests are hypothetical.

[4] Cic. *De Orat.* 1. 227; Livy, *Epit.* 49; *ORF*², pp. 67 f.

[5] Livy, *Epit.* 49; Cato, fgt. 197, *ORF*², pp. 79 f.

impetus for the passage that same year of the famous law, introduced by the tribune L. Calpurnius Piso Frugi, which established a standing court for the trial of extortion cases. This provided a new means of bringing rapacious governors to justice, and in the event also opened up a new avenue for politically inspired prosecutions.[1]

Secondly, the dispute had electoral consequences. Galba was the outstanding orator of the day and could point to his recent military successes in Spain, yet he did not attain the consulship until 144, though he was eligible to hold it in 148. There can be no certainty that he would have wished to stand against Postumius in 149, though it is likely enough; but in any case the long delay shows that Libo's attack had inflicted some damage on Galba's reputation and on his career.

But in a sense the most significant aspect of the episode is to be seen in the methods by which Galba defended himself:

> He almost lifted on to his shoulders his ward Quintus, the son of his kinsman C. Sulpicius Galus, so that he should move the people to tears by the living memory of his illustrious father; he committed his own two small sons to the guardianship of the people, and, like a soldier making his will on the eve of battle, said that he appointed the Roman people to be their guardian in their fatherless plight. So, though at that time Galba was being overwhelmed by popular ill-will and hatred, he secured his escape by means of these histrionics.[2]

'Thus', Cato complained, 'by stirring the pity of the populace for little children he snatched himself from the flames'; and Cato urged that the parading of children or women in this way should be entirely forbidden.[3] Cato's indignation may have led him to pass over other factors contributing to Galba's escape, and the appeal to prejudice may not all have been on one side;[4] but it is clear that both he and

---

[1] Refs. in *MRR* i, p. 459; cf. esp. Cic. *Brut.* 106. There are indications that Galba had engaged in direct plundering: Ps.-Ascon., p. 203 Stangl; Nepos, *Cato Mai.* 3. 4; cf. App. *Iber.* 60. Ferguson, 'The Lex Calpurnia of 149 B.C.', *JRS* 11 (1921), pp. 86 f., suggests that in addition to its ostensible purpose the law was deliberately intended to provide the Senate with a weapon against disobedient governors and was causally connected with the decision to create new provinces. The argument seems to infer motives too readily from *de facto* results.

[2] Cic. *De Orat.* 1. 228, from Rutilius Rufus.

[3] Cic. *Brut.* 90; Cato, fgt. 199, *ORF*[2], p. 80 = Fronto, p. 52. 12 Hout. Cato reported the affair at length in the last book of the *Origines*. Cf. Cic. *Brut.* 80; 89; Livy, *Epit.* 49; *Ox. Epit.* 49; Val. Max. 8. 1, abs. 2; Quint. *Inst.* 2. 15. 8.

[4] Other factors: App. *Iber.* 60 alleges bribery; nor was rational defence lacking: see p. 58,

Galba recognized not only that the exploitation of patronage and *clientelae* was insufficient to control the tribal assembly, and that the votes of many citizens might be determined by their own opinions, by self-interest, by rational arguments, or by prejudice, but also that much might be achieved by playing directly upon the emotions of the crowd. The deliberate incitement of irrational popular passion in public life may not have been entirely new, but Cicero's testimony to Galba's originality in the technique of emotive and digressive rhetoric shows that the practice was now more extensively exploited.[1] Such a trend, not easily reversible, could lead to highly disruptive consequences. Indeed, it almost certainly played a major part in the developments of the very next year.

with n. 5. On the other side Simon, *Roms Kriege*, pp. 61 f., notes the allegations that Galba had appropriated an excessive share of the booty: App. *Iber.* 60; cf. the possible echo in Val. Max. 6. 4. 2.

[1] Cic. *Brut.* 82.

VI

ELECTION TO THE CONSULSHIP

THE war against Carthage dragged on through 148 with little sign of progress. Piso, not attempting to assault Carthage itself or to join battle with Hasdrubal, turned to the reasonable but unspectacular task of reducing other cities which still adhered to Carthage. In this he met with only limited success and suffered some reverses, while on the other hand the Carthaginians were re-asserting themselves and even won over a Numidian chieftain with eight hundred cavalry. There are allegations that Piso hardened resistance by breaking faith with a surrendered town, that he allowed the morale and discipline of the army to deteriorate, and that the Carthaginians were enabled to regain confidence, to whip up support in the townships, and to make approaches to the Numidian rulers, who were temporizing, and to the Macedonian pretender Andriscus.[1] Even if these are exaggerations, it is likely enough that such complaints were circulating in Rome by the end of 148. In any case, it is no surprise that Piso's general lack of success produced a reaction at the consular elections. What is surprising, not to say astonishing, is the nature of that reaction; for popular pressure secured the election of Scipio Aemilianus, a man who was at least five years below the minimum age established by law and who had not yet held the praetorship, which was a legally established prerequisite, nor even the more junior but electorally important aedileship, for which he was at this very time a candidate.[2]

Scipio's election to the consulship of 147 is so familiar a fact that

---

[1] App. *Iber.* 110 f.; 113; 115 f.; Zon. 9. 29; Diod. 32. 18. For modern discussions see p. 56 n. 1.

[2] See esp. App. *Lib.* 112, which is the most detailed account preserved; Livy, *Epit.* 49; 50; also Livy, *Epit.* 56; Cic. *Phil.* 11. 17; *De Amic.* 11; Vell. 1. 12. 3; Val. Max. 8. 15. 4; *Auct. ad Her.* 3. 2; (Victor) *De Vir. Ill.* 58. 5; Florus, 1. 31. 12; Eutrop. 4. 12; Diod. 32. 9a; Zon. 9. 29; Plut. *Mar.* 12. 2; *Praec. Reip. Ger.* 10; 'Plut.' *Apophth. Scip. Min.* 4; App. *B.C.* 1. 19; 3. 88; 4. 92; *Iber.* 84. For the regulations see Astin, *Lex Annalis*, pp. 19 f. and 31 f.

it is necessary to emphasize how truly extraordinary it was. It is not only that he was doubly unqualified and still a junior senator. The whole affair defied precedent. The regulation imposing a minimum age had been in force for over thirty years, and the legal prerequisite of the praetorship for half a century; Scipio was the first man to be elected consul from such junior rank since Flamininus, consul in 198—and the prerequisite of the praetorship had probably been introduced as a direct reaction to Flamininus' controversial election. Since the Second Punic War the only precedent for allowing the plea of expediency to override constitutional laws was the recent but less far-reaching case of Marcellus' third consulship in 152.[1] And finally, Scipio was elected despite the opposition both of the presiding consul and of the Senate. In short, the election of Scipio was, to say the least, a remarkable and significant development in Roman public life, the causes and nature of which demand serious attention.

It is obvious that one of the basic reasons for the election of Scipio was discontent with the progress of the war, in the sense that without such discontent Scipio would not have been elected. On the other hand, such discontent is not by itself a sufficient explanation of this extraordinary event. For one thing, Scipio's personal qualities were highly relevant. It is certainly true, as modern writers have said, that he was elected consul on account of his military record. Apart from his earlier achievements, there is a long catalogue of his successes in Africa under Manilius: his skilful tactics saved the lives of troops who had been repulsed from a breach in the wall of Carthage; twice he took decisive action to save the Roman camp during night assaults; he alone proved able to protect foragers from the enemy's cavalry; enemy fortresses would surrender only to him, since he was the only tribune who kept his pledged word; he advised against the first, almost disastrous, expedition against Hasdrubal and, also unsuccessfully, suggested certain wise precautions; he saved the army during a difficult retreat across a river, rescued some cohorts which had been cut off (for which he was awarded the *corona obsidionalis*), and persuaded Hasdrubal to bury the corpses of three military tribunes; he acted as arbiter in the affairs of Numidia when Massinissa died; on the second expedition against Hasdrubal he procured the desertion of

[1] Flamininus: Astin, *Lex Annalis*, pp. 26 f. Marcellus: above, pp. 38 f.

Phameas, the Carthaginian cavalry commander, together with a large body of horsemen; finally he obtained large quantities of supplies for the army when it was desperately in need of them.[1] It is true that some exaggeration must be suspected in a tradition, derived from Polybius, which portrays Scipio as virtually the central figure, always right and frequently saving the army when it was endangered by the incompetence of others. In particular it is a reasonable guess that many of his exploits were undertaken not on his own initiative, as the sources imply, but on the instructions of his commander. Nevertheless, only a good record is worth exaggerating; Scipio's must have been genuinely impressive. Moreover, in judging its effect on the election it should be remembered that any exaggerations which there may be in the literary tradition could equally well have been current in Rome in 148. Indeed, reports of Scipio's exceptional achievements had already begun to circulate in Rome by the end of 149; for Cato, who died in that year, praised them with a famous quotation from Homer.[2]

Scipio's military record certainly played an important part; yet it is still not a sufficient explanation to say that he was elected consul on account of that. For the question 'Why did large numbers of people vote for Scipio?' implies another question: how did large numbers of people come to acquire and take seriously the notion of making consul a man who was so very junior and so very far from being legally qualified, when to do so would be startlingly novel, and when he himself was not only not a candidate for the consulship but seeking the aedileship? The idea was constitutionally outrageous, not to say absurd, yet it was accepted and acted upon by a large section of a notoriously conservative people. The impression inherent in the sources is that it originated and spread spontaneously among the masses, without incitement; a like impression is given of the belief of the army that Scipio 'was aided by the same deity that was

[1] To the account of App. Lib. 98–110 other sources add only the corona obsidionalis: Vell. 1. 12. 4; Plin. Nat. Hist. 22. 13, from Varro; (Victor) De Vir. Ill. 58. 4. See also Livy, Epit. 49 f.; Ox. Epit. 49 f.; Oros. 4. 22. 1 and 7 f.; Val. Max. 5. 2, ext. 4; Eutrop. 4. 10 f.; Polyb. 36. 8. 2 f.; 36. 16. 10; Diod. 32. 7 f.; 32. 17; Zon. 9. 27; Plut. Praec. Reip. Ger. 10; Cato Mai. 27. 5 f. The number of cohorts saved by Scipio is variously reported.

[2] Polyb. 36. 8. 7, from Suidas, s.v. ἀίσσουσιν, quoting Od. 10. 495; also in Livy, Epit. 49; Diod. 32. 9a; Plut. Cato Mai. 27. 6; Praec. Reip. Ger. 10; 'Plut.' Apophth. Scip. Min. 3; Suidas, s.v. Κάτων. For his death see p. 58.

supposed to have enabled his grandfather Scipio to foresee the future'; and we are informed that the opinion among the troops, about which many wrote home, that only Scipio would take Carthage, was θεόληπτος, divinely inspired![1] But if the sources convey the impression that he was the spontaneous choice of the *populus*, that is also the impression that Scipio himself would have desired and sought to create, whatever the truth of the matter. It cannot be *proved* false, but it would be barely credible even if the incident were considered in isolation, let alone in the light of the evidence for Scipio's ambition, for his wish to prove himself a worthy grandson of Africanus, and for his deliberate exploitation of popular appeal as a political weapon. Six years later, it will be recalled, Scipio's escort is said to have included men 'who frequented the Forum and were able to gather a crowd and to force all issues by shouting and inciting passions'.[2] Things may not have been so very different in 148.

It is unlikely that Scipio ever publicly stated that he wanted to be consul in 147—that would have spoiled the effect—but it is more than likely that, perhaps even while he was still serving under Manilius, he saw in the situation an unrepeatable opportunity to reach the heights of glory as the new Africanus, and that he and his friends arranged the implanting, spreading, and encouraging of the idea that he must be elected consul: that Carthage would be captured only by this able and heroic soldier, who alone had proved a match for the Carthaginians, this heir—this worthy heir—of Paullus and Africanus, who indeed had so inherited the power and influence of Africanus that he had arbitrated between nations and organized a kingdom; and who was said to be aided by the divinity which had aided Africanus himself.[3] Then at the last he could represent himself as bowing to the overwhelming force of public opinion that he should be elected.

If these were the major factors lying behind the popular desire to elect Scipio to the consulship, that desire had still to be given effect

---

[1] App. *Lib.* 104; 109. [2] Plut. *Aem.* 38. 4.
[3] App. *Lib.* 104. The play on superstition was surely deliberate. Note how Polybius, 6. 56. 6 f. and 10. 2. 13, regards the exploitation of superstition as neither immoral nor shameful, but positively respectable and profitable. Another manifestation of it in 148 is perhaps in Diod. 32. 18 (probably from Polybius), where Piso's failure through being distrusted is said to have been 'as though some divine agency were working against him'.

through the electoral process. Discussion of this must be prefaced with the accounts given by Appian and the epitomator of Livy.

Appian, *Lib.* 112: The elections were at hand, and Scipio was a candidate for the aedileship (for the laws did not yet permit him to be consul on account of his age), yet the people were electing him consul. This was illegal, and when the consuls showed them the law they persisted, and became vehement, and raised a clamour[1] that in accordance with the laws of Tullius and Romulus the people were sovereign in the elections and set aside or confirmed whichever they wished of the laws concerned with them. In the end one of the tribunes said that he would deprive the consuls of their right to conduct the election unless they complied with the wishes of the people. Then the Senate instructed the tribunes to repeal this law and to re-enact it after one year.

Livy, *Epit.* 50: Since he was debarred by his age from becoming consul, after a great struggle by the plebs, who were supporting him, and resistance to them for a considerable time by the senators, he was exempted from the laws and appointed consul.[2]

The first problem is to determine when and how the 'People' (by which must be understood presumably a clear majority of the people) *expressed* their wish to elect Scipio consul. Most modern accounts are too brief to deal with this question at all clearly, but the general notion seems to be that the election was held and that the desire of the people was revealed by the fact that enormous numbers voted for Scipio, although he was not eligible and not a candidate; the presiding consul, Postumius, refused to take account of these illegal votes and deadlock resulted.[3] Thus the popular desire would have been expressed by the orderly casting of votes and fully revealed when the results from the voting-units, the centuries, were reported to the consul.

It cannot have been so. If the voting had been carried through in this orderly way Scipio would not have been elected. Even if it be supposed that *professio*, the formal notification of candidature to the presiding magistrate, was not yet a legally obligatory requirement for election, and that votes cast for any qualified candidate could be

---

[1] ἐλιπάρουν καὶ ἐνέκειντο καὶ ἐκεκράγεσαν.

[2] *Quoniam per annos consuli fieri non licebat, cum magno certamine suffragantis plebis et repugnantibus ei aliquamdiu patribus, legibus solutus et consul creatus.*

[3] e.g. Hallward, *CAH* viii, p. 482. Virtually all modern accounts, including Hallward's, are of course incidental to discussions of the Third Punic War and cannot be expected to examine the election in detail. Appian uses the plural 'consuls', but only one consul can have presided and it is most unlikely that Piso left Africa.

taken into account, it simply is not credible that the presiding magistrate was not able to disregard, and have disregarded by the officials of the centuries, votes cast for a candidate who was patently not qualified.[1] And given that there must have been properly qualified candidates, and that, in the nature of Roman public life, these must have secured at least some votes in many, if not all, centuries, the result would have been that Postumius would have declared two of these candidates elected. But in fact it seems probable that at least since the 180's *professio* had been obligatory: in other words, it is very unlikely that votes for candidates not on the official lists were recorded, let alone counted, and the presiding magistrate, through a herald, asked the *rogator* of each century only about those candidates who were on the list.[2] In either event it follows that the orderly casting of votes would not have produced deadlock. The desire to elect Scipio consul was expressed first in some other way; and, since there were no other orderly and legal channels, that implies some fairly substantial public outcry or disturbance. Livy, it will be recalled, mentions a great and extended struggle, and Appian says that the people 'became vehement and raised a clamour that . . . the people were sovereign in the elections'. The precise course of events cannot be recovered, but there can be no doubt that it involved mobs cheering and shouting demands for the election of Scipio, and jeering at the consul who quite properly refused to regard him as eligible. Once again there comes to mind the description of Scipio's escort in 142, when he was a candidate in another election: 'men who frequented the Forum and were able to gather a crowd and to force all issues by shouting and inciting passions.'[3]

From this point on the course of the struggle is comparatively easy to trace.[4] Postumius persisted in his refusal to recognize Scipio as a candidate and proposed to carry through the election without regard to him. In this he was supported by the Senate (that is, by a

[1] Cf. Mommsen, *Röm. Staats.* i[3], pp. 471 f. and 480 f.

[2] Astin, 'Professio', *Historia* 11 (1962), pp. 252 f.; Cic. *De Orat.* 2. 260. Earl, 'Appian *B.C.* 1, 14 and "professio" ', *Historia* 14 (1965), pp. 325 f., esp. 330 f., doubts that in the second century *professio* was required by law, but he evidently accepts that the presiding magistrate could disregard votes cast for a legally disqualified candidate.

[3] Plut. *Aem.* 38. 4.

[4] The only source preserving details is App. *Lib.* 112; cf. *Iber.* 84. Livy, *Epit.* 50 makes it clear that the Senate supported Postumius.

majority of the senators), but his intention was thwarted by a tribune who threatened to veto the election unless Scipio was accepted as a candidate. The cry of those who pressed for Scipio was clearly that, according to a basic principle, the *populus* was sovereign in the elections and that therefore laws restricting the choice of the Roman People should remain valid only as long as they themselves thought fit. Although this argument was not new to Roman politics, there can be no mistaking the potential danger to order and stability ensuing from its successful use, in defiance of the Senate, to support a flagrantly illegal candidature. In a similar situation in 184, when only a suffect praetorship had been involved, the Senate had preserved the principle of law by abandoning the election,[1] but in 148 the prospect of the state being deprived at a crucial moment of all its senior officials compelled the senators to give way. They instructed the tribunes to introduce a bill suspending the relevant legislation for one year only, thereby in effect giving Scipio personal exemption from the legal requirements.

Inevitably Scipio was elected, his colleague being C. Livius M. Aemiliani f. M. n. Drusus. The final step was the allocation of provinces. When Livius asked that lots should be cast, one of the tribunes proposed that the appointment to the command against Carthage should be made by the People.[2] Livius' request is slightly surprising, for quite apart from earlier links between the families and the possibility that he was related to Scipio (conceivably, it has been suggested, his cousin), the enthusiasm for Scipio might have been expected to have ensured the election of a friendly and amenable colleague. Possibly Livius' bid for the command was not intended seriously; perhaps it was part of a scheme to demonstrate anew the popular will that Scipio should command, thereby enhancing his prestige and authority in the face of a hostile Senate. Or it may be that Scipio's opponents had been able to exert enough pressure through their *clientelae* to secure the election of one of their own number;[3] or perhaps Livius, elected as an ally, unexpectedly revealed ambitions of his own. The one certain point is the most significant:

---

[1] Livy, 39. 39; Astin, 'Professio', *Historia* 11 (1962), pp. 252 f.

[2] App. *Lib.* 112; Livy, *Epit.* 51; Val. Max. 8. 15. 4. Livius' family and position are discussed by Münzer, *Röm. Adels.*, pp. 225 f., esp. 235 f.

[3] Against this suggestion cf. p. 74 n. 1.

that once again the accepted constitutional procedure was overridden in order to secure the appointment of the man who commanded popular favour.

In the events which gave Scipio the consulship and the African command can be seen not only the working out of his own ambition but grave developments in Roman political life. In the first place there was the sacrifice of legal and constitutional restrictions on the plea of immediate expediency. For this there was the recent precedent of Marcellus' third consulship;[1] but the concessions made for Scipio were far greater than that made for Marcellus, and where Marcellus' consulship contravened the clear intention of the law but perhaps not its letter, Scipio's stood twice over in open contradiction to the letter. But more was involved even than this. There was the triumph of the argument that legal restrictions upon elections were valid only for so long as the People themselves wished. The tribunician veto had been used not merely for political ends but deliberately to threaten a serious crisis as a means of political blackmail.[2] In the previous year the usefulness of mass emotion had been demonstrated in Galba's escape;[3] now both mass emotion and popular outcries (though perhaps as yet without actual violence) had been proved to be effective political weapons, playing a major part in overcoming not only legal obstacles but the opposition of the Senate, which was at last successfully defied. Finally, though the winning and exploiting of popular favour had been a factor of increasing importance for some time past,[4] the practice had now been carried a great deal further and had been seen to offer enormous possibilities to the ambitious man.

Although clear antecedents can be found for all these developments, each of the trends was now carried an important stage further;

---

[1] pp. 38 f.

[2] The *leges Aelia et Fufia*, which were passed very close to this time, imposed a ban on the carrying of legislation between the proclamation and the holding of electoral assemblies. If this ban was already in force, the implications would be very serious; for the tribune in 148 would have been blackmailing the Senate into overriding yet another regulation, one which had been enacted only very recently, and which was almost certainly enacted for the express purpose of preventing last-minute legislation in the interests of particular candidates. However, it seems rather more probable that the ban had not yet been enacted, and that it was created as a reaction to Scipio's election, with the intention of preventing similar occurrences. Astin, 'Leges Aelia et Fufia', *Latomus* 23 (1964), pp. 432 f., esp. 437 f.

[3] pp. 59 f.

[4] pp. 28 f.

and the very success of the movement to elect Scipio revealed possibilities and provided precedents for the future. For all this much of
the responsibility must be assigned to Scipio himself. At the very
least, he gave tacit encouragement by his acquiescence: there is not
the faintest hint that he was in any way reluctant to take advantage
of the constitutional improprieties which were being perpetrated;
and, while from the nature of things proof cannot be absolutely
conclusive, there is every reason to suspect that he himself played
a very considerable and positive part in encouraging, inciting, and
engineering these improprieties.

VII

THE NEW AFRICANUS

ALTHOUGH election to the consulship was a major triumph for Scipio, when he sailed for Africa in the early months of 147 he must have been well aware that as yet his political eminence was by no means secure, that the course of the coming campaign could be decisive for his whole future career.[1] A military disaster, even if not his fault, would mean almost certain obscurity and impotence. Doubtless neither he nor others feared a real disaster, but if his progress was too slow, if the expected successes did not materialize, if he suffered even a minor reverse, the image of the brilliant scion of the Scipios might fade, the tide of popular favour could easily turn against him, and the next consular elections might be followed by his recall, leaving for someone else the glory of victory. It is a fair assumption that Scipio was very confident of success, but he cannot have been blind to the dangers in his path. It must therefore have been an unpleasant shock for him to learn immediately on his arrival how on that very day the naval commander, L. Hostilius Mancinus, had succeeded in landing a force on the precipitous coast of the Carthaginian suburb of Megara, actually within the city wall, at a point where the defences had been neglected.

The immediate problem was that Mancinus was in grave danger. If he suffered a disaster he himself would certainly be disgraced (if he survived), but equally there would be no lack of persons ready to

[1] For modern discussions of the campaign and of the military and topographical problems see p. 56 n. 1. The basic narrative source continues to be Appian, *Lib.* 113 f. The briefer narrative of Zon. 9. 29 f., which differs in a number of respects, has less authority than that of Appian. Few of Scipio's officers and companions are known. His principal *legatus* was C. Laelius (App. *Lib.* 126 f.; Cic. *Rep.* 2. 67; *De Amic.* 103; Zon. 9. 30). C. Fannius and the young Ti. Gracchus were serving under him (Plut. *Ti. Grac.* 4. 5 f.) and Polybius was present ('Plut.' *Apophth. Scip. Min.* 5 = Polyb. 38. 19; Amm. Marc. 24. 2. 16 = Polyb. 38. 19a. 3; Polyb. 38. 21; App. *Lib.* 132 = Polyb. 38. 22; Diod. 32. 24; Oros. 5. 3. 3 = Polyb. 38. 14. 3; Plin. *Nat. Hist.* 5. 9 = Polyb. 34. 15. 7). The fleet was commanded by a Serranus, presumably an Atilius, who was probably a *legatus*. Additional Note E, p. 340.

blame Scipio for failing to save him and his men. This crisis was soon overcome, since although Mancinus' position proved untenable, Scipio intervened rapidly and effectively to ward off the impending catastrophe and to make possible a safe withdrawal. But the incident had further implications, in that it enabled Mancinus to claim to have been the first to break into Carthage, thus threatening to deprive Scipio of some part of the credit for the capture of the city. It is improbable that Scipio allowed his actions at the time to be influenced by this, but there is little doubt that others asserted that he did so. The result was a dispute about the merits of Mancinus' exploit. The Polybian–Scipionic version evidently presented it as so reckless, foolish, and incompetently managed that the troops were withdrawn immediately and Mancinus was at once sent home; but there are clear indications that others thought the exploit more valuable, and a rival account actually asserts that Scipio left the troops entrenched in their position, with Mancinus himself in charge. It is a fair guess that the withdrawal was later alleged to have been unnecessary and motivated by Scipio's jealousy.[1]

After taking strong action to restore the discipline of the army, the blame for the poor state of which he placed squarely on his predecessor, Piso,[2] Scipio set about operations in earnest. His first assault on the walls did succeed in getting a force temporarily inside the suburb of Megara but ended in a withdrawal—though it is uncertain whether this was a defeat or a planned manœuvre.[3] Now, if not earlier, he decided that the first essential was to complete the blockade of the city in order to weaken the defenders by famine. Hence he spent three weeks building elaborate fortifications right across the isthmus which linked the city with the mainland. This was followed,

---

[1] The two accounts are in App. *Lib.* 113 f. and Zon. 9. 29. The latter, though more favourable to Mancinus, shares the tradition that initially Scipio saved him from great danger. Livy, *Epit.* 51, Ampel. 32, and the garbled account in Flor. 1. 31. 10 all reflect a tradition which attached some value to Mancinus' exploit. Cf. Plin. *Nat. Hist.* 35. 23 and below p. 99 on his candidature for the consulship. Zonaras does not mention the withdrawal at all, but this is probably due to the epitomizing process; Appian (from Polybius) leaves no doubt that it occurred. The important difference is whether or not it took place immediately. It is conceivable that the version represented by Appian has passed over an attempt to hold on, which was given up only after an interval of at least several days. The position probably proved untenable because of difficulties in supply and reinforcement created by the precipitous coast. For Mancinus' status see Additional Note E, p. 340.

[2] App. *Lib.* 115 f.   [3] Additional Note F, p. 341.

probably after an interval, by the construction of the famous mole to block the entrance to the harbours, a gigantic task involving the transport of enormous quantities of rock.[1] But such methods were slow. By the end of the summer the only visible gain was the commercial quay, captured with immense effort, and although the tighter siege was doubtless producing distress, the new emergency entrance which the Carthaginians constructed for their harbour probably enabled occasional ships to continue to run the blockade. These could be halted only by the winter weather and by dealing with the main sources of supply. So in the early autumn Scipio made a great and successful effort to reduce the crucial Carthaginian stronghold at Nepheris, the capture of which was followed quickly by the submission of most of the other centres which had held out hitherto.

In launching the Nepheris campaign Scipio was perhaps not unmindful of the need to achieve visible results quickly; for the slow methods adopted in the siege itself, if militarily necessary, were politically a liability. The situation emerges clearly from the abortive negotiations initiated at this time by Hasdrubal, the Carthaginian commander. Although Hasdrubal was no doubt impelled to open these by growing distress among the besieged, he made it plain that any terms had to include the preservation of the city, the one point which had really been at issue and on which Scipio could not possibly give way: clearly the siege was by no means over. Polybius is explicit that Scipio was induced to offer attractive personal terms to Hasdrubal by the proximity of the consular elections and the thought that he might be replaced if he did not end the war soon.[2] During the year of slow progress the popular enthusiasm which had carried him

[1] Baradez, 'Nouvelles recherches sur les ports antiques de Carthage', *Karthago* 9 (1958), p. 72 n. 52, estimates that the theoretical volume of material in the mole was about 6,000 cu. metres, but that allowing for subsidence the actual figure was likely to be in the range 12,000–18,000 cu. metres.

[2] Polyb. 38. 7. 6 f., esp. 8. 2 f.; cf. Diod. 32. 22; Zon. 9. 30. Zonaras mentions the negotiations before the expedition against Nepheris, but Polybius leaves no doubt about the sequence. De Sanctis, *Storia*, iv. 3, pp. 70 f., rightly draws attention to Scipio's failure to make any general offer of life and personal liberty to the populace as a whole. His suggestion that Scipio was confident he would not be replaced is contrary to the evidence of Polybius, but he may be nearer the truth in pointing to Scipio's need to satisfy the troops with as much booty as possible, including the proceeds from the sale of the populace. Cf. App. *Lib.* 75, 115, 116, 127, 133.

into office will certainly have waned significantly; the elections would be conducted without the presence and impact of his own forceful personality; and his opponents had had a year to make their preparations. The elections for the censorship, earlier in the year, pointed the way with the success of L. Cornelius Lentulus Lupus and L. Marcius Censorinus, neither of whom is likely to have been on good terms with Scipio.[1] The results of the consular elections themselves must have seemed to have justified any forebodings, for it is likely that among those defeated was Scipio's brother, Q. Fabius Maximus Aemilianus; and the men elected were Cn. Cornelius Lentulus, brother of the censor Lupus, though otherwise virtually unknown to us, and L. Mummius, a *novus homo*, who as praetor had fought in Spain with sufficient success (after an initial defeat) to earn a triumph, and who later was to be Scipio's unco-operative colleague in the censorship.[2] Despite this, and despite the eagerness of Mummius for military glory, Scipio was not replaced. The factors which favoured him can only be conjectured. Lentulus was perhaps handicapped by being associated, at least through his brother, with the moderate policy of Nasica Corculum (whom Lupus and Marcius now appointed Princeps Senatus).[3] There may have been disagreement between the consuls, or more general disunity preventing Scipio's opponents from making common cause. The law which had appointed Scipio to Africa will have played some part: at the least it had been a sufficient demonstration of popularity to induce caution in opponents, and its terms may well have made it difficult to replace Scipio without a further law. Probably, too, there was again a tribune supporting Scipio, ready to veto the appointment of a successor. Finally, Scipio will have given the best possible account of his progress, so it may have been a real consideration that Carthage

---

[1] Lupus: p. 92; Marcius had almost certainly stood as a rival of Manilius for the consulship of 149: p. 55.

[2] Fabius had been praetor in 149 and therefore was eligible for the consulship of 146. Lentulus' filiation is not preserved but there is little doubt that he was Lupus' brother: Münzer, *RE*, s.v. *Cornelius*, no. 177; cf. also the filiation of the cos. of 97, Cn. f. Cn. n. For Mummius' career in general see Münzer, *RE*, s.v. *Mummius*, no. 7a; for his censorship see below pp. 115 f. and 119 f.

[3] Lupus: p. 53. Nasica: Val. Max. 7. 5. 2; cf. Diod. 34/35. 33. 6; Plut. *Aem.* 15. 3. The date of his appointment is not recorded, but 147 is highly probable, as by then he was probably the senior eligible candidate.

might fall very soon: a successor to Scipio might then have the embarrassing experience of arriving to find the city just captured.[1]

A few months later there arose another issue of military command. The consul Mummius was appointed to take an army to Greece in order to quell the Achaean League, which had been involved in a protracted crisis and which now openly defied Roman wishes and embarked upon what was in effect a rebellion against Rome. Q. Caecilius Metellus Macedonicus was still in Macedonia with the army with which as praetor in 148 he had defeated Andriscus, the 'Pseudo-Philip', and supervised the formation of the new Roman province. He had been taking an active interest in developments in Greece and now he marched rapidly southwards, won several quick successes in central Greece and advanced as far as the Isthmus of Corinth. At that point Mummius arrived, took control of the campaign and sent Metellus away. He soon ended the war with a crushing victory, followed by the occupation of an undefended Corinth. Subsequently he supervised the notorious destruction of that city.[2]

Neither commander was at all pleased with the other, as is shown by the varying tone of the sources. In some Mummius is presented as arriving at Metellus' camp in great haste, ahead of his own troops, in order to secure the credit for a victory already virtually won by Metellus' efforts; elsewhere Metellus is pictured as making every effort, especially by offering terms, to finish the war before the arrival of the consul and thus to take upon himself the credit for victory.[3]

---

[1] There is a real possibility that before the end of 147 the consul Livius had secured the passage of a law by which commissioners were appointed to arrange the settlement of Africa. This would have emphasized the nearness of victory—and probably intentionally so. The lex agraria of 111, CIL i². 2, no. 585. 81, refers to land assigned to Utica by Xvirei quei ex [lege] Livia factei createive fuerunt. These are almost certainly the ten commissioners mentioned in App. Lib. 135. The law has been attributed to an otherwise unattested tribune of 146 (e.g. Niccolini, Fasti dei Tribuni della Plebe, p. 132; MRR i, p. 466) but it need not be tribunician and the consul of 147 could well have been its author. Cf. Badian, Foreign Clientelae, p. 138 n. 2.

[2] The main source for the Achaean crisis is Paus. 7. 11 f., with the campaigns of Metellus and Mummius in 7. 15 f. Numerous refs. to the commands of both men in MRR i, pp. 461 and 464 f. In general see De Sanctis, Storia, iv. 3, pp. 120 f., esp. 149 f. Metellus' concern with Greek affairs before his actual military intervention: Paus. 7. 13. 2 and 5; 7. 14. 7; Polyb. 38. 12. 1.

[3] The latter view in Paus. 7. 15. 1 f. and 11, and perhaps in Justin 34. 2. 1., the former in Val. Max. 7. 5. 4; Oros. 5. 3. 5; (Victor) De Vir. Ill. 60. 1 f.; 61. 2; Florus, 1. 32. 3 f.; cf. Vell. 1. 12. 1.

Doubtless Metellus felt that the appointment of Mummius was an unreasonable intervention in a situation which he was quite capable of handling and in which he had already been active; while to Mummius Metellus' advance must have seemed an equally unreasonable infringement of the *provincia* to which he himself had been assigned.[1] The heart of the trouble was the decision to send Mummius instead of instructing Metellus to act; and there must be a strong suspicion that this decision was prompted more by political than by military considerations. It is hard to believe that Metellus and his army could honestly have been judged incapable of acting effectively; Metellus is more than likely to have made representations that he should be given the task; if he had been, there would have been no need to levy fresh troops; and the need for rapid action was obvious. It seems only too likely that the ambitions of Mummius for military laurels were aided by some jealousy and hostility towards Metellus, aggravated perhaps by the latter's political association with Scipio, whose own position was for the time being unassailable.

In the spring of 146, probably a little earlier than the campaigns of Metellus and Mummius against the Achaeans, the struggle in Africa entered its last agonizing phase as Scipio launched his final assault against the starving defenders of Carthage. A force under Laelius captured a section of the wall and established the decisive foothold within. There ensued a week of continuous and horrifying house-to-house street-fighting, ending in the surrender from the central citadel of many thousands of wretched survivors, destined to be sold into slavery.[2] Hasdrubal, the Carthaginian commander, soon followed. The last defenders, the Roman deserters, wisely sought death in the flames of the temple of Esmun. Carthage had fallen: Rome had a second Africanus.

[1] Zon. 9. 31 reports that because Metellus feared that the Achaeans, who had already reached Thessaly, might attack Macedonia, he went out and routed them. This could be the hypothesis of a historian writing long after the event, but equally it could be a contemporary excuse for an action which was recognized to be in some degree improper.

[2] The number of prisoners is variously reported but probably totalled around 50,000: App. *Lib.* 130; Oros. 4. 23. 3; Florus, 1. 31. 16. The leading men were kept in open confinement: Zon. 9. 30; cf. Oros. 4. 23. 7. Zonaras says that the majority of the men perished in prison, but this is contradicted by Oros. 4. 23. 7 and in view of the promise reported in App. *Lib.* 130 would have been a breach of *fides*; cf. Cic. *Tusc.* 3. 53. De Sanctis, *Storia*, iv. 3, p. 74 n. 107, suggests that Zonaras refers only to those prisoners taken to Rome for the triumph.

A new Africanus—perhaps also a new Aemilius Paullus. When at the end Hasdrubal came before Scipio as a suppliant, the victor took the opportunity to remind those around him of the mutability of fortune and the folly of presumptuous words and deeds; even so Paullus had exhorted his *consilium* when Perseus was brought before him.[1] Nor is this the only echo. Like Paullus, Scipio made a point of taking none of the booty for himself;[2] before leaving the newly organized province, Scipio celebrated his victory with sacrifices and games, following, it is explicitly stated, the example of Paullus, who had held a great festival at Amphipolis; when the captured arms and equipment were burned in accordance with an ancient custom, Scipio dedicated them to Mars and Minerva, the deities honoured by Paullus at Amphipolis; and Scipio further followed his father's example in throwing the foreign deserters to wild beasts as part of the entertainment.[3]

Hasdrubal was no scion of a line of kings, Carthage ranked well below Macedon among the heirs of Greek civilization; but as an enemy of Rome it was more ancient and more feared than Macedon; its history had been long and its material success great; despite its final agony, it must have yielded considerable booty; and it provided an opportunity for one gesture which was both unique and imaginative. Representatives of the cities of Sicily were invited to claim from the spoils objects which the Carthaginians had plundered from them in the past.[4] Selection and identification cannot have been easy, for already a century had passed since the expulsion of the Carthaginians from the island, and most of the plundering must have been much earlier: Thermae received statues which had belonged to its predecessor, Himera, which were presumably looted in 408.[5]

[1] Polyb. 38. 20. 1 f.; Diod. 32. 23. Paullus: Polyb. 29. 20; Diod. 30. 23. 1; Plut. *Aem.* 27. 2 f.; Livy, 45. 8. 6 f.

[2] Polyb. 18. 35. 9 f.; 'Plut.' *Apophth. Scip. Min.* 7; *De Fort.* 1; Cic. *De Off.* 2. 76. Cf. also Plin. *Nat. Hist.* 33. 141; 'Plut.' *Apophth. Scip. Min.* 1; Aelian, *Var. Hist.* 11. 9. 5. Paullus: Polyb. 18. 35. 4 f.; Plut. *Aem.* 28. 10 f.; Cic. loc. cit.

[3] App. *Lib.* 133 and 135; Livy, *Epit.* 51; cf. *Ox. Epit.* 51; Val. Max. 2. 7. 13. Paullus: Livy, 45. 32. 8 f.; Plut. *Aem.* 28. 7 f.; Diod. 31. 8. 9; cf. Val. Max. 2. 7. 14. On the deserters see also p. 17 n. 4. On the burning of the equipment see Additional Note G, p. 341.

[4] App. *Lib.* 133; Livy, *Epit.* 51; Diod. 32. 25; 'Plut.' *Apophth. Scip. Min.* 6; Cic. *Verr.* 2. 1. 11; 2. 2. 3, 85 f.; 2. 4. 73 f., 84, 93, 97 f.; 2. 5. 124, 185 f.; Ps.-Ascon., p. 227 Stangl; *Schol. Gron.*, p. 334 Stangl; Val. Max. 5. 1. 6; Eutrop. 4. 12; *ILS* 8769.

[5] Cic. *Verr.* 2. 2. 85 f.; 2. 4. 73; *ILS* 8769.

Nevertheless, the offer was quite genuine, for many items were returned. No doubt Scipio's motives were mixed: perhaps they included a dramatic sense of the reversal of fortune; more pro-saically, he cannot have failed to recognize the utility of his action in building up a patron–client relationship;[1] and probably he was rewarding, in a cheap but acceptable way, the practical assistance given in the war by at least some Sicilian cities.[2] But above all his action was a grand and ostentatious gesture, not necessarily coolly calculated as such, but fully in keeping in a man who was just achieving his ambition to be a new Africanus and who had effectively employed extravagant gestures as a means of self-advertisement towards that end.

Another incident has received much attention from modern writers, though it perhaps made less impression on the ancient literature. It seems that some days or possibly even some weeks after the capture of the city Scipio gave the order to fire those parts of it which still stood, presumably a part of the complete devastation of the site which preceded the solemn imprecations against resettlement.[3] As he watched the beginning of the great conflagration his friend Polybius noticed that there were tears in his eyes and asked the reason: 'What', he evidently asked, 'could be finer than this?' Scipio turned, grasped the historian's hand, and replied: 'It is a fine thing, Polybius, but I have an unaccountable fear and dread lest some day someone else should give this same order about my own city.' And probably at this point he quoted from Homer: 'The day shall come when sacred Troy shall perish, and Priam, and the people of Priam of the ashen spear.'[4]

The incident should be interpreted with caution. There is no justi-fication for treating it as an intense emotional crisis, or for supposing that the mood here expressed was the dominant characteristic of

---

[1] The gifts were in Scipio's name, not in that of Rome: Cic. *Verr.* 2. 1. 11; 2. 4. 74 f., 78, 97; 2. 5. 186; *ILS* 8769. On the importance of this type of patron–client relationship see Badian, *Foreign Clientelae*, pp. 154 f.

[2] Tyndaris: Cic. *Verr.* 2. 5. 125; cf. 2. 4. 84. It is unlikely that other and larger cities failed to help. Cic. *Verr.* 2. 4. 93 suggests that Agrigentum gave assistance; cf. also 'Plut.' *Apophth. Scip. Min.* 6: τοὺς ἀπὸ τῶν πόλεων παρόντας.

[3] App. *Lib.* 2; 135; *B.C.* 1. 24; Zon. 9. 30; Cic. *De Leg. Agr.* 1. 5; 2. 51.

[4] Polyb. 38. 21; App. *Lib.* 132 = Polyb. 38. 22; Diod. 32. 24; Appendix II, no. 9. The quotation is *Iliad*, 6. 448 f. Discussion in Appendix IV.

Scipio's outlook from this time on, the key to the understanding of
the remainder of his career; indeed it is not legitimate to assume even
that this mood was his main reaction to the capture and destruction
of Carthage, that it was more than the mood of a particular moment.
Nor must the element of pessimism in his words be exaggerated: he is
conscious of the reversal of fortune which 'fate' may effect; he is
aware that one day Rome, like all earthly things, must perish, and he
fears that its end may resemble that of Carthage; but there is no
implication that the decline of Rome is already evident and advanced,
let alone that his own destruction of Carthage is hastening the process.
None of this is to deny that his utterance did represent his thoughts,
or at least an important part of his thoughts, at that moment. But
what is revealed, apart from acceptance of rather conventional ideas
of the mutability of fortune, is primarily a deep and genuine patriotism; and this it is reasonable to take into account in interpreting his
whole career.

Though Carthage had been captured and destroyed, there was
still much work for Scipio to do. He had to co-operate with the
customary commission of ten senators in planning the future of the
conquered and surrendered territories and in organizing the new
province of Africa; and when the commissioners had departed he had
to put the settlement into effect.[1] Less arduous and of less intrinsic
importance, but still a considerable task, was the management of the
booty, including the sale of the thousands of prisoners and of the
booty in kind. For a fixed number of days the troops were allowed
to plunder freely, though all gold and silver and all temple-dedications
were reserved, to be displayed at the triumph and to meet the cost of
the donatives and celebrations. Scipio allowed none of the booty to
become his private property, even refraining from the purchase of
items at the sale of booty in kind; also his slaves and freedmen were
forbidden either to participate in the looting or to purchase anything
for themselves.[2] The reasons for this careful abstention are not hard
to divine. Booty was a factor of immediate political moment:
Scipio will not have forgotten how discontent concerning it had

---

[1] App. *Lib.* 135; cf. p. 74 n. 1; Gsell, *Hist. anc.* iii, pp. 403 f.; cf. vii, pp. 1 f.; Romanelli,
Storia delle province romane dell'Africa, pp. 43 f.

[2] App. *Lib.* 133; Oros. 4. 23. 7. For Scipio's abstention see p. 76 n. 2.

very nearly deprived his father of his triumph over Perseus, although Paullus too is said to have taken nothing for himself from the spoils.[1] It is possible that the reservation of precious metals and dedications left none too much of value for personal plunder; the amounts going into the central fund will have been obviously greater (though whether or not they were really extraordinary must remain uncertain)[2] and Scipio will have been anxious to demonstrate to the troops, many of whom originally volunteered in the hope of enrichment, that this was in no way for his personal benefit: all would be available, when vows and proper expenses had been met, for the general distribution.

The political usefulness of booty was not confined to the donatives to the troops. It could adorn a triumph and pay for the triumph itself, for games, and for a temple, all likely to impress the urban populace. That Scipio gave games in Rome as well as in Africa may be taken for granted; his temple of *Virtus*, though no date is preserved, may well have been erected at this time; of the triumph which he celebrated on his return to Rome, probably late in 146, it is written that it was the most splendid of all, rich in gold, loaded with all the statues and votive offerings that the Carthaginians had assembled from every land.[3] It is conceivable that there is some exaggeration here. Perhaps the splendour was not entirely without precedent. There is no hint that the general character of the celebrations varied from the normal pattern. Yet a difference there must have been: an exceptional sentiment, a consciousness of the uniqueness of the occasion, must have been generated by this final triumph over the Carthaginians, celebrating the ultimate victory over Rome's greatest enemy. The granting of that triumph was the recognition of a new Africanus, a worthy successor to a great house, but in addition it conferred, or at least ratified, *gloria* such as no living man could hope to rival.

[1] Triumph: Livy, 45. 35 f.; Vell. 1. 9. 6; Plut. *Aem.* 30 f. Abstention: p. 76 n. 2.
[2] Additional Note H, p. 342.
[3] App. *Lib.* 135; other refs. to the triumph in *MRR* i, p. 467. The temple: Plut. *Fort. Rom.* 5; Scipio is referred to as Numantinus but it is unlikely that the temple followed his second triumph.

VIII

FRIENDS AND ENEMIES

THE emergence of the new Africanus, assured of a leading role in the political life of Rome, prompts a review of some of the other leading personalities of the period, of Scipio's friends and enemies, and of such political groupings as can be discerned. Modern scholarship has made it abundantly clear that in the Roman governing class personal and political relationships were inextricably entangled, with the consequence that the consideration of 'family-group' factions and of motivation by factional rivalry is indispensable to the understanding of Roman politics.[1] Hence it is desirable to associate a review of Scipio's friends and enemies with some discussion of the political groupings of the period, although with due recognition of the limitations and hazards involved. It is necessary to bear in mind that there were other political considerations besides factional advantage; that the evidence for relationships between persons is not especially plentiful, is sometimes ambiguous, and tends to be rather haphazard;[2] and that political groupings varied greatly in their coherence and durability. Above all, the scene must have been extremely complex. The multiplicity of ties of old allegiance, of obligation, of kinship, and of marriage, together with the lack of any clear distinction between personal and political relationships, must often have led to cross-ties and cross-obligations, to rival claims for support, to, so to speak, *factiones* being rather ill-defined at the edges. Political groupings cannot be assumed always to have been completely separate entities, tempting though it often is to think of them as simple units.

[1] See esp. Gelzer, *Nobilität*; Münzer, *Röm. Adels.*; cf. Scullard, *Roman Politics*, pp. 1 f.; 'Roman Politics', *BICS* 2 (1955), pp. 15 f.

[2] Throughout this study common hostility to a third person is not treated as sufficient evidence in itself of political alliance. In particular, hostility towards Ti. Gracchus and his associates is not regarded as proof of alliance with Scipio Aemilianus in any other respect or at any other time.

In any discussion of Scipio's friends the first to come to mind must always be Gaius Laelius, whose intimate association with him is attested repeatedly.[1] Slightly older than Scipio, Laelius was no rival to the brilliance of the former's career and military reputation, but he probably had the keener intellect of the two.[2] Very intelligent, exceptionally learned, genuinely cultured, calm and cheerful in disposition, Laelius displayed all these qualities in his quiet, elegant, carefully reasoned speeches, the published versions of which led later generations to judge him one of the ablest orators of his time, perhaps second only to Ser. Sulpicius Galba. Yet such qualities, though they might earn widespread respect, were scarcely likely to capture the public imagination; the careful, rather literary speeches will have made more impression on the educated than on the masses—indeed, even before a tribunal consisting of consuls and their *consilium* they proved less effective than the passionate vigour of Galba's rhetoric.[3] Furthermore, his father having been a *novus homo*, he did not enjoy the prestige and authority of distinguished ancestry. Nevertheless, he was no mere political satellite of his illustrious friend. Although the assertion that Scipio was merely the principal actor, Laelius the true author, was undoubtedly a slander inspired by political hostility,[4] it must derive from the basic truth that Laelius' intelligent judgements and advice were of immense value to Scipio. In matters of political calculation and intrigue a man endowed with Laelius' intellect and temperament is likely to have been masterly; the suggestion is surely right that it was from this as much as from his erudition that he acquired his nickname, Sapiens.[5]

Few other personalities of the period are as clearly distinguishable as Laelius. L. Furius Philus, for example, is a very shadowy figure; yet he not only shared the intellectual and cultural tastes of Scipio

---

[1] e.g. Cic. *De Amic.* 4 f.; *De Orat.* 2. 22; Val. Max. 8. 8. 1; Gell. 17. 5. 1; Plut. *Ti. Grac.* 8. 5.

[2] Cf. esp. Cic. *Brut.* 84. His age: Cic. *Rep.* 1. 18; *De Amic.* 15. Evidence for the assessment which follows collected by Münzer, *RE*, s.v. *Laelius*, no. 3; cf. *ORF²*, pp. 116 f. Much of it is Ciceronian and suffers from idealization, but there is sufficient distinctive material to justify the assessment. Cf. esp. Cic. *Brut.* 82–89; 91–94; *Pro Mur.* 66; *De Off.* 1. 90; 1. 108; *De Orat.* 3. 28; Hor. *Sat.* 2. 1. 72.

[3] Cic. *Brut.* 85 f.

[4] Plut. *Praec. Reip. Ger.* 11; *An Seni Sit Ger.* 27; Julian, *Orationes*, 8. 244 C.

[5] Münzer, *RE*, s.v. *Laelius*, no. 3, col. 407.

and Laelius but was very closely associated with them,[1] and he was
by no means insignificant in political life. His *gens* was of ancient
fame, and as consul in 136 he himself played a central role in the
crisis of the *foedus Mancinum*. Similarly Scipio's elder brother, Q.
Fabius Maximus Aemilianus,[2] was a personage of importance in his
own right: elder son of Paullus, adopted into the line of the great
Cunctator, he had served with distinction in the campaign against
Perseus and had been employed by Paullus on responsible missions;
later, as consul, he conducted campaigns in Spain with some success;
and at Numantia he served as senior *legatus* of his brother, with whom,
despite some possible hints of early jealousy on the latter's part,[3] he
remained closely associated,[4] even if his interest in matters cultural
and Hellenic did not extend so far as that of Scipio, Laelius, and
Furius.[5] Further than that we cannot penetrate into his character and
talents; yet it is enough to show that the association between this
capable head of the Fabian house and the flamboyant new Africanus,
the head of the Scipios, was of considerable import in public life.

The Fabian house provided a direct link with another important
group, the three Servilii brothers, who secured the consulship in turn
in three successive years, 142, 141, and 140.[6] The eldest of them, Q.
Fabius Maximus Servilianus, was by adoption the brother of Fabius
Maximus Aemilianus, and his link with Scipio is further emphasized
by the marriage of his son to the daughter of P. Rupilius, cos. 132,[7]
a *novus homo* of obscure origins who was a protégé of Scipio. The

---

[1] Münzer, *RE*, s.v. *Furius*, no. 78. The three grouped together: Porcius Licinus in Suet.
Ter. 1; Cic. *De Orat.* 2. 154; *Rep.* 3. 5; *Brut.* 258. It seems that his speeches were not available
to Cicero: *Brut.* 108.

[2] Münzer, *RE*, s.v. *Fabius*, no. 109.

[3] Polyb. 31. 23. 8 f. Numantia: App. *Iber.* 90.

[4] Cf. Cic. *De Amic.* 69. Fabius' son, the later Allobrogicus, evidently acquired in his
youth great notoriety for a manner of life very unlikely to have been approved by Scipio
(Val. Max. 6. 9. 4), but in 135 Scipio supported his candidature for the quaestorship (Val.
Max. 8. 15. 4) and in the next year almost certainly took him to Spain as his quaestor: App.
Iber. 84; Münzer, *RE*, s.v. *Fabius*, no. 110.

[5] He is never mentioned in the same manner as these three, an omission only partly
accounted for by the fact that he was dead before the dramatic date of Cicero's *De Republica*
and *De Amicitia* (Münzer, *RE*, s.v. *Fabius*, no. 109, col. 1794); but he did have some interest
in such matters, for he took his share of Perseus' library and in the earlier stages of the
association between Polybius and the two brothers he seems to have taken the lead: Plut.
Aem. 28. 11; Polyb. 31. 23. 5 f.

[6] Münzer, *RE*, s.v. *Fabius*, no. 115; s.v. *Servilius*, nos. 46 and 48 See pp. 315 f.

[7] App. *Iber.* 67; Val. Max. 2. 7. 3; Münzer, *RE*, s.v. *Fabius*, no. 111; *MRR* i, p. 499 n. 1.

Servilii had their limitations in political life. The youngest, Quintus Servilius, seemingly forceful, quick-tempered, harsh, unscrupulous, and probably self-consciously aristocratic in bearing, is most un-likely to have been personally popular;[1] and though he ended the Viriatic war in 139, he did so by procuring the treacherous assassina-tion of Viriatus himself, which offered opponents an opportunity to castigate his methods as shameful.[2] Earlier, his brother Servilianus (who also earned some notoriety for ruthlessness)[3] had been trapped by Viriatus and compelled to come to terms. Nor did any of the brothers excel as popular orators: Servilianus is not mentioned at all in this respect, while Cicero clearly indicates that Gnaeus and Quintus, though able speakers, were by no means outstanding in this field, achieving more for their clients through their prestige and social influence.[4] Herein doubtless lay their power and their value as allies, in their inheritance from a great patrician family, supplemented by forceful characters and by the spectacular achievement of their successive consulships.

In marked contrast to these patricians, in background and probably in temperament, was M'. Manilius, cos. 149, one of the oldest of Scipio's associates. He was the first of his family to reach the consul-ship and his record in military matters was by no means distinguished; but he had great knowledge and understanding of legal matters, so much so that he came to be regarded as one of the founders of Roman civil law. This he combined with wide experience and sagacity, so that, Cicero avers, his advice was sought and given readily on all manner of topics. Not a hero, but perhaps quietly popular, and cer-tainly a valuable adviser in political fields.[5]

The remainder of Scipio's associates can be grouped into three broad categories, of which the first is composed of persons who, though certainly linked with him, for various reasons were less important than those considered so far. There was P. Rupilius, said to have risen from very humble beginnings, who married his daughter to a Fabius Maximus and who, as a protégé of Scipio,

---

[1] Cf. Dio, fgt. 78; Livy, Ox. Epit. 54, 55.
[2] p. 127; cf. Vell. 2. 1. 3; Val. Max. 9. 6. 4; (Victor) De Vir. Ill. 71. 3 f.
[3] App. Iber. 68; Val. Max. 2. 7. 11; Oros. 5. 4. 12; Frontin. Strat. 4. 1. 42.
[4] Cic. Brut. 97.
[5] p. 55 with n. 3; Cic. Brut. 108; De Orat. 3. 133.

secured the consulship in 132. He earned notoriety for his part in the judicial persecution of the Gracchans, as well as more conventional fame for the suppression of the Sicilian slave rebellion and the new settlement for the island embodied in the *lex Rupilia*. To have secured such patronage and advancement he must have had considerable ability, but nothing is recorded either of his earlier career or of his character. He had a brother, Lucius, of whom nothing is known beyond the fact that he too stood for the consulship but was defeated, and that his candidature, like his brother's, was supported by Scipio.[1] Then there was C. Fannius M. f., son-in-law of Laelius, whose tribunate gained distinction through the influence of Scipio, and his namesake C. Fannius C. f.,[2] and L. Cassius Longinus Ravilla, a *nobilis*, though only by one generation, austere and stern, with a reputation for judicial severity, yet, it seems, a popular figure, who as tribune in 137 acted in co-operation with Scipio.[3] The poet Lucilius, intimate with Scipio and Laelius, if not a political figure in the conventional sense, used his pen for political ends in some of his earliest satires.[4] Also associated with Scipio were others who, though in several instances destined for distinction, were probably too young to have achieved much political influence in his lifetime: the two Fabii Maximi, sons of Aemilianus and Servilianus; Q. Mucius Scaevola, son-in-law of Laelius, through whom he obtained an augurate; Q. Aelius Tubero, one of Scipio's nephews, known for his exceptional enthusiasm for learning and for Stoicism but not very successful in public life; and younger still, P. Rutilius Rufus, who served as a military tribune under Scipio at Numantia.[5] Finally there was Sp. Mummius, whose more famous brother Lucius was no friend of Scipio but who himself is clearly presented as such by Cicero. It is very likely that this association, facilitated by the death of Lucius and

---

[1] Münzer, *RE*, s.v. *Rupilius*, nos. 4 and 5; esp. Cic. *De Amic.* 73; *Tusc.* 4. 40; pp. 82 and 230.

[2] Fraccaro, 'Sui Fannii dell' età graccana', *RAL* 19 (1910), pp. 656 f. = *Opusc.* ii, pp. 103 f.; 'Ancora sulla questione dei Fannii', *Athenaeum* 4 (1926), pp. 153 f. = *Opusc.* ii, pp. 119 f. His conclusions are preferable to those of Münzer, *RE*, s.v. *Fannius*, no. 7; 'Die Fanniusfrage', *Hermes* 55 (1920), pp. 427 f. Cf. also *MRR* i, p. 519 n. 2.

[3] Münzer, *RE*, s.v. *Cassius*, no. 72; esp. Cic. *Brut.* 97; pp. 130 f.

[4] Kappelmacher, *RE*, s.v. *Lucilius*, no. 4, esp. cols. 1623 f.; cf. also p. 313 n. 7.

[5] Münzer, *RE*, s.v. *Fabius*, nos. 110 and 111 (cf. p. 82 with n. 4); s.v. *Mucius*, no. 21; s.v. *Rutilius*, no. 34; Klebs, *RE*, s.v. *Aelius*, no. 155.

encouraged by a common interest in Greek learning, began when Spurius was a member of the embassy headed by Scipio in 140–139, an embassy whose tour of the eastern Mediterranean must have occupied more than a year.[1]

In the second category are those whose association with Scipio was broken and who became political opponents. In one case the occasion of the breach is accurately attested. Q. Pompeius, evidently able and unscrupulous, no mean orator and skilled at ingratiating himself with the electorate, was a *novus homo* who entered public life under the patronage of Scipio. Pompeius wished to stand for the plebeian consulship of 141, but Scipio, not surprisingly, preferred to support Laelius and expected Pompeius to wait. Pompeius was not willing to wait, and gained an initial advantage in canvassing by deliberately deceiving Scipio about his intentions. Scipio reacted to the deception with a scornful and insulting witticism. This probably marks the point at which Scipio formally broke off his *amicitia* with Pompeius —a development which can scarcely have surprised the latter. Pompeius must have come to terms with influential opponents of Scipio, for he went on to win the election and ten years later was elected to the censorship, achievements which would have been unthinkable in a *novus homo*, however wealthy and attractive, without aristocratic support.[2]

The second person in this category is Q. Caecilius Metellus Macedonicus, whose estrangement from Scipio evidently began in connexion with some public issue and may possibly have been conducted at first in a moderate spirit before developing into 'serious and well attested enmity'. The occasion of the estrangement is not specified, and the only firm indication of date is Metellus' defence of Aurelius Cotta when Scipio prosecuted the latter in 138. Probably the breach occurred not long before that date, after Metellus' consulship and proconsulship in 143 and 142; but the evidence is not so strong as could be wished.[3] As a political figure he was handicapped by a reputation for excessive severity (presumably in the sphere of military discipline) which earned him some unpopularity among the

---

[1] Cic. *De Amic.* 69; *Rep.* 1. 18; Münzer, *RE*, s.v. *Mummius*, no. 13. The embassy: p. 127. Scipio and L. Mummius: Ch. X, *passim*.

[2] pp. 121 f.; Miltner, *RE*, s.v. *Pompeius*, no. 12.   [3] pp. 312 f.

electors, but he also had important assets: *nobilitas* and descent from a famous family; eloquence of the first rank; marked military ability, which earned him the unusual honour of a praetorian triumph; a sense of magnificence which enabled him to make impressive, not to say spectacular, use of his Macedonian spoils; and perhaps one should add a wife whose 'conspicuous fecundity' enabled him to exploit the device of political marriage and helped to make his family the most powerful in the political life of the next generation.[1]

Then there were the Sempronii Gracchi, related to Scipio through the marriage of Cornelia (by birth his cousin and also sister of his adoptive father) to the elder Tiberius. That powerful personality seems often to have pursued an opportunist policy, varying his political associations at different stages of his career. He was dead by this time, but his family renewed and strengthened its association with the Scipios. The younger Tiberius accompanied Scipio to Carthage, and Scipio married his sister, Sempronia.[2] But later Tiberius married a daughter of Appius Claudius Pulcher, Scipio's most dangerous rival, with whose father the elder Tiberius had been associated for a time; the marriage between Scipio and Sempronia was childless and became a very unhappy relationship;[3] and Gaius, the younger brother, married a daughter of P. Licinius Crassus Dives Mucianus,[4] who was no friend of Scipio. In this case too the date of the estrangement is not known. It might have been in 137–136, as a consequence of the dispute concerning the *foedus Mancinum*, and certainly it cannot have been later than that; but there is a very real possibility that Tiberius' marriage took place much earlier, around 143,[5] and there is no reason why the breach should not have occurred at that time.

The last person known to fall into this category is C. Porcius Cato, one of Scipio's nephews. All that is known is that he supported

---

[1] pp. 100 and 105. Eloquence: Cic. *Brut.* 81; *De Orat.* 1. 215. Wife: Val. Max. 7. 1. 1. In general, Münzer, *RE*, s.v. *Caecilius*, no. 94. There is no independent evidence concerning the associations of Macedonicus' brother, L. Metellus Calvus, cos. 142, but presumably the two were political allies.

[2] Cornelia and Sempronia: p. 13. The younger Tiberius at Carthage: Plut. *Ti. Grac.* 4. 5. The father's opportunism: Earl, *Tiberius Gracchus*, pp. 49 f. Date of his death: p. 36 n. 1.

[3] App. *B.C.* 1. 20.

[4] Plut. *Ti. Grac.* 21. 2; *C. Grac.* 15. 5; 17. 6; Just. *Dig.* 24. 3. 66.

[5] Plut. *Ti. Grac.* 4. 2 f.; Livy, *Epit.* 58; Vell. 2. 2. 3; App. *B.C.* 1. 13. The date: pp. 319 f.

Tiberius Gracchus in 133, and the passage in which this is mentioned implies that he was already an *amicus* of Tiberius.[1] It is a reasonable assumption that in earlier years he must have had close ties with Scipio, but there is no way of knowing whether or not these were loosened before 133, when his attitude would have ensured a breach; his friendship with Tiberius suggests that they were, but there is no means of knowing whether this friendship was of recent creation or of long standing.

The final category consists of other persons whose co-operation and support Scipio is likely to have enjoyed but for whom the positive evidence for such association is in varying degrees inadequate. Most of them are somewhat misty figures, though not necessarily without influence and importance. Thus the Acilii, who rose to *nobilitas* as clients of the Scipios, had provided two recent consuls to whom Scipio may have been able to look for support during the 140's.[2] The Livius who was Scipio's colleague in the consulship of 147 may have been both a supporter and a relative.[3] It is likely that the Atilii, now represented by the Serrani, followed their old associates the Fabii into alliance with the Scipios.[4] The Octavii, a fairly recent addition to the aristocracy, had had close links with the Scipios and the Aemilii, which may help to account for the stand taken against Tiberius Gracchus by Marcus Octavius, their sole representative in this period.[5]

Last of all, there was P. Cornelius Scipio Nasica, the son of Corculum. Impetuous in character and pungent in speech, he evidently lacked the tactful affability needed to ingratiate himself with persons of humbler rank and was apt to betray strong aristocratic prejudices, which doubtless gave great point to the nickname Serapio, scornfully

[1] Cic. *De Amic.* 39.

[2] A Glabrio in 154 and a Balbus in 150; cf. Scullard, *Roman Politics*, for the career of M'. Glabrio, cos. 191, father of the cos. suff. of 154; but the next Glabrio to make his mark was the associate of C. Gracchus. On the Acilii see Münzer, *Röm. Adels.*, pp. 91 f.

[3] But it is not certain that he was either: p. 67.

[4] A Serranus was almost certainly a *legatus* under Scipio in 147: Additional Note E, p. 340. The co-operation of Sex. Atilius Serranus, cos. 136, with his colleague Furius Philus (Cic. *De Off.* 3. 109) is not strong evidence since they were acting upon the instructions of the Senate.

[5] Earl, 'M. Octavius', *Latomus* 19 (1960), pp. 657 f., esp. p. 661 (though not all the arguments are valid). In 168 Cn. Octavius and Paullus co-operated closely: Livy, 44. 19. 4, 21. 3, 22. 16, 35. 8 and 13; 45. 6. 12, 28. 8, 29. 3.

applied because of his resemblance to a lowly *victimarius* of that name.[1] Nevertheless, as the heir of the second great branch of the Scipios, and through his mother a grandson of Africanus himself, he was a person of no small importance. Although he failed to secure the aedileship (probably at the elections in 146),[2] he recovered quickly, became consul in 138 and was appointed Pontifex Maximus when he himself was absent from Rome. In view of this and of his prominent role in the crisis of 133, it is particularly unfortunate that there is virtually no direct evidence of his political associations. By *c.* 135 his son had married a daughter of Metellus Macedonicus, but there is no means of knowing whether the marriage took place before or after Metellus' breach with Aemilianus.[3] Nasica's opposition to the Gracchans does not necessarily mean that he co-operated with Aemilianus at other times. It has to be remembered that Aemilianus had not supported Corculum's policy towards Carthage and had been the final agent in the execution of the rival policy; also that there are some hints that in Aemilianus' earlier years there were family tensions. On the other hand Corculum had been actively associated with Aemilianus' father, Aemilius Paullus, with his brother Fabius, and probably with his intimate friend Laelius;[4] and the ties by blood, by adoption, and by the common heritage of a great patrician family were very close and must have been very significant in the social and political atmosphere of Rome. On the whole it seems reasonable to suppose, albeit tentatively, that these ties asserted themselves and that there was some degree of co-operation between the two Scipios.

At this point it is convenient to pause and to take note of certain more general features. In the first place, Scipio plainly had an eye for talent. The overwhelming majority of his known associates ultimately reached the consulship, and three protégés, Pompeius, P. Rupilius, and Rutilius Rufus, were notable choices. Secondly, it would certainly be a mistake to think that Scipio's relationships with his *amici* were of a uniform kind. Men like Pompeius, the Rupilii,

[1] Münzer, *RE*, s.v. *Cornelius*, no. 354. Cf. esp. Cic. *Brut.* 107; *De Off.* 1. 109; Livy, *Epit.* 55; Val. Max. 3. 7. 3; 7. 5. 2; 9. 14. 3; Plin. *Nat. Hist.* 7. 54; cf. 21. 10.

[2] p. 101.   [3] p. 314.

[4] Polyb. 29. 14 f.; Livy, 44. 35. 14 f., 36. 9 f., 38. 1 f., 46. 1 f.; 45. 33. 8, 34. 8; Plut. *Aem.* 15 f.; Cic. *De Amic.* 101.

and Rutilius Rufus, for all that they had resources and talents to offer, were essentially clients, followers of a powerful leader, owing their advancement very largely to his patronage; and even such men as the Fannii and L. Cassius Longinus must have stood in a relationship of considerable dependence upon him. Laelius and Furius, on the other hand, though also unmistakably followers with undivided loyalties, were also personal friends, constant companions, and intimate counsellors; while men from great aristocratic families, like the Servilii brothers and Scipio Nasica, are much more likely to have regarded themselves and to have behaved as allies and associates than as followers, and the firmness and intimacy of such alliances may well have varied considerably. Such men may have been ready enough to assist Scipio in order to avail themselves of his immense prestige, but they would never have allowed themselves to appear as his political henchmen. And these are the men who had the most to bargain with, the family influence, the *clientelae*, to offer or to withhold; and they are the men most likely, in the complex but limited network of the aristocracy, to have had links of various kinds with others besides Scipio. To keep the support of such men required more than a glamorous or a dominating personality, or the threat of with-holding favour; there was need of skilled political leadership.

And here is seen one of Scipio's failings; for the fact is that he proved inadequate in one of the prime tasks of any political leader—the tactful handling and conciliation of his associates and supporters. Pompeius, of course, as a *novus homo* deserting his patron, is an unusual phenomenon, and if he stood alone it might be suspected that he was quite exceptionally difficult and unscrupulous and that none of the responsibility for the breach lay with Scipio. But Pompeius does not stand alone. There was Metellus Macedonicus, no less able than Pompeius and far more distinguished, whose dispute with Scipio widened into actual hostility; there were Tiberius and Gaius Gracchus, Scipio's kinsmen and brothers-in-law, of whom Tiberius married the daughter of none other than Appius Claudius; and there was C. Porcius Cato, Scipio's nephew, whose hereditary ties Scipio clearly failed to strengthen and preserve.

The qualities demanded by military leadership and by political leadership do not entirely coincide. Beyond doubt Scipio was endowed with a good measure of the former, and it must not be thought that he was without talent in the latter field: for nearly twenty years he remained a dominant political figure, numbering among his allies and supporters many men of remarkable ability. Nevertheless, the defection of such associates as Pompeius, Macedonicus, the Gracchi, and C. Cato, all of very considerable immediate or potential value, does indicate that there were certain shortcomings in his leadership. And if the sources of this weakness are sought, at least part of the answer is surely to be found in the all-too-ready wit, the sharp tongue, the self-assertion and arrogance which, as was observed in an earlier chapter, must have hindered the healing of differences and made him more prone to embitter enmities than to win over opponents.

An examination of Scipio's opponents has to embrace two questions: who were his opponents, and what political relationships existed between them. The first question can be answered fairly easily, for a considerable list can be compiled even of men explicitly attested as opponents. Chief among them was Ap. Claudius Pulcher, patrician, coeval of Scipio and his equal in family distinction, fluent and rather passionate as an orator, ambitious, determined, ingenious, and unscrupulous. He was defeated by Scipio at the elections for the censorship in 142, became Princeps Senatus at the next census, when he himself was in office, and is stated to have been an *inimicus* of Scipio, with special reference to the years after 133.[1] Another patrician *inimicus* was Ser. Sulpicius Galba, probably the ablest orator of the day, noted alike for his forceful and passionate rhetoric and for the ruthlessness he displayed as praetor in Spain. As a young man he had attacked Scipio's father, Paullus, and he and his fellow consul in 144 were the objects of one of Scipio's insulting witticisms, when the latter's intervention helped to prevent either of them obtaining an important command in Further Spain.[2] The other consul, L. Aurelius Cotta, a shadowy figure, was later prosecuted by Scipio in person;[3] and another Sulpicius, P. Galus, probably related to Galba, was scathingly criticized by Scipio on the score of his luxurious and

---

[1] Münzer, *RE*, s.v. *Claudius*, no. 295; cf. esp. Cic. *Brut.* 108; *Rep.* I. 31; *Pro Scaur.* 32; cf. pp. 111 f.

[2] Münzer, *RE*, s.v. *Sulpicius*, no. 58; cf. pp. 58 and 104 f.

[3] Klebs, *RE*, s.v. *Aurelius*, no. 98; pp. 104 and 129.

effeminate way of life.[1] Others lashed by Scipio's tongue were
L. Mummius, the conqueror of Achaea and Scipio's colleague in the
censorship, where his very different approach angered and embittered
Scipio,[2] and Ti. Claudius Asellus, who was attacked by Scipio in the
censorship and who as tribune of the plebs in 140 retaliated by
prosecuting Scipio.[3]

Two Hostilii Mancini may be added to the list: Lucius, whose
canvass for the consulship of 145 offended Scipio by extensive
propagation of the claim that he, Lucius, had been the first to break
into Carthage; and the unfortunate Gaius, consul in 137, whose
degradation in the following year was the culmination of a process in
which Scipio played no small part.[4] In 145 the tribune C. Licinius
Crassus, attempting to change the method of appointment to the
priestly colleges, was faced with Laelius as his principal opponent.[5]
M. Aemilius Lepidus, the patrician consul of 137, whose size and
weight earned him not only his nickname Porcina but a gibe about
his physical unsuitability for the activities of war, was the leading
opponent of the *lex Cassia tabellaria*, which was supported and
probably inspired by Scipio.[6] And L. Calpurnius Piso, consul in
Africa in 148, will not have been on good terms with the man who
repeatedly castigated his incompetence and failure.[7]

In other instances the evidence is less direct or is confined to the
years after 133, but it still leaves little doubt about the relationship.
There were the Postumii Albini, patrician and powerful. Aulus, the
consul of 151, despite his philhellenism, was criticized, not to say
caricatured, by Polybius with a savagery which would have been
quite impossible if the friendship of Aulus or of members of his
family had counted for anything with Scipio or his associates;[8]
Postumii were twice attacked or mocked by Lucilius,[9] and Spurius,

---

[1] Appendix II, no. 20.
[2] Ch. X, esp. pp. 119 f.; Münzer, *RE*, s.v. *Mummius*, no. 7a.
[3] pp. 120, 127, and 175 f.
[4] pp. 99 and 131 f.; Münzer, *RE*, s.v. *Hostilius*, nos. 18 and 20.   [5] p. 101.
[6] p. 131; Diod. 33. 27; Klebs, *RE*, s.v. *Aemilius*, no. 83.
[7] pp. 61 and 71; Münzer, *RE*, s.v. *Calpurnius*, no. 87.
[8] Polyb. 39. 1. 1 f.; Münzer, *RE*, s.v. *Postumius*, no. 31.
[9] 1326–38 M. and 848 f. M., the latter from Book 29 and therefore probably written
c. 133–129 (cf. refs. at p. 313 n. 7). Neither of the individuals is identifiable with any great
degree of probability. Cf. Münzer, *RE*, s.v. *Postumius*, nos. 28, 29, and 68.

the consul of 148, will scarcely have improved relationships by his opposition to Scipio's election to the consulship, even if it be supposed that his objections were genuinely founded upon constitutional and not at all upon personal considerations.[1] Another patrician who must have enjoyed great influence was L. Cornelius Lentulus Lupus, censor in 147 and Princeps Senatus from 130: he is a shadowy personality, never mentioned in any connexion with Scipio, but he was a major target for the satires of Lucilius.[2] The two brothers P. Mucius Scaevola and P. Licinius Crassus Dives Mucianus, alike eminent lawyers, were both associated with the agrarian legislation of Ti. Gracchus in 133 and both are attested as leading opponents of Scipio thereafter; moreover, Mucianus gave one daughter in marriage to Gaius Gracchus and another to the son of Ser. Sulpicius Galba; and Galba assisted Mucianus' candidature for the aedileship.[3] Q. Fulvius Nobilior, whose consulship in 153 was marred by a disastrous defeat in Spain, is mentioned in an unflattering light by Polybius, was prominent in defence of Galba in 149, and as censor in 136, even if not wholly identified with his colleague's policy, must have co-operated in nominating Appius Claudius as Princeps Senatus in preference to more senior men, including Scipio.[4] The other branch of the Fulvii, the Flacci, provided two consuls (in 135 and 134) about whom almost nothing is known, but the dynamic M. Fulvius Flaccus, cos. 125, was deeply involved in Tiberius Gracchus' agrarian programme and in 132–129 clashed especially with Scipio. And almost exactly the same can be said of C. Papirius Carbo, eloquent and energetic, who as tribune in 131 found his principal opponents in Scipio and Laelius.[5]

There remain a few cases where the evidence is more tentative, though suggestive. Thus by 136 a Q. Marcius Philippus had married a Claudia of the Appii Claudii, probably a daughter of Scipio's great rival.[6] D. Iunius Brutus, a lawyer who also won great military fame,

---

[1] pp. 65 f.

[2] Hor. Sat. 2. 1. 62 f.; Münzer, RE, s.v. Cornelius, no. 224; cf. MRR i, p. 501 n. 1.

[3] Münzer, RE, s.v. Mucius, no. 17; Licinius, no. 72; cf. esp. Cic. Rep. 1. 31; De Orat. 1. 239; Brut. 98; 127; p. 191.

[4] p. 37; Polyb. 35. 4. 2; Livy, Epit. 49; Münzer, RE, s.v. Fulvius, no. 95.

[5] pp. 191 f., 232 f., 238, and 241; Münzer, RE, s.v. Fulvius, no. 58; s.v. Papirius, no. 33.

[6] Cic. De Domo, 84; cf. Münzer, RE, s.v. Marcius, no. 75.

was related by marriage to M. Aemilius Lepidus Porcina and co-operated with him in military campaigns.[1] An account of the campaigns conducted by L. Licinius Lucullus, cos. 151, is patently hostile to him and equally sympathetic towards Scipio.[2] Finally, although P. Popillius Laenas became notorious for his part in the persecution of the followers of Tiberius Gracchus in 132, in which Laelius and P. Rupilius were also deeply involved, this is not evidence that he was previously associated with Scipio, and there is some reason to think that his cousin Marcus, cos. 139, was disliked by Scipio.[3]

The second question concerning Scipio's opponents, their political relationship to each other, is much more difficult to answer satisfactorily. There just is not enough information preserved. However, it is possible to discern something of one group of men linked with each other and centred upon the powerful personality of Appius Claudius, men who had an inheritance of ties among their families but who also formed new ties in their own generation.[4] As Claudius became the father-in-law of Ti. Gracchus, so P. Licinius Crassus Mucianus was the father-in-law of C. Gracchus, and both he and his brother P. Mucius Scaevola were associated with Claudius and Ti. Gracchus in the agrarian programme of 133. Another daughter of Mucianus was married to the son of Ser. Sulpicius Galba, and in 149 Galba had been defended by Q. Fulvius Nobilior, who in turn helped to make Claudius Princeps Senatus; and a member of the other branch of the Fulvii, M. Fulvius Flaccus, was also closely involved in the agrarian programme of 133. The association of these men and their families clearly had more coherence and foundation than simply

---

[1] pp. 133 and 146; Münzer, RE, s.v. Iunius, no. 57.

[2] App. Iber. 49–55; cf. 60, 61.

[3] Volkmann, RE, s.v. Popillius, nos. 22 and 28. For 132 see p. 230. Cf. Lucil. 621 M.: percrepa pugnam Popili, facta Corneli cane. The reference is evidently to the reverses suffered by Marcus in Spain (p. 129). The fragment is from Book 26, and therefore was published c. 131 (cf. refs. at p. 313 n. 7), after Publius' co-operation with Laelius and Rupilius. One can only guess at the explanation: perhaps the co-operation of 132 had not endured, or perhaps Marcus had not shared his cousin's attitude.

[4] References concerning these individuals are given earlier in this chapter. For discussions of earlier generations see esp. Münzer, Röm. Adels. and Scullard, Roman Politics. Some details are controversial but there is no doubt that there had been links between these families. This discussion does not follow the elaborate conjectures of Münzer, Röm. Adels., pp. 270 f., concerning the marriages of Crassus Mucianus and Brutus Callaicus.

common hostility towards Scipio, but it does not follow, any more than with Scipio's allies, that the bonds were uniformly close; indeed such men as these are perhaps unlikely to have preserved over a long period complete and unbroken unity, though it so happens that from the period under discussion there survive no traces of disunity within this particular group.

*Aemilius Lepidus is another leader from a great and powerful family who is known to have opposed Scipio, and at the same time his part in the affair of the Marcian aqueduct in 143 suggests that he was not on good terms with Ap. Claudius.[1] Perhaps he, together with his kinsman Brutus Callaicus, represents a third and distinct focal point of forces in political life,[2] but the evidence is too scanty for any degree of assurance. In the case of other prominent persons, such as Lentulus Lupus, L. Mummius, and the Popillii, it is even more insubstantial, to the point where speculation is quite unprofitable; though it is suggestive that when Fulvius Nobilior appointed Claudius Princeps Senatus in 136 he was passing over not only Scipio Aemilianus but also Lentulus Lupus, who was probably the senior candidate. On the other hand Metellus Macedonicus and Q. Pompeius, two of the better-known personalities of the period, provide a salutary illustration that the scene was complex and liable to change. Both these men were at one time politically associated with Scipio and later became opponents of him; both of them opposed Tiberius Gracchus in 133, when there is every reason to suppose that Gracchus was supported by Appius Claudius; yet the two of them were manifestly engaged in a feud with each other,[3] despite which they found themselves as colleagues in the censorship of 131. Furthermore, in 130–129 Metellus was one of Scipio's leading opponents, but on the news of Scipio's death his public position changed abruptly: he bewailed the loss to the state and instructed his sons to carry Scipio's bier.[4]

*There remains the possible identification of another focal point in

---

[1] pp. 109 f.

[2] Münzer, *Röm. Adels.*, pp. 237 f., esp. pp. 240 f., holds that Lepidus renewed and strengthened the family alliance forged in 179 with the Claudian–Fulvian group; but there is no positive evidence, except perhaps Münzer's unacceptable view that in 143 the Decemviri, with whom Lepidus clashed, were hostile to Claudius as well: p. 106 n. 6.

[3] p. 129.   [4] p. 244.

the Postumii Albini, who secured consulships in 154, 151, and 148. They were certainly not on good terms with Scipio, and there is good reason to believe that the previous generation of their family had been opponents of the Claudian–Fulvian faction in the 170's;[1] later a Spurius Postumius is said to have been a rival of Ti. Gracchus in seeking renown in the law-courts, and since some went so far as to allege (very implausibly) that this rivalry was the chief inducement underlying Gracchus' agrarian proposal of 133, it can be inferred that the rivalry was intense and that Postumius did not support the agrarian bill.[2] An ancient and famous patrician family, the Postumii were well fitted to play an independent role in politics and it is a reasonable hypothesis that they did so.

With the Postumii were probably associated the Calpurnii Pisones, who had previously achieved the consulship only once, in 180, but who now became very prominent indeed, with consuls in 148, 139, 135, and 133. The significant pointer is that the first two consuls, those of 180 and 148, both had Postumii as their colleagues, which could be an extraordinary coincidence but more probably indicates an old family helping a new one to power. In line with this relationship are the patent hostility of Scipio towards Caesoninus, the consul of 148, and some indications that Frugi, the consul of 133, was no friend of the Claudian faction.[3] One other family may be mentioned tentatively in conjunction with the Postumii and the Calpurnii. This is the Hostilii Mancini, the reason being that L. Hostilius Mancinus, in 145 only the second of his family to reach the consulship, was almost certainly a *legatus* under L. Calpurnius Piso Caesoninus in 148.[4]

The Postumii probably had other close allies, and plausible guesses could be offered as to the identity of some; but they would be no more than guesses and therefore would bring little profit. Nor should it be forgotten that there is a large element of hypothesis running through this whole chapter. Yet for all the limitations in detail, something of the general picture has emerged. Politics in this period are not to be thought of in terms of two clearly defined monolithic parties, 'pro-Scipio' and 'anti-Scipio'. That is not to deny that the

[1] Additional Note I, p. 342.   [2] Plut. *Ti. Grac.* 8. 8.   [3] pp. 318 f.
[4] Additional Note E, p. 340.

question of whether one was associated with Scipio or opposed to him was always of major importance, and on occasion perhaps the overriding issue. But despite the outstanding pre-eminence of Scipio and Appius Claudius, the simple notion of two coherent factions just does not fit the facts; it seems that there were several persons or families who could be thought of as the nuclei of factions. Scipio's opponents did not necessarily have anything in common apart from their opposition to himself; and it would be surprising if they had never allowed other issues or quarrels amongst themselves to override that common opposition. Moreover, the possibility of powerful nobles and factions striking bargains over the use of their influence and their *clientelae* meant that there was always some fluidity in the situation, a fluidity increased both by new quarrels and defections, as in the cases of Metellus and Pompeius, and by the complex nexus of kinship, traditional ties, and *beneficia*, which not infrequently must have made men feel obligations in more than one direction.

IX

FROM TRIUMPH TO CENSORSHIP

SCIPIO's triumph over Carthage was a peak of both public and personal success; the achievement of a great ambition was here magnificently symbolized. Nevertheless, this could not be the final culmination either of career or of ambition. Not only did there lie ahead the further prize of the censorship, but a leading member of one of the great aristocratic families will have taken it for granted that he would go on to use his achievements as the basis of power and influence, to be a *princeps civitatis.* That Scipio would be a major political figure cannot have been in doubt; the question was rather how great would be his influence on elections and government: to what extent would his support assist the election to high office of friends and allies or his intervention effectively sway the decisions of the Senate. There was much in his favour. The way had been eased by the death of most of the political giants of the 150's: the elder Gracchus, probably towards the end of the decade, M. Aemilius Lepidus in 152, Cato in 149, and M. Claudius Marcellus, drowned at sea in 148.[1] There were still powerful and active politicians—for example, the Postumii, led by two recent consuls, and the Lentuli brothers, the one just concluding his censorship, the other his consulship—but none is likely to have wielded such influence as the really dominating personalities of the earlier period, of whom only Nasica survived, now Princeps Senatus, yet surely somewhat discredited and with his influence diminished. The new Africanus, on the other hand, enjoyed the unrivalled advantage of the prestige and authority conferred by his victory and triumph. He could present himself not only as a victorious hero but also as the 'people's choice', who, though lacking in years and technically ineligible, had been raised to high office by popular insistence that he alone could meet the crisis—and who had justified the confidence placed in him.

[1] Lepidus and Gracchus: pp. 35 f.; Cato: p. 58; Marcellus: Livy, *Epit.* 50; *Ox. Epit.* 50; Cic. *In Pis.* 44; *De Divin.* 2. 14; *De Fato*, 33; Ascon., p. 12 C.

Yet not everything on the political scene was favourable. In the first place, his aristocratic allies at this time were neither numerous nor outstanding.[1] Of the really great families there were only the closely linked Fabii Maximi and Servilii Caepiones. Also very distinguished, though less so than these two, were the Sempronii Gracchi, the Caecilii Metelli, the Furii, and probably the Livii; but the head of the Gracchi, the younger Tiberius, was still only sixteen or seventeen, and the other three, like the Fabii, had suffered eclipse for a generation. Moreover, while these families included several men of great ability, at this date they contained only one man who was already of consular rank, Scipio's own former colleague Livius. There was also the Princeps Senatus, Nasica Corculum, but in view of recent events the extent to which he was prepared to co-operate with Scipio must remain uncertain. Scipio's other known or possible allies, including a few consulars, all seem to be either *novi homines* or of only comparatively recent nobility.[2] These weaknesses were in part accidental, but also they may be attributable, perhaps in no small measure, to Scipio's early neglect of some of the traditional methods by which *amicitiae* and *clientelae* were developed; certainly they will have aggravated the general consequences of that neglect, both in the Senate and in the assemblies. Furthermore, the very swiftness and drama of Scipio's rise to the highest ranks, not to mention the methods employed to that end, were such as to provoke resentment and jealousy, and to encourage co-operation against him. The hostile factions and the *clientelae* which they controlled must have been formidable—at least for so long as they could work together. Much was going to depend also upon the political value of Scipio's personal prestige—or the extent to which it could tempt men to default on obligations laid upon them by ties of kinship and patronage —and particularly on the extent to which in the assemblies it could sway those voters who were not effectively tied by social obligations. Even in this last field all was not as secure as Scipio would have wished. Already it was virtually certain that before long Mummius would be celebrating a triumph magnificent with all the treasures of

[1] For Scipio's relationships with the individuals and families mentioned in this passage see further Ch. VIII and Appendix VIII.

[2] Manilius, cos. 149, is certain. Other consulars who may have been friendly are the two Acilii, Glabrio, cos. suff. 154, and Balbus, cos. 150.

Corinth, likely to equal and perhaps to surpass Scipio's in everything except the lineage of the victor and the reputation of the vanquished;[1] and as an immediate and visible irritant, there in the Forum was L. Hostilius Mancinus, now a candidate for the consulship, displaying diagrams of Carthage and of the assaults upon it, with the aid of which he explained in detail to the onlookers his version of what had happened. His audience will have heard that he was the first to break into Carthage, that this was an achievement of considerable value, and probably that it was bungled by Scipio. It is no wonder that he roused Scipio's anger, particularly as he emerged victorious from the election.[2]

That election, for the consuls of 145, was held under the shadow of a fresh crisis in Further Spain. In 147 fighting had broken out once more against the Lusitani, who, after an initial reverse at the hands of the praetor Vetilius, had found a leader of outstanding ability in the famous Viriatus. They had inflicted a grave defeat upon Vetilius, who was himself killed, and another upon his quaestor. In 146 Vetilius' successor, C. Plautius, had also fared very badly, had incurred heavy casualties, and was reported to have retired into winter-quarters in the middle of summer.[3] In addition, it is possible that reports had already been received of the further disaster suffered by a certain Claudius Unimanus.[4] Thus there must have been a general awareness that one of the consuls to be elected was likely to be sent with a consular army to restore this dangerous situation. The successful patrician was Q. Fabius Maximus Aemilianus, Scipio's brother. Although he seems to have been reasonably competent and had served with some distinction in the Third Macedonian War, it is unlikely that he had to his credit any recent or spectacular military achievements; certainly he will have had no opportunity for such

[1] ILS 20; Livy, Epit. 52; Cic. Pro Mur. 31; Ps.-Ascon., p. 237 Stangl; (Victor) De Vir. Ill. 61. 2; Eutrop. 4. 14. 2; Vell. 2. 128. 2; Tac. Ann. 14. 21; App. Lib. 135; cf. Plin. Nat. Hist. 33. 149; 37. 12. Degrassi, Inscr. Ital. xiii. 1, p. 557. For Mummius' distribution of the treasures see pp. 115 f.

[2] Plin. Nat. Hist. 35. 23; pp. 70 f.

[3] For Viriatus and the Viriatic war see esp. Schulten, 'Viriatus', NJA 39 (1917), pp. 209 f.; Gundel, RE, s.v. Viriatus; Simon, Roms Kriege, pp. 87 f.; De Sanctis, Storia, iv. 3, pp. 222 f.; App. Iber. 61 f. Vetilius and Plautius: App. loc. cit.; Livy, Epit. 52; cf. Ox. Epit. 51; Oros. 5. 4. 2 f.; Diod. 33. 1. 3; cf. 33. 2. On the chronology see Additional Note J, p. 343.

[4] Oros. 5. 4. 3 f.; Flor. 1. 33. 16; (Victor) De Vir. Ill. 71. 1. Additional Note K, p. 344.

in Sicily, which had been his province when he was praetor.[1] But if the conqueror of Carthage, immediately after his own triumph, had not been able to ensure the election of a brother who was also a Fabius Maximus, his prospects of political influence would have been limited indeed.

There is no record of who opposed Fabius for the patrician place, but a defeated plebeian is known. Q. Caecilius Metellus had recently demonstrated his considerable talent as a commander by his victory in the Fourth Macedonian War, celebrated by the adoption of the name 'Macedonicus' and by a triumph, which for a praetor was a comparatively rare honour; and he could point also to his victories in Greece in the spring of 146.[2] In himself therefore seemingly a strong candidate, he almost certainly had the further advantage of being recommended and assisted by Scipio;[3] and all this on an occasion when military considerations should have weighed heavily. Yet he was defeated by Mancinus, virtually a *novus homo*, a man accused by Scipio of having exhibited at Carthage recklessness and incompetence. A negative explanation is recorded: that 'he was hated by the plebs on account of excessive *severitas*', which probably means harsh military discipline.[4] Since the voters must have been conscious that several thousands of them would be selected to serve under one of the consuls of 145, this reputation, whether justified or not, was understandably a handicap. On the positive side a marked contrast was offered in the *comitas*, the friendliness and affability, of Mancinus' illustrated talks; and furthermore it is safe to assume that Mancinus did convince some people of the competence and merit of his services at Carthage. Finally, it is reasonable to suppose that at this time, shortly after Scipio's return to Rome, those who were hostile to him were able to achieve a considerable measure of co-operation, so that

[1] In 149: Polyb. 36. 5. 8.

[2] p. 74. The triumph: Livy, *Epit.* 52; Cic. *In Pis.* 58 and 61; *Pro Mur.* 31; *De Fin.* 5. 82; Vell. 1. 11. 2 f.; Val. Max. 7. 1. 1; 7. 5. 4; 8. 5. 1; Eutrop. 4. 14; Plin. *Nat. Hist.* 7. 142 f.; App. *Lib.* 135; Florus 1. 30. 5.

[3] For his relations with Scipio see pp. 85 and 312 f.

[4] (Victor) *De Vir. Ill.* 61. 3; cf. Livy, *Ox. Epit.* 52; Val. Max. 7. 5. 4. An incident during Metellus' subsequent campaign in Spain became a classic example of military *severitas*: Vell. 2. 5. 2 f.; Val. Max. 2. 7. 10; Front. *Strat.* 4. 1. 23; (Victor) *De Vir. Ill.* 61. 4; cf. also Front. *Strat.* 4. 1. 11. But he was not entirely callous: 'Plut.' *Apophth. Caec. Met.* 1; cf. Val. Max. 5. 1. 5; Livy, *Ox. Epit.* 53.

a good many leading men are likely to have been pressing their clients to vote for Mancinus.

The consular elections in 146 thus showed Scipio to be by no means overwhelmingly influential; even so soon after his triumph an opponent had been able to win one of the consulships, and that opponent none other than Mancinus. In the praetorian elections the success of C. Laelius arouses no surprise; but it was probably in this year (though conceivably two years later) that P. Scipio Nasica, later known as Serapio, Corculum's son, failed to secure the curule aedileship, a failure which can scarcely be attributed entirely to Serapio's ill-concealed aristocratic prejudices and the tactless wit which led him when shaking the horny palm of an artisan to ask its owner if he walked on his hands;[1] his defeat points also to the diminished influence of the Princeps Senatus himself.

Soon after these elections—perhaps only a few weeks later, at most a few months—one of the tribunes of 145, C. Licinius Crassus, proposed a bill under which vacancies in the priestly colleges would be filled by popular election instead of by co-optation. Since the priestly colleges had political significance, both the bill and the dispute it occasioned were political in character. In the course of a speech on the subject Crassus reinforced the 'popular' nature of his proposal by the calculated innovation of turning around on the *rostra*, thereby addressing directly the mass of the people instead of the more limited and more select company who could be fitted into the comparatively small space of the *comitium*. Nevertheless, the bill was rejected by the assembly, the chief public opposition having come from Laelius, whose speech became famous.[2] Various

---

[1] Val. Max. 7. 5. 2. Valerius confuses several Nasicae, but Cic. *Pro Planc.* 51 leaves little doubt that the anecdote pertains to Serapio. For his character cf. p. 87. Assuming that the curule aedileship was still held by patricians and plebeians in alternate years, Serapio must have been a candidate for the aedileship of either 145 or 143. Since he was consul in 138 he must have been praetor in 141 at the latest, which leaves 143 as the latest year for the intended aedileship. His parents were married after the death of Africanus in 183 (Polyb. 31. 27. 3. Livy, 38. 57. 2 must be wrong. Africanus' death: Scullard, *Roman Politics*, p. 152 n. 1), so he cannot have been old enough for the aedileship of 147 (for the age requirement see Astin, *Lex Annalis*, pp. 31 f., esp. p. 37).

[2] Cic. *De Amic.* 96. Laelius' speech: ORF², fgts. 12–16, pp. 117 f. Crassus' innovation is mentioned in Varro *De Re Rust.* 1. 2. 9; Plut. *C. Grac.* 5. 4 f. attributes it to C. Gracchus, presumably because he was the first to follow the practice regularly. Cicero and Plutarch leave no doubt about the significance of the gesture. The curious wording of Varro (*primus*

hypothetical suggestions could be offered about the circumstances and implications of the episode, but so little is known with certainty that comment is best confined to one significant feature.

This feature is the expectation of Crassus and his supporters (not necessarily all of those who were hostile to Scipio) that the change to popular election would be to their advantage; and on the other side Laelius and, it may be presumed, Scipio felt that their interests would be threatened. This points again to the limitations of Scipio's influence, even at elections in the tribal assembly. Nor was it only a matter of his opponents manipulating their *clientelae.* Crassus' innovation on the *rostra* shows that he was hoping to win much support by stimulating popular enthusiasm and by emphasizing the right of voters to make their own decision. In the event he miscalculated and was defeated, perhaps in part because the forces against him were too strong, but also because Laelius was able to play upon religious fears, dwelling upon the tradition of established institutions and practices and the gratification with which they were viewed by the gods. But this very line of defence is itself a recognition of the utility of appealing to the independent judgement, the prejudice, or the emotions of voters. If Scipio and his friends were making 'popular appeal', in its widest sense, a key factor in their success, others were certain to compete with them, indeed might well feel driven to do so.

After he had successfully opposed Crassus, Laelius set off for his province, which was Hither Spain, Hispania Citerior. Here he won a victory over the Lusitanian leader Viriatus, who was probably already making incursions into Citerior.[1] It was a remarkable coincidence, but probably fortuitous, that when Scipio's closest friend went to Citerior his brother, the consul Q. Fabius Aemilianus, was given the command in the other Spanish province, Further Spain,

---

populum ad leges accipiendas in septem iugera forensia e comitio eduxit) has aroused some discussion, but the inference that at the time Crassus was proposing agrarian laws is both unnecessary (so, rightly, Tibiletti, 'Storia agraria', *Athenaeum* 28 (1950), pp. 236 f., and Scullard, 'Scipio Aemilianus', *JRS* 50 (1960), p. 63 n. 19) and improbable, for the wording and context of Cic. *De Amic.* 96 imply strongly that it occurred when Crassus was speaking to his bill concerning the priestly colleges. (The punctuation and translation of the Loeb edition tend to obscure this point.)

[1] Cic. *De Off.* 2. 40; *Brut.* 84. It is possible that prior to his departure Laelius attempted and failed to carry the proposal for reform mentioned in Plut. *Ti. Grac.* 8. 5, but this could equally well have been in 140. It is discussed in Appendix VII.

Ulterior. This appointment was considered highly desirable, carrying with it the conduct of the Lusitanian war, which was the only immediate opportunity for winning military glory. On the other hand Fabius was handicapped by the composition of his two fresh legions, which were levied from inexperienced young men; all who had served recently in Africa, Macedonia, and Greece were exempted.[1] Although this exemption was probably reasonable, Fabius must have been very reluctant to dispense with the services of experienced veterans; and the fact that he was obliged to do so is a reminder that military conscription was politically significant. Whereas troops could be found fairly readily for campaigns which were expected to be short and profitable, as against Carthage, there was strong aversion to service for a long period in a theatre where conditions were likely to be severe, casualties heavy, and booty slight; and as the Spanish wars between them dragged on for more than a decade this aversion certainly grew. Political leaders were faced here with a difficult problem, which was rendered both more pressing and more intractable by awareness that those liable for conscription were also voters in the assemblies.

For Fabius himself the immediate consequence of the exemption granted to the veterans was that, so far from undertaking major offensive operations during his first campaigning season, he positively avoided engaging in full-scale battle. It is said that the time was spent in training and disciplining the new troops, a task probably requiring all the more care in view of the damage inflicted on their morale by an early defeat. For that defeat the account of Appian (derived perhaps from Polybius) would acquit Fabius of all responsibility, emphasizing that it was incurred by a subordinate while Fabius himself was journeying to sacrifice at Gades; whether the Roman public took the same note of this careful distinction is a good deal more doubtful. In short, to many Romans Fabius' record in 145 must have sounded—or could easily have been made to sound—highly unsatisfactory.

Dissatisfaction with Fabius was probably an important factor in the elections at the end of the year. Scipio must have been dismayed

---

[1] App. *Iber.* 65 (the only narrative of his activities); cf. Livy, *Epit.* 52 and *Ox. Epit.* 52; Vell. 2. 5. 3; perhaps Florus 1. 33. 17. The attraction of the command is seen in the quarrel between the consuls of 144: p. 104. Fabius and Mancinus are likely to have been assigned their provinces by lot. Nothing is known of Mancinus' activities.

at the result, for the new consuls were Ser. Sulpicius Galba and L. Aurelius Cotta, both of them enemies,[1] while Metellus Macedonicus, a year further from his triumph and presumably still hampered by his unfortunate reputation, suffered a second successive defeat.[2] Very little is known about either the career or the qualities of Cotta. As tribune he had unsuccessfully attempted to use his sacrosanctity to shield himself from his creditors, an episode which can scarcely have assisted his electoral prospects. He was a skilled orator, but so were many leading Romans of this period. Stronger recommendations he may have had, but nothing is recorded of them, so that it is tempting to suppose that his success was due at least in part to being associated with Galba in the canvass.[3] Galba, it will be recalled, had been praetor as far back as 151 and thus was four years late in reaching the consulship. This delay can be attributed in no small measure to the impression made by the attempt to prosecute him for the massacre and enslavement of great numbers of Lusitanians.[4] By the end of 145, however, not only will the effects of that attack have diminished considerably but Galba's record will almost certainly have been a positive recommendation: here was a man who had proved in the field that he could defeat the Lusitanians and whose 'strong' methods probably seemed to many Romans precisely what was needed in the present situation. Furthermore, in projecting a favourable image of himself he had the advantage of being the outstanding orator of his day, a leader in the technique of arousing mass emotion. If in addition to these various factors it may be assumed that at this stage the majority of Scipio's opponents were still co-operating and thus supporting Galba through their *clientelae*, the latter's success and Scipio's inability to sway the election are adequately accounted for.

It was certainly intended to press home the advantage gained in the election: one of the new consuls was to supersede Fabius in the command against Viriatus. At this point, however, Galba and Cotta quarrelled about which of them should go to Spain; for some reason the matter was not decided by sortition, so there followed a contentious debate

[1] p. 90.

[2] (Victor) *De Vir. Ill.* 61. 3; cf. Livy, *Ox. Epit.* 52; Val. Max. 7. 5. 4.

[3] The grandfathers of these men had been consuls together in 200. Tribunate: Val. Max. 6. 5. 4; cf. *MRR* i, p. 450. Eloquence: Cic. *Brut.* 82.

[4] pp. 58 f.

in the Senate. Scipio seized his opportunity, driving home his point with one of those pungent witticisms almost calculated to ensure that his opponents really were enemies: 'I consider that neither should be sent, because the one possesses nothing and for the other nothing is enough.' The outcome was that neither consul was sent and Fabius was left to carry on for another year, a political victory which Scipio owed as much to the disunity of his opponents as to his own *auctoritas*.[1] Fabius, for his part, made good use of his second campaigning season and retrieved his reputation. He defeated Viriatus twice, inflicted heavy casualties, and captured two towns.[2] Nevertheless, the war, so far from being finished, spread to Citerior; for it must have been during 144 that Viriatus successfully fomented a new Celtiberian rebellion which was to become famous as the Numantine war.[3]

So little information has been preserved about the year 144 that, apart from the activities of Q. Marcius Rex, which will be examined shortly, the only political topic remaining for consideration is the election for 143, at which the fortunes of Scipio's associates began to improve. Admittedly, the successful patrician was Ap. Claudius Pulcher, Scipio's most serious rival, but under the most favourable circumstances there could have been little prospect of preventing the election of this ambitious and determined heir of the patrician Claudii.[4] It is more significant that Claudius' colleague was Metellus Macedonicus, successful at the third attempt. Obviously a number of factors were operative, such as the turn of events in Spain, probably a shortage of recent plebeian praetors with adequate military prestige, and presumably a positive attempt by Metellus to counteract his reputation for *severitas*; perhaps also the impression made by the spectacular buildings erected from the Macedonian spoils.[5] But the most important development was almost certainly serious disunity among the hostile factions, of which the first known sign is the quarrel between Galba and Cotta and of which there are other traces in the following years. Indeed, even without these indications such a development might reasonably have been conjectured, for Metellus'

---

[1] Val. Max. 6. 4. 2 = Appendix II, no. 12.   [2] App. *Iber.* 65.

[3] App. *Iber.* 66 and 76 f. Since one of the consuls of 143 was sent to Citerior, the rebellion must have reached serious proportions before the end of 144.

[4] Cf. p. 90.

[5] Vell. 1. 11. 3 f.; 2. 1. 2; Plin. *Nat. Hist.* 34. 64; 36. 40; cf. 34. 31; Cic. *Verr.* 2. 4. 126.

was not an isolated success but the first of a series which gave to associates of Scipio five or six out of eight major magistracies in the years 142–140.[1]

It is a measure of the gravity of the Celtiberian rebellion, and also, perhaps, of Fabius' success in containing Viriatus, that Hither rather than Further Spain was selected as a consular province for 143. This command, with its opportunity to win military laurels, fell to Metellus.[2] Claudius, left in Italy, in due course found opportunity to go north to Cisalpine Gaul and to campaign against the Salassi, an Alpine tribe living in the Aosta region.[3] He had been sent to settle a dispute between the Salassi and their neighbours, and it is alleged that he attacked them without good pretext, actuated by jealousy of his colleague and by a desire for a triumph.[4] No doubt political polemic has made the most of these charges, but there may be some truth in them; subsequent events suggest that Claudius was not above allowing personal ambition to weigh heavily in his decisions. What is beyond doubt, however, is that his first invasion resulted in a serious defeat, with heavy losses.[5] Such a military reverse was of necessity also a political reverse, and it was presumably because there were those in Rome who were prepared to exploit this (probably by urging that Claudius should be recalled) that the Decemviri were impelled to consult the Sibylline books, in which they claimed to find that whenever the Romans were about to make war upon the Gauls they should sacrifice within the enemy's borders. There can be no doubt that the Decemviri were intervening on behalf of Claudius.[6] Simultaneously they raised a dispute about the Marcian aqueduct which looks suspiciously like a deliberate attempt to create a diversion, and in any case their pronouncement was itself favourable to

---

[1] Six if Metellus Calvus, cos. 142, is rightly presumed to have been associated with Scipio.

[2] For the Celtiberian (Numantine) war see esp. Schulten, *Numantia*, i, pp. 353 f.; *Gesch. von Numantia*, pp. 65 f.; Simon, *Roms Kriege*, pp. 101 f.; De Sanctis, *Storia*, iv. 3, pp. 233 f. For Metellus' campaigns cf. also Additional Note L, p. 344, and p. 123.

[3] Livy, *Epit.* 53; Oros. 5. 4. 7; Dio, fgt. 74. 1; cf. Obsequ. 21.

[4] Dio, fgt. 74. 1; cf. Strabo, 4. 6. 7.   [5] Oros. 5. 4. 7; Obsequ. 21.

[6] The sources (Obsequ. 21; Dio fgt. 74. 1), though brief, leave no doubt about this. Münzer seems to accept this in *RE*, s.v. *Claudius*, no. 295, but argues to the contrary in *Röm. Adels.*, pp. 240 f. His later view is improbable and is perhaps influenced by a marked tendency to treat the politics of this period in terms of only two groups, pro-Scipio and anti-Scipio.

him, calculated to absolve him from any charge of military incompetence and finding the cause of the disaster in a religious
technicality—and at that a technicality of which Claudius could
reasonably have been unaware. Moreover, the mistake could be
rectified without difficulty, enabling Claudius to resume his campaign
with the morale of his troops restored. Two members of the college
were sent to him, assuredly to explain matters both to the consul and
to the troops. Then Claudius began a new offensive, in which he
killed many of the Salassi and devastated their territory.

But his opponents were not to be foiled so easily. When he
returned to Rome they were strong enough to ensure that the Senate
refused his request for funds to celebrate a triumph.[1] He could not
appeal to the assembly, since at least one of the tribunes was hostile,
so the choice before him was—or should have been—between
abandoning his claim altogether or celebrating a triumph at his own
expense on the Alban Mount. But, ambitious, determined, and unscrupulous, and doubtless convinced of the merits of his claim, he
decided that he would triumph in Rome; and he succeeded in doing
so. There was indeed a precedent: a century and a half earlier L.
Postumius Megellus had celebrated a similar unauthorized triumph.
Presumably Claudius advanced some technical argument to the
effect that it was not illegal to do this, but the fact is that the ambition
and private judgement of an individual overrode the judgement of
the Senate, thus striking a new blow both at the authority of the
Senate and at accepted procedure, procedure so well established as to
have virtually, if not actually, the force of constitutional law.[2] Yet
Claudius went further still. Senatorial authority was maintained not
merely by the prestige of the Fathers but by the powers of willing
tribunes. So it was intended to be on this occasion: a tribune proposed
to veto the triumph and to enforce his veto by dragging Claudius
from his chariot; attempted defiance should result in the consul being
hauled ignominiously from his triumphal procession to prison.
Claudius foiled this by having with him in his chariot a daughter
who was a Vestal Virgin, so that the tribune could not reach him

[1] Oros. 5. 4. 7; Dio, fgt. 74. 2.
[2] For the legal conditions governing triumphs see Mommsen, *Röm. Staats.* i³, pp. 126 f.
Postumius: Livy, 10. 37. 6 f.; Dion. Hal. 17/18. 5. 3. The consuls of 223 were refused
a triumph by the Senate but had it authorized by the assembly: Zon. 8. 20.

without violating the sacred person of the Vestal and thereby rousing the fears and passions of the superstitious mob.[1] Thus the veto was successfully defied. The device employed by Claudius is of little importance in itself; opportunities to use it would of necessity be rare, and in practice this occasion seems to be unique. What matters is the stimulus Claudius gave to the idea that it was desirable and practicable to search for means of circumventing the tribunician veto.

If Claudius was to remain a serious rival to Scipio he had to vindicate his pretensions to military ability. To that end a triumph was highly desirable, and once he had claimed one he certainly could not afford to submit to the Senate's decision that it was unmerited. He did succeed in celebrating it, but in the intense struggle he followed his rival's methods to the extent of furthering his personal ambition by overriding legitimate constitutional obstacles placed in his path. No doubt the obstacles seemed to Claudius tricks of the political game, infuriating and unreasonable, at least in their present use; it might well be argued that a better case could be made for him than for Scipio in 148. Yet none of this alters the fact that his actions were symptomatic of—indeed, through the accumulation of example, were a contribution to—the development in political struggles of an attitude of mind which in its essence was incompatible with the existing pattern of government.

The rejection of Claudius' triumph by a majority of senators does not mean that this body was now falling under the influence of Scipio and his friends; rather it is an indication of growing disunity among other factions. Some senators will have felt sincerely that a triumph should not be awarded to a general who had suffered losses as great as those inflicted on the enemy, while others will have been motivated more by jealousies, quarrels, and feuds, revived or new. It matters little which was the more important element: the incident itself will have generated fresh tensions and hostilities, and the plain fact is that Scipio's opponents were proving unable to maintain a united front, a feature which is illustrated further by the affair of the Marcian aqueduct.

In 144 the Senate had decided upon action to improve the supply of water to the city. Instead of waiting for the appointment of

[1] Cic. Pro Cael. 34; Val. Max. 5. 4. 6; Suet. Tib. 2. 4; cf. Oros. 5. 4. 7.

censors, two years away, it instructed the urban praetor, Q. Marcius
Rex, to undertake badly needed repairs to the two existing aqueducts,
Appia and Anio (Vetus), and to bring to the city such other waters
as he could. The latter instruction he chose—and may well have
been intended—to fulfil by providing a third aqueduct, the famous
Marcia, named after himself despite the fact that it was probably the
completion of an earlier project rather than a completely new construction. Since Marcius' work was not finished at the end of 144, the
Senate authorized the prorogation of his magistracy for 143—a
remarkable procedure in that the prorogation of a magistracy to be
exercised within the city is almost without parallel. In none of this,
nor in the grant of substantial funds for the task, is there any hint of
opposition.[1] That is not proof that there was none, but at least
Marcius obviously had the backing of a safe majority of senators, and
it is conceivable that there was no opposition to these extraordinary
but sensible measures to meet a presumably urgent need. But during
143 the Decemviri, when consulting the Sibylline books about
'another matter'—obviously Claudius' defeat at the hands of the
Salassi—'discovered' that the oracles were opposed to Marcius'
project of extending his new aqueduct to the Capitol. Textual
difficulties leave some doubt about details, but it seems likely that
according to the Decemviri one of the earlier aqueducts should have
been used instead. In the subsequent senatorial debate Marcius
enjoyed the eloquent support of M. Aemilius Lepidus, himself
probably praetor in 144 or 143, and secured a favourable vote.[2]

No doubt the Decemviri were actuated by more than one consideration, but it does look very much as if the 'discovery' was

---

[1] The chief source is Frontin. *De Aquis*, 1. 7; cf. also Plin. *Nat. Hist.* 31. 41; 36. 121; Plut.
Coriol. 1. 1. For the prorogation see Mommsen, *Röm. Staats.* i³, p. 637 n. 1. Stuart, 'Pliny,
Historia Naturalis XXXI, 41', *AJPh* 64 (1943), pp. 440 f., and 'The Denarius of M'. Aemilius
Lepidus', *AJA* 49 (1945), pp. 226 f., esp. pp. 242 f., argues plausibly that Marcius did not
erect an entirely new structure but completed the one left unfinished by the censors of 179
(Livy, 40. 51. 7 f.).

[2] Frontin. *De Aquis*, 1. 7. 5; cf. Livy, *Ox. Epit.* 54, referring to the completion of the
project in 140. The objection raised by the Decemviri is discussed by Stuart, 'P. *Oxyrhynchus*
668. 188–90', *CPh* 39 (1944), pp. 40 f., and Astin, 'Water to the Capitol', *Latomus* 20
(1961), pp. 541 f. Schöne, 'Zu Frontinus', *Hermes* 6 (1872), pp. 248 f., would make Lepidus
speak on behalf of the Decemviri (reading *collegio* for *collega*). This is rightly rejected by
Münzer, *Röm. Adels.*, pp. 239 f., who also recognizes that Lepidus is almost certainly Porcina,
cos. 137; see also *MRR* i, p. 473 n. 1.

deliberately designed to distract attention from the misfortunes of Appius Claudius, whom the Decemviri were supporting at that very time; possibly also it was a counter-attack against men who were critical of Claudius. But, except in so far as they were arousing superstitious fears, they were on poor ground. The extension to the Capitol was almost certainly intended to fulfil a genuine need, not merely the ambition of Marcius, while technical considerations made use of the Appia impossible and of the Anio very difficult and expensive.[1] Furthermore, it was not only the prestige of Marcius himself that was at stake. Since he had probably completed the aqueduct begun by the censors of 179, M. Aemilius Lepidus and M. Fulvius Nobilior,[2] it looks very much as if the Lepidi retained their interest in the project and as if it is no coincidence that Marcius' chief advocate belonged to that family. There is no means of knowing whether the Fulvii Nobiliores felt themselves similarly involved, but in any case there can be little doubt that the quarrel started by the Decemviri both reflected and aggravated the disunity among Scipio's rivals; and since the majority of the Decemviri had favoured Claudius and were probably still working on his behalf in their opposition to Marcius' plan, it is a fair guess that Marcius and Lepidus were among those who subsequently refused to vote a triumph for Claudius. In view of such quarrels it is certainly no surprise that the next consular election resulted in a double success for Scipio's associates.

The plebeian consul for 142, L. Caecilius Metellus Calvus, is very little known, and details of his qualifications and earlier career are entirely lacking. It is simply to be presumed that he was politically tied to his more illustrious brother, Macedonicus, and thus was probably still allied to Scipio; furthermore, Scipio's intimate friend Laelius, who was also eligible for the consulship of this year, did not stand against Calvus.[3] It is not difficult to see why Calvus should have been given preference. The Metelli were important allies and men of distinguished ancestry, more likely to take offence and less readily conciliated than one so close as Laelius. The latter will surely have acquiesced in avoiding so obvious a source of strain, particularly

---

[1] Astin, 'Water to the Capitol', *Latomus* 20 (1961), pp. 541 f., esp. pp. 547 f.

[2] p. 109 n. 1.

[3] Cic. *Tusc.* 5. 54 shows that Laelius suffered only one repulse, and that is known to have been in 142 (pp. 146 f.).

if Calvus had already had to wait until his brother could secure election.

The patrician consul, Q. Fabius Maximus Servilianus, is a little less obscure, though there is no record of his previous career either. Perhaps of even more exalted lineage as a Fabius than by being born a Servilius Caepio, he was adoptive brother of Fabius Aemilianus; thus he was linked closely to Scipio himself. He had two brothers by birth, who were to win the patrician consulships of the next two years, so demonstrating that with three consulships in three years the Servilii Caepiones were indeed a power to be reckoned with.[1] Servilianus was evidently not an outstanding orator, and he was to meet with military defeat at the hands of Viriatus; nevertheless, besides his family advantages, he probably had some useful qualities. Despite his reverses, his performance in Spain suggests some military talent[2]—quite apart from the ruthless efficiency perhaps implied by his readiness to cut off heads and hands;[3] while his work on pontifical law, in twelve or more books, indicates at the least painstaking industriousness and conscientiousness.[4]

It is unfortunate that more cannot be discerned of the circumstances of this election;[5] it is not even possible to guess at the identity and importance of any of the defeated candidates. Yet it is clear that the result must have distressed Scipio's opponents, and above all the presiding consul, Appius Claudius. For in 142 an election was to be held for new censors, and Claudius wanted the patrician place. It was obvious that his chief rival would be Scipio, and the outcome of this consular election did not augur well for his hopes. On the other hand the very shock may have assisted in rallying behind him the great majority of those who disliked Scipio: many who had disapproved of Claudius' triumph would prefer him to the all-too-successful

---

[1] On these men and their relationship with Scipio see pp. 82 f. and 315 f.

[2] App. *Iber.* 67 f.; for various reports cf. Oros. 5. 4. 12; Livy, *Epit.* 53 and 54; *Ox. Epit.* 53 and 54; Diod. 33. 1. 3 f.; Charax, fgts. 26 f. *FGrH*; Obsequ. 22 and 23; perhaps Florus 1. 33. 17.

[3] App. *Iber.* 68; Oros. 5. 4. 12; Frontin. *Strat.* 4. 1. 42; Val. Max. 2. 7. 11. The last asserts, with what justification is unknown, that Servilianus' harshness was contrary to his natural gentleness and clemency.

[4] Macrob. *Sat.* 1. 16. 25 = Servilianus, fgt. 4. He was also the author of an annalistic history.

[5] Additional Note L, p. 344.

conqueror of Carthage. That such a rally did occur seems certain; either there was no third patrician candidate or, if there was, his intervention was insignificant.[1]

Anecdotes throw some light on the electoral clash between the two great aristocrats. The fundamental character of the struggle is clear: the authority and prestige of the greater part of the aristocracy, the strength of many ties of social loyalty and obligation, the resources of great *clientelae* were thrown behind Claudius in a struggle to outweigh the fame and glamour of the new Africanus and the talents of his low-class, rabble-rousing helpers. But Claudius knew he would need more than social pressure. He could point, of course, to his recent triumph over the Salassi, but in character and circumstance it could scarcely match the emotional assets of the conquest of Carthage; he had to do at least some damage to the image of Scipio which was established in the popular mind. He tried pouring scorn on the low social status of many who accompanied Scipio to the Forum, suggesting that he was an unworthy heir of his father: 'O Paullus Aemilius, groan beneath the earth when you learn that your son is escorted to the censorship by Aemilius the herald and Licinius Philonicus the tax-collector.'[2] Gibes of this kind may have had some effect, for the election was to be in the *comitia centuriata*, and in any case there was a strong element of social deference in the Roman character; but other insults recoiled upon Appius. He asserted that he greeted all Romans by name, whereas Scipio knew hardly one of them—an exaggeration, no doubt, but probably aimed at a genuine weakness deriving from Scipio's early distaste for the affairs of the Forum. Scipio's retort was scornful and stinging: 'You are right; for my concern has been not to know many but to be unknown to none.'[3] When Claudius attempted, as it seems, to impugn Scipio's reputation for bravery, or at least to present himself as the more valorous, Scipio urged the people to send them both to the Celtiberian war, as either legates or tribunes, and to use the soldiers as witnesses and

---

[1] The anecdotes discussed below suggest a direct contest between Scipio and Claudius. Plut. *Aem.* 38. 3 f. indicates that the greater part of the aristocracy was backing Claudius, and indeed the story would be pointless unless this was so. With others backing Scipio, there can have been few to support any third candidate.

[2] Plut. *Aem.* 38. 4 f.; *Praec. Reip. Ger.* 14.

[3] Appendix II, no. 13.

judges of the bravery of each of them.[1] It was an utterly unrealistic suggestion, but the responsibility for saying so, and thus of refusing the challenge, was laid firmly upon Claudius.

The victor was Scipio. Once more, despite the structure of the *comitia centuriata*, skilful exploitation of popular appeal had more than compensated for comparative weakness in *amicitiae* and dependent social machinery. Yet the victory was only partial. There is no record of whom Scipio would have liked to have as his plebeian colleague; nor is it possible to guess: Metellus Macedonicus was still in Spain, and no other consular believed to have been associated with Scipio stands out as an obvious choice. The one certain thing is that Scipio had not supported and did not want the man who was elected, L. Mummius.[2] Scipio's popularity is here seen to be a very personal advantage, less effective in influencing decisions in which he himself was not involved directly. On the other hand, the success of Mummius is less surprising than it may appear at first sight. That he was a *novus homo* is true, but he was now Mummius Achaicus and was the first *novus homo* to win a *cognomen* of this type in virtue of his military achievements[3]—a *cognomen* significantly on the pattern of 'Africanus' and 'Macedonicus'. If his victory was not to be compared with Scipio's, it surely had much more emotional appeal than Appius' defeat of the Salassi, while the triumph with which it was celebrated, resplendent with the wealth and art of Corinth, can scarcely have been less impressive than Scipio's, nor the entertainments and donatives less lavish.[4] Moreover, Mummius had been as careful to refrain from enriching himself from the treasures of Corinth as Scipio had been from those of Carthage; and, though the main distribution of artistic treasures was yet to come, his handling of the booty will already have contributed to the reputation he earned (or created for himself) of being mild, abstemious, and generous—traits which his enemies maliciously attributed to sloth, weakness, and lack of culture.[5] The abuse can have

[1] Appendix II, no. 14.

[2] Appendix II, no. 17 makes it impossible that Scipio could have given any support or encouragement to Mummius.

[3] Vell. 1. 13. 2.

[4] To the references given at p. 99 n. 1 add Cic. *De Off.* 2. 76; *Parad. Stoic.* 38; Frontin. *Strat.* 4. 3. 15.

[5] Abstention, etc.: Livy, *Epit.* 52; Cic. *De Off.* 2. 76; *Parad. Stoic.* 38; Frontin. *Strat.* 4. 3. 15; (Victor) *De Vir. Ill.* 60. 3; Strabo, 8. 6. 23; Dio, fgt. 76. Abusive comments: Vell. 1. 13.

made little impact at the time; Mummius' personal popularity must have far outstripped that of any other plebeian who may have contested the election. If in view of these assets he benefited from the tendency to rally against Scipio and enjoyed the backing of a large section of the aristocracy and their dependents,[1] it is easy to understand how lack of distinguished ancestors did not prevent his becoming censor at the first opportunity.

The success of Mummius was an annoying limitation upon Scipio's own success, not merely because it demonstrated the limited nature of his personal influence with the electorate but also because he would have a colleague liable to veto some of his actions; for Scipio intended his censorship to be memorable for efficiency and thoroughness, an ambition which did not harmonize at all well with the attitude and plans of Mummius.

3 f.; Plin. *Nat. Hist.* 35. 24; Val. Max. 6. 4. 2; (Victor) *De Vir. Ill.* 58. 9; Plut. *Lucull.* 19. 5; cf. Strabo, 8. 6. 23. Münzer, *RE*, s.v. *Mummius*, no. 7a, protests against uncritical acceptance of these hostile verdicts and attempts with some success to refute them, though he trusts too readily the Greek dedicatory inscriptions and the verdict of Polybius, 39. 6.

[1] Mummius' political associations are unknown, except for a possible link with L. Licinius Lucullus (Dio, fgt. 76. 2; Strabo 8. 6. 23), which in turn may hint at a link with the Postumii (Lucullus, a *novus homo*, had a Postumius as his colleague in the consulship). Combined support for Mummius could well have been the *quid pro quo* for combined support of Claudius.

X

CENSOR

THERE can be little doubt about the attitude of mind in which Mummius entered upon his censorship. Presumably he was ready to take some part in the necessary duties of leasing state property and concluding contracts for such items as the collection of revenue, the repair of existing buildings and the construction of new amenities;[1] but he had no intention of incurring ill will by exercising disciplinary powers against senators, equites, or anyone else, or even, in many cases, by assenting to such action on the part of his colleague.[2] His prime intention was to win further fame for himself by his munificence in distributing the artistic treasures looted from Corinth. He 'adorned Rome'; a new temple of Hercules Victor rose in celebration of the victory of 146; statues, monuments, and paintings were given to and displayed in shrines throughout the city, in the neighbouring towns, up and down the peninsula, even in the provinces, as far afield as Italica in Spain;[3] Rome saw, on the Capitol, its first gilt ceiling;[4] some buildings were so impressively furnished that they thereby became known as *aedificia Mummiana*;[5] over a century later Strabo could hold that the majority and the best of the dedicatory

---

[1] Cic. *Brut.* 85 mentions one such contract, in no way remarkable in itself. The only major building project known for certain is the completion of the Pons Aemilius, begun in 179: Livy, 40. 51. 4. Scipio's temple of Virtus may belong to this time: Plut. *Fort. Rom.* 5. For Mummius' temple of Hercules see below, n. 3.

[2] Dio, fgt. 76. 1; cf. Cic. *De Orat.* 2. 268 and below on Ti. Claudius Asellus.

[3] Livy, *Ox. Epit.* 53; Cic. *Verr.* 2. 3. 9; *De Off.* 2. 76; *Orator*, 232; Frontin. *Strat.* 4. 3. 15; Plin. *Nat. Hist.* 35. 24; (Victor) *De Vir. Ill.* 60. 3; Vitruv. 5. 5. 8; Strabo, 8. 6. 23; ILS 20, 21[a-d]. The temple is undated, but the contract must have been placed either during the censorship or earlier; if earlier, the temple must have been approaching completion by 142.

[4] Plin. *Nat. Hist.* 33. 57. Broughton, *MRR* i, p. 474, says that this was probably the work of both censors, but Pliny's phrase *censura L. Mummi* seems to suggest that Mummius alone was responsible.

[5] Festus, 125 L.: *Mummiana aedificia a Mummio dicta*. The reference cannot be to buildings erected by Mummius, since that would presuppose extensive building activity of which there would certainly have been some other trace in the surviving sources.

offerings in the city had come from Corinth.[1] Rome and all Italy were 'crammed with *ornamenta*'—and, it may be added, with inscriptions recording the name of the donor.[2]

This lavish display was not at all the kind of censorship which Scipio had envisaged. Manifestly he could not have competed with Mummius, whose resources were unique, but that in itself was probably not especially distressing; he was certainly very angry with his colleague, but perhaps not envious of him. For his own plans looked for a censorship that would be strict and thorough. After a general call for a return to the *mores maiorum* and a warning against lack of respect towards the censors, the revision of the Senate, the examination of the equites, and indeed the whole social review (*regimen morum*) were to be conducted with rigorous severity. Admittedly it has been suggested that political rivalries played a substantial part in his attempts to expel senators and equites from their respective orders, since the three potential victims who are positively identified all bore the gentile names of hostile families.[3] Possibly Scipio, like many another, found it easier to recognize moral turpitude among his enemies than among his friends, but the supposition that his motives were basically factional would be unwarranted. On the contrary, there is every probability that his criticisms of licence, luxury, and other failings were entirely sincere.[4]

What lay behind this serious approach? One explanation which has been put forward is that, influenced by the theories of Polybius, Scipio was especially concerned to preserve the balance of the 'mixed constitution', to prevent—or to delay for as long as possible—developments which eventually could lead to the fatal transfer of public deliberation from the Senate to 'the People'. This is unlikely, for although it is not incompatible with the recorded events of the censorship, some of Scipio's actions at other times strongly suggest that such a concern did not enter into his practical thinking.[5] Nor indeed is so specialized a theory needed to account for his attitude.

[1] 8. 6. 23.

[2] Cic. *Orator*, 232; (Victor) *De Vir. Ill.* 60. 3; cf. *ILS* 20, 21[a-d].

[3] Münzer, *Röm. Adels.*, p. 265; *RE*, s.v. *Mummius*, no. 7a, col. 1205.

[4] They correspond closely to what is known of Scipio's personal standards and character: pp. 16 f.; cf. also Appendix II, no. 57 and esp. no. 53.

[5] Appendix V.

The *regimen morum* was, after all, an accepted part of the censors' duties, and although there were differences of thoroughness, efficiency, and impartiality it was certainly nothing new for a censor to be conscientious and strict.[1] Scipio's career, and especially his military activities, show him to have been predisposed to conscientious thoroughness. As a holder of one of Rome's greatest magistracies he clearly took himself very seriously; a distinct note of pomposity is discernible, doubtless intimately linked with his old eagerness to prove himself a worthy heir to the names and *dignitas* of his forebears, as well as with pride in distinction already achieved: the censorship of the new Africanus must be no ordinary affair, but, in his own words, in all respects 'worthy of the majesty of the state'.[2] The implication that such a spirit governed his handling of the entire range of censorial duties is scarcely to be doubted, even though the character of the surviving evidence tends to direct attention chiefly to the *regimen morum*.[3]

Nevertheless, this latter was a sphere in which Scipio was subject to special influences. His own upbringing, character, and prejudices would have combined with normal Roman conservatism and admiration for the *mores maiorum* to predispose him to severity, quite apart from any rational formulation of why the practices which he condemned were harmful to the state. Yet a sense of safeguarding the state was almost certainly present, for the notion that growing vices lead to national decline was obvious and old: corruption in the governing class would soon spread through and rot the whole society; licence and luxury, besides exciting avarice and corruption, would undermine the virility of the people, make them soft and effeminate; the toughness and discipline of the army would decay. Such ideas would have had a natural appeal to a Roman, particularly as he would have seen military efficiency as a key factor in the power and success of his city; and that they were current in Rome, and

---

[1] Mommsen, *Röm. Staats.* ii[3], pp. 375 f. Kienast, *Cato*, pp. 79 f., draws attention to the severity, or intended severity, of censors in 184, 179, 174, and 169. He is perhaps too ready (p. 85) to infer from the absence of evidence that subsequent censors were comparatively unimportant. For attacks on luxury see p. 120, with n. 3.

[2] Appendix II, no. 17a; for pomposity and pride see also nos. 19 and 23; cf. no. 15.

[3] The census figure for 142 shows a rise, which is contrary to the general trend of this period. One possible explanation is that the registration procedure was organized more efficiently on this occasion. See Appendix XII, esp. p. 338 n. 1.

therefore familiar to Scipio, is indicated not only by such recorded attacks on luxury as the censorships of Cato and the elder Gracchus,[1] and the three sumptuary laws—the first as far back as 182, the latest as recent as 143[2]—but also by positive signs that in the middle of the second century Roman leaders did feel a need to maintain and protect military hardiness. In 157 a major motive behind the decision to make war on the Dalmatians was that the Senate 'did not want the men of Italy to become at all effeminate by reason of the long peace';[3] and some six years later Scipio Nasica Corculum successfully opposed the provision of seating in the theatre precisely for the reason that it might undermine the hardiness of the people.[4] Subsequently, uneasiness about possible military inadequacy will have been encouraged by the initial reverses in Africa and Macedonia in 149 and 148, by several serious reverses in Spain, and by the general success of Viriatus, who had proved able not merely to hold out but on numerous occasions to secure the initiative. As for Scipio Aemilianus himself, he will have found the idea that the virtuous and simple life is the basis of military power presented as a constant theme of Xenophon's *Cyropaedeia*—the book which he 'always had in his hands'—and the conclusion of the same book describes with great emphasis the gloomy consequences of departure from such standards.[5] Furthermore, his own personal experiences will have shown him that all was not well in the military sphere and will have encouraged him to see as immediately relevant the ideas to be found in Xenophon. In 151 the reluctance of the young aristocrats to serve in Spain had matched the unwillingness of the rank and file; it seems probable that Scipio thought that Lucullus' conduct of the subsequent campaign was influenced adversely by the quest for booty;[6] and in 147 Scipio had

---

[1] For numerous references to Cato's censorship in 184 see *MRR* i, p. 374; for Gracchus' attitude in 169 see Plut. *Ti. Grac.* 14. 4. Cf. also the widely reported action of Fabricius in 275; references collected in *MRR* i, p. 196. The early currency of such ideas is perhaps implied by the very existence of the *regimen morum*.

[2] They were the *leges Orchia* (182), *Fannia* (161), and *Didia* (143): Macrob. *Sat.* 3. 17. 2 f., and other references collected in *MRR* i, pp. 382, 443, 472.

[3] Polyb. 32. 13. 6 f. Even if he has exaggerated its importance, this view must have been held by senators with whom he was in close contact.   [4] p. 48.

[5] Cf. also the occurrence of the idea in Diod. 33. 28a. 2, but this eulogistic account (probably from Poseidonius) of Scipio's embassy in 140 is too idealized to be strong evidence.

[6] The idea is prominent in App. *Iber.* 51–55, which is very favourable to Scipio and hostile to Lucullus.

to begin his command of the African army with a rigorous restoration of order, hitting hard at indiscipline, avarice, and extravagant living.

Scipio as censor, then, is to be understood neither as a self-conscious defender of the mixed constitution nor as an isolated social reformer, but rather, not unlike Cato forty years earlier,[1] as one naturally disposed to carry out his duties seriously and conscientiously, and encouraged to do so by ideas long current and probably widely accepted, which his own experiences will have tended to confirm, of the need to protect the basic military qualities of the Romans.

Chance deprived Scipio of the opportunity to make the opening pronouncement of the censorship, for the customary sortition established that it was Mummius who in due course would complete the *lustrum* and who thereby had the right to summon the first *contio*.[2] Of Mummius' speech to the people no fragment, no echo has survived, but it is a safe assumption that it gave an indication of his attitude and intentions sufficiently clear to diminish somewhat the impact of Scipio's subsequent stern admonition—of which a little is known.[3] An exhortation to return to the *mores maiorum*, its tone is revealed by two anecdotes used by Scipio to emphasize the necessity for the utmost respect and solemnity in the presence of the censors—and to warn that a joke or a yawn during formal proceedings could bring severe punishment. Possibly he argued that a strict census would be a major contribution to general security; certainly he vigorously attacked and condemned various practices which he alleged to be contrary to the *maiorum instituta*, among them the use of adoption to obtain the legal privileges of fatherhood, a topic which probably reflects not only the traditional duty of the censors to encourage the birth-rate but also special concern about the shortage of man-power for the army.[4]

The turn of events must have caused Scipio some disappointment already, and more disappointments were to follow. All that is known

---

[1] Kienast, *Cato*, pp. 68 f., esp. pp. 79 f.

[2] The opinion that it was Mummius is maintained in Appendix X; for the procedure see Varro, *De Ling. Lat.* 6. 87 and Mommsen, *Röm. Staats.* i³, p. 40 n. 3 and p. 42 n. 4.

[3] Appendix II, nos. 15 and 16; cf. no. 56 = ORF², fgts. 13-15, pp. 124 f.

[4] The meaning of the passage is discussed in Appendix IX. For the man-power question see pp. 167 f.

of the revision of the Senate is that Mummius reprieved a number of senators whom Scipio wished to expel.[1] The same happened at the review of the equites, though here Scipio's attitude is illustrated by four known cases in which he wished to take action: his rhetorical skill was employed in a biting attack upon the dandyish dress and manners of P. Sulpicius Galus, who was accused of promiscuous homosexuality;[2] luxurious living was the charge against an unnamed eques, who found himself the object of a sharp and rather pompous witticism;[3] C. Licinius Sacerdos was alleged to have committed perjury;[4] and Ti. Claudius Asellus was accused of spendthrift extravagance and doubtless of many other faults besides; it seems that he too, when he attempted to defend his record, was answered with an insulting witticism.[5] Whether Mummius allowed Galus and the unnamed eques to be deprived of their horses is unknown; the charge against Licinius was waived by Scipio himself because he could find no witness to support it; but Asellus was certainly among those who were reprieved by Mummius.[6] The same pattern was repeated in the registration of those of humbler status: again Scipio wished to be severe, again Mummius applied his veto. A centurion was to be removed from his tribe for allegedly absenting himself from the battle of Pydna—an event so far in the past that it is difficult to avoid the conclusion that Scipio was motivated by personal spite. To the man's defence that he had been guarding the camp Scipio curtly retorted: 'I don't like people who are over-scrupulous.'[7] The reply was arrogant and contemptuous, no matter whether it was spoken in

[1] Dio, fgt. 76. 1, referring to all classes; cf. Festus, 360 L.

[2] Appendix II, no. 20.

[3] Appendix II, no. 19. The elaborate confection mentioned is taken by De Sanctis, *Storia*, iv. 3, p. 258, to be the essence of the charge, from which he infers a petty and narrow outlook in Scipio. But it is much more likely that Scipio accused the eques of luxurious living in general and simply made this particular instance the subject of his witticism. Similarly the sleeves of Sulpicius Galus' tunic may seem a trivial target, but they were not the main burden of Scipio's attack, and in a particular generation certain features of dress can be widely regarded as symbolic of immorality and degeneration. Much the same may be said about Scipio's horrified complaints found in Appendix II, no. 53.

[4] Appendix II, no. 21. Possibly the alleged perjury related to statements made before the censors themselves (cf. Mommsen, *Röm. Staats.* ii³, pp. 373 f.; Plut. *Pomp.* 22. 8), in which case the real basis of the charge may have been some other form of misconduct.

[5] Gell. 3. 4. 1; Appendix II, nos. 22 and 26.

[6] Cic. *De Orat.* 2. 268 = Appendix II, no. 28, discussed in Appendix X.

[7] Appendix II, no. 23.

tones of smug mockery or of sharp impatience; but if it was in the latter tones, it may have reflected also the mounting exasperation which Scipio undoubtedly felt.

The increasing sense of frustration and irritation aroused in Scipio by his colleague's interventions, by the repeated blows to his pride, will have been heightened by the spectacle of Mummius' energetic ostentation and by a certain degree of precedence which this *novus homo* probably enjoyed by virtue of being the elder.[1] Scipio's feelings were given public expression in a characteristically damning witticism: 'I would perform all my tasks in a manner worthy of the majesty of the state, if the citizens had either given me a colleague or not given me one.'[2] Conceivably this could have been a sudden angry outburst, but the other known incident was unmistakably a calculated insult. When Scipio gave a banquet for his friends on the occasion of the dedication of a temple of Hercules, he did not invite his colleague, an omission surely the more pointed in the light of Mummius' personal interest in that deity.[3] Indeed, it requires no great stretch of the imagination to suspect that our Greek source has only half the story, that the temple dedicated was Mummius' own, and perhaps even that Scipio absented himself from the official celebrations and entertained his friends at a rival gathering, to which Mummius was pointedly not invited. Such conjectures apart, however, the story as it stands confirms that Scipio's witticism about his colleague is not to be taken as an isolated spasm of bad temper; the relationship between the censors became very strained indeed.

To the disappointments of the censorship itself was added a humiliating reverse in factional politics. For the plebeian consulship of 141 Scipio put forward his intimate friend C. Laelius, who already had been obliged to wait a year and who had a strong claim on his support. Laelius' candidature ran counter, however, to the ambitions of a certain Q. Pompeius. Pompeius was a *novus homo*, the first of several to enter public life or achieve high office under the patronage of Scipio. Of his background virtually nothing is known. He

---

[1] Mommsen, *Röm. Staats.* i³, p. 40 n. 4 *fin.*, with reference to Plut. *Pomp.* 22. 8. If such precedence was a matter of courtesy rather than of invariable practice, Scipio may not have been willing to accord it to his colleague, but that in itself would have been a further cause of friction.   [2] Appendix II, no. 17.

[3] Plut. *Praec. Reip. Ger.* 20; Mummius' temple to Hercules Victor: *ILS* 20.

evidently put his not insignificant rhetorical gifts to demagogic uses, for he was among those whom the later *populares* claimed as their exemplars; his care and skill in the electoral technique of recognizing and greeting members of the public was noted by Rutilius Rufus;[1] and his general success suggests that he had to his credit some very popular achievement. His talents were clearly such as to make him very useful to Scipio—and he was unwilling to wait any longer for his reward. His resolve to stand against Laelius necessarily involved a breach with Scipio and, it may be safely assumed, an understanding with men hostile to Scipio, the support of at least some of whom would be essential for success, even though the calm, precise, intellectual Laelius was probably not a rival likely to fire the public imagination.

Desertion of a patron in this manner would have been offensive enough in itself, but to it Pompeius added a large measure of deception. It seems that on the day on which Laelius was to commence his formal canvass Scipio and other associates gathered in readiness to escort him to the Forum. Their start was delayed by the non-arrival of Pompeius, who was expected to accompany them and to use his talents and popularity on behalf of Laelius. Then came reports that Pompeius was already in the Forum, busy shaking people by the hand and soliciting support not for Laelius but for himself. The start which he thus gained will have ensured that he made the first impact and that he had a clear field in which to do so, while the impact itself will have been the more profound because of the unexpectedness of the candidature and probably because Pompeius appeared on his own behalf at the very time when Laelius and Scipio were expected. The belated arrival of these latter must have been something of an anticlimax. Inevitably Scipio's associates were angry with Pompeius, and although Scipio himself found in the incident material for another of his witticisms, it was no light-hearted joke but an insulting pun on Pompeius' filiation; and when it came to the election, the success of the second of the three Servilii, Cn. Caepio, though welcome, will scarcely have assuaged the bitterness of seeing Pompeius defeat Laelius.[2]

---

[1] Cic. *Brut.* 96; *Acad. Pr.* 2. 13; Rutil. Ruf., fgt. 7.

[2] 'Plut.' *Apophth. Scip. Min.* 8 = Appendix II, no. 25; Cic. *De Amic.* 77; *Tusc.* 5. 54; cf. pp. 311 f.

The cumulation of this unhappy incident, shot through with intrigue, upon all the tensions of the censorship, and upon the fears and stresses generated by the devastating plague of 142,[1] must have added a good deal of extra rancour to the hostility between Scipio and his opponents. But something more serious seems to be indicated than the general raising of the political temperature or the defection of one able supporter, or even than the loss of face involved in the defeat of Laelius. Seen in conjunction with other breaches, with Metellus Macedonicus, the Gracchi, and C. Cato, the incident is a symptom of a certain inadequacy in Scipio's political leadership which at various times cost him valuable support.[2]

In the early months of 141 Scipio and his friends must have experienced added despondency on account of developments in Spain. At that time the latest news available of Fabius Servilianus in Ulterior was probably that his first dashing offensive had been halted, that Viriatus had repelled his army in disorder, had almost captured his camp, and had driven him back to his starting-point at Itucca.[3] True, Metellus Macedonicus in Citerior had done well, subduing the greater part of Celtiberia, but he had not been able to complete the task;[4] Termantia and Numantia still held out, and it was Pompeius, not Caepio, who was to take up the command, to all appearances virtually assured of the glory of concluding the war and celebrating a triumph. Later in the year, as the final humiliation of the censorship, Scipio had to endure seeing his despised but doubtless satisfied colleague perform the ceremony of the *lustratio*;[5] and as the censors retired from office it was at least likely, and probably already certain,

---

[1] Oros. 5. 4. 8 f.; Obsequ. 22.   [2] See further pp. 89 f.

[3] It has often been held that the commander in Ulterior in 142 was the other consul, Metellus Calvus, and that Servilianus succeeded him in 141. Simon, *Roms Kriege*, pp. 70, 80 f., 118, accepting this, infers that Calvus must have fared very badly, which would have been just as depressing for Scipio. But in fact it is highly probable that Calvus did not go to Spain and that Servilianus went in 142. The point of division in Appian's account of the latter's activities is not certain, but it is natural to assign *Iber.* 67 to 142, with the first part of Oros. 5. 4. 12; cf. Obsequ. 22. See Astin, 'The Roman Commander', *Historia* 13 (1964), pp. 245 f. On Itucca, which Servilianus may actually have lost again, see Simon, op. cit., p. 117 n. 26.

[4] App. *Iber.* 76. For the campaign of 142 see Schulten, *Numantia*, i, pp. 354 f.; *Gesch. von Numantia*, pp. 67 f.; Simon, *Roms Kriege*, pp. 105 f. Livy, *Ox. Epit.* 53 probably indicates that he was troubled by Lusitanian raids: Astin, 'The Roman Commander', *Historia* 13 (1964), esp. pp. 248 f.

[5] Appendix X.

that among the tribunes taking office in December would be Ti. Claudius Asellus, bent on avenging himself by bringing against Scipio a prosecution which might easily wreck the latter's political future—as it was certainly intended to do.[1] All in all, Scipio's eighteen months in office had been a period not only of personal frustration and unhappiness but of serious political misfortunes, not the least of which must have been a considerable decline in prestige.

[1] pp. 127 and 175 f.

XI

140–134: SUMMARY OF EVENTS

THIS chapter has a number of purposes. One is to make clear the character and the limitations of the information available concerning the years between Scipio's censorship and the tribunate of Tiberius Gracchus. In particular it will be seen that except for the wars in Spain only a few apparently isolated and disconnected events are known.[1] Secondly, it is hoped to convey the general outline of the wars in Spain, the political significance of which will emerge later. Thirdly, the general chronological relationship of events to each other will be established and available for reference. Finally brief narratives will be given of certain episodes of which only some aspects are examined in later chapters.

Q. Pompeius, who in 141 succeeded Metellus Macedonicus in Hither Spain, made little headway in his campaign against Numantia and Termantia. Despite a few successes, probably late in 141, his difficulties tended to worsen throughout 140 and culminated in a demoralizing and unsuccessful attempt to winter with an army of recruits in a bleak camp close to Numantia.[2] Meanwhile in Further Spain Q. Fabius Maximus Servilianus at first fared better. In 141, recovering from his earlier reverses at the hands of Viriatus, he

---

[1] There are some incidents which it is impossible to relate to other known events and the political impact of which cannot be assessed at all, even though it is evident that they must have made some impact. One such incident in 141 was the defeat of a Roman army in Macedonia by the Scordisci: Livy, *Ox. Epit.* 54. Another was the prosecution and suicide of L. Hostilius Tubulus, who as praetor in 142 is said to have flagrantly accepted bribes in the course of his judicial duties: Cic. *De Fin.* 2. 54; Ascon., p. 23 C.; cf. Münzer, *RE*, s.v. *Hostilius*, no. 26.

[2] App. *Iber.* 76 f.; Livy, *Ox. Epit.* 54; Oros. 5. 4. 13; Dio, fgt. 77; Diod. 33. 17. Livy, *Epit.* 54 (*Termestinos subegit*) is misleading, but this is probably due to the epitomator rather than to acceptance of Pompeius' false claims, which Schulten suggests, *Numantia*, i, p. 357. For the Spanish campaigns of 141–134 see Schulten, 'Viriatus', *NJA* 39 (1917), pp. 223 f.; *Numantia*, i, pp. 355 f.; *Gesch. von Numantia*, pp. 69 f.; Simon, *Roms Kriege*, pp. 108 f. and 119 f.; De Sanctis, *Storia*, iv. 3, pp. 228 f. and 239 f.; on the chronology of Servilianus see Astin, 'The Roman Commander', *Historia*, 13 (1964), pp. 245 f., esp. p. 253 n. 35.

entered Baeturia and marched to the west and north, though on his return he was still engaged in recovering control of the Baetis valley. But a new offensive in the early months of 140 proved disastrous. Viriatus routed the Roman troops and trapped them in a position from which there was no escape. Servilianus was obliged to negotiate a treaty by which the Lusitanians were to hold such territory as was at that time in their possession and Viriatus was recognized as a 'friend of the Roman people'.[1] Although this treaty was ratified at Rome, Servilianus' successor, his brother Q. Servilius Caepio, one of the consuls of 140, reported unfavourably on the arrangements and was given authority to provoke Viriatus into renewing hostilities. Probably before the year was out, the peace was broken and Caepio had taken the offensive.[2]

The other consul of 140 was C. Laelius, and it may have been in this year that he attempted to introduce his proposal for some kind of reform, probably agrarian in character and directed mainly to the man-power problem. The attempt was abortive, since Laelius was forced to withdraw in the face of strong opposition.[3] A number of other events are more securely dated to 140.[4] L. Cornelius Lentulus made a last attempt to prevent the extension of the aqua Marcia to the Capitol, but the majority of senators once more approved the project, which was completed before the end of the year.[5] Another decree of the Senate, sponsored by Ap. Claudius Pulcher, evidently laid it down that there should not be more than one levy in the year. This is likely to have been controversial, especially as it probably amounted to a refusal to send reinforcements to Q. Caepio for his renewed campaign against Viriatus.[6] Earlier Caepio had clashed with Ti. Claudius Asellus, now tribune of the plebs, who had attempted to veto his departure from Rome. Although our source is

[1] App. Iber. 68 f.; Livy, Epit. 53 and 54; Ox. Epit. 53 and 54; Oros. 5. 4. 12; Diod. 33. 1. 4; Charax, fgt. 27 FGrH; cf. Obsequ. 23; Val. Max. 2. 7. 11; Frontin. Strat. 4. 1. 42. For bibliography see p. 125 n. 2.

[2] App. Iber. 70; Diod. 33. 1. 4.   [3] Appendix VII.

[4] A certain D. Iunius Silanus was accused of corruption during his praetorship in Macedonia; condemned and repudiated by his father, T. Manlius Torquatus, he committed suicide: Livy, Epit. 54; Ox. Epit. 54; Cic. De Fin. 1. 24; Val. Max. 5. 8. 3.

[5] Frontin. De Aquis, 1. 7. 5; Livy, Ox. Epit. 54. On the text of the latter see Stuart, 'P. Oxyrhynchus 668. 188–90', CPh 39 (1944), pp. 40 f.; cf. Astin, 'Water to the Capitol', Latomus 20 (1961), p. 544 n. 2. For the earlier dispute see pp. 108 f.

[6] Livy, Ox. Epit. 54, where delectus is restored with great probability. Cf. p. 144.

marred by a hopeless manuscript corruption, it seems that Caepio used a lictor and a threat of force to deter Asellus from enforcing his veto.[1] But the biggest political struggle of the year was probably Asellus' prosecution of Scipio Aemilianus. Although many details are obscure there can be no doubt that Scipio's political future was at stake. He was acquitted, but the fact that Scipio delivered several speeches suggests that a decision was not reached easily.[2]

It was probably in the spring of this year that Scipio left Rome as the senior member of an embassy, with L. Caecilius Metellus Calvus and Sp. Mummius as his colleagues and the philosopher Panaetius as a personal companion. The embassy must have had very wide terms of reference, since it visited many countries in the eastern Mediterranean, including Egypt, Cyprus, Syria, Rhodes, and various places in Greece and Asia Minor. In view of the length of the journey it is unlikely that Scipio was back in Rome before the late summer of 139. The results of the embassy are largely unknown, though they almost certainly included Roman recognition of Antiochus VII, who shortly afterwards established himself on the Seleucid throne.[3]

In 139 (consuls Cn. Calpurnius Piso and M. Popillius Laenas) Q. Caepio procured the assassination of Viriatus and compelled a large army under Viriatus' successor to surrender. He thereby virtually ended the Lusitanian war, although there was still resistance for his successor to put down in the rugged country to the north.[4] Earlier in the year Viriatus had attempted to negotiate with the new governor of Hither Spain, the consul M. Popillius Laenas.[5] Popillius had been

---

[1] Livy, Ox. Epit. 54. There are serious difficulties about all suggested restorations of the impossibly corrupt line 184, but a reference to a lictor (who must be the consul's, since tribunes did not have lictors) and the verb terruit or deterruit are certain.

[2] Appendix II, nos. 26, 27, and 28; Gell. 3. 4. 1; cf. 4. 17. 1 = Lucil. 394 f. M.; pp. 175 f.

[3] Cic. Rep. 3. 48; Acad. Pr. 2. 5; Justin, 38. 8. 8; Strabo, 14. 5. 2; Diod. 33. 28a; 'Plut.' Apophth. Scip. Min. 13 = Appendix II, no. 29; 14; Plut. Cum Princ. Phil. 1 = Poseid. fgt. 30 FGrH; Val. Max. 4. 3. 13; Athen. 6. 273a = Polyb. fgt. 76 BW = Poseid. fgt. 59 FGrH; 12. 549d = Poseid. fgt. 6 FGrH (where Athenaeus erroneously writes 'Poseidonius' for 'Panaetius'); cf. 'Lucian' Macrob. 12; Lucil. 464–6 and 1291 M. (Victor) De Vir. Ill. 58. 7 incorrectly states that Laelius went. For the date see esp. Astin, 'Diodorus and the Date of the Embassy', CPh 54 (1959), pp. 221 f. Antiochus VII sent very substantial assistance to Scipio in 134 (Livy, Epit. 57), which suggests that he felt himself to be under a considerable obligation. See further pp. 138 f. and 177.

[4] App. Iber. 74 f.; Livy, Epit. 54; Ox. Epit. 54; Oros. 5. 4. 14; other refs. in MRR i, p. 482.

[5] Diod. 33. 19; Dio, fgt. 75; (Victor) De Vir. Ill. 71. 2.

enabled to turn his army against the Lusitanians because of an enforced lull in hostilities in Celtiberia. When he arrived to take up his
command he found that Pompeius had engaged in negotiations with
the enemy. The outcome had been that the Numantines had gone
through the motions of making a *deditio*, but they insisted that they had
done this only because Pompeius had concluded a *de facto* treaty with
them. Despite the testimony of some of his own staff, Pompeius
strenuously denied that there was any such treaty. Popillius referred
the matter to the Senate, which on the one hand decided that
Pompeius had negotiated a treaty, thus rejecting his story and ad-
ministering a sharp rebuff, but on the other hand refused to ratify this
treaty.[1]

Another controversial event of this year was the enactment of a *lex
tabellaria*, which laid it down that voting in elections was to be by
written ballot. Although Gabinius, the tribune who proposed the
measure, was certainly the object of derogatory abuse, nothing else is
known of the struggle which must have centred upon this bill, nor
is it possible to ascertain the political associations of its author.[2]
Finally, the praetor peregrinus of 139, Cn. Cornelius Scipio Hispanus,
issued an edict expelling all 'Chaldaeans' from Rome and Italy,
'because by their lies and by a deceitful interpretation of the stars, for
their own profit they were bewildering weak and foolish minds'. In
addition Hispanus is said to have expelled the Jews because their
religious practices were corrupting Roman customs; but doubts
have been raised as to the authenticity of this latter expulsion. It is
conceivable that the edict is a symptom of some unrest; that at a time
when economic and social hardships were becoming more apparent,
the astrologers were sharpening fears and discontents; but it is highly
improbable that they were consciously engaged in conspiratorial
or seditious activities, and it is by no means impossible that the

---

[1] App. *Iber.* 79, 83; Livy, *Epit.* 54; Cic. *De Fin.* 2. 54; *Rep.* 3. 28; Vell. 2. 1. 4; 2. 90. 3;
Eutrop. 4. 17. 1; Flor. 1. 34. 4; Oros. 5. 4. 21; cf. Dio, fgt. 79. 3; Cic. *De Off.* 3. 109. See
pp. 148 f.

[2] Cic. *De Leg.* 3. 35; *De Amic.* 41; Livy, *Ox. Epit.* 54. Gabinius is probably the man who
served under Metellus Macedonicus in 146 (Polyb. 38. 12. 1) and son of the man who served
as a *praefectus* under Anicius in 168 (Livy, 45. 26. 2); both items suggest but by no means
prove a possible association with Scipio. Gabinius is probably also the author of the law
which required the Senate to devote its meetings in February to the reception of embassies:
Carcopino, *Mél. Glotz*, i, pp. 120 f.

protective and paternalist motives attributed to the praetor are quite genuine.[1]

The consuls of 138 were P. Cornelius Scipio Nasica (Serapio) and D. Iunius Brutus. Brutus succeeded Caepio in Further Spain and began the long series of successful campaigns in western and north-western Spain which were to earn for him a triumph and the *cognomen* Callaicus.[2] Meanwhile in Celtiberia Popillius achieved no more success than his predecessor Pompeius, and suffered a considerable reverse when he attempted a direct assault upon the walls of Numantia.[3] Pompeius himself, back in Rome, was facing another crisis in his stormy career: prosecution for maladministration in Spain. The prosecution witnesses included Q. Metellus Macedonicus, who was involved in a personal feud with Pompeius, and his brother L. Metellus Calvus, and also the brothers Gnaeus and Quintus Servilius Caepio; but despite this formidable array of consulars Pompeius was acquitted.[4]

Another unsuccessful prosecution for maladministration was that of Aurelius Cotta, who had been consul in 144, by Scipio Aemilianus in person. This time Metellus Macedonicus appeared as the leading speaker for the defence, which succeeded only after seven re-hearings. It was alleged, and apparently widely believed, that Cotta owed his escape in no small measure to bribery.[5]

But the year also saw political clashes of a different kind. During the winter 139–138 there was difficulty with the corn supply for the city. Early in 138, as the situation worsened, a tribune, C. Curiatius, publicly urged the consuls to propose to the Senate the purchase of corn by the state and the appointment of special *legati* to undertake the task. Probably nothing was done; at least, Nasica opposed the plan, evidently on the ground that it would prove ineffective. In

[1] Val. Max. 1. 3. 3; Livy, *Ox. Epit.* 54. Cramer, 'Expulsion of Astrologers', *C & M* 12 (1951), pp. 8 f., esp. pp. 14 f., and *Astrology in Roman Law and Politics*, p. 58, overestimates the political significance.

[2] App. *Iber.* 71 f.; Livy, *Epit.* 55, 56; *Ox. Epit.* 55; other references in *MRR* i, pp. 483, 485, 487, and, for the triumph, p. 488 n. 5. See p. 146.

[3] App. *Iber.* 79; Livy, *Epit.* 55; cf. *Ox. Epit.* 55; Frontin. *Strat.* 3. 17. 9; cf. Lucil. 621 M.

[4] Cic. *Pro Font.* 23; Val. Max. 8. 5. 1. The recriminations between Macedonicus and Pompeius are reflected in the contrast between App. *Iber.* 76 and Val. Max. 9. 3. 7. Cf. Dio, fgt. 82.

[5] Appendix II, no. 30. *Septies ampliata*: Val. Max. 8. 1, abs. 11; alleged bribery: C. Gracchus in App. *B.C.* 1. 22.

doing so he provoked a public outcry,[1] and at some point in the disputes of this year the mocking Curiatius saddled him with the nickname Serapio, from his resemblance to a lowly *victimarius* of that name.[2] Nor was the corn supply the only inflammatory topic of the moment. A levy was held, probably at least in part to provide fresh troops for Brutus to take to Spain. The occasion was marked first of all by the public scourging, on the instructions of the consuls, of deserters from Spain. Public action of this kind was a recognition of unrest over the levy, an endeavour to forestall by severe example attempts to desert or to avoid the levy. Then Curiatius and another tribune, S. Licinius, demanded that each tribune should be allowed to exempt ten persons from the levy, and when the consuls refused this concession the two tribunes imposed a fine and imprisoned the consuls. Subsequently the fines were remitted, and the imprisonment cannot have lasted long; whether or not the tribunes won their point is not recorded.[3] It is quite likely that the tensions surrounding this levy were heightened by the news of the death of Viriatus, which perhaps raised the hopes of many that no new levy would be needed, or that if they could avoid this levy they might escape altogether service in the Spanish wars. But even when this special circumstance is taken into account, it remains evident that the recruiting problem was assuming serious dimensions.

It is possible that Curiatius died before the end of his year of office; at any rate, some very popular tribune died, and his funeral seems to have caused crowds to gather.[4]

In the following year, 137 (consuls M. Aemilius Lepidus and C. Hostilius Mancinus), a second *lex tabellaria* was passed, the *lex Cassia*, which provided that voting should be by ballot in all popular trials except where the charge was *perduellio*. The tribune who proposed the bill was L. Cassius Longinus Ravilla, but its true author was probably Scipio Aemilianus himself; at the least he was Cassius'

---

[1] Val. Max. 3. 7. 3.

[2] Val. Max. 9. 14. 3; Plin. *Nat. Hist.* 7. 54; cf. 21. 10; Livy, *Epit.* 55, which suggests that this may have occurred during the dispute over the levy.

[3] Livy, *Epit.* 55; *Ox. Epit.* 55; Cic. *De Leg.* 3. 20; Frontin, *Strat.* 4. 1. 20. As in 151, the action taken against the consuls implies that they had attempted to defy the tribunician veto: p. 43.

[4] Livy, *Ox. Epit.* 55.

leading supporter. The opposition, which very probably commanded a majority in the Senate, was headed by the consul M. Aemilius Lepidus and secured the support of one of the tribunes, M. Antius Briso. Antius' veto caused some delay, but eventually some form of private pressure applied by Scipio induced him to withdraw and permit the passage of the bill.[1]

In the later part of this year the dominating feature of the political scene was the crisis of the *foedus Mancinum*.[2] The consul Mancinus, who had succeeded Popillius in Hither Spain, suffered a number of reverses in his operations against the Numantines, until finally, with the whole of his demoralized army, he was trapped in an exceedingly dangerous position. He extricated his troops only at the price of a formal treaty, the details of which were negotiated by his quaestor, Ti. Sempronius Gracchus.[3] Furthermore, the Numantines, not surprisingly after their experiences with Pompeius, insisted that Mancinus and his staff should solemnize the agreement with suitable oaths.[4] Mancinus was recalled to Rome to face a storm of indignation and protest; for not only was the whole episode a grave blow to Roman prestige, but early in the Numantine war it had been decided that a *deditio*, formal capitulation, would be the only acceptable termination.[5] In the ensuing argument Mancinus and his staff at first defended their action and urged ratification of the treaty. They argued that it had saved numerous Roman lives, that it preserved all Rome's former possessions in Spain, and that it should be judged not in terms of the ideal objectives but in terms of what was possible in view of the danger that was threatening.[6] At the same time the fundamental causes of the disaster were asserted to be the poor state

[1] Cic. *Brut.* 97; 106; *De Leg.* 3. 35 f.; 3. 37; *Pro Sest.* 103; cf. *De Amic.* 41; Ascon., p. 78 C.; *Schol. Bob.*, p. 135 Stangl; Ps.-Ascon., p. 216 Stangl. The opposition of the Senate is suggested especially by Cic. *Pro Sest.* 103.

[2] The fullest accounts of this episode are in App. *Iber.* 80 and 83, and Plut. *Ti. Grac.* 5 f. Numerous other references collected by Münzer, *RE*, s.v. *Hostilius*, no. 18, and Broughton, *MRR* i, pp. 484 f. See also Simon, *Roms Kriege*, pp. 145 f. Cf. below pp. 150 f.

[3] Plut. *Ti. Grac.* 5. 5 f.; Dio, fgt. 83; Vell. 2. 2. 1; (Victor) *De Vir. Ill.* 59. 4; Mart. Cap. 5. 456; cf. Oros. 5. 8. 3.

[4] App. *Iber.* 80. Implied also in Val. Ant. fgt. 57 = Gell. 6. 9. 12; Flor. 2. 2. 2; Livy, *Epit.* 56; Plut. *Ti. Grac.* 7. 2; Cic. *Pro Caec.* 98; Dio, fgt. 79.

[5] pp. 148 f.

[6] Dio, fgt. 79. 2; cf. 83. 2; that Gracchus argued for ratification is implied also by Plut. *Ti. Grac.* 7. 5; Vell. 2. 2. 2; Claud. Quad. fgt. 73.

to which Pompeius had reduced the army and the religious consequences of rejecting Pompeius' treaty.[1] But it soon became apparent
not only that a majority of the Senate favoured repudiating the
treaty but that a majority for repudiation could be secured in the
assembly. One of the consuls of 136, Scipio's friend L. Furius Philus,
with Scipio and Laelius in his *consilium*,[2] held an inquiry into the
affair, probably to consider not so much whether the treaty should be
repudiated as how this might be done. In Roman eyes the difficulties
were not legal, since the unauthorized action of a commander could
not bind the Roman people unless they chose to ratify the agreement;[3] and although the inadequacy of this legal basis to cope with
emergencies arising at a great distance from Rome posed moral problems, notably in respect of *fides*, these were evidently submerged. The
real difficulty lay in the oaths, and the divine wrath which might be
incurred if these were violated. But Rome had a well-established
method of coping with this problem, even if a precedent for its
application to a consul could be found only by citing, or mis-
representing, the affair of the Caudine Forks, nearly two centuries
previously. The person responsible for the oaths was himself repudiated and surrendered, or at least offered, to the other party.[4]
Furius and his fellow consul, Sex. Atilius Serranus, evidently laid

---

[1] App. *Iber.* 83. This is confirmed by the subsequent attempt to hand over Pompeius as
well as Mancinus.   [2] Cic. *Rep.* 3. 28.

[3] Whatever may have been the case earlier, the principle was firmly established by this
time: Polyb. 6. 14. 10 f.; Mommsen, *Röm. Staats.* iii, p. 343; admitted even by Neumann,
RE, s.v. *Foedus*, col. 2826.

[4] The primary purpose of the device was certainly religious: Cic. *Pro Caec.* 98; Livy,
Epit. 56; Plut. *Ti. Grac.* 7. 2. The surrender of the consuls responsible for the Caudine
treaty is mentioned as a precedent for the treatment of Mancinus (App. *Iber.* 83; Plut. *Ti.
Grac.* 7. 2; Flor. 1. 34. 7; cf. Vell. 2. 1. 5; Oros. 5. 7. 1). The extent to which the accounts
of the Caudine affair have been influenced or inspired by the events of 137 has been widely
discussed since Nissen's basic article, 'Der Caudinische Friede', *RhM* 25 (1870), pp. 1 f.,
esp. pp. 50 f. Cf. esp. Neumann, *RE*, s.v. *Foedus*, cols. 2821 f.; de Visscher, 'La deditio
internationale et l'affaire des Fourches Caudines', *CRAI* (1946), pp. 82 f. Nissen, op. cit.,
p. 60, and esp. Simon, *Roms Kriege*, pp. 152 f., are probably correct in their belief that,
whatever really happened in 321-320, the main features of the story were well established
before 137. There were also other, more recent precedents for the procedure. In 266 and
188 the Romans handed over, through the agency of the Fetials, men guilty of violating
foreign ambassadors (Livy, 38. 42. 7; *Epit.* 15; Val. Max. 6. 6. 3; 6. 6. 5; Dio, fgt. 42; 61;
Zon. 8. 7); and in 236 a *legatus*, M. Claudius Clineas, whose unauthorized treaty with the
Corsicans was repudiated, suffered much the same fate as Mancinus, except that in addition
he was subsequently exiled (Dio, fgt. 45; Zon. 8. 18; Val. Max. 6. 3. 3; Amm. Marc.
14. 11. 32).

three separate bills before the assembly, proposing the handing over respectively of Mancinus, of his staff, and of Pompeius. The vote against Mancinus was a foregone conclusion, and, whether by reason of prudence or of more sinister pressures, Mancinus was actually induced to support the bill himself. Pompeius resisted strenuously, as he was bound to do since he maintained that he had made no treaty to be repudiated, and the assembly accepted his case. The popular Tiberius Gracchus used his rhetorical skill to procure the escape of himself and the rest of Mancinus' staff, contending that the full responsibility lay with Mancinus alone.[1] There is a strong suspicion that the bill concerning the staff was separated from that concerning Mancinus himself precisely in order to achieve this result.[2] Mancinus alone, therefore, was taken to Spain by Furius and the Fetial priests, to be exposed naked for the Numantines to take if they wished. Rejected unharmed by them, he returned to Rome to become the focus of intense legal argument about his status and his civic rights.[3] By that time another dispute had arisen, though this is less well recorded. Mancinus' successor in Hither Spain, his fellow-consul Lepidus, had also been recalled, to be prosecuted and fined. He had made war on the Vaccaei, contrary to instructions and, according to his opponents, without provocation. In co-operation with Brutus he attempted to besiege Palantia but was compelled to abandon it with heavy losses; no doubt his marked lack of success facilitated his condemnation.[4]

It was at about this time, perhaps actually in 136, that the great slave rebellion broke out in Sicily.[5] Already the use of numerous

---

[1] For these proposals and Pompeius and Gracchus see Cic. Rep. 3. 28; De Off. 3. 109; Plut. Ti. Grac. 7. 3 f.; Vell. 2. 1. 5; (Victor) De Vir. Ill. 64. 2; Eutrop. 4. 17. 1; Mart. Cap. 5. 456; cf. Quint. Inst. 7. 4. 13; App. Iber. 83.

[2] Cf. Plut. Ti. Grac. 7. 3 f.

[3] Cic. De Orat. 1. 181; 1. 238; 2. 137; Pro Caec. 98; Top. 37; Dig. 49. 15. 4; 50. 7. 18; cf. (Victor) De Vir. Ill. 59. 4.

[4] App. Iber. 80 f.; Oros. 5. 5. 13; Livy, Epit. 56; Obsequ. 25; cf. Diod. 33. 27. Schulten, Numantia, i, p. 365 n. 2, plausibly infers from App. Iber. 82 that the retreat from Palantia coincided with the lunar eclipse of 31 March–1 April 136. Simon, Roms Kriege, pp. 164 f., argues that the whole campaign belongs to the early months of 136, but this is uncertain.

[5] The most important evidence is contained in substantial fragments of Diodorus: 34/35. 2 = Poseid. fgt. 108 FGrH. Other references collected by Münzer, RE, s.v. Eunus, no. 1. Both the date and the character of the outbreak have been much discussed. The evidence for a very early date, e.g. 139, seems insufficient (essentially Diod. 34/35. 2. 1 and

slaves to tend the herds and flocks of the great estates had given rise to widespread brigandage; for slaves so employed had to have considerable freedom of movement and to some extent had to be armed. In addition very large numbers of slaves were employed in the profitable agricultural operations of the great landowners, both Roman and Sicilian, who dominated the island's life. To the harsh conditions and treatment endured by many of these slaves must be added the fact that many of them had once been free men. The rebellion started with an uprising among the despairing slaves of a particularly brutal owner named Damophilus. Led by a Syrian named Eunus, who had mystical pretensions, they seized the town of Enna and massacred many of the free inhabitants. Encouraged by this initial success the rising spread rapidly. Soon there were sufficient rebels, many of them no doubt experienced soldiers who had been captured in the recent wars, to form a sizeable army. Under able leadership they embarked on the desperate enterprise of trying to occupy the whole island and to hold it against Rome. Eunus created a political organization, modelled, it seems, upon Seleucid Syria, and even issued coinage. Several other towns were captured and several successes were won against the armies of a series of Roman praetors. In 134 it was found necessary to give the command against the slaves to a consul, and so also in 133, but the rebels were not finally crushed until 132. In the meantime news of their early successes sparked off abortive risings in Italy, Delos, and Attica,[1] though all of these were put down rapidly.

Censors were elected in 136. The successful candidates were Ap. Claudius Pulcher and Q. Fulvius Nobilior (cos. 153). Virtually

the list of four praetors in Flor. 2. 7. 7; but Livy, *Ox. Epit.*, which deals with 138 and one item of 137, does not mention the war). Livy's account under 134 clearly implied that the full-scale war began earlier (Livy, *Epit.* 56; cf. Obsequ. 27; Oros. 5. 6. 1 f., under 135, perhaps antedated from Livy), which, together with Flor. 2. 7. 7 and perhaps App. *B.C.* 1. 9, makes a date later than 136 difficult to envisage; but so also is a date much before 136. But there can be no certainty. See esp. Rathke, *De Bellis Servilibus*, esp. pp. 25 f.; Ciaceri, *Processi politici*, pp. 55 f. (esp. pp. 70 f. for earlier bibliography); Münzer, loc. cit.; Last, *CAH* ix, pp. 11 f.; Carcopino, *Hist. rom.* ii. 1, pp. 186 f.; Broughton, *MRR* i, p. 483 and addenda; Green, 'First Sicilian Slave War', *P & P* 20 (1961), pp. 10 f.; Forrest and Stinton, 'First Sicilian Slave War', *P & P* 22 (1962), pp. 87 f.; and, for the character of the outbreak, Vogt, *Struktur der antiken Sklavenkriege*. Cf. also Capozza, 'Le rivolte servili', *AIV* 95 (1957), pp. 79 f.

[1] Diod. 34/35. 2. 19; Oros. 5. 9. 4 f.; Obsequ. 27; 27b.

nothing is known of their activities, except that Claudius wished to pursue a rather more severe policy than his colleague; but their differences cannot have been comparable to those between Scipio and Mummius and did not amount to a political cleavage, for Fulvius nominated his colleague to be Princeps Senatus.[1]

The known events of the next year, 135, are few in number and mostly military in character. At least one praetor was engaged in fighting the rebel slaves in Sicily, while another, M. Cosconius, campaigned successfully against the Thracian Scordisci.[2] One of the consuls, Ser. Fulvius Flaccus, defeated the Vardaei in Illyricum.[3] The other consul, Q. Calpurnius Piso, took command in the Numantine war; at best he made no progress, and there is a strong possibility that he suffered a serious defeat.[4] In any case, even if he did not suffer such a defeat, the cumulative effect of years of continual lack of success, punctuated by defeats and disasters, resulted at the end of this year in the election of Scipio Aemilianus to a second consulship. At this date second consulships were prohibited, so once again Scipio was in effect exempted from the provisions of the law.[5]

Scipio's fellow consul in 134, C. Fulvius Flaccus, took over the command against the Sicilian slaves, possibly after a praetor of this year had already failed; but Flaccus seems to have achieved very little.[6] Otherwise all that is known about the events of 134 concerns the activities of Scipio, which are recorded in unusual detail.[7] When

---

[1] Dio, fgt. 81; cf. Festus, 360 L.; Livy, *Epit.* 56. For Claudius as Princeps Senatus see Plut. *Ti. Grac.* 4. 2 and *MRR* i, p. 486 with n. 2.

[2] Livy, *Epit.* 56.   [3] Livy, *Epit.* 56; App. *Illyr.* 10.

[4] The brief notice in App. *Iber.* 83 makes no mention of the defeat, but cf. Obsequ. 26: *in Numantia res male gestae, exercitus Romanus oppressus.* A possible but not very probable explanation is that Obsequens has presented as a single event a Livian summary of the general situation in the years before Scipio's second consulship (cf. Livy, *Epit.* 56).

[5] Livy, *Epit.* 56; App. *Iber.* 84, which incorrectly states that the legal difficulty was that Scipio was under age. Cic. *Rep.* 6. 11 says that Scipio was elected in his absence, but this is probably a false inference (see the context); Val. Max. 8. 15. 4 has the circumstantial detail that he was supporting his nephew's candidacy for the quaestorship. See also Cic. *Div. in Caec.* 69; *De Amic.* 11; Val. Max. 2. 7. 1; 4. 3. 13; Oros. 5. 7. 1; Vell. 2. 4. 2; 'Plut.' *Apophth. Scip. Min.* 15; Gell. 16. 8. 10; Eutrop. 4. 17. 2; *ILS* 43; cf. Flor. 1. 34. 2.

[6] Livy, *Epit.* 56; Oros. 5. 9. 6. The initial appointment of a praetor in 134 would help to ease the chronological problem posed by Flor. 2. 7. 7 (see p. 133 n. 5).

[7] In particular App. *Iber.* 84 f. has a very full account, quite out of proportion to the rest of his history. This may have its origin in the work of Rutilius Rufus, who served under Scipio and whose history is mentioned in *Iber.* 88; but he is not the only possible source. See p. 4 with n. 4.

the Senate refused either to give him ready cash or to allow him to levy fresh troops, he acidly commented that his own resources and those of his friends would provide the money, but he complained about the lack of fresh troops in view of the low morale of those in Spain.[1] Nevertheless he was allowed to take volunteer contingents sent by cities and kings on account of their personal relationship to him, and he was able to enrol a bodyguard of five hundred clients and friends, so that in all he took four thousand fresh troops.[2] When he reached the province he set about systematically disciplining and training his army, a process which bequeathed a considerable fund of anecdotes.[3] By late summer he had begun his carefully contrived programme of pillaging and devastation, designed to deprive the Numantines of the harvest of their own and of neighbouring territories. This involved a long march to the west, but before winter set in he was back at Numantia, and soon established the two camps which were the bases for the construction of the massive series of forts, palisades, and towers with which he encircled the city. The siege was long but highly organized and relentless; probably in July or August 133 those of the defenders who had not starved to death or committed suicide finally surrendered, and their city was razed to the ground. The war was ended, it is said, within fifteen months of Scipio's arrival in Spain.[4] And at about this same time, though whether before or after the fall of the city is unknown, Scipio learned how the political life of Rome had been convulsed by the tribunate and the death of Tiberius Gracchus.[5]

[1] Appendix II, no. 32.

[2] App. *Iber.* 84; cf. 89; Livy, *Epit.* 57; Cic. *Pro Reg. Deiot.* 19; *Schol. Clun.*, p. 272 Stangl; Vell. 2. 9. 4; Sall. *Iug.* 7. 2. There has been much discussion about the originality of Scipio's ἴλη φίλων (App. *Iber.* 84) and its relationship to the praetorian cohort, to the development of which he, or possibly the elder Africanus, made a major contribution (Festus, 249 L.): Durry, *RE*, s.v. *Praetoriae cohortes*, col. 1612; De Sanctis, *Storia*, iv. 3, pp. 260 f.

[3] Appendix II, nos. 33–41; cf. 47. Livy, *Epit.* 57; App. *Iber.* 85 f.; Val. Max. 2. 7. 1; (Victor) *De Vir. Ill.* 58. 6; Eutrop. 4. 17. 2; Oros. 5. 7. 4 f.; Frontin. *Strat.* 4. 1. 1; 'Plut.' *Apophth. Scip. Min.* 16; Flor. 1. 34. 8 f.; cf. Lucil. 398 f. and 407 f. M.

[4] The basic account is App. *Iber.* 87 f. See esp. Schulten, *Numantia*, i, pp. 366 f.; iii, pp. 9 f.; *Gesch. von Numantia*, pp. 85 f.; Simon, *Roms Kriege*, pp. 180 f. Schulten's excavations fully confirmed the accuracy of Appian's account of the siege-works. The chronology is calculated from the fifteen months of Vell. 2. 4. 2, from the assumption that Scipio reached Spain about April 134, and from references to harvests and winter quarters in App. *Iber.* 87 and 89. Oros. 5. 7. 5 seems to imply that Scipio remained inactive until the spring of 133, which cannot be correct.   [5] Plut. *Ti. Grac.* 21. 7.

XII

FOREIGN POLICY AND THE SPANISH WARS

1. *Foreign Policy*

BETWEEN the destruction of Corinth in 146 and the acquisition
of the kingdom of Pergamum in 133, Roman foreign policy
was dominated by the two long wars in Spain, the Viriatic and
the Numantine. Admittedly these may have been thought of rather
as rebellions to be suppressed, and therefore in a sense internal matters; but in their demands upon Rome's resources, in many of the
problems which they posed, and in the kinds of deliberation and
decision which they required these were essentially foreign wars,
fought to determine the future relationship between the Roman state
and these Spanish peoples, and highly significant for Rome's whole
position in the Iberian peninsula. By good fortune they are reported
in what for this period is quite considerable detail. By contrast, other
aspects of foreign affairs in these years are shadowy in the extreme.
Not enough is recorded to permit the reconstruction even of the
broad outlines of the policies pursued, let alone to throw light on
personal attitudes and divergences of opinion lying behind the actions
taken. This relative silence is probably not entirely accidental but
reflects a genuinely quiet period. It is a reasonable guess that preoccupation with the Spanish wars, and in the later years also with the
Sicilian slave rebellion, led to an acceptance of the need for cautious
policies elsewhere and the avoidance of unnecessary military en-
tanglements. Certainly there was some fighting, but Appius Claudius'
campaign against the Salassi in 143,[1] for all its interest, was scarcely
a major development in foreign policy, and in 143 or 142 the victory
of Tremellius Scrofa over a pseudo-Philip or pseudo-Perseus was no
more than the suppression of rebellion within the Roman province of
Macedonia.[2] The other known wars, in Macedonia and Illyricum,

[1] pp. 106 f.   [2] Additional Note L, p. 344.

were presumably essentially defensive and uncontroversial, part of the disturbances almost endemic on the frontiers of the Balkan provinces.[1] In the political field the Roman Senate must have taken some interest in the war between Attalus II and the Thracian Diegylis,[2] in the death of Attalus II and the succession of Attalus III to the Pergamene throne, in the latter's assertion of his authority against his predecessor's powerful advisers,[3] and in the intrigues, and especially in the rebellion of Galaestes about 140, which afflicted Egypt in the years following the accession of Ptolemy VII Euergetes, who in 145 had secured his position with Roman assistance.[4] More complex difficulties were presented by the disintegrating Seleucid kingdom of Syria, torn by civil war and menaced from the east by the advancing power of Parthia. After the battle of Oenoparas in 145 it seemed that Demetrius II might establish himself in control, but the unpopularity of his methods facilitated the rebellion of Diodotus Tryphon in the name of the child Antiochus VI, son of Alexander Balas. A few years later, when Antiochus was dead, Tryphon proclaimed himself king, though his control was never complete even when Demetrius was captured by the Parthians in 140–139. The Senate refused to recognize Tryphon as king, and it is uncertain whether it ever recognized Antiochus or Demetrius. The situation in Syria was one of the problems investigated by Scipio Aemilianus and his colleagues on their embassy to the east in 140–139, and they probably recommended Roman recognition of Antiochus VII, who shortly afterwards overthrew Tryphon; indeed it is not impossible that his bid for power was encouraged by Scipio.[5] But apart from this the results even of this famous embassy are largely untraceable. It is said in a general way that it settled numerous disputes and engendered great good will, and it looks as if Attalus III felt himself especially indebted to Scipio, but

---

[1] p. 135.   [2] Diod. 33. 15; Strabo, 13. 4. 2; Trog. *Prol.* 36.

[3] Strabo, 13. 4. 2; Diod. 34/35. 3; Justin, 36. 4. 1 f.; cf. Magie, *Roman Rule in Asia Minor,* i, pp. 30 f.; De Sanctis, *Storia,* iv. 3, p. 209.

[4] De Sanctis, *Storia,* iv. 3, pp. 185 f.

[5] De Sanctis, *Storia,* iv. 3, pp. 190 f., 196 f., and 201 f.; Bevan, *The House of Seleucus,* ii, pp. 223 f.; Bouché-Leclercq, *Histoire des Séleucides,* i, pp. 347 f.; Seyrig, *Notes on Syrian Coins,* pp. 12 f. Whether the Senate ever recognized Demetrius depends upon the authenticity of the letter in 1 Macc. xv. 15 f. and of the list of addressees appended to it. The Senate's attitude to Tryphon and Antiochus VI is indicated by Diod. 33. 28a. 1, but this does not prove that Antiochus was recognized when he was alive. For Scipio's embassy and the connexion with Antiochus VII see p. 127.

that is all.[1] Whether or to what extent any of these Hellenistic matters aroused controversy at Rome is entirely unknown. All that can be said—and it is a significant point—is that nothing is known which is likely to have constituted a prolonged and burning issue, and that no development is recorded which is likely to have made a deep impact on the internal affairs of Rome. Thus for the understanding of Roman politics in these years the lack of information about relations with the Hellenistic world may not be as serious as it at first seems; in fact it may be a true reflection of the comparative unimportance of these matters.

The converse is true of the Spanish wars. Admittedly much of our greater knowledge is due to the accident that Appian's *Iberica* is virtually the only surviving continuous narrative of these years; but it is also true that most of the information recorded in the Epitome of Livy is concerned with Spain or with matters related to it, and that there are a considerable number of other pertinent passages, such as fragments of other historians, passing references in Cicero, and anecdotes in Valerius Maximus and elsewhere. Even without Appian most of the military and political crises of the wars would be known, albeit imperfectly. All this suggests that the topic bulked large in the minds both of later writers and of contemporaries. Nor is this surprising, for the wars plainly had considerable and varied repercussions in the political life of Rome.

It has long been recognized that among these repercussions were serious strains upon the economic and especially the man-power resources of Rome, and that these strains have some bearing upon the great political crises of 133. For this reason the senatorial leaders, and especially Scipio Aemilianus, have been criticized on the ground that they persisted in prosecuting the wars until total victory was achieved, even though there were opportunities to terminate the wars earlier through negotiated settlements.[2] It is therefore pertinent to consider in what respects and to what degree Roman policies and

---

[1] Diod. 33. 28a. 2 f.; Cic. *Pro Reg. Deiot.* 19; *Schol. Ambros.*, p. 272 Stangl.

[2] e.g. Meyer, *Kleine Schriften*, i[2], pp. 401 f.; Schulten, *Numantia*, i, pp. 274 f.; Kornemann, *Livius-Epitome*, pp. 108 f.; Blázquez, 'La Conquista de Hispania', *Klio* 41 (1963), pp. 168 f., esp. 184 f.; cf. Bilz, *Die Politik*, pp. 49 f., who notes that for many years Scipio was not in a position to control policy, but believes that until 137 there was a real choice and that Scipio approved of the policy of total subjection.

objectives were politically controversial; how far, in fact, the Romans felt themselves faced with a serious choice of policies.

Several aspects of this problem require separate treatments of the two wars, but first there is a negative point which applies to them equally, namely that it is very unlikely that imperialism and expansionism as such were at issue. The Celtiberians were unequivocally rebels, and, in view of Galba's conquests in 150, it is highly probable that the Lusitanians were regarded in much the same light; moreover they were accused, with great plausibility, of extensive raiding of the prosperous lowland areas which were under direct Roman control.[1] The wars as such, then, and the principle of subjecting these peoples to Roman authority are unlikely to have occasioned dispute. But if this much is common, there are marked contrasts between Roman policies in the Viriatic war and those adopted in the Numantine war. One of these is seen in the treatment of the defeated enemy. When the bulk of the Lusitanians surrendered to Q. Servilius Caepio in 139 they did so under an assurance that they would not be enslaved; Caepio and his successor Brutus then gave them land and settled them in agricultural communities. On the other hand, Scipio Aemilianus refused to give any assurance whatsoever to the Numantines and enslaved all the survivors. It may be objected that between those events there intervened six years of additional warfare, during which Roman attitudes may have hardened; but there is another contrast which is truly contemporary. Probably as early as 142, and certainly before 139, it had become established Roman policy that the Numantine war could be terminated only if the enemy made a *deditio*; yet as late as the summer of 139, after eight years of costly and often humiliating warfare, a negotiated settlement with Viriatus was not entirely out of the question. The Viriatic war occasioned atrocities and much devastation, and there is no reason to suppose that Rome's methods of warfare were any less ferocious than usual; but Roman policies were relatively moderate, by comparison not only with Galba's excesses in 150 but with the attitude adopted in the contemporary Numantine war. And if the moderation is only relative, the contrast is still there.

[1] App. *Iber.* 61 f. Schulten, 'Viriatus', *NJA* 39 (1917), pp. 218 f., identifies the scene of Vetilius' operations and defeat as far to the south in Roman territory.

2. The Viriatic War

No reason is recorded for the relative moderation of Roman policy in the Viriatic war; it is possible only to guess. It may be, for example, that the outcry against Galba's brutalities[1] had left some sense of uneasiness or even of guilt, and this may have been reinforced by the manner in which the treaty of 140 was nullified;[2] possibly also policy was affected by respect and even admiration for the talents and personal qualities of Viriatus himself.[3] But also, although Rome had formulated the concept of the *deditio*, her policies were often characterized by pragmatism and she was no stranger to the idea of waging war for limited objectives. Leading senators may have been conscious of the great numbers and loose organization of the Lusitanians—in contrast to the Celtiberian cities of Termantia and Numantia—and of the difficulty of achieving an absolute military victory over such a large area of difficult terrain. Further, many may have realized that much of the Lusitanian restlessness sprang from land-hunger and could be resolved by resettling them in agricultural communities. It was in the expectation of just such resettlement that the Lusitanians had surrendered to Galba, and in 147 it seems that they would have agreed upon such terms with Vetilius if Viriatus had not played upon memories of the treachery of Galba and of the massacre from which he himself was one of the few survivors.[4]

The breaking-off of those negotiations and the subsequent successes of Viriatus, including the defeat and death of Vetilius himself,[5] injected into the situation important considerations of Roman prestige. Under such circumstances it would be surprising if the senators had been all of one mind in their view of what would constitute an acceptable end to the war, yet it is unlikely that this became a serious political factor before 140. That does not exclude disputes about who should command, or recriminations about the successive defeats, but policy as such was probably not greatly at issue. This is suggested first by the complete absence of indications of controversy of that

---

[1] pp. 58 f.   [2] pp. 126 and 143.

[3] Cf. App. *Iber.* 75; Livy, *Epit.* 54; Diod. 33. 7 and 21a; Flor. 1. 33. 13 and 15; (Victor) *De Vir. Ill.* 71.

[4] App. *Iber.* 59 f.; 61. Cf. also App. *Iber.* 75; Livy, *Epit.* 55; Strabo, 3. 3. 5; Schulten, 'Viriatus', *NJA* 39 (1917), pp. 211 f.

[5] p. 99.

kind,[1] but especially by the plain fact that prior to 140 the military situation was hardly ever such as to permit a settlement on terms which could conceivably have been acceptable to Rome. What the Lusitanians had rejected in the shadow of defeat by Vetilius they were scarcely likely to accept while they were repeatedly repelling Roman armies, often carrying war and devastation far into Roman territory, plundering, and even exacting tribute from the inhabitants, and at times seizing towns well south of Corduba. Even the successful campaign by Fabius Maximus Aemilianus in 144 was offset by the rebellion of Celtiberia, and in the next two years the Romans again fared badly.[2] In 141 Fabius Maximus Servilianus' work of consolidation seemed to offer better prospects, but this was largely a matter of recovering and securing territory which had been lost to the Lusitanians. And when he launched a new offensive in the spring of 140 he was quickly routed and trapped in an impossible position. It was in order to save his army from total destruction that he negotiated the treaty which accepted the territorial *status quo*, recognized the independence of the Lusitanians, and designated Viriatus a friend of the Roman people.[3]

This treaty was ratified at Rome. There is no indication of serious opposition, and probably there was not very much. Admittedly no one can have anticipated a settlement which not only recognized the independence of the Lusitanians under Viriatus but left them in control of a substantial part of Baeturia,[4] but in view of the circumstances in which the treaty had been made many senators no doubt felt at least that the opportunity might as well be taken to regroup, especially as the Numantine war continued to absorb men and resources. Moreover it is likely that discontent with the levy was manifesting itself,[5] in which case it could have been politically

---

[1] There is no reason to suppose that the objectives of the war were at issue in the controversy concerning the command in 144: pp. 104 f. and Appendix II, no. 12.

[2] pp. 105 and 123, and Additional Note L, p. 344.

[3] pp. 125 f., for this and the renewal of the war.

[4] The town of Arsa, captured by Q. Caepio when he renewed the war (App. *Iber.* 70) was in Turdetania, i.e. central or southern Baeturia: cf. Hübner, *RE*, s.v. *Arsa*, no. 3. Hence it was probably in the area controlled by Rome at the outbreak of the war: App. *Iber.* 61.

[5] Cf. Ap. Claudius' resolution in 140 prohibiting a second levy; also Claudius Asellus' attempt to interfere with Caepio's departure for Spain could be plausibly explained by such difficulties: pp. 126 f.

imprudent to reject an opportunity for peace in one of the two wars. But it was one thing to ratify the settlement as a temporary expedient, quite another to view it as a satisfactory and permanent solution. Although Viriatus had been shrewd enough to realize that there would have to be some accommodation with the Romans, he was exceedingly optimistic if he expected this particular arrangement to endure indefinitely. Like many another leader he perhaps failed to comprehend the enormous, even if often latent, preponderance of Roman power; or, if he was aware of it, he did not grasp its full significance for his people. Situated as they were on the borders of a militaristic empire, with no other great power to play off against Rome, in the long run they could hope to enjoy political independence only with the good will of Rome and only in such measure as the Romans saw fit to allow them. The treaty of 140 was not conducive to such good will, either in its terms, which probably even included the cession of Roman territory, or in the manner in which it was concluded. It was the product of a humiliating defeat, immensely damaging to Roman military prestige. Provided that her strength permitted, it would have been astonishing if Rome, in which political advancement was inextricably entwined with military training and experience, had not found occasion to reverse this situation. The only cause for surprise is that the opportunity was found so very soon.

Q. Servilius Caepio, Servilianus' brother and successor, probably heard of the treaty first when he reached Spain. In the following few months he presumably devoted himself to restoring the morale of his army and assessing the situation. His conclusion was that the war both could and should be resumed immediately, that the treaty was not only unsatisfactory but did not correspond at all even to the immediate military potential of the two parties; and this judgement was to be fully vindicated by his own rapid and successful drive when hostilities were renewed. His first reports must have reached the Senate not long after the treaty had been ratified. The Senate first authorized secret arrangements to irritate and provoke Viriatus, then, presumably on the excuse of some technical breach, declared the treaty void and renewed the war. And here policy towards Viriatus must have become a major political issue; for it is virtually inconceivable that these decisions can have been reached without serious divergences of opinion, both about their expediency and about the principles involved. One indication of controversy is the report that Caepio agitated for the decision in frequent dispatches,[1] but it is almost certainly reflected also in two further episodes.

The first of these is Appius Claudius' sponsorship, in 140, of the decree of the Senate which laid it down that there should be only one levy in the year.[2] There certainly was one levy in 140, since substantial reinforcements and replacements reached Pompeius in Citerior, and it is possible that Caepio too had been allotted some of the troops enrolled on that occasion. But now there had been a request for a second levy, and in all likelihood this had been made by Caepio in view of the impending resumption of hostilities. There are many possible motives which may have led Claudius to propose his motion and induced a majority of senators to vote for it: an unwillingness to arouse further resentment at the unpopular levies; a desire to conserve man-power; in some cases possibly the irrational influence of dislike of Caepio himself; and a conviction, perhaps encouraged by Caepio's own dispatches, that he did not really need the extra troops. But however big a part was played by such considerations, it is difficult to believe that Claudius would have initiated this resolution if he had whole-heartedly approved Caepio's plans. Of course, the resolution could have been much more than this: it could have been an attempt to forestall the proposal to renew the war, or, if it came later, to prevent by an indirect device the implementing of the decision already taken. At the least, however, it strongly suggests that Claudius was much less enthusiastic than Caepio about the early resumption of hostilities.

If the element of hypothesis in all this is uncomfortably large, the second episode is much more straightforward. In the spring of 139, as Caepio's successful drive was developing, a truce in the Numantine war enabled M. Popillius Laenas to turn his forces also against Viriatus, who was thus hard pressed by two Roman armies. Under the circumstances it is not surprising that he attempted to negotiate; what is surprising is that, before there was any clash with the army from Hither Spain, he sought to open negotiations with Popillius—

---

[1] App. *Iber.* 70.   [2] p. 126.

not with Caepio, his main opponent—and that Popillius responded. Popillius had a difficult task, for he had to formulate a settlement firm enough to stand a good chance of ratification and yet not so severe that Viriatus would reject it out of hand, so he adopted the familiar technique of making demands only one at a time. Viriatus was persuaded to execute or to hand over various leaders demanded by Popillius—presumably those alleged to have violated Servilianus' treaty—and possibly to meet other conditions; but, understandably enough in view of past Roman behaviour, he refused the demand for the disarming of his troops—a condition which in practice he might have been unable to enforce but which the Roman Senate would almost certainly have regarded as essential.[1]

This episode is significant not merely for its hint of personal friction between Popillius and Caepio, nor yet for the element of unscrupulous ambition in Popillius' attempt to steal the honour of ending the war, but rather because it indicates a real difference in the policies of the two commanders. For Viriatus clearly had strong hopes of obtaining more lenient terms from Popillius than from Caepio and, despite the fact that Popillius' terms themselves proved too severe, a man who was already so well versed in Roman duplicity is likely to have had very strong grounds for such hopes before going so far as to surrender some of his leading lieutenants.

During its last two years, then, the Viriatic war raised divisive issues of policy. One of the main considerations involved was the need to salve Roman pride and to restore the prestige of Roman arms after Servilianus' misfortune. On the other side there was the degree of impropriety involved in deliberately provoking a breach of the treaty—for *fides* was still an important concept at Rome. And there were questions of expediency posed by the demands on man-power and resources made by the Numantine war, and by the strategic undesirability of fighting both wars at once. These considerations were relevant not only to the decisions as to whether, when, and by what means the war was to be resumed but also as to what would constitute acceptable conditions for ending it. Here there was evidently a divergence between the advocates of more lenient and more severe policies. Probably some felt that to restore Roman prestige

---

[1] Diod. 33. 19; Dio, fgt. 75; (Victor) *De Vir. Ill.* 71. 2.

a formal *deditio* must be achieved, and possibly the future of Viriatus himself was at issue. But the difference was not all that great, and once war was resumed it was perhaps not so sharp as to be a dominating issue. It does not look as if Popillius' terms could have been characterized as 'mild'; and it was Caepio, evidently the protagonist of the sterner policy, who, after procuring the assassination of Viriatus, facilitated the *deditio* of the Lusitanian army by a guarantee against enslavement and who initiated the process of resettling the Lusitanians in agricultural communities.[1] The process may not have been entirely pleasant, but it was related to one of the Lusitanians' basic needs, and it was better than enslavement or massacre. It is doubtful if Popillius' terms would have proved much better in practice, except for Viriatus himself.

The work of resettling Viriatus' followers was completed in 138 by Caepio's successor, D. Iunius Brutus.[2] But the fighting was not yet ended. For at least two full years, and perhaps longer, the army of Further Spain campaigned under the command of Brutus. Four phases can be distinguished. First, in 138, Brutus used a mixture of terrorism and clemency to subdue the Lusitanians who lived between the rivers Tagus and Durius, where numerous plundering bands were still operating. Second, in 137, he crossed the Durius and penetrated far into northwestern Spain, winning a great battle against the Callaici on 9 June. Then he co-operated with Aemilius Lepidus in his attack on the Vaccaei, participating in the ill-fated siege of Palantia and in the ignominious retreat in the spring of 136.[3] The fourth phase was the further repression of communities which had already surrendered, many of whom rebelled when Brutus was preoccupied elsewhere. It is not clear whether this fourth phase came in the latter part of 137 or after the siege of Palantia in 136; indeed the word 'phase' is probably misleading, since there may well have been such activity at both times. Reports of Mancinus' defeat by the Numantines and of the failure at Palantia are equally likely to have encouraged rebellions. Whether Brutus' campaigns continued through 136 is unknown; it has been suggested that they continued to 134 or 133, but it is unlikely that he remained in Spain beyond the spring of 135 at the latest.

---

[1] App. *Iber.* 75.   [2] Livy, *Epit.* 55. For Brutus' campaigns cf. p. 129.   [3] p. 133.

There is one indication that Brutus was the object of some controversy: Scipio Aemilianus delivered a speech, which was afterwards published, 'concerning the *imperium* of D. Brutus'.[1] Nothing is known about its contents, its date, or its outcome; all that emerges is that at some time there was a debate about the extension or termination of Brutus' command. An obvious occasion is after the siege of Palantia, when Lepidus was relieved of his command and summoned home. It is entirely possible that there was a simultaneous move to recall Brutus, Lepidus' kinsman and partner in the venture. If so, the attack was at best only partially successful. Brutus had to his credit very considerable achievements which put him in a much stronger position than Lepidus, and in due course he was awarded a triumph.

Whether or not this was the occasion of Scipio's speech, Brutus' participation in the war against the Vaccaei certainly involved him in a controversial issue; but the episode is more closely related to the Numantine war and is better discussed in that connexion. There is no reason to suppose that Brutus' main activities were particularly controversial. Given the situation when he took up his command, a large part of his campaigns must have been regarded as inevitable in order to preclude further trouble from the Lusitanians. His march north of the Durius could have incurred some criticism as being unnecessary, but it seems to have been designed largely to terrorize the inhabitants into quiescence and in any case was of short duration and cannot be said to have put much extra strain on Roman resources. If the debate in which Scipio spoke was concerned with this rather than with the Palantia episode, the matter is scarcely likely to have been at issue for long or to have been of fundamental significance.

3. *The Numantine War*

The Celtiberian uprising which Viriatus incited in 144 was in great part suppressed by Metellus Macedonicus in 143 and 142.[2] It is likely that this was achieved by a combination of military efficiency and a moderately lenient policy. Even the Termantines and Numantines, it seems, made approaches and were granted favourable terms: they were to resume their formal status as 'friends and allies of the

---

[1] Appendix II, no. 31.   [2] p. 123 and Additional Note L, p. 344.

Roman people', on condition that each town provided three hundred hostages, gave a great number of cloaks, hides, and war-horses, and surrendered all its weapons. But on the appointed day, after fulfilling all the other conditions, they balked at the surrender of their arms, and thereby broke the compact and renewed the war.[1] By the end of Metellus' period of command they were the only Celtiberians still in rebellion.

It was probably this last-minute breach of agreed terms which led the Roman Senate to decide upon its inflexible policy towards these two towns. For it is evident that from an early stage in the war, certainly before 139, the only conclusion which would be acceptable to the Senate was the unconditional surrender of the enemy, and once this was established it is unlikely that there was at any time, except in the very special circumstances of 137–136, any significant body of opinion in favour of a negotiated settlement.

This policy is seen at work in the actions of Q. Pompeius. In the winter 140–139, after two seasons of generally unsuccessful campaigning, he opened discussions with the Numantines and Termantines in an attempt to end the war before his period of command expired.[2] In practice he was negotiating a settlement, and it seems certain that in the presence of his staff he agreed upon terms and gave undertakings sufficiently formal for the Numantines to interpret them as a treaty. At the same time, Pompeius insisted that they must make a *deditio*, as this would be the only satisfactory conclusion to the war; so they did this, apparently confident that this was only an outward formality which would not affect the settlement to which they had agreed. But when the new commander, Popillius, arrived, Pompeius denied outright that he had agreed to any terms. Faced with the Numantine claim that a treaty had been agreed and also

[1] Diod. 33. 16. Schulten, *Numantia*, i, p. 360 n. 3, and *Gesch. von Numantia*, p. 74, interprets this as Pompeius' own version of the treaty which the Numantines alleged he made in 140–139; but Cavaignac, 'L'Ambassade de Scipion', *RN* 13 (1951), pp. 132 f., rightly observes that the two are radically different. In particular the undertaking that the Numantines should be 'friends and allies' is incompatible with Pompeius' account of his actions (p. 128, and below). Simon, *Roms Kriege*, p. 114 n. 19 and p. 115 with n. 23, retains the association with Pompeius and is thereby led into tortuous and unsatisfactory hypothesis.

[2] p. 128. In the remainder of the discussion of this episode references to the Numantines are to be understood to include the Termantines. After this episode Termantia is not mentioned again during the war and evidently made an early *deditio*: cf. Schulten, *Numantia*, iii, p. 57; Simon, *Roms Kriege*, p. 114 n. 19.

with the supporting testimony of some of Pompeius' own staff, Popillius referred the matter to the Senate. In the dispute which followed, Pompeius made no attempt to defend the alleged treaty as a reasonable settlement; instead he insisted that there had been a true *deditio* and that no treaty had been negotiated. This behaviour is comprehensible only if he knew from the outset that there was no chance of a negotiated settlement being accepted. It was inevitable that when the majority of senators decided that a treaty had been negotiated they should refuse to ratify it.

Although it was established Roman policy that the war could be terminated only by a *deditio*, there was still room for differences of opinion about the treatment to be accorded to the Numantines after the *deditio*. The affair of Pompeius, however, is not evidence for disagreement even of that kind. His negotiations were not an attempt to secure for the Numantines better terms than he was supposed to offer; he was not attempting to repeat what Marcellus had done twelve years earlier.[1] The crux of the dispute was Pompeius' denial that he had agreed to a treaty; thus it was primarily a dispute between Pompeius and the Numantines, and it became a clash between him and other Romans only when the latter accepted the Numantine rather than Pompeius' version of events. The dispute would have taken a very different course if Pompeius had been concerned to achieve a moderate settlement of the war. There was of course a certain resemblance to the actions of Marcellus, who had conferred with Numantine leaders shortly before they made their *deditio* and who had treated their persons, if not their property, with leniency; but the favourable political settlement which followed was not within his absolute discretion and it is a safe assumption that once the required *deditio* was achieved he used his political skill and influence to persuade the Senate to adopt a moderate attitude. Memories of Marcellus may have influenced the Numantine response in 139, but it is clear that Pompeius gave undertakings which it was not in his power to fulfil and that he misled the Numantines about his intentions and about the implications of what they were doing; and this he did in order to secure a *deditio* as proof of his own success, for political reasons. Perhaps he had unscrupulous hopes that in the

[1] p. 42.

process he would weaken the resources and morale of the Numantines sufficiently to make it difficult for them to resume the war and
so leave them with no alternative but to accept whatever arrangements the Senate decided upon; or possibly he was cynically prepared to saddle them with the technical responsibility of going back
on the *deditio*. However that may be, the ensuing controversy was
not a clash between moderate and severe policies towards Numantia
but an argument about whether Pompeius had actually achieved the
deditio which he claimed.

The issues of the Numantine war erupted into a new crisis two
years later, when the *foedus Mancinum* raised a fresh dispute.[1] The
situation and the immediate issues were very different from those of
139, yet in a sense much the same conclusions can be drawn about the
general features of Roman policy. In many ways Mancinus' treaty
was parallel to that made between Servilianus and Viriatus a few
years before. Like Servilianus', it had been made to avert a major
disaster, yet did not correspond to the ultimate potential strength of
the two parties; and, like Servilianus', it had had to be negotiated by
a commander who lacked ultimate authority for this purpose and
yet who was precluded by circumstance and geography from consulting the proper authorities in Rome—only in this case there was
the added complication of the oaths taken by Mancinus and his
staff. At first sight an obvious way out of the difficulties of the situation would seem to have been to ratify the treaty as a temporary
expedient, in the confident expectation that occasion and justification could soon be found to resume hostilities and reassert Roman
authority, just as had happened in the case of Servilianus' treaty.
Admittedly there were other considerations: the military problems
elsewhere were less pressing than those which had prevailed in 140;
Mancinus himself was by no means as distinguished as Servilianus
and is unlikely to have commanded as much personal support—
some of his political associates may well have considered him ex-
pendable; doubtless there was considerable anger that he had not
merely presented a treaty for ratification but had taken oaths, as the
Numantines insisted, which were intended to prejudge the issue;
there was much justification for feeling that the circumstances were

[1] pp. 131 f.

shameful and very damaging to the prestige of Roman arms; and emotional reactions of this kind offered magnificent scope for exploitation by personal and political enemies. On the other hand Mancinus and his supporters, among them the eloquent and popular Tiberius Gracchus, were not without a case, and they certainly argued for ratification. They could claim with some plausibility that they were not responsible for the low morale of the troops and that this was the basic cause of the trouble. Theirs was a treaty which had saved a Roman army from annihilation, which would end a war that had imposed severe burdens and necessitated frequent levies for a particularly unpopular field of service, and which apparently would have restored the situation that had obtained at the beginning of the war; and in this last respect it was probably distinctly less objectionable than Servilianus' treaty. Above all there was the complication of the oaths, and the dire religious consequences which a superstitious people might fear if these were violated. Yet, in spite of all this, the treaty was rejected not only by the Senate but, probably quite decisively,[1] by the assembly. The strength of the sentiment against it is at first sight surprising, but becomes much more intelligible and perhaps almost inevitable when it is realized that any negotiated settlement, however favourable, had for long been considered out of the question. Thus the predetermined and widely accepted Roman policy towards Numantia was almost certainly a major element in the reaction to the *foedus Mancinum*.

In this instance there is clearly a sense in which the immediate issue was a choice between a moderate and a severe line of action, since one group advocated acceptance of the settlement and the other rejected it as shameful and unacceptable. Yet it is by no means clear that this reflects a long-term or pre-existing division of opinion. Plainly Mancinus did not of his own accord offer the Numantines a moderate settlement; whether or not he and his staff favoured a moderate policy in principle, they were under duress and if they were to extricate the army they had no choice but to assent to moderate terms. Similarly the fact that they argued for ratification is

---

[1] It is difficult to believe that Scipio and his supporters would have proposed handing over also the popular Pompeius unless they felt that the tide of public sentiment was running strongly in their favour.

sufficiently explained by respect for the oaths they had taken, by desire to defend their *fides* and *dignitas*, and by general concern for their future political prospects. Naturally they argued that the treaty offered a reasonable settlement, particularly since their opponents, led by Scipio and his friends, were talking freely of shame and disgrace—doubtless without clear distinction between the circumstances and the terms of the treaty. Yet the one source that reports some arguments for acceptance includes a plea that account should be taken not of what ought to have happened but of what was possible;[1] and according to another source Mancinus asserted that the fundamental causes of the disaster were gross mismanagement by Pompeius and evil auspices resulting from the rejection of Pompeius' treaty.[2] These are not arguments for the principle of a moderate settlement; on the contrary, their tenor is that the settlement was fundamentally unsatisfactory but that it was the best that could be obtained in the immediate circumstances. In other words, there is no known element in the dispute which could not have arisen entirely from the immediate situation and from the incompatibility of that situation with the predetermined policy of insisting upon a *deditio*. There is nothing which requires or especially suggests the hypothesis of a preexisting conflict about moderate or severe policies; and although the evidence does not preclude such a conflict, it does hint that it would have played little part in this dispute.

The next political conflict which had its origin in Hither Spain followed hard upon the heels of the Mancinus affair, indeed was under way before that episode was complete. In 136 M. Aemilius Lepidus was recalled and fined because of his unauthorized attack upon the Vaccaei.[3] It was asserted that there had been no provocation, that there was no truth in Lepidus' allegations that the Vaccaei had helped the Numantines, that his true motive was personal glory, and above all that his actions were contrary to explicit instructions. Lepidus himself evidently maintained that the Vaccaei really had been assisting the Numantines, that the Senate's instructions reached him only after the campaign had begun, so that it could not be abandoned without serious loss of prestige and consequent spread of

---

[1] Dio, fgt. 79. 2.   [2] App. *Iber.* 83; cf. Dio, fgt. 79. 3.
[3] p. 133.

the war, and that the Senate would have taken a different view if it had realized that the campaign was already under way and also that Brutus, with the army of Further Spain, was co-operating with him. Quite apart from the probable intrusion of Lepidus' ambitions and of factional hostility, this dispute was clearly a matter of expediency and not of principle. The issue was not whether Rome should extend her empire but how the Numantine war should be fought: whether advantage should be taken of the lull in that war to deal with actual or potential allies of the Numantines, or whether every effort should be made to avoid spreading the conflict. Once again a dispute which must have been a major political event neither requires nor suggests the existence of a long-term division of opinion concerning the fundamentals of Roman policy.

The war against Numantia entered its final phases with the assumption of the command by Scipio and the organization of the great siege, remorseless and efficient without, full of horror and agony for those within.[1] Scipio refused to give any promise which might mitigate the full implications of the *deditio*; his only concession, when the *deditio* came at last, was to grant one extra day so that those who wished to commit suicide might do so. The act of surrender in itself fulfilled one of the established objectives of Roman policy and simultaneously posed the further question of what should be done with the conquered people, city, and territory. Scipio, who had plenty of time to consider the matter, had already decided upon his immediate actions. This small hill-town suffered the same fate as the great commercial cities of Carthage and Corinth: the city was razed to the ground and the few survivors were enslaved.

Nevertheless, Scipio's actions did not go uncriticized. The one moderately detailed account which survives, that of Appian, not only indicates that the city was razed before the customary advisory commission was sent out but actually states that Scipio did this on his own responsibility, 'with the Romans not yet having arrived at a decision about Numantia'.[2] The reason for this explicit emphasis can only be that there was some criticism on the score that Scipio

[1] pp. 135 f.
[2] App. *Iber.* 98. White, in the Loeb edition, translates 'the Romans knowing nothing about the transaction as yet', but this cannot be correct.

had acted without authorization. Furthermore, Appian goes on to mention three alternative motives for the razing of the city: 'either because he thought that it was for the advantage of the Romans, or because he was given to passionate anger and was vindictive towards captives, or because, as some hold, he believed that great disasters are the foundation of far-famed glory'. In practice it is likely enough that Scipio's motives were compounded of all three of these elements. Harshness and ambition were by no means foreign to his nature, yet it would be unreasonable to question that he regarded the destruction of Numantia as in the best interests of Rome. His career is marked by sufficient instances of severity to leave little doubt that he believed in securing Roman rule by examples of terrorism, and in a passage almost certainly derived from Polybius in which this idea is expounded as a general principle of empire, Numantia is given as a specific example.[1] But although Scipio's sincerity may be accepted, the fact is that two of the opinions recorded by Appian are manifestly hostile, and strongly suggest that there were some who criticized Scipio not only because he acted without authorization but also because of the severity of his measures. And this in turn implies that there was some argument about policy towards the defeated enemy.

Nevertheless, it would be unsafe to infer that this had been a seriously divisive issue over an extended period in the past. It has been observed already that it did not play a significant part in the disputes centred upon Pompeius and Mancinus; and though the existence of this issue would not be incompatible with those episodes, to which it was not really relevant, its late development is suggested by the fact that no decision had been reached even by as late as the summer of 132. Several interpretations are possible. To start with, although the evidence suggests that both by temperament and by opinion Scipio was inclined towards the infliction of severe punishments, it does not follow that from an early stage in the war he had judged it necessary to destroy Numantia utterly. He may have done so, but equally he may have arrived at this extreme only as the war dragged on and inflicted more and more damage on Roman prestige.[2] Again, it is possible that the arguments about the destruction of

---

[1] Diod. 32. 4; cf. p. 331.
[2] Termantia was not destroyed: Schulten, *Numantia*, iii, p. 57.

Numantia were largely recriminations after the event, based not on principle but on political expediency, exploiting an opportunity to attack Scipio's character. And finally, since the clear objective of the *deditio* was established and at the same time was proving extremely hard to achieve, it would be entirely understandable if the question of what was to happen after the *deditio* received comparatively little attention until victory was achieved or at least was manifestly close; and this possibility is all the more plausible in view of the fact that the Senate had taken no decision on the matter. On the other hand it may have taken no decision simply because the majority of senators were content to wait for the opinion of the advisory commission which would be sent, which would imply that before the event the issue had not been hotly contested at all. From this welter of conjectures one point emerges clearly: if it is impossible to prove conclusively that the fate of Numantia was not a major political issue over a substantial period, nevertheless that it was such an issue is only one among several possible hypotheses, and by no means the most attractive.

4. *Decisions and Consequences*

The discussion so far in this chapter has attempted to identify the main features and objectives of Roman policy in the Spanish wars, and to show that, so far as can be ascertained, neither they nor other aspects of foreign policy induced a long and persisting cleavage about basic principles or objectives. There remains the question of how far the course of events in Spain lay within the control of the Romans themselves, to what extent they could in practice have adopted different policies and thereby have minimized the consequences of the wars for their own society.

The Spanish wars, and their repercussions in the affairs of Rome, are not to be understood as the products of a policy of aggressive imperialism to which a policy of containment would have been a realistic alternative. They were rather the product of the very fact of the Roman presence in Spain, of the inherited situation, and of the desire of the Lusitanians and Celtiberians to modify that situation. The Romans could have avoided war only by yielding some measure of Roman authority, and it would never have occurred to the senators, or probably to the masses, that they should do this.[1] There is no sign whatsoever that the alternatives of expansionism or containment were ever an issue in respect of these wars, nor is there reason to expect them to have been; the Romans simply did not think of these struggles in such terms.

Similarly, although the great length of the wars was injurious to the existing fabric of Roman society, by and large they were not prolonged because of insistence on a severe policy when a practicable alternative was available. An earlier termination of hostilities on a more moderate basis was scarcely ever a realistic possibility. It was excluded by the background to the wars themselves, by the presuppositions which governed Roman thinking, and by the long series of failures and defeats which were humiliating and galling, yet did not correspond to the true power-relationship of the contestants. This is true of most of the Viriatic war and of the whole of the Numantine war after about 142.

It might be objected that insistence on the *deditio* of the Numantines did prolong the war unnecessarily, since the Numantines were willing to negotiate terms as early as 139. Viewed in the abstract this is so; but the point is that in Roman eyes a negotiated settlement was simply not a realistic possibility. Once the Numantines had repudiated the agreement of *c.* 142, the Romans could not be expected to contemplate anything but a *deditio* (unless, of course, they proved physically incapable of achieving this, which possibility probably never occurred to them). The issue of the war had now become not merely the reassertion of Roman authority over Numantia but the maintenance of Roman military prestige. The policy seems to have been uncontroversial and taken virtually for granted. And once the decision had been taken, the ending of hostilities on any terms short of a *deditio* would have seemed a partial defeat; every extra year of war, every reverse, can only have deepened Roman determination.

Again, it might be objected that the policy of insisting upon a *deditio* was placed at issue in 137–136, when the *foedus Mancinum* was under discussion. At that time there was a direct choice of rejecting or accepting a treaty, and a treaty which was probably not unduly objectionable in its actual terms; and there was a group pressing for

----

[1] p. 140.

ratification of this treaty. But this pressure came from those whose personal prestige was at stake, and others did not share this basic motive. In the light of the circumstances and of the policy which hitherto had been taken virtually for granted, it is not hard to understand how ratification would have seemed to a large majority to be unreasonable and even outrageous. It would have been an admission of defeat not only in this one campaign but in relation to an established objective of the whole war; and that this would have been so was implied even in the arguments of Mancinus and his associates.[1] Furthermore, for these very reasons, even in the very unlikely event of ratification, it is very difficult to believe that this would have achieved more than a short respite in hostilities.

There was one occasion when there was a real possibility that a less bellicose policy might have been adopted and that this might have mitigated the effects of the wars upon Rome herself. That was in 140, when the decision was taken to renew the war against Viriatus. Here again it is no surprise that Servilianus' treaty did not prove enduring, but it had been ratified and there was an obvious case for delaying resumption of the struggle until the Numantine war was finished. Resuming it at that particular time involved three or four more years of virtually inevitable fighting which had to be conducted simultaneously with the struggle against Numantia. It is possible that delay would have eased somewhat the strain upon Roman manpower and perhaps have avoided the crisis over the levy of 138. On the other hand, it does not necessarily follow that it would have been safe to reduce the size of the army in Further Spain even if the treaty had remained in force, and the potent political trends which manifested themselves in the dispute over the levy of 138 are apparent also in other events;[2] so it is by no means certain that the decision to renew the Viriatic war added very greatly to the deleterious consequences of the Spanish wars as a whole.

At no other time was there any possibility that greater moderation on the part of the Romans would reduce the duration of the Viriatic war. It has been observed earlier in this chapter that in general Roman policy was relatively moderate and that the military situation virtually precluded any settlement for the first seven years.[3] Once

---

[1] pp. 151 f.   [2] pp. 185 f.   [3] pp. 140 and 141 f.

fighting had been resumed in 140, the struggle against Viriatus and his immediate followers did not last very long and could not have been curtailed significantly. Even if Popillius had offered more lenient terms in 139, this would have made a difference of only a few months. Brutus perhaps engaged in more extensive warfare than was strictly necessary, but even so he cannot have prolonged hostilities by a great deal; and his co-operation in the attack on the Vaccaei, which seems to be the clearest instance, was an unauthorized venture which met with official disapproval.

Within the context of the Roman objectives, which in general could not have been other than they were, the reasons for the length of the wars were the difficulty of the terrain, the remarkable resilience of the enemy, and Rome's failure to apply her full potential strength quickly and consistently, a failure which manifested itself particularly in the mediocre performance of several commanders and in the consequent demoralization of the armies. This failure could have been rectified in two ways: first by a much more massive military effort; but that would have increased enormously the immediate strains imposed on man-power and resources, and thus might have done nothing to mitigate the repercussions of the wars; second, by much more efficient generalship, such as if the commanders throughout had been of the calibre of Metellus Macedonicus or Scipio Aemilianus; but that is equivalent to saying that the wars could have been shortened and the strains eased if Rome had had a totally different structure of government and military command, or alternatively if she had been unusually fortunate in the talents of the consuls of those years.

The conclusion stands then. Underlying the policies pursued in the Spanish wars were attitudes of mind which were largely taken for granted. Given these attitudes, together with the actual military situations, more moderate policies could not have been seriously contemplated; nor, within the established system, could anything else have been done which would have both shortened the wars and mitigated the strains they imposed upon Rome. It follows that responsibility for what happened cannot properly be attributed to any one political group or personality, and that it is misleading to single out Scipio Aemilianus in this respect. It is quite true that his character and career suggest that he will have approved entirely of the policies pursued; it is true that he was ruthless in his treatment of Numantia, and that he played a major role in the episode of the *foedus Mancinum*, or at least in determining what should be done about those who had taken the oaths. It is even conceivable that he often took the lead in pronouncing judgement on the situations and in formulating the decisions, though there is very little evidence for this. The point is that there is no reason to suppose that the decisions would have been different if he had been entirely silent. And that is so not merely because in practice he rarely enjoyed sufficient political strength to dominate the decisions of the Senate, but above all because in general no other decisions could have been regarded as realistic possibilities. Furthermore, it has been pointed out that the one significant decision to which there was a serious alternative was the abandonment of Servilianus' treaty in 140; yet in all likelihood this issue arose only after Scipio had left Rome on his embassy, and when the decision was taken he was probably in Egypt or Syria. Thus he cannot have been responsible for the forfeiture of this one possible opportunity to reduce the repercussions of the Spanish wars upon Roman politics and society.

Those repercussions took two main forms. There were first the increased social problems and tensions, resulting from the long and unprofitable drain upon resources. And one source of these tensions, discontent with the frequent levies for service in arduous and hazardous campaigns, focused attention and concern upon the increasing difficulty of raising adequate armies—a problem which arose primarily from an obsolete but deeply rooted method of recruiting. The repercussions manifested themselves secondly in the disputes and conflicts of the Roman aristocrats. Not only were the Spanish commands and the prize of victory the objects of ambition, but in these years the reverses in Spain provided a good proportion of the weapons with which the politicians belaboured each other and exacerbated their rivalries. And if these conflicts were not about the basic issues of foreign policy or the objectives of the wars themselves, no more were they all the opportunist exploitation of superficial misfortunes, though no doubt there was plenty of recrimination of that kind. The major conflicts arose out of substantial crises in the wars themselves, crises in which the emotion and self-interest of individuals were deeply involved but which also concerned the prestige and fortunes of the state.

It was not inevitable that the Spanish wars should make such an impact, or at least that it should be so profound: in 147 the Lusitanians might have accepted Vetilius' offer of resettlement; Viriatus might have died several years earlier than he did; the Numantines might have carried through the agreement of c. 142, instead of changing their minds at the last moment; or the Roman magisterial system might have produced a few more commanders of above-average ability. But none of these things occurred, and thus the long years of warfare, with all their consequences, were all but inevitable; for, given the predisposed attitudes of the Roman leaders and the institutional framework within which they were working, they had very few opportunities—probably only one—to take a decision which both seemed a serious alternative and might have mitigated the repercussions. And so the wars dragged on, complicating social problems, heightening tensions, exacerbating personal hostilities, and thereby contributing to the development of a major internal crisis.

XIII

SOCIAL AND ECONOMIC PROBLEMS

1. *Agrarian Changes and the Levy*

IN the middle years of the second century Rome was experiencing the increasing pressure of several social problems. It has always been recognized that deeply involved in these problems was the changing pattern of agriculture, characterized by the growth of large estates worked largely by slave labour. This was accompanied by a reduction in the demand for hired free labour and a steady decline in the number of peasant farmers; not only tenants but peasant proprietors were being dispossessed.[1] The origins of these trends lay in the great influx of wealth which had occurred since the Second Punic War. Much of this new wealth passed directly into private hands and was invested in land. At the same time the acquisition of numerous prisoners from large-scale foreign wars, together perhaps with easier access to the slave-trade of the eastern Mediterranean, had facilitated the supply of slave labour. In 146 the wealth of Carthage and of Corinth may have given new impetus to the trend, but

---

[1] The main accounts are App. *B.C.* 1. 7 f.; Plut. *Ti. Grac.* 8. 1 f.; cf. Livy, 42. 1. 6; 19. 1 f.; cf. Sall. *Bell. Iug.* 41. 7 f. Cato's *De Agri Cultura*, concerned with the operation of a farm of moderate size as an investment, takes it for granted that the permanent labour force will consist of slaves, supplemented by free labour hired only for special occasions, notably for harvesting. It is a reasonable assumption that many of the features of Sicilian agriculture indicated in Diod. 34/35. 2 (esp. 1 f., 27 f., 32, 34, 36, 38) were paralleled in parts of Italy; for similar brigandage by slave shepherds, as early as 185, cf. Livy, 39. 29. 9. Earl, *Tiberius Gracchus*, pp. 23 f., esp. pp. 29 f., attempting to minimize the extent and significance of these developments, points out that the term *latifundium* does not appear in Latin until the elder Pliny; but great extension of the boundaries of existing holdings was not necessarily the only form of expansion. Scullard, *JRS* 54 (1964), p. 199, rightly notes the possibility of investment in many medium-sized farms, such as Cato's model, and in the present chapter the term 'great estates' is to be understood to include such multiple holdings. In general see esp. Last, *CAH* ix, pp. 2 f.; McDonald, 'Rome and Italy', *CHJ* 6 (1939), pp. 124 f., esp. pp. 137 f. and 142 f.; Brunt, 'The Army and the Land', *JRS* 52 (1962), pp. 69 f. (who draws attention to the probable importance of tenant farming and to the connexion between military service and agricultural distress).

at most this will only have accelerated a process already sufficiently advanced to carry on under its own momentum; for by then the great estates must have been producing much surplus wealth which could be reinvested in yet further accretions of land.

*One consequence of these agricultural changes was that the employment of huge numbers of slaves, often in terrible conditions and with inadequate control, constituted a latent menace to public safety. There had been some disturbances early in the century,[1] and it would be surprising if the brigandage which developed in Sicily did not occur in Italy also. Nevertheless the dangers inherent in the situation were evidently not appreciated to the full until they were forcibly demonstrated by the great rebellion in Sicily, as well as by the lesser uprisings which followed in Athens, Delos, and Italy itself.[2] That such uprisings could in time be suppressed was obvious, but the need was to prevent them and their attendant horrors from occurring in the first place.

*The other general consequence of the growth of the great estates was that many peasants were dispossessed of their farms. The tenant farmer suffered from the direct economic competition of the new methods; the landowner often found it more profitable to work his land by slave labour than to lease it. Even the peasant proprietor may have suffered from economic competition, but in any case the development of the great estates can only have encouraged the abandonment of many small farms, partly because it provided a ready market for those who wished to sell, and partly as a result of the pressures which can be applied by powerful and grasping interests. At the same time the towns, and especially Rome itself, could offer a positive alternative to rural life;[3] for the influx of wealth had led to great public and private expenditure of money and thereby had created new opportunities for earning a livelihood, accompanied by the attractions of frequent free entertainments.

A further factor was hastening this whole process, and exacerbating the anxieties and distress of the peasant farmers. This was the system of military conscription, which was derived from, and was suited to, the local wars and rudimentary civil organization of

[1] Livy, 32. 26. 4 f.; 33. 36. 1 f.; 39. 29. 8 f.
[2] pp. 133 f.; cf. App. B.C. 1. 8 f.   [3] See further p. 165.

a much earlier period.[1] In theory the Roman army was a citizen militia: when an army was needed, citizens were conscripted at a formal levy. Those liable for conscription were all whose property was valued at or above a certain minimum figure, and this in effect ensured that the burden fell largely on the peasant farmer and his sons; and each man, until he reached the age of forty-six, was liable for conscription for up to a total of no less than sixteen years' service, plus an extra four in the event of grave emergency. But by the second century Rome's military needs were entirely different. Most wars were now far from home and necessitated the continuous employment of the same troops for several years, all the year round; a greater number of commitments demanded greater numbers of troops; and in some areas it was actually necessary to maintain standing armies.[2] In short, a high proportion of those selected in the levies were being conscripted into a spell of several years' uninterrupted professional service; and although there are some foreshadowings of the system tried in the later Republic, which made more use of long-term, volunteer professionals irrespective of property-classification, this had not yet developed very far.

The consequences of this state of affairs are obvious. Many a family dependent on a small farm must have been deprived of vital manpower for years on end; many a veteran must have returned to find serious neglect or an alarming accumulation of debt, and in a proportion of cases sale, and then probably migration to town or city, must have followed rapidly.[3] It was a situation which necessarily became steadily worse, for in the great majority of cases men who had lost their farms were no longer available for the levy; thus the

[1] The problems of recruitment which arose during the second century are examined further in section 3 of this chapter, pp. 167 f. In general see esp. Smith, *Service in the Post-Marian Roman Army*, ch. i.

[2] Afzelius, *Die römische Kriegsmacht*, pp. 34 f., esp. pp. 47 and 61, has traced the legions serving in the period 200–168. In those years the number of legions scarcely ever dropped below eight. Only about a quarter of the legions which were enrolled served for a single year; almost half served for three or more years. In Spain, where the personnel of the legions was changed gradually by means of *supplementa*, a period of about six years' service became standard: see p. 169 n. 3.

[3] The anecdote in Val. Max. 4. 4. 6 about Regulus seeking to return from Africa to repair the misfortunes of his estate, even if apocryphal and anachronistic, clearly illustrates what could happen. Cf. Sall. *Bell. Iug.* 41. 7 f.: *populus militia atque inopia urgebatur . . . interea parentes aut parvi liberi militum, uti quisque potentiori confinis erat, sedibus pellebantur.*

numbers liable to conscription tended to decline and a correspondingly heavier burden lay upon those who remained. In the early
decades of the second century this process was masked by other
factors, notably by the settling of *proletarii* in colonies as *adsidui*, liable
to military service; by the extension of citizenship to a number of
communities; and probably by a natural recovery of the population
level after the massive losses of the Second Punic War. Then after
168 there ensued a long period when military demands were relatively light, so much so that the desire to give more men battle-
experience could be spoken of as a serious reason for undertaking the
Dalmatian war of 156.[1] Hence in these years, although a net decline
in the number of *adsidui* was now a reality, there was probably no
great difficulty in raising the troops required, with the result that the
trend did not force itself upon people's attention.[2] But a new phase
began with the Dalmatian war. From 156 onwards Rome was continuously at war, often engaged in three or even four wars at once,
much of the fighting being both difficult and costly; the acquisition
of Macedonia imposed a new permanent commitment; between 154
and 132 there was only one short interval, of only two or three
years, in which there was no war in distant Spain, where men
served for six years on end; and for at least twelve years Rome was
waging war in both Spanish provinces at the same time. It is not
hard to envisage the impact of all this upon the class liable for conscription, or what it meant in terms of the decline in the numbers
of small-holders, which by about 140 was evidently accelerating
drastically.[3]

It is not to be thought that all dispossessed peasants and rural poor
automatically migrated to Rome, but there is little doubt that for
many years past significant numbers had found relief in this way, and
at various times the wealth expended in the city may even have made
it a positive attraction.[4] But now, at the very time when the pressures on the peasant farmers were so great and dispossession was

[1] Polyb. 32. 13. 6 f.

[2] p. 168; Appendix XII. In the light of the figures for 200–168 (cf. p. 163 n. 2), Smith,
Service in the Post-Marian Roman Army, p. 3, supposes that after 168 Rome's minimum
permanent requirement was 8+ legions (= *c.* 42,000 citizens); but this is probably true only
from the later 150's onwards. In the interval it is unlikely that this number was needed often,
and is conceivable that at times only four may have been required.

[3] pp. 337 f.   [4] p. 165.

probably increasingly common, the city failed to supply this alternative. For, as will appear shortly, from about 140 increasing
financial stringency and other factors were creating a serious urban
crisis. If the experiences of the past still led some to move to the city,
they will have found growing distress and poor prospects for themselves. Thus the urban crisis itself contributed to the hardships of the
rural poor.

2. The Urban Crisis

The social developments which followed the Second Punic War
were not confined to the rural areas. Rome itself was changing. The
expenditure of the new wealth which flowed in from the provinces
and from foreign wars enabled it to support a growing urban
population. Part of this increase was provided by an influx of rural
poor, who found an alternative source of livelihood in the expanding
building trade, the developing import and retail services, and in the
manufacture of tools, equipment, and domestic utensils.[1] As early as
187 the Latin allies were complaining of the numbers of their citizens
who had migrated to Rome, and all who had done so since 204 were
sent home; yet in 177 the same complaint was heard again, and new
action was needed.[2] It is true that the Latins may have been attracted
in part by the prospect of acquiring full Roman citizenship; but the
migration of many thousands of them presupposes that there was
a living to be made; and if this was so for Latins, the opportunity was
there also for Roman citizens. In 179 a need was felt for a new
aqueduct, and although the project could not be completed on that
occasion, the fact and the manner of the construction of the aqua
Marcia in 144–140, followed after only fifteen years by the Tepula,[3]
strongly suggest a substantial increase in population.[4]

[1] Cf. Frank, *Economic Survey*, i, pp. 175 f.; note also that for many of the items listed in
De Agr. Cult. 135 Cato recommends the purchase of those manufactured at Rome, and for
the remainder he mentions various other towns.

[2] Livy, 39. 3. 4 f.; 41. 8. 6 f.

[3] pp. 108 f. Tepula: Frontin. *De Aquis*, 1. 8. 1.

[4] Brunt, 'The Army and the Land', *JRS* 52 (1962), pp. 69 f., writing principally about the
first century but with some reference to the pre-Gracchan period, expresses doubts about the
generally accepted hypothesis of a substantial drift into Rome, but he perhaps under-
estimates the opportunities for free persons to make some sort of livelihood in the rapidly
expanding city of the second century. Although conditions may often have been attractive
only in contrast with destitution in the countryside, that would have been enough to

As the urban masses grew in number, so the means of maintaining them became more complex, and hence more vulnerable to recession or other changes of economic fortune. Such changes did occur during the 130's.[1] In the later 140's the wealth which had come from Carthage, Macedonia, and Corinth had been spent freely upon expensive projects, above all upon the costly aqua Marcia. But none of this money was brought back to the treasury by means of taxes, and the reserves were being rapidly reduced. At the same time Rome was engaged in two Spanish wars which, so far from being profitable, were almost certainly a serious financial drain.

These wars dragged on for year after year, and the outbreak of the Sicilian slave rebellion, around 136, will have created even greater demands. At the end of 135 or early in 134, when Scipio was about to assume the command against Numantia, the Senate refused to provide him with any cash from the treasury, allocating instead certain revenues which were still to be collected.[2] However much this decision may have been influenced by jealousy and spite, the formal excuse can only have been that the reserves were insufficient and could not be substantially reduced, so that Scipio must await future income. In other words it clearly implies that the reserves were, at best, comparatively low. Under these circumstances there can only have been a substantial curtailment of public expenditure within the city during the 130's, contrasting markedly with the lavish spending of the immediately preceding years. Opportunities for employment were reduced, which in turn created a recession in the trades and cut the doubtless already meagre incomes of many. Large numbers probably became dependent upon the charitable distributions of the great houses and upon casual work in the countryside, available chiefly at harvest-time. This would have been serious enough in itself, but it so happened that it coincided with other grave difficulties.

Already in the early months of 138, Rome was experiencing a

produce a significant drift. For Brunt's opinion that the supporters of Tiberius Gracchus were mostly rural, see Additional Note M, p. 345. None of this is to deny Brunt's contention that very large numbers remained in the countryside.

[1] Cf. Boren, 'The Urban Side of the Gracchan Economic Crisis', *AHR* 63 (1958), pp. 890 f.

[2] 'Plut.' *Apophth. Scip. Min.* 15 = Appendix II, no. 32.

serious and worsening shortage of corn, which inevitably meant higher prices. It was now that one of the tribunes, C. Curiatius, summoned the consuls, Scipio Nasica Serapio and D. Iunius Brutus, to a *contio* at which he urged them to propose to the Senate that the state should purchase corn through the agency of special *legati*; and when Nasica attempted to argue against the plan, the crowd roared its anger and discontent.[1] Probably the situation improved later in 138, but around 136 a new crisis was created by the slave rebellion in Sicily, the island whose exports of grain to Rome were so great that Cato had called it 'the nation's storehouse, the nurse at whose breast the Roman people is fed'.[2] Even if it were possible to make up the volume of grain with imports from elsewhere, a drastic rise in prices was bound to occur. And the rebellion was not brought under control for several years. It so happens that there is no record of any manifestation of popular discontent over the grain supply in these years (that is, after 138), but the available sources are such that this silence proves only that there was no shattering eruption. This protracted grain crisis coincided with a phase of financial stringency and recession. It is of immense importance that by the end of 134 large sections of the urban population were suffering severe hardship, with considerable numbers perhaps actually threatened with death by starvation, and that the mood of many must have passed beyond discontent to wretched despair.

3. Recruitment and Man-power

From 151 onwards Rome frequently experienced difficulty in recruiting troops. In 151 itself grave disputes led to the incarceration of the consuls and the use of sortition in the levy; in 145 Fabius Maximus Aemilianus was able to recruit only men with no previous experience; in 140 Appius Claudius initiated his decree that there should be only one levy in the year; in 138 deserters from the Spanish army were severely punished as a public example, and further disturbances concerning the levy again led to the incarceration of the consuls; in 134 Scipio Aemilianus was refused permission to hold a levy, on the

[1] pp. 129 f.
[2] Cic. *Verr.* 2. 2. 5. For the rebellion see pp. 133 f. Interference with grain production was inevitable; cf. Cic. *Verr.* 2. 3. 125 for loss of crops.

ground that Italy would have been stripped of men;[1] and the diffi-culty of finding sufficient recruits is explicitly attested as a factor underlying Tiberius Gracchus' proposals in 133.[2]

The problem did not make a sudden and unheralded appearance in 151. There are occasional signs of difficulties in earlier years,[3] and particularly in 169,[4] when the Third Macedonian War was absorbing large numbers of men in campaigns that were proving to be far from easy. Nevertheless, the problem was now much more serious; indeed, the frequent indications between 151 and 133 strongly suggest that it was becoming acute, whereas the evidence for earlier years does not. Even in 169 the difficulty was overcome quickly by the applica-tion of greater energy and efficiency;[5] and neither then nor at other times do we hear of disorder and tribunician intervention such as occurred in 151 and 138.

It is obvious that a large part of the trouble lay in the reluctance of men to be conscripted, and one reason for that reluctance was cer-tainly the arduous, unprofitable, and dangerous character of the warfare. It is significant that in 171 and 150–149, when the Third Macedonian and Third Punic wars respectively seemed to promise easy campaigns with much booty, there were numerous volunteers.[6] But service in Spain was a different matter; it was not for nothing that the Celtiberian war of 154–151 became known as the 'fiery war',[7] and the later struggles were similarly characterized by great hardships and heavy casualties. The hope of considerable booty might still have been a palliative for conscription, but Spain could no longer offer even this. The campaigns were against the compara-tively poor highland and inland communities, already bled of much of their resources by long wars with Rome. In 151 Lucullus was seriously disappointed in his hopes of rich plunder, and in 132 all that

---

[1] For these events see pp. 42, 103, 126, 130, and 136. Probably the list should include also the attempt by Claudius Asellus to veto the departure of Q. Caepio in 140 (pp. 126 f.), which may be explained very plausibly as an attempt to prevent recruits being taken to Spain.

[2] App. *B.C.* 1. 7 f., esp. 11; cf. 1. 27; Plut. *Ti. Grac.* 8. 4.

[3] Livy, 34. 56. 9 (193 B.C.); 36. 3. 4 f. (191); 39. 29. 10 (185); 40. 36. 13 f. (180); 42. 10. 12 f., cf. 18. 6 (172). In several of these instances special circumstances may have been operative, as the pestilence of 182–180, and it would be unwise to infer that the recruiting problem became general and serious very early in the century.

[4] Livy, 43. 14. 2 f.   [5] Livy, 43. 14. 3 f. and esp. 15. 1.

[6] Livy, 42. 32. 6; App. *Lib.* 75.   [7] Polyb. 35. 1; Diod. 31. 40.

Scipio could offer as a donative to the troops who had destroyed Numantia was the meagre sum of seven *denarii* each.[1]

Another reason for the reluctance evident at the levy was the period of service for which men were conscripted. In the majority of cases this was several years, often as many as six.[2] For this the nature and location of the wars were in part responsible, and here again Spain is outstanding. It would have been military and economic nonsense to send large numbers of troops to Spain and then replace them after only one or two years, and there was a natural desire to keep experienced troops as long as possible. In practice six years seems to have become the standard term of service in this theatre.[3] Yet these men were recruited under a system designed to raise armies for short local wars and very little adapted to the new conditions. They were still treated as a citizen militia; a contribution towards the cost of equipment and food was deducted from their not very substantial pay;[4] and no regular provision was made for them upon discharge. In earlier times the peasant had returned to his farm after an absence of a few months, or possibly only a few weeks; but these men were away for years on end, at a time when the pressures upon the peasant farmer were in any case great and the threat of dispossession very real. Nor was that all; there was yet a further consequence of the citizen militia concept. Discharge at the end of a term of service, even of six years in Spain, did not confer immunity from the levy. Each man might be selected again, for a total of up to sixteen years, until he reached the age of forty-six; and even then he could be called upon for a further four years in the event of grave emergency.

---

[1] Lucullus: App. *Iber.* 54; Scipio: Plin. *Nat. Hist.* 33. 141.

[2] p. 163 n. 2.

[3] App. *Iber.* 78. Smith, *Service in the Post-Marian Roman Army*, p. 7 n. 4, thinks that this passage implies that 'six years was an unusually long period of continuous overseas service in Spain with continuous fighting'. The passage might mean this, but equally well it could mean that men who had served for six years had completed the standard period of continuous service in Spain. Two items confirm the latter interpretation. First, Smith himself, op. cit., p. 6, has deduced from the figures for *supplementa* for Spain from 195 to 168 that the average period of service was 6/7 years. Second, in 180, when troops in Spain were said to be threatening mutiny if they were not discharged, the compromise settlement included the discharge of all who had served in Spain for more than six years continuously: Livy, 40. 36. 10, cf. 40. 35. 6 f., 10 f. The dispute of 180 illustrates the pressure to retain experienced troops; cf. also Livy, 39. 38. 5 f. for a similar dispute in 184.

[4] Polyb. 6. 39. 15; cf. Plut. *C. Grac.* 5. 1.

And not only were veterans liable to recall, but there was a strong incentive for the officials who were conducting the levy to prefer such men, since there were obvious attractions in having a good proportion of trained and experienced soldiers among the recruits. Moreover, after 164 the numbers of the *adsidui*, the class liable for conscription, were in general declining, and that in turn increased the chances both of initial selection and of subsequent recall.[1]

These were powerful reasons for discontent with the levy, and they can be discerned at work in the difficulties which arose. In 151 fear of the 'fiery war' in Celtiberia is alleged to have reached paralysing proportions, and the lot was used to determine which of the recruits should enjoy less burdensome service—and probably also shorter service, though this is not stated. But in addition the claim of the tribunes to prevent the levying of certain individuals suggests very strongly an attempt to protect those who were in especial difficulties as a result of previous service.[2] In 145 both the possibility and the unpopularity of early recall were recognized in the exemption from the levy of that year of all who had served recently in Africa, Macedonia, and Greece; the result was an army of tiros which considerably handicapped the operations of Fabius Maximus Aemilianus, or so it was alleged.[3] The issue of recall was probably central also in the disputed levy of 138, since the tribunes who intervened made demands similar to those of 151. Immediately after this levy the unpopularity of service in Spain led to the public chastisement, in the presence of the recruits, of deserters from the Spanish armies.[4] One final testimony to the discontent is that Tiberius Gracchus is alleged to have proposed, and someone shortly afterwards certainly enacted, a reduction of the total period of service for which a man might be conscripted.[5]

There was also, however, a further element in the situation: a shortage of man-power and an actual decline in the numbers of recruits available. This is not to be understood in the sense that it was ever actually impossible to find the number of recruits desired, nor was the total citizen population necessarily insufficient to support

[1] Appendix XII; cf. below.
[2] pp. 42 f.   [3] p. 103.   [4] p. 130.
[5] Plut. *Ti. Grac.* 16. 1; Ascon., p. 60 C.; Smith, *Service in the Post-Marian Roman Army*, pp. 8 f.

armies of the size required; but there certainly was a shortage in the sense that the class of peasant farmers could meet the demands made upon it only at the cost of great hardship and suffering. Furthermore, there were evidently fears that if a really great crisis occurred the number of recruits available might actually prove insufficient, and certainly that this situation might soon arise if the number of *adsidui* continued to decline. With much justice it might be said that the fundamental problem was not one of man-power but one of an antiquated and inadequate method of recruiting armies; but there is a real sense in which there was a shortage, and a growing shortage, of man-power in that section of the population from which the Roman armies of this period were in fact recruited—and that is how the Romans themselves viewed the problem.

The decline in numbers could scarcely be overlooked, since it was revealed by the census statistics, and was especially apparent in the figures for 136;[1] but also there is positive evidence that the man-power problem was recognized and was the subject of genuine concern. In 131, for example, Metellus Macedonicus as censor harangued the assembled people on the subject of increasing the birth-rate. Emphasizing that the safety of all was at stake, he exhorted men to marry for the purpose of begetting children, and he even went so far as to advocate compulsory marriage for that end.[2] Earlier, in 142, Scipio Aemilianus himself had attacked those who used adoption in order to obtain privileges pertaining to parenthood.[3] In 140 Appius Claudius introduced his proposal that there should be only one levy in the year, which, whatever the underlying motives, implies a recognition that resources were limited.[4] In that same year, or perhaps in 145, Laelius put forward his abortive proposal which our source explicitly designates as an attempt to combat a decline in the free population.[5] In 134 came the refusal of the Senate to allow Scipio to hold a levy, on the ground that Italy would have been stripped of men; and although this decision is likely to have been much influenced both by political jealousy and by fear of slave uprisings, it plainly presupposes a known shortage of potential recruits.[6] The

---

[1] Appendix XII.
[2] p. 237.
[3] Appendix II, no. 16, discussed in Appendix IX.
[4] p. 126.
[5] Plut. *Ti. Grac.* 8. 4 f.; Appendix VII.
[6] p. 136.

legislation of Tiberius Gracchus is stated by both the main sources to have been linked with the shortage of men for the army.[1] Finally, a decade later a law of Gaius Gracchus forbade the enlistment of persons under seventeen years of age;[2] armies do not enlist boys when they can find men.

The recruiting problem was not solved for another generation. The long delay is not inexplicable. No doubt one reason was in-grained conservatism, an inability to visualize the need for a complete break with the traditional system. Yet there may have been more rational causes as well. There was perhaps real difficulty in envisaging a full distinction between the soldier and the civilian: in the military state there was the tight hold of the concept of the army as the people in arms. It is even possible that there was a conscious unwillingness to create a situation in which, as a result of reliance upon long-term professionals, large sections of the male population might never be practised in arms. However that may be, the solution was not delayed because senators were unaware of the problem; awareness of it is one of the great political factors of the period. Metellus Macedonicus was not a lonely voice crying in the wilderness, even if his advocacy of compulsory marriage was a purely personal idiosyncrasy. Rome, with her highly developed military institutions, her extensive use of conscription, her insistence on military service as a prerequisite for state office, her emphasis on the military functions of her highest officials, her public triumphs, her huge conquests, and her great struggles against Carthage and the Hellenistic powers, was self-consciously a military state. The governing aristocracy as a whole was fully aware of the man-power problem, and few can have lacked real concern.

4. Tensions and Trends

It is evident that the social problems which are the subject of this chapter were all becoming increasingly pressing during the 130's. Serious tensions were developing simultaneously in several sections of the community. The class liable for conscription, the rural poor, and the urban masses were all gravely discontented, for different

[1] p. 168.   [2] Plut. C. Grac. 5. 1.

reasons but at the same time. Ominously, the early months of 138 saw both a major dispute over the levy and the controversy about the grain supply, with its outcry against Nasica. This conjunction is given further emphasis by the fact that the same tribune, Curiatius, led the public agitation on both issues.[1] The discontent and the problems from which it sprang were immediate and evident to all; and, whether or not the fact was fully discerned by the politicians of the day, whose military traditions perhaps directed their attention above all to the problem of maintaining military power, this accumulation of tensions constituted a potential threat to stability and to the existing pattern of political life.

Furthermore, these tensions were among the factors which encouraged certain more general trends in political attitudes and behaviour. Since the levies were all authorized and ordered by the Senate, the resentment and discontent which they aroused in these years contributed substantially to the undermining of the moral authority of that body, to the increasing readiness to challenge, oppose, and circumvent its will. Linked with the crumbling of a psychological barrier was the readiness of tribunes to interfere in the levy. This certainly happened in 151 and 138; and when in 140 Ti. Claudius Asellus attempted to veto the departure of the consul Caepio it is very likely, though unattested, that his intention was to prevent the departure of troops for Spain.[2] To what extent factional animosities and other ulterior motives lay behind these tribunician interventions cannot possibly be determined, but in any case this is in a sense a minor question. The main point is that the difficulties and the discontent encouraged tribunician intervention against the wishes of the majority in the Senate. Moreover, both in 151 and in 138 the tribunes went so far as to impose their veto in order to obtain the concessions they were demanding; and in order to enforce the veto they even fined and imprisoned the consuls. Tribunes were thus encouraged to go to great lengths in their conflicts with other authorities; and this in turn encouraged another trend, another changing attitude. For it was possible for military leaders to take the view that when tribunes interfered in this manner with the levy they were in serious conflict with the fundamental interests of the state; and

[1] pp. 129 f.   [2] pp. 42 f., 126 f., and 130.

that in turn contributed to the growth of the idea that it was desirable
to find some way of overriding or circumventing the tribunician
veto. It is no accident that the issue of the levy was involved in
at least two, and probably in three, of the four known attempts to
override the veto which occurred between 151 and 134.[1]

[1] Three if Asellus' veto in 140 is so interpreted (above).

XIV

POLITICAL STRUGGLES AND POLITICAL METHODS

1. *Fluctuations in Fortune*

SCIPIO's censorship, it will be recalled, had not been the brilliant success for which he had hoped. In addition to the frustrations created by his unco-operative colleague, he suffered a major disappointment when Laelius was defeated by Q. Pompeius in the election for the consulship of 141; and the general trend of events in the early months of 141 seemed unfavourable.[1] Later in the year, however, the outlook improved. In Further Spain Fabius Maximus Servilianus had recovered from his set-back and was making steady if not spectacular progress; in Hither Spain Pompeius, already in difficulties, was perhaps not going to win an easy triumph after all; and at the consular elections the successful candidates were Laelius and the third of the Servilii brothers, Q. Caepio.[2] The election of Laelius in particular was a source of personal pleasure for Scipio; there were immediate practical advantages in having both consuls well-disposed; and for the future Laelius' political acumen and Caepio's social influence would each gain added value from their status as consulars. All this was a welcome prelude to another struggle, the prosecution of Scipio, early in 140, by Ti. Claudius Asellus.[3]

Several important details of this trial are unknown. There is no record of who, apart from the two principal antagonists, spoke either for the prosecution or for the defence; there is no record of the formal charge; it is not known whether there was or was not a direct relationship between the formal charge and Asellus' allegation that the censorial *lustrum* was evil and accursed, *malum infelixque*;[4] nor is

---

[1] Ch. X, esp. pp. 123 f.   [2] pp. 125 f.   [3] p. 127.
[4] Cic. *De Orat.* 2. 268 = Appendix II, no. 28; Gell. 4. 17. 1 = Lucil. 394 f. M.

there any indication of the misfortunes which lay behind the accusation of *infelicitas*,[1] nor yet of the fault by which Scipio was supposed to have brought this about. On the other hand several important facts are clear: the case was tried by the People and, since the proposed penalty was a fine, it can be inferred that they assembled by tribes in the *concilium plebis*; presumably as a gesture of contempt for both prosecutor and charge, Scipio did not adopt the unshaven, unkempt appearance customary for defendants;[2] two extracts from speeches and a devastating witticism show Scipio striking back at Asellus with accusations of spendthrift extravagance and depravity, perfidy, and irresponsibility;[3] the issue was fought hard, for Scipio delivered several speeches against Asellus;[4] and finally, though it is nowhere stated explicitly, it is certain that Scipio was acquitted.

The prosecution was a manifestation of a personal feud: Asellus was bent on revenge for Scipio's attempt to humiliate him during the censorship. But it could not avoid being much more than this, being in fact a full-scale trial of political strength. Neither Scipio nor his enemies could be unmindful of the way in which the public career of the elder Africanus had been brought to an ignominious end. Now the second Africanus was being attacked in a similar manner and at a crucial point; for if a tribal assembly, where Scipio's outstanding prestige and popular appeal might be expected to be at their most effective, could be induced to vote for his condemnation, the blow would be virtually irreparable—quite apart from the crippling financial consequences of a heavy fine. To secure the necessary votes Asellus doubtless looked in part to the *clientelae* and influence of numbers of leading senators, not least Ap. Claudius Pulcher. Probably he hoped also that Scipio's prestige and popularity had been diminished not only by the passage of years since the victory over Carthage but also by his attempt to conduct a severe censorship and by his comparatively unsuccessful tenure of that office. But in addition Asellus set out positively to undermine Scipio's popularity,

[1] Possibly there is some connexion with the plague attested for 142: Oros. 5. 4. 8 f.; Obsequ. 22.

[2] Gell. 3. 4. 1; 6. 11. 9 = Appendix II, no. 26.

[3] Appendix II, nos. 26, 27, and 28; no. 22, with the insulting implication that Asellus was stupid, is usually associated with the trial but more probably belongs during the censorship.

[4] Cf. Appendix II, no. 27 and comment.

asserting that recent misfortunes were of supernatural origin and had been provoked by Scipio. In the event the attempt failed; and any damage done by Asellus' attacks may well have been compensated by the focusing of attention upon Scipio's personality and achievements, now capped by the formal approval of a majority of voters. The new Africanus was not yet vulnerable to attacks of this kind.

Within a few months, or possibly even a few weeks, of his acquittal Scipio set off on his embassy to the countries of the eastern Mediterranean.[1] His appointment to lead this embassy was in itself a notable success. It is true that the Hellenistic world, and especially Syria and Egypt, had been unsettled in recent years, so that there was need of investigation and diplomatic action; true also that multiple-purpose embassies were quite common. But an embassy of such remarkably wide scope, though not unprecedented, was certainly very unusual, and had to be given considerable authority and discretion in its actions. Perhaps many senators were ready to support the idea as a means of removing Scipio from the political scene for a considerable time, but none the less he himself must have been anxious to go. The Hellenistic world, especially Alexandria, Pergamum, and Athens, held many attractions for a man of Scipio's tastes, and in addition the embassy offered him an opportunity to inform himself about a wide range of problems and to exercise a considerable influence on Roman policy. There is no reason to doubt that all the personal and the official purposes of the embassy were fulfilled, or that it was entirely successful; and, if details are few and the extent of the influence which accrued to Scipio cannot be properly estimated, it is suggestive that both Attalus III of Pergamum and the Seleucid Antiochus VII seem to have felt themselves under obligation to him.[2] During the next few years, when in certain other respects his rivals were in the ascendant, he probably had an authoritative share in the formulation of policies and decisions concerning the Hellenistic world, relatively uncontroversial though these may have been.

It is not difficult to discover events between the spring of 140 and the later months of 137 which may be reckoned as reverses for Scipio or alternatively as successes or assets for his rivals. Of the six consuls of 139–137 only one, Scipio Nasica Serapio in 138, is likely

---

[1] pp. 127 and 138 f.   [2] Antiochus: p. 127 n. 3; Attalus: p. 138.

to have been well disposed; the other five were all either certainly or very probably hostile.[1] In 140, probably even before Scipio left Rome, there occurred the episode in which the consul Caepio successfully defied Asellus' attempt to veto his departure for Spain— a Pyrrhic victory which is far more likely to have aroused enthusiasm for Asellus than for Caepio and his friends. Q. Fabius Maximus Servilianus' treaty which temporarily halted the war with Viriatus was plainly the product of defeat and was soon nullified and castigated as shameful. Appius Claudius' opposition to a second levy, whatever his motive, was bound to win him much popular support; similarly the inauguration of the new aqueduct must have added to the popularity of Q. Marcius Rex and of those who had supported him, including M. Aemilius Lepidus.[2] In 138 the failure of the attempt to prosecute Q. Pompeius was certainly a disappointment for Scipio, whoever may have initiated the prosecution; worse, and undoubtedly a humiliation for Scipio, his own prosecution of Aurelius Cotta failed after numerous rehearings; and the consul Scipio Nasica, ever tactless, clashed fiercely with tribunes on the two delicate issues of the levy and the corn supply, in the process getting himself temporarily imprisoned, provoking one attested public outcry against himself and assuredly others as well, and into the bargain acquiring an unedifying nickname.[3]

Naturally not all the reverses were on one side. In 139 the majority in the Senate sharply rebuffed Q. Pompeius by preferring the Numantine account of his negotiations to his own;[4] and in 138 the consul Brutus was as much involved as his colleague Nasica in the disputes concerning the levy. Likewise there were a few positive successes for Scipio in this same period. The *lex Gabinia* of 139 which introduced the ballot may have been one such, though the political associations of Gabinius are too uncertain for this to be asserted with

---

[1] But the election of men ill-disposed towards Scipio does not always mean that men closely associated with him were defeated. No close-knit faction could have put forward two fully qualified candidates each year. For the consular and censorial posts of 139–133 Scipio must have given support to some other friendly candidates besides the four who were successful (Nasica, the consuls of 136, and Scipio himself), but there is no indication of whom he supported or on what occasions.

[2] For these events of 140 see pp. 126 f.; note that this was perhaps also the year of the failure of Laelius' plan for reform.

[3] pp. 129 f.   [4] p. 128.

confidence.[1] In the same year Q. Servilius Caepio virtually ended the Viriatic war, though the assassination of Viriatus himself, which was the key to Caepio's victory, left the way open for derogatory remarks about his unworthy methods.[2] The election of Nasica to the consulship was another success, even if his performance in the office did lead to disputes. And in 137 there was the *lex Cassia*, which extended the ballot to most popular trials, and was probably a response to the adverse judgements of the previous year. Scipio supported this and may have been ultimately responsible for it. In the struggle he showed himself powerful enough both to induce the tribune Antius to withdraw his veto and, together with the austere but popular Cassius, to carry the assembly against strong opposition, probably from a majority of senators, led by the consul M. Aemilius Lepidus.[3]

In the later months of 137 the news of Mancinus' defeat and his treaty with the Numantines loosed a massive political storm[4] and ushered in a short period of exceptional success for Scipio. Two of his associates secured the consulships of 136, and one of them, his intimate friend Furius Philus, held an inquiry into the affair, with Scipio and Laelius in his *consilium*; subsequently it was under Furius' supervision that Mancinus was offered to the Numantines. Scipio himself seems to have emerged as the dominating figure in the crisis, powerful enough to have had a major influence upon the decisions taken and especially upon the decision that Mancinus' fate should not be shared by his staff, among them his quaestor Tiberius Gracchus.[5] How far Scipio controlled the subsequent affair of Lepidus it is impossible to say, but at the least the recall and prosecution of the recalcitrant proconsul will have given him a great deal of satisfaction.[6] Nevertheless, despite the personal triumph of being elected to the consulship of 134, these successes were limited. Even in the midst of the Mancinus affair the attempt to embroil Pompeius failed. The censors elected in 136 were Ap. Claudius Pulcher and Q. Fulvius Nobilior; and Fulvius proceeded to nominate Claudius as Princeps Senatus. The five men who, in addition to Scipio himself, were elected to the consulships of 135–133 are all to be reckoned among his opponents; even his own success was marred by the election of

[1] p. 128.   [2] pp. 83 and 127.   [3] pp. 130 f.   [4] pp. 131 f.
[5] Cf. Plut. *Ti. Grac.* 7. 3 f.; Cic. *Rep.* 3. 28.   [6] p. 133.

a Fulvius as his colleague. In the Senate the proportion of friendly consulars declined seriously in the 130's; and the jealousy and ill will felt towards him by the majority in that body found expression in 134 in the refusal of funds and reinforcements for his Numantine campaign.[1] Furthermore, while Scipio himself met with these various reverses, his leading opponents were doing well, at least in the centuriate elections. Not only did Claudius obtain the censorship and become Princeps Senatus, but he had a Fulvius as his colleague and in each of the following three years secured the election of a political ally to the consulship: in 135 Ser. Fulvius Flaccus, in 134 C. Fulvius Flaccus (very possibly brother of his predecessor; both were Q. f.), and in 133 P. Mucius Scaevola. This remarkable success for Claudius and his associates, and for the Fulvii in particular, is matched by the achievements of the Calpurnii Pisones. They were a fairly 'new' family, whose first consul held office in 180 and the second in 148, but who now secured consulships in 139, 135, and 133. It has been suggested that the Calpurnii were closely linked with, indeed were protégés of, the Claudii and Fulvii. If this were so, the success of the 'Claudians' in 135–133 would be astonishing, for they would have held every consulship except the place won by Scipio himself. It is more likely, however, that in this generation the Calpurnii were not so closely associated with the Claudii and Fulvii but looked elsewhere for intimate allies, probably to the Postumii. That, of course, does not exclude the possibility that there was some co-operation in order to defeat friends and protégés of Scipio; for the Calpurnii were no friends of the new Africanus.[2]

There were, then, marked fluctuations in political fortune between 140 and 134, and the known events, together with the consular *fasti*, indicate that for much of the time, though not for all of it, the balance of advantage was tilted against Scipio. It is a safe hypothesis for these years, as it was seen to be for the later 140's, that one broad factor of great importance in these fluctuations was the extent to which other politicians were prepared to co-operate with each other against Scipio. It has been observed elsewhere that the pattern of politics was certainly not that of a simple confrontation between a 'Scipionic' group and a single, monolithic 'anti-Scipionic' group. It

[1] p. 136.   [2] pp. 95 and 316 f.

was at once much more complex and much more fluid than that.[1]
But so long as the new Africanus, ambitious, proud, and thrustful,
remained a powerful force, there was the possibility that other political leaders and groups might often co-operate specifically to thwart
him; and the degree to which they achieved such co-operation
was bound to have a substantial effect upon his fortunes. In this
respect it is very suggestive that the short phase in which Scipio
seems to have had the greatest success and to have exercised the
greatest influence, especially in the Senate, was during the dispute
about the *foedus Mancinum.* For this was an issue calculated both to
arouse passions and to divide Scipio's opponents. Clearly many who
did not have close links with Scipio or who were actively hostile
shared the view that Mancinus' treaty should be repudiated. There is
reason to think that Metellus Macedonicus, who by this time had
broken with Scipio, was one such, and Q. Pompeius another;[2] indeed
the fact that Mancinus charged Pompeius with the fundamental
blame for the defeat shows both that there was a breach between
them and how it was widened. Under these circumstances it is not
surprising that Scipio and his friends should have taken the lead. He
was certainly not encumbered by friendship or obligation towards
Mancinus, and the involvement of his kinsman Tiberius Gracchus
was no great handicap: a way could easily be found to exculpate
Gracchus and lay all the responsibility upon Mancinus; and if Gracchus had already married the daughter of Appius Claudius,[3] Scipio
would have had little compunction about humbling him, provided
that the disgrace was not so great as to reflect upon the whole family.
And who more fitted to pronounce upon the military inexpediency
and the national dishonour of the treaty than the conqueror of
Carthage?

And so for a short time Scipio dominated the scene. When it was
evident that the consuls elected for 136 would have the responsibility
of handling the problem, two of his associates won the contest—

[1] pp. 95 f. Also the successful moves against Mancinus and Lepidus, both opponents of
Scipio, are intelligible only on the hypothesis of a moderately fluid pattern.

[2] Despite their personal hostility towards himself and each other Furius took them as
legati to Spain, presumably to witness that the exposure of Mancinus was carried out
properly: Dio, fgt. 82; Val. Max. 3. 7. 5.

[3] pp. 319 f.

a success unique in the 130's; and so he and Laelius could assist in the inquiry conducted by Furius; hence he was credited with helping to save Mancinus' staff and blamed for not saving Mancinus himself.[1] But as soon as the immediate crisis was over the elections, as we have seen, once more began to go against Scipio. Doubtless there remained a legacy of ill will among those who had been deeply involved, but as a live dispute the affair rapidly degenerated into a technical legal discussion of whether Mancinus had forfeited his citizenship or was entitled to *postliminium*.[2] If the advocates of the treaty had every reason to feel anger towards Scipio, those who had sided with him on this one issue had no reason to continue to support him. In short, his successes, springing from an intense but ephemeral crisis, did not repair his real political weaknesses. As in the years immediately following his triumph, his rivals, potential or active, continued to be more numerous than his reliable allies, and to dispose of greater *clientelae* than he could command. Hence, so long as dislike and jealousy impelled a moderate degree of co-operation against him, he was at a constant disadvantage in the Senate and in the *comitia centuriata*.

There is, however, another aspect of this essential continuity in the fundamentals of Scipio's political position from 145 to 134. This is his continued ability to win and exploit popular favour. There must be the strongest suspicion that the two ballot laws, of 139 and 137, were a conscious attempt to enhance the importance of this factor; and, whether or not Scipio had any connexion with the *lex Gabinia*, he played a major part in securing the passage of the *lex Cassia*. Furthermore, the very fact that this law was carried against the powerful opposition of *principes*, led by a consul, and probably against the wishes of a majority of senators, emphasizes the value of popular support as a political asset.[3] The same factor can be seen at work in 140, in Claudius Asellus' deliberate attempt to undermine Scipio's popularity by playing upon superstitious fears and prejudices; and it is significant that the attempt failed.[4] But the really far-reaching importance of this factor, its enormous potential as a political weapon, was brought to the fore by Scipio's second consulship and his appointment to the command against Numantia.[5]

[1] Cic. *Rep.* 3. 28; Plut. *Ti. Grac.* 7. 3 f.   [2] p. 133.
[3] p. 131.   [4] p. 175 n. 4.   [5] p. 135, with refs. in n. 5.

Before Scipio could be elected consul for 134 it was necessary to rescind the law which prohibited second consulships. The required legislation was carried even though the majority of senators were in practice opposed to it;[1] then, despite that same opposition, despite all it implies in the mobilization of *clientelae* against him, despite the influence which his opponents manifestly wielded in the centuriate assembly, Scipio was elected consul; then, despite the hostile Senate, he was given the command against Numantia, surely by a special resolution of the tribal assembly.[2]

No detailed account of this election has survived, but there can be little doubt about the methods employed: the incitement of popular feeling; the accusations that this terrible war, with its constant levies and its severe campaigns, had been needlessly prolonged by the incompetent fumbling of the commanders (none of them political associates of Scipio, except the now hostile Metellus Macedonicus, and Furius with his special task in 136); the assertions that Rome had been disgraced by the shameful treaty of Mancinus; and there will have been no mincing of words about the ill-fortune of the current commander, by coincidence another Calpurnius, possibly actually the brother of the reviled consul of 148—a point certainly not to be missed. Only Scipio, it was claimed, could bring this wearisome war to an acceptable end, only the conqueror of Carthage could be trusted to avenge the defeats and salvage the military pride of Rome;[3] once more constitutional restrictions must yield to what was represented to be urgent necessity. Nor did the parallel with 148 end there. Once more Scipio undertook no orthodox candidature; once more he did not 'seek' the consulship but appeared (contrived to appear?) as the

---

[1] See below, p. 184.

[2] No source attests a special resolution, except for a possible hint in Oros. 5. 7. 1. Val. Max. 8. 15. 4 asserts *eidem senatus bis sine sorte provinciam, prius Africam, deinde Hispaniam dedit.* The ascription of the decision to the Senate is no more convincing for 134 than for 147, concerning which Valerius is certainly wrong; it is hard to believe that the Senate which refused Scipio men and money facilitated his appointment. On the other hand, behind Valerius' statement probably lies some special procedure, and indeed it seems wildly improbable that Scipio would have risked sortition, even if the Senate had declared Hither Spain a consular province.

[3] App. *Iber.* 84 barely hints at the political struggle but reveals the argument clearly. Several other sources state or imply that Scipio's election was brought about by the shame of the earlier reverses: Livy, *Epit.* 56; Vell. 2. 4. 2; 'Plut.' *Apophth. Scip. Min.* 15; Oros. 5. 7. 1; Eutrop. 4. 17. 2; cf. Cic. *Rep.* 6. 11; Cassiod. *Chron.*

spontaneous choice of the Roman People. And not of the People alone. The Senate was persuaded—by what means is not recorded, but the method of 148 comes readily to mind—to instruct the tribunes to arrange the special legislation required before Scipio could be elected: he was responding to the call of both Senate and People.[1]

This picture is scarcely to be taken at its face value. Certainly the popular enthusiasm was there, but to accept that it was entirely spontaneous is another matter: given Scipio's record and character, deliberate incitement seems as probable in 135 as in 148; and the true opinion of the Senate is revealed clearly enough by its subsequent refusal to provide Scipio with funds or to allow him to hold a levy.[2] Yet, if the picture is misleading, the fact remains that it was created, and a great political victory was won.

For Scipio's opponents the defeat was alarming. Despite all their efforts, despite their considerable advantages, he had been carried on a tide of popular feeling across constitutional barriers to the high— and, at this date, irregular—honour of a second consulship, and to a special military command; soon he was likely to be celebrating a second triumph and enjoying the credit of having ended victoriously a long and vexatious war, in the conduct of which others had failed conspicuously. The consequent feelings of jealousy, frustration, and anger found immediate expression in the refusal of men and money, a decision which, however plausible the excuses, represents a willingness on the part of at least some to prolong the war in order to damage Scipio's reputation. Curiously enough, Scipio's friend Polybius had noted the power to withhold funds as a means by which the Senate might coerce recalcitrant consuls.[3] The device was no small impediment, but insufficient, it soon became apparent, to block Scipio's path. For the future, the incentive was strong indeed to discover some method of countering Scipio's hold on the popular imagination and the immense enthusiasm which he could inspire.

2. *Trends and Attitudes*

In the first section of this chapter political struggles have been examined mainly in terms of the extent to which Scipio and his

---

[1] App. *Iber.* 84.   [2] p. 136.   [3] Polyb. 6. 15. 2 f.

opponents experienced success or failure. In this second section the emphasis is placed upon the methods and devices employed in those struggles and upon certain trends which may be discerned in political behaviour. Naturally much was done that conformed to a long-standing pattern. There was nothing essentially new or startling in the series of prosecutions of leading men—Scipio, Pompeius, Cotta, Lepidus, and, at some date unknown, also Laelius[1]—nor in the denigration of opponents for military failure, nor in the exploitation of religious prejudices for political ends, nor in Scipio's use of private pressure to secure the withdrawal of a tribune's veto;[2] though it is perhaps as well to be reminded that such methods, so evident in these years, were an accepted part of political life. But the pattern was not static. For the most part the changes which can be observed were not so much sudden, drastic innovations, breaking radically with established practices, as several parallel trends, each advanced step-by-step by a succession of developments associated with exceptional or pressing circumstances, so that inhibitions and restraints were gradually modified, and new attitudes of mind steadily evolved and became widely accepted.

In the previous chapter it was observed that the psychological barrier of the Senate's moral authority was being undermined by public discontent, especially with regard to the levy.[3] This same process was much assisted by Scipio's reliance upon popular appeal to circumvent a predominantly hostile Senate. The outstanding instances are his two consulships and the two military commands associated with them, all of which he obtained in defiance of the wishes of the Senate; but there were certainly other instances as well, of which the passage of the lex Cassia was probably one and that of the lex Gabinia may have been another. Moreover the authority of the Senate can only have been further impaired when the same man, denied reinforcements and money, reacted by collecting virtually a private army of clients and volunteers, by expending the private fortunes of himself and his friends, and by obtaining assistance from Hellenistic monarchs. Nor was Scipio the only political leader who defied the will of the Senate: in 143 his greatest rival, Appius Claudius Pulcher, celebrated the triumph which the Senate had

[1] pp. 127, 129, and 133. Laelius: ORF², p. 119.   [2] p. 131.   [3] p. 173.

refused him.[1] As each successful defiance demonstrated that, despite all the difficulties, a hostile majority in the Senate could be circumvented, so each in turn contributed to the growing readiness to make more such attempts.

This trend was accompanied by the growth of a similar readiness to circumvent or set aside constitutional impediments which were formally established in law. Significant stages in this development were the second consulships of Marcius Figulus and Nasica Corculum in 156 and 155, and the third consulship of Claudius Marcellus in 152;[2] but much the biggest contributions were the two consulships of Scipio Aemilianus, both of which showed that, given sufficient popular support, it was possible to overcome direct constitutional prohibitions even in the face of powerful opposition. Something of this same development is probably to be seen also in the apparent attempts to tamper with constitutional procedures in the interests of a particular faction; for there must be the strongest suspicion that this motive was deeply involved in the unsuccessful proposal of Crassus in 145[3] and in the Gabinian and Cassian ballot laws. Hand in hand with all this went an increasing readiness to attempt to overcome that recurrent constitutional impediment, the tribunician veto. For this there were several reasons. Because the tribunate had long since become an accepted part of the constitution, the veto came to be taken for granted as an ordinary political device; but its use for factional purposes, or for purposes which might be judged essentially factional by the impeded party, caused much frustration and impatience; furthermore, its use to obstruct the elections in 148, to interfere with the levy, and to hinder the departure of a consul to his allotted military command, could all give rise to feelings that it was being used against the fundamental interests of the state; and finally, in practice the veto was the most important legal barrier against defiance of the Senate or manipulation of constitutional rules and procedures for partisan interests, with the result that the growing readiness to attempt these things led to increasing conflict with the veto.

Resentment of the veto manifested itself in at least four attempts within fourteen years to ignore or to nullify it. It was one thing to

---

[1] pp. 107 f.   [2] pp. 38 f.   [3] pp. 101 f.

use private pressure to persuade a tribune to withdraw his veto, as Scipio did in 137, but a very different thing to attempt to ignore it outright, as was done by consuls in 151, 140, and 138, or to exploit a religious device and technicality to prevent it being enforced, as did Appius Claudius in 143;[1] even more remarkable, in 140 the consul Caepio actually threatened to resist by force Claudius Asellus' attempt to enforce his veto. Admittedly, Caepio seems to have had a particularly hot temper,[2] but even so it is highly significant that irritation at interference through the veto had reached the point where an unusually rash and impetuous consul could go so far. Moreover, the success of at least two of these attempts can only have encouraged the further development of the trend. Admittedly these successes depended on special, even unusual circumstances, and outright defiance was shown to be in general impracticable; an effective means of nullifying the veto had yet to be found. But the search was on, and events had shown it to be neither impossibly outrageous nor wholly unprofitable.

Lastly, there are hints of another trend, one which substantially increased the risk of disorder. It was no novel or unfamiliar phenomenon for a political crowd at Rome to give expression to strong feelings by shouting and barracking. As it happens, between 151 and 134 the only attested instances of this are the expressions of support for Scipio in 148 and the outcry against Nasica over the grain in 138,[3] although there were other occasions on which such outbursts are certain to have occurred, notably during the disputes over the levies of 151 and 138. But during these years the enjoyment of popular appeal acquired increased value as a political factor, and in this respect the events of 148 left no doubts as to the usefulness of popular demonstrations, of cheering and shouting crowds; and if popular appeal was to be exploited in this way, it was scarcely possible to preserve in practice a strict divorce between taking advantage of such demonstrations and actually stimulating them. It is indeed difficult to believe that the crowds of 148 were not deliberately incited, and it is highly significant that by 142 Scipio could be accused of having in his company men who were 'able to gather a crowd and to force all

[1] pp. 43, 107 f., 126 f., 130, and 131.   [2] p. 83.
[3] pp. 66 and 129 f.

issues by shouting and inciting passions'.[1] If there was a growing habit of using agitators to stimulate noisy demonstrations and to arouse passions, there was plainly a possibility that one day things might get out of control, especially in a city with virtually no police force beyond the few attendants of the magistrates. When crowds are accustomed and encouraged to express their strongest political wishes in this way, it is no great step to public disorder.

3. On the Eve of a Crisis

In conclusion it will be as well to summarize the general political situation on the eve of the tribunate of Tiberius Gracchus. In the factional rivalries of the time, embittered by the prosecutions and feuds of recent years and by the affair of Mancinus, Scipio held a leading position but was by no means all-powerful. His rivals, chief among them Appius Claudius Pulcher, could often preponderate in the Senate and in the comitia centuriata, provided that they were willing to co-operate against him. In fact they did enjoy considerable success in centuriate elections; but at the end of 135 they had experienced the shock of Scipio's election to a second consulship and their inability to prevent him securing the Numantine command; and now they faced the likely prospect of his return to a second triumph, once more a popular hero. Angered by his ambition, his pride, and his stinging witticisms, jealous of his success, resentful of his ability to overcome constitutional obstacles, they had been forcefully reminded that the peculiar advantage he enjoyed was his ability to command and to stimulate great personal popularity. In the political struggle popular appeal had been made one of the key factors. With this development had come others. Long-established psychological barriers were crumbling. Men were more ready to question the authority of the Senate, politicians were conscious that, though difficult, it was not impossible to use the 'popular' elements in the constitution to circumvent a hostile majority in the Senate. There was a growing readiness to attempt to override legal and constitutional barriers, and in particular to seek some means of circumventing the tribunician veto. There had been, it seems, some use of agitators to incite popular enthusiasm, and the

[1] p. 30.

populace was becoming increasingly accustomed to expressing its feelings in noisy demonstrations. On top of all this, and aggravated by the Spanish and Sicilian wars, there were very serious political problems: a 'demographic' problem which was giving much concern to the military leaders of the state, and urgent social and economic problems which were causing grave distress and discontent among many citizens, both urban and rural. In short, the accumulation of intense factional tensions, of new trends in political behaviour, and of serious political problems provided the material for a major crisis in the life of the Roman Republic.

XV

THE TRIBUNATE OF TIBERIUS GRACCHUS: THE STRUGGLE FOR THE AGRARIAN LAW

1. *The Tribunate of Tiberius Gracchus*

AMONG the ten tribunes of the plebs who assumed office on 10 December 134 B.C. was Tiberius Sempronius Gracchus, eloquent and energetic, son of the distinguished consul of 177 and 163 and, through his mother Cornelia, grandson of Scipio Africanus. Within a few months Tiberius had introduced, steered through the assembly, and put into operation a highly controversial bill for agrarian reform, had defied the opposition of the majority in the Senate, overcome a tribunician veto by contriving the deposition from office of a fellow tribune, arranged by *plebiscitum*, without consulting the Senate, to employ for his agrarian scheme the treasure bequeathed to Rome by Attalus III of Pergamum, sought to have himself re-elected tribune for the ensuing year, and been battered to death in a riot in which a considerable number of his supporters also perished—the first bloodshed in the long agony of the Roman Revolution.[1] Whether Tiberius is admired or blamed, this bloody and startling culmination, so foreign to the character of political disputes for many generations past, has led to frequent emphasis upon the new and revolutionary nature of his programme or, more commonly, of his methods. This emphasis needs to be qualified by an examination of the events of these few months in the light of the political activities and developments of the previous years. Too often the novelty of the resort to force has distracted attention from this significant background. Event after event had a recent and often a close precedent and may be seen as a logical advance in one or

[1] The main sources are App. *B.C.* 1. 7–17 and Plut. *Ti. Grac.*, supplemented by scattered references elsewhere, esp. in Cicero. Cf. Greenidge and Clay, *Sources*², pp. 1 f. On the relationship between the accounts of Appian and Plutarch see Appendix XI.

other of the current trends in political behaviour. In 133 the progression of such trends, often in their essence incompatible with the existing basis of political stability, combined with the powerful pressure of urgent issues and with a situation of intense factional hostility to produce a violent climax which, though in a sense a sudden shock, yet fits into place as the comprehensible outcome of what had gone before; Rome toppled over a brink which she had been approaching remorselessly for years.

2. *Allies and Objectives*

It has always been evident that in presenting his agrarian bill Tiberius did not stand alone. On the contrary, he had distinguished and powerful associates. Of the leading men whom he is said to have consulted when drafting his bill, three are named, all of them from important consular families.[1] The most notable is the Princeps Senatus himself, Ap. Claudius Pulcher, Tiberius' father-in-law, shortly to become one of the agrarian commissioners appointed under the terms of Tiberius' bill. The others are two brothers, both outstanding as lawyers: P. Licinius Crassus Dives Mucianus, father-in-law of Tiberius' brother Gaius, destined shortly to succeed Tiberius himself as agrarian commissioner, to become Pontifex Maximus, and to achieve the consulship of 131; and P. Mucius Scaevola, also shortly to become Pontifex Maximus, and about to enter office as one of the consuls of 133, the first permissible year after his praetorship. Also from a consular family was M. Fulvius Flaccus, consul in 125, who quickly emerged as one of the Gracchan leaders and by 129 had become an agrarian commissioner.[2] Another supporter of Tiberius, much younger, was C. Porcius Cato, consul in 114, grandson of the Censor and of Aemilius Paullus, and thereby a nephew of Scipio Aemilianus; and yet another was C. Papirius Carbo, also an agrarian commissioner by

---

[1] Plut. *Ti. Grac.* 9. 1; Cic. *Acad. Pr.* 2. 13. Cf. pp. 90 and 92. The fact is generally acknowledged but does not always receive the attention it deserves. Earl, *Tiberius Gracchus*, pp. 8 f., esp. p. 14, offers an assessment similar to the present one in several respects.

[2] pp. 233 and 238. A Fulvius Flaccus, who is very likely to have been this man, is said to have warned Tiberius of the trend of the senatorial debate immediately before the outbreak of violence: Plut. *Ti. Grac.* 18. 2.

129, consul in 120, his family certainly of praetorian standing and possibly consular.[1]

Thus of the six aristocratic associates of Tiberius who are named, all attained the consulship, at least five, in addition to Tiberius himself, were from (five different) families of consular standing, one was the Princeps Senatus, and two were shortly to become Pontifex Maximus. Nor is this likely to have been the complete list; in the train of such men there will have been others of senatorial rank whom the sources happen not to name: another Ap. Claudius Pulcher was suffect consul in 130;[2] the family of the *novus homo* M. Perperna, consul in 130, was very probably under the patronage of the Claudii;[3] and a Marcius Philippus had married an Appia Claudia, probably a daughter of the Princeps Senatus himself.[4] But however it may be in such hypothetical cases, it is evident that those of Tiberius' associates who are identified positively are a distinguished and important group of politicians.

How far the agrarian bill was the product of Tiberius' own initiative it is impossible to say. Clearly he was an enthusiast for it, and since it stood in his name it was inevitable that it should be linked closely with him; but it is perfectly possible that his prior consultations with others concerned not only points of detail and legal phrasing but matters of substance and principle, and even that the true origin of the bill lay in collective deliberation rather than in Tiberius' personal initiative. In any event, the preparatory advice and support of the Princeps Senatus and two of the most learned and scrupulous students of law certify that the bill was not the wild scheme of a hotheaded visionary, that it was in no sense subversive. Nor was it revolutionary in the sense of attempting the redistribution of private property; for so far from proposing the confiscation of privately

[1] Cic. *De Amic.* 39; pp. 232 f. and 238. In Cic. *De Orat.* 3. 74 Carbo is *nobilissimus*, on which see Gelzer, *Nobilität*, p. 25; Münzer, *RE*, s.v. *Papirius*, cols. 1004 f. and 1016.

[2] Münzer, *RE*, s.v. *Claudius*, no. 11, plausibly conjectures that he was a cousin of the Princeps Senatus and that he is the Appius of Cic. *De Orat.* 2. 284, whose witticism about the *lex Thoria* suggests a favourable attitude towards Tiberius' agrarian proposals.

[3] Münzer, *Röm. Adels.*, pp. 95 f., where the arguments are persuasive because Perperna was a *novus homo*; also the close links between the Perpernae and the Valerii Flacci suggest that all three families were very close in 132–130 as well as later.

[4] Cic. *De Domo*, 84; Münzer, *RE*, s.v. *Claudius*, no. 386. Tentative suggestions could be extended: e.g. the two Fulvii who were consuls in 135 and 134, and the Antistii, from whom came Claudius' wife. For the position of the Calpurnii see pp. 316 f.

owned land, it actually offered guaranteed perpetual tenure of the legally permissible maximum holding of public land.[1]

The essence of the plan, as is well known, was that a commission of three should allocate to landless citizens small holdings of publicly owned land, *ager publicus*, which had never been systematically distributed or rented out; and since wealthy investors had taken over much of this land, either by direct farming or by pasturing much larger herds and flocks than the law specified, the commissioners were to reclaim all in excess of the maximum holding permitted by law to any one person.[2] Of course vested interests were threatened by the plan and many, perhaps most, wealthy men faced loss of income and even of invested capital; and naturally opponents of the scheme made the most of the difficulties, hardships, and moral injustices which would ensue—the disputed titles, obscured boundaries, plots bought in good faith from previous occupiers, buildings erected, and capital invested. The true extent of these problems can never be known, but some exaggeration may fairly be suspected in Appian's famous account, and the work of redistribution does not seem to have been hampered unduly.[3] Moreover, the claim that purchases and investment had been made in good faith, though no doubt true in some cases, is itself somewhat suspect as a general statement. In 196 and 193 there had been extensive prosecutions of graziers, evidently for violating the restrictions concerning pasturing on public land, and the fines had sufficed to pay for expensive and ostentatious public works; in 173 action had been taken against landowners who had extended their boundaries to include public land in Campania; and in 167 Cato referred to the limitations on holdings in terms

---

[1] App. *B.C.* 1. 11. Plut. *Ti. Grac.* 9. 2, cf. 10. 4, states that Tiberius at first proposed to pay compensation for public land recovered from private hands, but this is very questionable and is generally rejected. Cf. Additional Note O, p. 346.

[2] App. *B.C.* 1. 9; Plut. *Ti. Grac.* 8; 13; Greenidge and Clay, *Sources*[2], pp. 4 f. The powers of the commissioners to adjudicate upon the status of land were conferred by a separate *lex iudiciaria*: Livy, *Epit.* 58; Macrob. *Sat.* 3. 14. 6. Appian's assertion that land was to be distributed to Italians (i.e. as well as to citizens) is controverted by Badian, *Foreign Clientelae*, pp. 169 f.

[3] App. *B.C.* 1. 10, cf. 18; similar complaints in Flor. 2. 1. 7; cf. Cic. *Pro Sest.* 103. Most of the surviving Gracchan *termini* were erected not later than 130: Degrassi, *Inscr. Lat. Lib. R.P.* i, nos. 467–75. For discussion of the regulations governing the use of *ager publicus* see esp. Tibiletti, 'Il possesso dell' *ager publicus*', *Athenaeum* 26 (1948), pp. 173 f., esp. pp. 191 f., and 27 (1949), pp. 3 f.

which make sense only if they were well known and on occasion enforced.[1]

Nevertheless, though the difficulties and the moral injustices of the scheme may have been overstated, it remains true that many, and perhaps most, wealthy men faced financial loss, in some cases perhaps serious loss. But this fact is itself a measure of the serious intent of those who, in preparing and supporting the scheme, not only knew that they would be faced with the opposition of powerful vested interests—opposition which a few years earlier had induced Laelius to abandon his scheme—but very probably themselves were willing to incur similar loss; for it is difficult to believe that among the seven distinguished families represented by the bill's known supporters, to say nothing of other possible supporters, there were not several who had profited from the extension of their estates over public land. Whatever the objectives at which these men were aiming, they certainly did not regard them lightly.

But if it can be asserted with certainty that the promoters of the bill were very serious in their purposes, the attempt to discover what those purposes were is bound to involve hypothesis. Motives are reported in the sources, but allowance must be made both for the possibility that some of these are *post eventum* conjectures and for the influence of the extensive propaganda, hostile and friendly, which was provoked by Tiberius' tribunate; furthermore, the declared purposes of a political venture are by no means necessarily the sole or the paramount purposes. Nor can it be assumed that there was a single 'real' motive, to which any others were at best subsidiary, insufficient in themselves to have led to action; for behind such a major venture it is reasonable to expect a complex of several motives, not necessarily fully analysed and distinguished one from another by the promoters themselves; and since the motives in question are not those of one individual but of a group of individuals, it is more than likely that there was some variation in motive or in the relative importance of different motives among the members of the group.

[1] Livy 33. 42. 10 f.; 35. 10. 11 f.; 42. 1. 6, 19. 1 f.; Gell. 6. 3. 37 = *ORF*², Cato, fgt. 167, pp. 65 f. No doubt enforcement at this date was mainly in respect of very profitable land from which the state might derive revenue.

Some of the motives attributed to Tiberius Gracchus must certainly be rejected. In the light of the known terms of the agrarian bill and the number and distinction of its promoters, the opposition's charges that Tiberius' aims were subversive and revolutionary, like the later accusations that he was aiming at a tyranny, carry little conviction and for the most part were surely deliberate slanders.[1] Similarly, assertions that Tiberius was incited by Diophanes the rhetorician and Blossius of Cumae almost certainly have their origin in attempts to give some plausibility to allegations of outrageous behaviour and subversive intentions on the part of a young noble of such talent and distinction; doubtless these men gave Tiberius loyal support and encouragement, and on that account subsequently became convenient scapegoats, but it is highly improbable that they were a major influence in the deliberations of a galaxy of nobles headed by such men as Ap. Claudius Pulcher and P. Mucius Scaevola.[2] There is more to be said in favour of the view that, fired by rivalry with contemporaries, by the stinging exhortations of his ambitious mother, and by a deep sense of grievance at the blow which his *dignitas* had suffered in the Mancinus affair in 136, Tiberius was angrily determined to achieve political prominence and recover his prestige.[3] Such determination would have given him drive and forcefulness, would have marked him out as a very suitable choice to exploit the tribunate on behalf of his associates, but by itself it would scarcely account either for the promotion of a bill which was bound to arouse strenuous opposition or for the serious co-operation of

---

[1] Plut. *Ti. Grac.* 9. 3; for the later charges pp. 213 and 228. Boren, 'The Opposition View', *AJPh* 82 (1961), pp. 358 f., holds that the fear of tyranny was genuine, but his arguments are not convincing.

[2] Plut. *Ti. Grac.* 8. 6; 17. 5; 20. 4 f.; cf. Cic. *De Amic.* 37; *Brut.* 104; Val. Max. 4. 7. 1. Gelzer, *Gnomon* 5 (1929), p. 300, rightly attaches little importance to the alleged Stoic influence of Blossius, but is inclined to see as more important the even mistier figure of Diophanes. It is true that Cicero, *De Amic.* 37, asserts that Blossius was not a *comes* but a *dux illius furoris*, but the anecdote upon which he is commenting contains no suggestion that Blossius was anything more than a devoted follower and agent of Tiberius; similarly in *Brut.* 104 Diophanes is mentioned only as an exceptionally well qualified teacher of rhetoric, with no hint that he was also a political mentor. On Blossius' Campanian background cf. Dudley, 'Blossius of Cumae', *JRS* 31 (1941), pp. 94 f.

[3] Plut. *Ti. Grac.* 7. 6; 8. 7 f.; but the motives are given as alternatives, not an accumulation. Other refs. to the Mancinus episode only: Cic. *Brut.* 103; *De Har. Resp.* 43; Vell. 2. 2. 1 f.; Oros. 5. 8. 2 f.; Flor. 2. 2. 2; Quint. *Inst.* 7. 4. 13; Dio, fgt. 83. 2 f. (cf. Boissevain's note ad loc.).

Claudius and the others: these men did not court a clash with powerful vested interests primarily in order to restore Tiberius' *dignitas*, desirable though that objective may have seemed.

*The declared purposes of the agrarian bill seem to have been three: to provide relief for the poor by settling them on small farms; to increase the number of citizens of sufficient census rating to qualify them for the levy, and thus to relieve the recruiting difficulties; and to reduce the number of slaves employed on the land in order to lessen the danger of slave uprisings. Much may have been said about this last—the Sicilian slave war was still raging, and so far the Roman forces had made little headway—but it is doubtful if the authors of the bill can have regarded it as more than a subsidiary objective, a welcome additional benefit accruing from a scheme designed primarily for other purposes.[1] The complex process of resettlement would have been a peculiarly indirect approach to the problem; and *although the transfer of a substantial amount of public land from large-scale operations to peasant farming was bound to bring about some reduction in the number of slaves employed in agricultural enterprises, it is questionable whether this could have been sufficient to effect more than a marginal reduction in the potential danger.

*The second objective, to alleviate the recruiting problem, is likely to have been more fundamental. The advocates of the bill perhaps needed to handle this topic with some care. On the one hand those citizens already liable to military service must have welcomed a scheme which promised greatly to augment their numbers, and a certain proportion of the assignees themselves may have seen soldiering as the most attractive way of escape from their poverty and hence may have been interested in acquiring land only in order to qualify themselves for military service. On the other hand, it is far from certain that the great majority of assignees would have welcomed the prospect of becoming liable to conscription, even though the inalienability of their plots protected them against expropriation during absence on service. In recent years it had been painfully apparent that much of the warfare was arduous, dangerous, and unprofitable, and that the levy had been highly unpopular among those already subject to it. Farming offered neither ease nor riches, but still it was

---

[1] It recurs in App. *B.C.* 1. 8–10 but is absent from Plut. *Ti. Grac.*

a positive attraction, and it would scarcely have been tactful, nor would it have facilitated the enactment of the bill, to have suggested too forcefully that the poor were to be given land in order that many of them might speedily be enlisted in the army. But however this difficulty was to be overcome, the alleviation of the recruiting problem was certainly a declared, a genuine, and a very important purpose of the scheme. This is evident from the prominence it is given in the sources and from the extensive indications that the problem was serious and widely recognized to be so.[1]

*The third declared purpose, the relief of the economically distressed, pervades the narrative accounts of Appian and Plutarch and is also mentioned elsewhere.[2] It is the self-evident basis of plans for extensive agrarian resettlement, and it is this which made the scheme so attractive to great numbers of impoverished citizens. It is impossible to determine how far this purpose was inspired by humanitarian considerations or by anxiety to relieve an explosive situation; but since there is every reason to believe that the distress was very great and very obvious, it could easily have been just as important a consideration as the recruiting problem in the formulation of the scheme. No doubt some of the supporters of the proposal attached more weight to one objective than to the other, but there are no good grounds for supposing that in general one was only secondary and subordinate to the other.[3]

The agrarian scheme, then, was declared to be a serious contribution towards the solution of two major problems, and was expected also to ease the dangers of a third. Behind it there lay also calculations of the political advantages which might be gained from the venture. This is not necessarily incompatible with a genuine desire to

---

[1] App. *B.C.* 1. 7 f., esp. 11, 27; Plut. *Ti. Grac.* 8; pp. 167 f. and 171 f. Inalienability: App. *B.C.* 1. 10, 27.

[2] Esp. App. *B.C.* 1. 9, 10, 27; Plut. *Ti. Grac.* 8. 10; 9. 4 f.; Cic. *De Leg. Agr.* 2. 81; *Pro Sest.* 103; Diod. 34/35. 6. 1. Additional Note M, p. 345.

[3] Earl, *Tiberius Gracchus*, ch. ii, who argues that the creation of more *adsidui* was the one real purpose of the scheme, adopts an unduly optimistic view of the condition of rural Italy and takes insufficient account of economic distress. He emphasizes the inalienability provision as being economic nonsense, intelligible only as a device to ensure that the assignees retained their new status. But it is unsafe to assume that the scheme made sound economic sense as that is understood today. App. *B.C.* 1. 10, cf. 27, gives a perfectly intelligible motive for the provision, which reappeared in later agrarian schemes: Gabba, *Appiani B.C. Liber Primus*, p. 26.

resolve the problems themselves; indeed, although the outlook of individuals will have varied, it is *a priori* reasonable to suppose that the motives of the scheme's sponsors were compounded of both elements. The very nature of such unpublicized political calculations makes it difficult to find evidence of them, but there are some suggestive hints. In the first place there are the frequent references to Tiberius' ambition, and in particular the large group of passages which refer to his proposals as a reaction to his loss of face in the Numantine affair.[1] This interpretation was evidently widespread, and it presupposes that the scheme could plausibly have been expected to bring considerable political benefits to Tiberius; and if to Tiberius, also to those who were associated with him. In the second place there are the indications that the division between supporters and opponents of the proposals corresponded very closely to existing factional divisions and did not cut across them. This is most apparent in the case of the bill's supporters, amongst whom can be discerned a complex of ties of marriage, kinship, and *amicitia*, as well as a record of co-operation in previous generations of their families; the only known supporter who does not fit smoothly into this pattern, C. Porcius Cato, is known to have been an *amicus* of Tiberius; and no person whose natural associations would have been with this group is named as an opponent of Tiberius.[2] It is not possible to be so precise about the opposition, partly because hostility towards Tiberius was common to a number of persons and groups who were mutually antagonistic among themselves. Also there is the possibility that some of them might not have been opposed to the agrarian scheme itself and became hostile only when Tiberius threatened to depose a fellow tribune, or even later. Thus Plutarch mentions the hostility of Q. Pompeius, Q. Metellus Macedonicus, and T. Annius only after the affair of the Pergamene treasure, thus at a very late stage, and with no necessary reference back to the original agrarian proposals;[3] similarly Scipio Aemilianus' intimate friend Laelius and his protégé P. Rupilius, together with P. Popillius Laenas, played a major part in the persecution of the humbler Gracchans after Tiberius' death but are not mentioned in connexion with earlier events; and

---

[1] p. 195 n. 3.   [2] pp. 86, 93, and 191 f.
[3] Plut. *Ti. Grac.* 14. 3 f.; p. 213.

Q. Aelius Tubero, Scipio's nephew, is said to have broken his *amicitia* with Tiberius, though at what stage is not stated.[1] On the other hand, nothing in the evidence implies that any of these persons were not opposed to the agrarian reform itself, and in all probability most of them were opposed to it: it is clear from the course of events that the majority of senators, and therefore presumably the majority of *principes*, were hostile to the scheme; a passage in Plutarch's account seems to reflect a tradition which associated the whole affair with a quarrel between Tiberius and Scipio Aemilianus; the fanatical opposition of Scipio Nasica at least suggests the possibility that Aemilianus' associates in general took the same view; and although there is almost no indication of the immediate associations of the tribune who vetoed Tiberius' bill, M. Octavius, his family had been connected closely with Aemilius Paullus and the Scipios.[2] Thus the cumulative evidence for division along factional lines, and in particular for a clash between the associates of Appius Claudius and those of Scipio Aemilianus, is quite considerable. It seems a safe assumption that the 'Claudians' were expected to obtain some significant political advantage *vis-à-vis* their rivals.

That advantage was plainly a substantial gain in popularity with the masses. Admittedly the many citizens settled by the commissioners in the more distant parts of Italy, however grateful towards their benefactors, could be expected to exercise their votes in the assemblies only on rare occasions; but numbers of them could be brought in for special events, particularly for elections, and doubtless others were settled in areas nearer to Rome. Even those who did not receive or did not want land might be expected to favour the men who had exerted themselves on behalf of the distressed masses and to be sensible of the improvement effected in their lot by the removal of many competitors; while those who were already liable for conscription might be expected to appreciate efforts to spread their burden more widely. True, there was a price to be paid: the probability that others would combine in opposition, and consequently that, for a time, the Senate would have a hostile majority; the certainty that the scheme would anger many with vested interests and

---

[1] p. 230. Aelius: Cic. *De Amic.* 37.
[2] Plut. *Ti. Grac.* 7. 5 f. Nasica: Plut. *Ti. Grac.* 13. 3. Octavius: p. 87.

therefore would provoke hostility among the wealthy, whose votes weighed heavily in the *comitia centuriata*. No doubt it was hoped that this would be mitigated by the strength of existing bonds of clientship, by the favour of many existing *adsidui*, and by the new *adsidui* who would soon acquire effective votes in the centuriate assembly—and subsequent electoral successes suggest that such hopes were justified.[1] The price might well seem worth paying when the returns might be expected to include not only important benefits for the state but a marked access of political strength in the very sphere which Scipio had so successfully exploited and in which he had proved to be so frustratingly powerful. And just at this time there was an additional factor to fortify these considerations. It was apparent that the Numantine war would soon be ended; many troops would be returning, after a long absence, with little booty and a derisory donative—in the event Scipio could give them no more than seven *denarii* each.[2] If Tiberius' bill were enacted, many of these men would find their economic salvation in the work of the agrarian commissioners—from the hands of Appius Claudius and his associates.

The tribunate of Tiberius Gracchus came at a time when factional hostilities are likely to have been particularly intense, when Scipio's second consulship and Numantine command had fired anew the jealousy and anger inspired by his record, his ambitions, and his character, when his opponents had been reminded forcefully that his peculiar advantage was his ability to stimulate great popular enthusiasm for himself, so that popular appeal had become a key political factor. Under such circumstances the popular appeal of the agrarian scheme was bound to be a major consideration in the minds of its promoters. On the other side, its significance cannot have been overlooked by the friends and associates of Scipio, least of all by the shrewd and calculating Laelius. They were faced with a serious challenge, made all the harder to meet by the absence of Scipio himself. Acceptance of the scheme, mere quiescence, evidently seemed insufficient: it would not have prevented the 'Claudians' earning their 'debt of gratitude'; those whose interests were threatened would

---

[1] Not at the elections for 132, but frequently in the following years: ch. XVII *passim*.
[2] p. 231.

have found other champions; and the majority of consulars and *nobiles* would have been no more ready than before to look kindly upon Scipio. The decision was taken, it seems, to oppose the scheme vigorously. The compensations for the inevitable loss of popularity might include new alliances and new influence among the wealthy and powerful, and perhaps there was some hope that a triumph over Numantia would repair some of the damage.

But the opponents of the bill are no more likely than its promoters to have been motivated solely by considerations of political expediency; nor can it be supposed that they all took their stand after a cool and rational appraisal of the issues. Their motives will have been a mixture, compounded in different proportions in different individuals—a confusion of emotion and reason, anger and fear, self-deception and self-interest, calculations of political advantage and genuine disapproval of the scheme as such. Some will have believed quite honestly, and others will soon have persuaded themselves, that the scheme was not a suitable means for attaining its professed objectives.

Tiberius Gracchus' agrarian bill, then, focused upon itself—and not unintentionally—all the tensions and passions of contemporary politics: the genuine concern about urgent problems, the despairing distress of the urban and the rural poor, the smouldering discontent of the classes liable for conscription, and the ambitions, jealousies, fears, and anger of personal and factional rivalry; it roused the anxious self-interest of many who faced financial loss; and it created a situation in which the struggle for and against the bill would focus all these passions and tensions upon a single issue, and simultaneously would of necessity heighten and exacerbate them.

3. *The First Stages in the Struggle*

Tiberius decided, presumably with the concurrence of Appius Claudius and others involved in the scheme, to take his agrarian proposals direct to the assembly, without consulting the Senate first. There have been suggestions that this in itself was a revolutionary step, a blow at the authority of the Senate, and thereby a major cause of opposition to the bill. This was not so. To take a bill direct to the assembly was not illegal (a point not in dispute), and equally was not the revival of a right obscured by long disuse. Admittedly since the Second Punic War it had been uncommon, but some attempts had been made and a few had succeeded; recently the *lex Cassia* of 137 was almost certainly an instance. The reason why such attempts were infrequent was plainly that they were especially likely to be vetoed by a tribune.[1] By contrast, the prior recommendation of the Senate was not only a near-necessity in practice but probably also a positive aid in deterring opposition and adverse votes; thus there were very strong practical reasons for seeking the approval of the Senate. Nevertheless, there need be no mystery about Tiberius' failure to do this. The obvious explanation is that he judged his chances of securing a favourable majority in the Senate to be slender or, more probably, non-existent.[2] To have a measure enacted by the assembly despite the disapproval of the Senate was certainly very difficult, but it was not absolutely impossible. In a sense this had been done with the legislation which had enabled Scipio to stand for the consulships of 147 and 134, and there is little doubt that the *lex Cassia* of 137 was a clear example.

When Tiberius formally promulgated his bill, very soon after he had begun his tribunate, both sides began to make preparations for the crucial meeting of the assembly, preparations which included encouraging as many clients and supporters as possible to travel from the more distant areas to Rome. Appian paints a vivid picture of the consequent state of affairs:

While the two sides (the poor and the rich in the city) were each making such complaints and hurling accusations at each other, a great mass of others who had an interest in the land, whether as inhabitants of colonies or of *municipia* or in some other way, and who shared the same apprehensions, crowded in and took sides with one or other of the factions. Emboldened by their numbers and exasperated against each other, they caused incessant disturbances as they awaited the voting on the law, some intending that they would in no wise allow it to be enacted, others that they would enact it at all costs. In addition to personal interest a spirit of rivalry infected both sides as they made preparations against each other for the appointed day.[3]

---

[1] pp. 44 f., with Additional Note C, p. 340. *Lex Cassia*: pp. 130 f.
[2] App. *B.C.* 1. 12 is not reliable evidence to the contrary.
[3] App. *B.C.* 1. 10. Cf. also Diod. 34/35. 6. 1 = Poseid. fgt. 110b *FGrH*.

Whether this account is derived from a contemporary description or is the imaginative creation of a later writer, the situation it depicts is entirely plausible. This is true even of the disturbances (στάσεις), provided that they are not thought of in terms of the gang-fights of a later period. The city, already overcrowded, was now crammed with thousands of extra men, many of them rough peasants, and most of them were there for the sole purpose of voting for or against the agrarian bill; a high proportion of voters felt a keen and some-times a desperate personal interest in the outcome, and they were con-stantly reminded of their interests by the speeches and exhortations of the protagonists. In such circumstances outbreaks of brawling, often no doubt drunken, were virtually inevitable.

It must soon have become obvious to Tiberius' opponents that neither public exhortation nor pressure upon clients would suffice to defeat the bill. The crowds streaming into Rome, the great throngs flocking after Tiberius when he appeared in public, the evident enthusiasm of the audiences which listened to his emotive speeches,[1] left no doubt as to the outcome of a vote: Tiberius could be thwarted only by the veto of one of the other tribunes. M. Octavius proved suitably determined and willing to incur the inevit-able odium; and so when the assembly met to vote upon the bill, Octavius vetoed the proceedings.[2]

Naturally Tiberius (and no doubt large sections of the crowd) professed great indignation and anger,[3] but it is hard to believe that anyone can have been very surprised. The promoters of the bill must have considered beforehand what action they would take in this situation. At first more or less 'traditional' forms of pressure were applied—similar no doubt to those by which Scipio had

[1] Emotive in content rather than in manner and delivery: Plut. Ti. Grac. 2. 2 f.; 9. 4 f., cf. 10. 1; App. B.C. 1. 9, 11. His retinue can hardly have been less now than in his last days, when it was regularly several thousand strong: Semp. Asell. fgt. 6; cf. Plut. Ti. Grac. 20. 2.

[2] This first assembly, recorded in App. B.C. 1. 12, is not mentioned explicitly in Plut. Ti. Grac. 10. 2 f. but is clearly implied. Octavius: Additional Note N, p. 346. Geer, 'Notes on the Land Law', TAPhA 70 (1939), pp. 30 f., attempts to identify the calendar dates of this and the two following assemblies. He suggests 29 January, 18 and 19 February, or less probably 4, 24, and 25 April; but he presupposes a degree of accuracy in detailed phrases, esp. Appian's ἐς τὴν ἐπιοῦσαν ἀγοράν, which must leave his results very hypothetical. Cf. Fraccaro, Studi, i, p. 108; Gabba, Appiani B.C. Liber Primus, p. 36; Earl, Tiberius Gracchus, p. 84.

[3] App. B.C. 1. 12; Plut. Ti. Grac. 10. 4.

persuaded Antius to withdraw his veto in 137. In this instance social and family pressures were not likely to achieve much, but constant argument and reiteration of the case for the bill, though perhaps unlikely to convince Octavius by logic, steadily strengthened the pressure of public opinion. A similar purpose was served by Tiberius' dramatic offer to use his own fortune to compensate Octavius for his large holdings of *ager publicus*, a gesture patently intended to proclaim that Octavius' motives were essentially selfish. Then, since Octavius refused to yield despite the obvious risk to his future political prospects, Tiberius tried another kind of pressure: he forbade all magistrates to transact public business of any kind until a vote had been taken on the agrarian bill, and by sealing the *aerarium* he made a special effort to cause financial difficulties. Thus to all intents and purposes he proclaimed a *iustitium*, a suspension of public business, as a means of political blackmail.[1]

This was a drastic step, but it was by no means new or revolutionary. As far back as 184 there had been a close parallel, when tribunes had threatened to veto all business in the Senate if a rival tribune used his veto against a certain resolution.[2] Tiberius' action went further than this, but only in the breadth of its application. Also it was directly comparable to—and no more irresponsible than—the threat to veto the elections of 148 and thus to deprive the state of its senior magistrates at a crucial juncture. But Tiberius' suspension of business proved less effective. At this time of year, with the magistrates safely elected and no major crisis in foreign affairs, there was probably little public business which could not be held over for a few weeks. Faced with stalemate and the prospect of long delay, extra-urban voters, especially the poorer among them, would soon begin to disperse to their homes. In a contest to keep clients and other voters in Rome an obvious advantage would lie with the side which by and large commanded the support and the resources of the wealthier sections of the citizen body, that is to say, with Tiberius' opponents. Meanwhile they could sow doubts and excite some sympathy by publicly mourning and deploring the interference with the orderly conduct of affairs. Thus, at least among the politicians, hopes could not have been high that at the next assembly Octavius would give way in face

---

[1] Additional Note O, p. 346.   [2] Livy, 39. 38. 9.

of the *iustitium*. When the day came he persisted in his veto; the stalemate remained unbroken, and unless the veto could be circumvented the agrarian bill was lost.

To meet this eventuality Tiberius had a simple but drastic plan, but first the deadlock was referred to the Senate. Octavius' renewed veto had provoked uproar in the crowd and mutual recriminations amongst the tribunes. This scene of disorder was ended when two consulars, perhaps genuinely alarmed at the tensions being generated and genuinely anxious for compromise, appealed to Tiberius to lay the matter before the Senate. Plainly failure to respond to this appeal would have been a tactical error, giving a plausible basis for charges of irresponsible obstinacy; and, although Tiberius can have had few illusions about the outcome, there was now nothing to be lost by taking the problem to the Senate. In practice the agrarian scheme probably left little room for compromise, since the fundamental issue was whether the regulations governing the use of public land were to be enforced effectively. Moreover, at this stage the opposition, commanding a majority in the Senate, must have felt that they had the upper hand: provided that they remained firm and gave Octavius sufficient encouragement the bill would be defeated. The debate proved fruitless, serving only to re-emphasize the deadlock. It was at this point, surely a well-chosen moment, that Tiberius revealed his plan—logical, simple, yet drastic and unprecedented: the veto could not be defied, therefore it must be removed; events had shown that it could be removed only by removing the tribune who was imposing it; so Tiberius proposed that Octavius be declared no longer a tribune of the plebs.[1]

4. *The Deposition of Octavius*[2]

The removal of a magistrate from office was not without precedent. Quite apart from cases where the discovery of a technical fault, a *vitium*, in the conduct of an election had been in reality a pretext for

[1] On events from the second assembly onwards see App. *B.C.* 1. 12; Plut. *Ti. Grac.* 11; Greenidge and Clay, *Sources²*, pp. 6 f.; Additional Notes P and Q, pp. 347 f.

[2] Narratives in App. *B.C.* 1. 12 and Plut. *Ti. Grac.* 11. 4 f., to which further reference will be given only on special points. Other refs.: Cic. *Pro Mil.* 72; *De Leg.* 3. 24; Ascon. p. 72 C.; Livy, *Epit.* 58; Oros. 5. 8. 3; Vell. 2. 2. 3; (Victor) *De Vir. Ill.* 64. 4; Diod. 34/35. 7. 1 = Poseid. fgt. 110d *FGrH*; cf. Cic. *De Nat. Deor.* 1. 106; Flor. 2. 2. 5.

dismissal, there were stories, some of them almost certainly true, of unsatisfactory magistrates of earlier ages who had abdicated under strong pressure or actual compulsion; there was even a story that in one instance reluctant tribunes had been induced to abdicate, though this was said to be because they had been involved in the treaty of the Caudine Forks and had nothing to do with their conduct in office.[1] But induced abdication is not abrogation, and the abrogation of the powers of magistrates was not practised. On the other hand, it was a recognized method of terminating pro-magistracies—this actually had been done in the case of Aemilius Lepidus, as recently as 136—and, although the *mos maiorum* presented a very serious impediment, it seems unlikely that the abrogation even of actual magistracies, let alone of tribunates, was clearly and explicitly prohibited by legislation; more probably the legal position was vague, with the consequence that in 133 rival interpretations could be advanced. The disagreement as to whether L. Tarquinius Collatinus, one of the first pair of consuls, abdicated or had his *imperium* abrogated may well derive from a search for precedents at this time.[2] But although the question of precedents was no doubt important in the arguments of 133, the move to depose Octavius is best understood in the light of current political attitudes and practices.

In the first place, for whatever purposes the tribunate may have been used in practice, in name the function of the tribunes was 'to perform the will of the plebs and especially to seek after their wishes'. This was no revivalist notion of Tiberius but a matter of common parlance, for this was the account given to Polybius; probably most tribunes, whatever their true motives, regularly claimed that their actions were in the interests of the masses, thereby simultaneously recognizing and keeping alive the traditional notion of

[1] A consul in 458: Livy, 3. 29. 2 f.; Dion. Hal. 10. 25. 2; Val. Max. 2. 7. 7; cf. Zon. 7. 17. The whole college of military tribunes with consular power in 402: Livy, 5. 9. 1 f. Possibly Camillus, dictator in 368: Livy 6. 38. 9; cf. Plut. *Cam.* 39. A dictator in 249, *coactus abdicare*: *Fasti Cap.*; Livy, *Epit.* 19. The tribunes: Livy, 9. 8. 13 f.; 9. 10. 1 f.; cf. Cic. *De Off.* 3. 109. Cf. Additional Note R, p. 348. The unreliable Florus, 2. 2. 5, asserts that Octavius was terrified into abdicating, but this is contrary to the whole tenor of other accounts and particularly to indications that he denied the validity of his deposition (pp. 208 f.).

[2] Mommsen, *Röm. Staats.* i³, pp. 628 f.; Additional Notes R and S, pp. 348 f. Lepidus: App. *Iber.* 83. Earlier attempts to abrogate pro-magistracies are recorded for 209 (Livy, 27. 20. 11 f.; cf. Plut. *Marc.* 27) and 204 (Livy, 29. 19. 6).

their duties;[1] and the recent interventions in respect of the levy and the grain supply will have helped to foster a sense of its reality. But also, because of the manner in which and the purposes for which the tribunician veto had often been employed in practice, there had been developing that unmistakable tendency to seek and to countenance means of circumventing the veto. Thirdly, recent developments had encouraged and given currency to the notion that urgent considerations of public interest could justify overriding the spirit of the law and even temporarily setting in abeyance particular laws: and if this could seem justifiable on such grounds, so also could action contrary to the *mos maiorum*. And finally, Scipio's two consulships had been achieved on the claim that it was the right of the People, the *Populus*, to make, change, adapt, or set aside the regulations governing eligibility for office, in other words to choose whomsoever they wished and to treat the regulations only as a general guide which in special cases could be overridden.[2] This had two aspects: if the *Populus* could in effect override electoral regulations, it could certainly take action which was not explicitly in conflict with any law, even though it was contrary to the *mos maiorum*; and at the same time these events had propagated the notion that the *Populus* had the right to have whomsoever it wished in office. And if this is not quite the same as removing whomsoever it wished from office, still it comes very close, and it will be recalled that as recently as 136 a promagistrate had been deprived of his *imperium*.

Several of these points, and the events in which they found concrete expression, were very important for rational argument in support of Tiberius' plan; but their deeper significance lies in the widespread attitudes of mind which they reveal. When it is realized that such notions as these were not only current but widely accepted and had been the basis of action, it is much less surprising that it occurred to Tiberius and his associates to break the deadlock by having Octavius deposed, or that, in this moment of great tension and frustration, huge numbers of voters were prepared to accept a step apparently so novel and drastic.

Both the surviving narratives indicate that Tiberius announced his

---

[1] Polyb. 6. 16. 5; Taylor, 'Forerunners of the Gracchi', *JRS* 52 (1962), p. 20 with n. 10.
[2] pp. 183 and 185 f.

proposal that Octavius should be deposed only after the deadlock had been discussed by the Senate, but it is unlikely that the idea first occurred to him then. Just when the plan was formulated cannot be known—and presumably never was known by more than a handful of close associates[1]—but it would be surprising if it were not before the second assembly at which Octavius exercised his veto, and the possibility could easily have been considered before the tribunate even began. However that may be, the project was handled with great skill. It was announced at the crucial moment when passions had reached a high pitch and the deadlock, the impossibility of compromise, had been demonstrated decisively; during its execution frequent appeals were made to Octavius to withdraw his veto and avert the crucial vote; probably Octavius was even invited to propose the deposition of Tiberius before Tiberius put his own proposal to the assembly; and one final appeal was made dramatically just before the vote of the eighteenth tribe completed the majority against Octavius. Octavius could scarcely have responded, nor can Tiberius have had great hopes that he would do so. To have proposed the deposition of Tiberius would have been to invite a humiliating adverse vote and at the same time to admit the propriety of Tiberius' own proposal; similarly to have given way before the threat would have been a humiliating defeat, would have cost him the good will of the powerful men who had encouraged him, and in itself would have come close to admitting the propriety of Tiberius' proposal. From Tiberius' point of view, however, the frequent appeals served to give maximum publicity to the contumacy and obstinacy of Octavius, publicity which would not only help to ensure a massive vote but which would also be some insurance for the future; for there was a real risk that, when the passions of the moment had subsided, there might be some reaction of sentiment against what had been done.

As was to be expected, the voting went heavily against Octavius; the first eighteen tribes, constituting the necessary majority, all voted for his deposition. Octavius himself maintained that the vote was

[1] Like the agrarian scheme itself, the plan could have owed as much to collective deliberation as to Tiberius' own inventiveness; the ingenious mind of Appius Claudius, for example, could well have made a substantial contribution; cf. his actions in 143: pp. 107 f. See Additional Note T, p. 349.

invalid.[1] His grounds are not stated, but whatever they were Tiberius found arguments against them sufficient to convince the masses for the moment. Nevertheless, Octavius' determination was of great significance,[2] in that it crystallized the issue and forced Tiberius to commit himself irretrievably in action. For when the voting was completed and Octavius was declared to be no longer a tribune, he refused to leave the tribunal, so that Tiberius was obliged, if he were not to lose his case by default, to have him removed forcibly. On the assumption that the vote was valid this was a logical and necessary consequence; but those who claimed that the vote was invalid could argue with equal logic that Tiberius had violated the sacrosanctity of a tribune, and it was not to be long before this powerful new weapon was put to good use.

The moment of deposition was significant in another way: it was marked by the first open violence. Passions has been raised to great intensity by harsh economic and social pressures and by the keen sense of self-interest which many felt in the proposed law, by the great tension of the struggle and the long delay, during which the determination and obstinacy of Octavius had been demonstrated repeatedly, so that he had become the focus of frustration, anger, and hatred. At such a moment, in a setting where shouting and jeering were familiar phenomena, it was no great step, when the termination of Octavius' sacrosanctity was proclaimed by his forcible removal from the tribunal, for a section of the crowd to make an angry rush at him. Shielded by friends and servants Octavius managed to escape unharmed; Tiberius himself probably hastened to intervene. There is a story that one of Octavius' slaves suffered hideous injury, but it is at least possible that this is an exaggeration, or even a complete fiction, emanating from later recriminations and propaganda; in any event there were evidently no other serious casualties. Thus the affair seems to have been a brawl rather than a riot,[3] and it had no

---

[1] Diod. 34/35. 7. 1 = Poseid. fgt. 110d *FGrH*; also implied by Octavius' refusal to leave the tribunal. Additional Note U, p. 350.

[2] Cf. Cic. *Brut*. 95: *qui iniuria accepta fregit Ti. Gracchum patientia.*

[3] Cf. Fraccaro's word, *tafferuglio*: *Studi*, i, p. 118; *Athenaeum* 9 (1931), p. 306 = *Opusc.* ii, p. 65. The forcible removal of Octavius and the brawl are recounted only by Plutarch, but Fraccaro, locc. citt., and Gabba, *Appiani B.C. Liber Primus*, p. 39, *contra* Carcopino, *Autour des Gracques*, pp. 26 f., rightly recognize that Appian's brief phrase, διαλαθὼν ἀπεδί-δρασκε, so far from indicating voluntary and peaceful withdrawal, harmonizes well with

immediate impact on the course of events. Nevertheless its psychological impact must have been considerable. The temper of the mob, the potential for violence, had been revealed. It is most improbable that either party to the dispute had been or was now contemplating the use of violence to achieve its ends; but the leaders in the struggle, on both sides but especially among Tiberius' opponents, must have feared that at subsequent moments of great tension they too might become the centre of such a brawl; the customary retinues made up of clients, freedmen, and slaves could now be looked upon not merely as symbols of status but as a useful means of protection; and the huge crowd which accompanied Tiberius himself is likely to have aroused particular apprehensions that it might get out of hand. If no one was planning to initiate violence, many must have been thinking in terms of defending themselves.

Plutarch's version. It remains true that the latter is presented dramatically and it is possible that it has been coloured by exaggerations, such as the blinding of Octavius' slave, but even this is not certain.

XVI

THE TRIBUNATE OF TIBERIUS GRACCHUS:
THE CATASTROPHE

THE deposition of Octavius and the appointment of an amenable successor[1] opened the way for the enactment of the agrarian law, for a subsidiary law conferring or augmenting the judicial powers of the three commissioners who were to operate it, and for the appointment of the commissioners themselves (Tiberius, his brother Gaius, and Appius Claudius). Although all this was achieved smoothly, the struggle was by no means over. The opposition, angry and embittered, remained intent on thwarting the scheme and on destroying Tiberius' political influence. An opportunity was found in the commissioners' need for money. If the scheme was to proceed at all rapidly considerable expense would have to be incurred in surveying and determining boundaries; further, an impoverished family, without the financial resources to purchase tools and seed or to maintain itself until the first adequate harvest, would not derive much benefit from the gift of a plot of land. Unless these matters were attended to speedily and efficiently there was a real danger that the project would prove ineffective. If that happened the disappointment of high hopes, no doubt excessively high in many simpler minds, would lead to a damaging reaction against Tiberius and his colleagues. If in the previous year it had been possible to claim that the *aerarium* had no funds to spare, so it could be also in 133: on the proposal of Scipio Nasica the Senate refused to allow Tiberius a public tent and gave him a derisory expense allowance.[2] Presumably the

---

[1] The name of the successor is variously reported: Plut. *Ti. Grac.* 13. 2, 'Mucius' (which is usually preferred); App. *B.C.* 1. 12, 14, 'Quintus Mummius'; Oros. 5. 8. 3, 'Minucius'. Cf. Earl, 'M. Octavius', *Latomus* 19 (1960), pp. 666 f., and bibliography given there.

The basic sources for this chapter are App. *B.C.* 1. 13–17 and Plut. *Ti. Grac.* 13–21; cf. Livy, *Epit.* 58; Oros. 5. 8. 3 f. Other refs. collected by Greenidge and Clay, *Sources*[2], pp. 7 f.; Münzer, *RE*, s.v. *Sempronius*, no. 54 cols. 1417 f.; *MRR* i, p. 494. Detailed references are given only on special points.

[2] Plut. *Ti. Grac.* 13. 3: nine obols a day. On Scipio's funds in 134 see pp. 136 and 184.

same was done for the other two commissioners, Appius Claudius and Gaius Gracchus. In effect it was precisely the device which had been used against Scipio Aemilianus the year before. Scipio had overcome it by drawing upon his own resources and those of his friends; but his friends had included several monarchs and he also had at his disposal the resources of a province. The commissioners did not have to pay an army, but their immediate expenses were bound to be very considerable; it is hard to believe that their private fortunes could have sustained the agrarian programme for very long.

At this critical juncture an envoy, Eudemus, arrived from Pergamum with the news that Attalus III had died and had bequeathed his estate and kingdom to Rome. Tiberius, possibly assisted by the fact that he was the patron with whom Eudemus lodged,[1] saw an opportunity to secure funds from an outside source. He put through the assembly a law which appropriated Attalus' personal fortune for the assistance of those who were being resettled on the land.[2] The anger of his impotent opponents is readily understood. He had overcome the obstacle which they had placed in his path and thereby he had transformed the prospects of the agrarian scheme. Moreover, they could argue that by tradition such matters were entrusted to the Senate and that Tiberius had insulted that body by taking them direct to the assembly. Indeed it is probably true that in the broad perspective of events this law marks an important extension of the field in which the authority of the Senate was being ignored or defied; but, seen in its context, it was certainly not intended as a revolutionary step, a conscious attack on the Senate as such.[3] The opposition had exploited their advantage as the majority in the Senate to place a major financial impediment in the way of the agrarian scheme, and Tiberius' action is to be understood simply as an attempt to counter this; he sought and found a device, entirely within the bounds of law, to overcome the impediment.

[1] Plut. *Ti. Grac.* 14. 1 f.; Badian, *Foreign Clientelae*, p. 174. But it is not certain that Tiberius gained great advantage from this; in particular it is not proven that Eudemus put loyalty to his patron before the interests of the Roman state.

[2] Additional Note V, p. 350.

[3] Plut. *Ti. Grac.* 16. 1 and Val. Max. 3. 2. 17 attribute such a purpose to Tiberius, though not with specific reference to this law. This is plainly connected with the later charges that he was seeking a *regnum*: p. 228.

With anger and bitterness intensified by the realization that neither the agrarian scheme nor Tiberius himself was vulnerable so long as he enjoyed sufficient popularity to control the assembly, his enemies were determined to undermine his position and to that end made strenuous efforts to discredit him. Something is known of the attacks made by three eminent consulars. Metellus Macedonicus attacked Tiberius' character by contrasting his allegedly disorderly conduct with the stern and sober uprightness of his father. Q. Pompeius asserted that Eudemus of Pergamum had given Tiberius a diadem and a purple robe, believing that he was going to be king of Rome. Neither Pompeius nor any other senator can seriously have believed that Tiberius was aiming at monarchy, nor is this what Pompeius is reported to have said. Pompeius' fiction—for such it surely was— was an attempt to characterize Tiberius' actions as outrageous and un-Roman by showing that to an outsider like Eudemus they resembled those of an autocrat. This is the first hint of the charge that Tiberius actually was aiming at a *regnum*, which afterwards was used extensively, with appropriate comparisons with such misty figures as Spurius Cassius and Spurius Maelius, to justify the killing of Tiberius and many of his supporters. But so far as is known Pompeius himself did not make that direct charge, and it is doubtful if much use was made of it before Tiberius' death.

The third consular, T. Annius Luscus, delivered a devastating speech against Tiberius in the Senate, and when Tiberius brought him before a *contio* Annius scored a notable success in verbal repartee. In both instances his argument concerned the deposition of Octavius: first, that it had been an insulting attack on a colleague who by law was sacrosanct and inviolable; second, that, if the veto could be circumvented in this way, the ability of the tribunes to protect the individual citizen had been gravely impaired. It seems that in reply to this attack Tiberius felt obliged to deliver a public speech, very defensive in tone, justifying his actions. Annius had challenged Tiberius to a *sponsio*, a judicial wager, on the question; others went further and, looking to a long-familiar political weapon, threatened to prosecute Tiberius when his period of office expired.[1]

---

[1] Plut. *Ti. Grac.* 14 f. On Metellus also Cic. *Brut.* 81; Annius, Livy, *Epit.* 58 and *ORF²*, pp. 104 f. Charges of attempted tyranny: p. 228; cf. Additional Note, Z, p. 353. Threats of

There was a considerable danger that such a prosecution might succeed. Popular enthusiasm could not be maintained indefinitely at the extreme intensity which had been reached during the struggle for the agrarian bill, and the constant repetition of charges that the efficiency of the tribunate had been impaired and sacrilege committed was likely to arouse genuine anxieties among the mass of the People; doubts and hesitations would grow; meanwhile Tiberius' opponents had several months in which to concert their efforts and use social pressures to the full; and, having the initiative, they would be able to choose a favourable time to bring the prosecution. Tiberius was seriously afraid that some time in 132 his enemies might be able to muster enough votes in the assembly to have him condemned. He decided, or was persuaded, that he must secure immunity from prosecution and that the best—or the only—way to achieve this was to be elected to the tribunate for a second year. In order to stimulate the necessary enthusiasm and support he may have promised new legislation, perhaps including a reduction in the total length of compulsory military service.[1] There was a clear possibility that he might succeed in the election—if his candidature was allowed to pass unchallenged. Thereby he precipitated a new dispute, centred upon another issue in which the requirements of the law were uncertain and controversial and upon which all the energies and passions of both sides could be focused.

Possibly Tiberius' opponents feared that his re-election might lead to a recovery of his waning prestige and open the way for extended political dominance by the 'Claudian' faction, though whether they really envisaged Tiberius maintaining his popularity and influence through an indefinite series of tribunates is perhaps more doubtful.[2]

prosecution: Plut. *Ti. Grac.* 16. 1; App. *B.C.* 1. 13; Dio, fgt. 83. 7 f.; Oros. 5. 8. 4 (naming Pompeius); cf. Cic. *De Leg.* 3. 24.

[1] Additional Note W, p. 351.

[2] Earl, *Tiberius Gracchus*, pp. 104 f., cf. pp. 112 f., places much emphasis on this possibility, but even in 133 it was not self-evident that Tiberius would succeed in the election. Moreover his actions as tribune could still be restrained and thwarted by the veto of opposing tribunes, which for long had been the principal means of keeping the potentialities of the tribunate in check. Tiberius had circumvented it once, but even on the agrarian issue the deposition of Octavius had proved to be an extremely hazardous undertaking. It was precisely because this very action seemed likely to lead to his destruction that Tiberius had been driven to seek a second tribunate; there was little likelihood either that he would attempt to repeat the device or that it would succeed a second time.

But in any case the attempt to secure re-election was highly provocative. The anger and bitterness felt towards Tiberius had created a desire for revenge as an end in itself, over and above the fact that his political destruction would be a major step in halting the agrarian programme. The prospects of achieving this had begun to appear very good indeed, and now, suddenly, they seemed likely to be confounded by a wholly unexpected move. And it was unexpected because it was in startling contrast to established practice and even, some held, to the requirements of the law.

In early times there certainly had been no barrier to immediate repetition (*continuatio*) of the tribunate, which had occurred on not a few occasions during the Struggle of the Orders. But in later years various regulations had prescribed increasingly restrictive conditions of eligibility for magistracies, including the prohibition of *continuatio*;[1] and although these restrictions had been waived during certain emergencies, notably during the Second Punic War, subsequently they had been reimposed and reinforced. It seems likely, therefore, that the legal issue was whether the prohibition of the *continuatio* of magistracies applied also to the tribunate, which technically was not a magistracy but which in practice was assimilated closely to the magistracies.[2] As for the *mos maiorum*, while distant ancestors had sanctioned *continuatio* of the tribunate, so far as is known there had been no instance for nearly two and a half centuries. That is a measure both of the gravity with which Tiberius regarded the threats against himself and of the shocked surprise with which his almost desperate decision must have been greeted.

It is evident that Tiberius was endeavouring to subordinate, if not actual constitutional law, at least long-established constitutional practice to a particular political issue. With much justice it might be asserted that both the action itself and the attitude of mind which lay behind it constituted a long-term threat not only to the existing pattern of government but to order and stability in general; and this was so not merely because they might increase the possibilities of using the tribunate to defy the Senate but because such actions and attitudes, if they proliferated, could progressively undermine respect for any form of constitutional government. Yet even in this Tiberius

---

[1] Mommsen, *Röm. Staats.* i³, pp. 517 f.   [2] Additional Note X, p. 351.

was an innovator only in a limited sense; he is certainly not to be thought of as a conscious revolutionary. It was at least possible to argue that he was acting within the terms of the law; it is not at all clear that his attempt at a second tribunate was any more improper in this respect than the means by which Nasica Corculum had achieved both a censorship and a second consulship less than ten years after his first;[1] nor was it any more liable to undermine constitutional regularity than the setting aside of undisputed legal regulations governing candidature for the consulship—twice in the interests of the same man, Scipio Aemilianus. If Tiberius was prepared to subordinate accepted constitutional practice to immediate and pressing political interests, this was neither novel nor out of tune with the times. In recent years, it has been observed in earlier chapters, there had been an increasing readiness to do precisely this,[2] so that Tiberius was reflecting a not uncommon attitude of mind. That is not to deny that his attempt had both novelty and significance; but it does mean that, however unexpected his particular proposal, his thinking was not fundamentally revolutionary, that he was a politician of his times. The most critical differences from other recent manifestations of this attitude of mind are perhaps two: first and above all, the tremendous accumulation of passions and tensions focused upon this one issue; second, the very fact that it was possible to argue that Tiberius was acting within the law. Scipio Aemilianus' two consulships had been so unmistakably contrary to law that it had been necessary to put special measures through the assembly, to use methods the legal validity of which was undeniable; but on the present issue the legal position was ambiguous, so that each side could claim the support of the law as it stood.

This ambiguity enabled men whose passions and interests were deeply involved to believe quite honestly, or to persuade themselves, that Tiberius was within his rights, or alternatively that his attempt at *continuatio* was illegal. Tiberius' opponents could convince themselves and proclaim loudly that the outcome which they were so anxious to prevent would conflict not only with their desires and interests but with the requirements of the law; but equally the Gracchans could convince themselves and proclaim that attempts to

[1] pp. 38 f.   [2] pp. 68, 183, and 186.

prevent the assembly re-electing Tiberius if it wished to do so were improper and a violation of the rights of the assembly. There is no need to emphasize the potential danger of a situation of great political tension in which each side could convince itself that the success of its opponents would be a violation of law and order.

It is scarcely surprising that Tiberius' opponents met with some success in their strenuous efforts to prevent his re-election. It was because he had already lost much support over the issue of the deposition of Octavius that he had been driven to seek a second tribunate; and now this candidacy was itself being castigated as illegal. On top of that the election happened to coincide with harvesting operations, which hindered many of Tiberius' potential supporters from returning to the city.[1] The total effect was that on the day designated for the election, the day expected to see the climax of the struggle, the opposition had real hopes that the assembly might not re-elect Tiberius.

Although the two surviving accounts differ about what actually happened at the assembly that day, they do agree on certain points: the voting began but did not progress very far; some of the tribunes were hostile to Tiberius, and there was a substantial dispute between these and Tiberius' supporters; the assembly was adjourned to the next day, and this adjournment was procured by the Gracchans because in some way things were not going well for them. One account, brief and imprecise, implies that the voting was going against Tiberius and attributes all the difficulties to the naked obstructionism of the Gracchans, but the alternative version, with its greater detail, is likely to be nearer the truth. When the first two tribes voted for Tiberius the hostile tribunes intervened with the objection that re-election would be illegal; probably they imposed a veto on further proceedings until Tiberius' candidature was disallowed. The presiding tribune, Rubrius, not an outright opponent of Tiberius but paralysed by doubts about the legal niceties of the situation,[2] was persuaded by Tiberius to hand over the presidency to

---

[1] It should cause no surprise that indigent casual labourers were unwilling to forfeit earnings at this time. Moreover, those who hired such labourers were in a position to exercise some pressure, especially if there was a surplus of labour so that men who went to vote might find themselves replaced.

[2] Appian, *B.C.* 1. 14, does not mention the veto explicitly, but its use at this point would

Mucius,[1] the tribune who had replaced Octavius. This complicated the dispute still further, because the opposition claimed that the new president should be selected by lot, not designated by Rubrius. It was in this phase of the dispute that things were not going well for Tiberius, no doubt because the opposition's case was strong and commanded considerable sympathy, so that if Mucius had proceeded immediately he would have risked forfeiting much-needed support.[2]

Whatever the details, it is plain that Tiberius felt he could not press the dispute further until he had aroused as much public enthusiasm as possible. He had the election postponed until the next day; then, dressed in mourning, he went round the Forum soliciting sympathy and support. To heighten the effect he took with him his young son and commended his family to the care of those whom he met. This was no anticipation of the next day's lynching. The device had been used before, by Ser. Sulpicius Galba in 149, and it is a safe assumption that Tiberius' purpose was fundamentally the same as Galba's: to secure sympathy and votes in order to escape a conviction which would have sent him into exile.[3] It seemed that he had succeeded. That evening he was accompanied to his home by a vast and encouraging crowd. There were good prospects that on the next day the crisis would be resolved in his favour; instead there was an outbreak of violence in which he was killed.

The surviving accounts of that final day of Tiberius' tribunate differ on many points, often irreconcilably, with the result that any reconstruction of the events is inevitably hypothetical in important respects. This is no cause for surprise. The events themselves were

accord with what he says and is the best explanation of why Rubrius should have been perplexed only at this point. The opposition, having waited to see whether, as they hoped, the voters would reject Tiberius, now resorted to the legal technicality, which they probably backed up with their veto. Rubrius is likely to have been further perplexed by the question of whether or not the veto was admissible in these circumstances: cf. Mommsen, *Röm. Staats.* i[3], pp. 286 f.; Bleicken, *Volkstribunat*, p. 76 with n. 2 on the requirement to ensure that successors were elected.

[1] The name is not certain (p. 211 n. 1) but for convenience 'Mucius' will be used.

[2] It is likely also that he was faced with a veto by the opposition; any attempt to proceed in spite of it, e.g. on the ground that it was not valid at tribunician elections (see p. 217 n. 2), would have required careful preparation to ensure that popular support was not alienated. On the two accounts of this assembly see Additional Note Y, p. 352.

[3] p. 59.

characterized by confusion and disorder, and to the difficulties con-
fronting even a contemporary who wished to ascertain the facts
must be added the patent interest of each side in ascribing to their
opponents as much as possible of the blame for the catastrophe; it
may be doubted if there was ever a primary account which was not
tendentious. Certainly both the surviving narratives are in some
degree tendentious, and since each could have preserved authentic
information passed over by the other neither can be trusted consistently to the automatic exclusion of the other.[1] There are a number
of points which are fixed: that the assembly met on the Capitol; that
the Senate was in session while the assembly was being held; that
there was a major disturbance in the assembly, involving some
violence, and that linked with this (though in what way is variously
reported) was Tiberius' gesture of putting his hand to his head; that
at some stage supporters close to Tiberius broke up some staves to
make truncheons; that the assault on the Gracchans was inspired and
led by Scipio Nasica; and that when this assault came the crowd
broke and ran without resistance. But agreement hardly stretches
further, and this is not sufficient to establish a firm, clear framework.
Hence the interpretation which follows, though, it is hoped, shown
to be plausible, is necessarily hypothetical and does not attempt to
embrace every controversial detail.

This interpretation is founded upon two propositions. The first is
that it is very unlikely that at the beginning of the day either side was
planning to initiate violence in order to achieve its ends. After the
catastrophe, of course, it was very much to the interests of each side
to accuse the other of being the first to resort to force. Thus Appian
reports that Tiberius pre-arranged a signal which he would give if
force were needed, and that when opposing tribunes obstructed his
re-election he gave the signal, whereupon his supporters, breaking
up staves to make truncheons, drove their opponents from the
assembly. On the other hand Plutarch, whose account of the catastrophe is in general more favourable to the Gracchans, states that the
breaking of staves was a defensive precaution and that it followed
a report that Tiberius' enemies were preparing to attack and kill
him; Tiberius' gesture has become an attempt to indicate to those

[1] Appendix XI.

who could not hear him that his life was endangered, and there is no reference to the opposition being driven from the assembly; the first actual violence mentioned, apart from disturbances on the edge of the crowd, is the assault led by Nasica.[1] Thus each side accused the other not only of initiating violence but of planning it; yet the indications are that neither did so. For it is evident that both sides were unprepared for violence, that both had to improvise weapons. Admittedly Tiberius' opponents are said to have had slaves and attendants armed with staves and clubs, but since this information comes from Plutarch's pro-Gracchan account it should be treated with caution, and if it is correct the probability is that such attendants were intended to protect their masters or patrons against brawls and personal assaults, a precaution encouraged by the assault on Octavius. There were no metal weapons, and the wooden ones cannot have been plentiful since the senators themselves used the legs and fragments of broken benches. Similarly the only weapons of the Gracchans were pieces of the staves belonging to the tribunes' attendants, which cannot have been very numerous and were confined to a small group around Tiberius himself.[2]

The second proposition is that it is even more improbable that when Nasica and his followers emerged from the temple of Fides they had any intention of killing Tiberius, let alone large numbers of his supporters. After the event, of course, no one had an interest in denying that the killing was planned. For the Gracchans the charge was an invaluable political asset, while for their opponents to have attempted to defend their actions by asserting that they had not been planned would have been most inadvisable, virtually an admission that they were in the wrong. Their need was to present their actions as entirely justifiable, and this could be the more plausibly maintained by letting it be thought that there had been deliberation and conscious decision. But in reality to have set out to kill citizens without trial would have been, to say the least, a grave risk, both personal and political, and furthermore quite unnecessary; their central interest was to prevent Tiberius being re-elected tribune, and to that

[1] App. B.C. 1. 15; Plut. Ti. Grac. 18. 3 f.; for the gesture see Additional Note Z, p. 353.
[2] In general the accounts agree about the nature of the weapons: App. B.C. 1. 15 f.; Plut. Ti. Grac. 19. 1, 7 f.; cf. Livy, Epit. 58; Oros. 5. 9. 2; Vell. 2. 3. 2; Val. Max. 1. 4. 2; Diod. 34/35. 7. 2.

end they needed to break up the assembly which they believed was being conducted in an illegal manner. Moreover, one of the minor but significant points upon which our two versions are agreed is that when the anti-Gracchan senators came out of the temple and advanced into the assembly they were unarmed; the broken benches which they used to arm themselves were those in the assembly. That does not suggest that they deliberately set out to kill.

The day began with crowds massing on the Capitoline hill for the resumed election. Plutarch paints a vivid and plausible picture of the scene: of the cheer which greeted Tiberius' arrival, of the crowd swaying backwards and forwards, of disturbances caused by partisans of each side trying to force their way into the crowd, and of a din which hampered proceedings and made it difficult for speech to be heard over any distance. Meanwhile the Senate was meeting near by. The subject of its debate at this stage is unknown, but it is a fair conjecture that it concerned the action to be taken if Tiberius attempted to push through his re-election despite arguments that this would be illegal and despite a tribunician veto. Perhaps some were already advocating that if he attempted this he should be prevented by forcible dispersal of the assembly. Possibly it was some such proposal that the senator Fulvius Flaccus reported to Tiberius; but that is purely a guess: as reported in Plutarch the message—that, although they had failed to secure the approval of the consul, Tiberius' enemies were planning to lynch him and for that purpose were arming many of their followers—is patently a Gracchan apologia and is distinctly improbable in content. Its true nature is unknown, and we cannot even be certain that the pro-Gracchan account places it at the correct point in the sequence of events.[1]

How then did the violence begin? Why did Tiberius' immediate supporters arm themselves by breaking up the staves of the attendants? Both the surviving narratives seem to be influenced by *post eventum* justifications, both are, at the least, over-simplifications. That the Gracchans simply took the initiative by driving away the opposing tribunes is incredible: conceivably they might have tried to

---

[1] Plut. *Ti. Grac.* 18. 2 f. Valgiglio, *Plutarco. Vita dei Gracchi*, p. 97, suggests that the message belongs after the breaking of staves and the outbreak of violence, and that in the version followed by Plutarch it has been placed earlier in order to strengthen the Gracchan case.

carry on despite the veto, asserting that it was improper at a tribunician election; but there was nothing to be gained by an unprovoked and sacrilegious attack on tribunes. Removing a tribune from office, with the full approval of the assembly, had already proved a costly enough venture. On the other hand, it is not easy to believe that they improvised weapons only in response to a reported plan to lynch Tiberius and that they stood quietly on the defensive. More general considerations apart, something drastic occurred to provoke the assault led by Scipio Nasica.

There seem to be three plausible possibilities. First, the disturbances on the edge of the crowd may have developed into brawls and thence into a more general fight in which the Gracchans got the best of it. Secondly, the breaking of staves may have followed a message from Fulvius that the other faction was considering dispersing the assembly; and this action in itself may have provoked or exacerbated disturbances among an already excited crowd, and may have given rise also to rumours that the Gracchans were preparing to resort to force. Thirdly, Appian implies that the opposing tribunes attempted to veto the proceedings at the assembly, which is exactly what is to be expected; if, on the argument that such a veto was improper, Mucius and Tiberius attempted to carry on, their opponents would have been obliged either to let the matter go by default or to enforce their veto through the agency of their attendants; and then Mucius and Tiberius would have been faced with the choice of submitting or resisting. And if they decided to resist (not unprecedented; the consul Q. Servilius Caepio had resisted Ti. Claudius Asellus, only seven years before),[1] the behaviour of their supporters would be readily intelligible: they would have armed themselves not to drive their opponents from the assembly but to resist the enforcement of a veto which they asserted to be invalid. The report of such a confrontation alone might have been sufficient to provoke Nasica and others to action. But it may have gone beyond a confrontation; an exchange of blows, once begun, would not have been easy to stop; serious disorders and fighting could have broken out amongst the crowd, and the obstructive tribunes might even have been driven from the assembly, as Appian asserts they were.

[1] pp. 126 f.

Whatever the actual origin and extent of the disorders, the reaction when they were reported in the Senate is easily imagined. To Tiberius' enemies it seemed that he was prepared to resort to violence rather than abandon a candidature which they held to be illegal. In their view Tiberius was using force to override constitutional obstacles, and this had to be resisted; law and order had to be restored. Nasica, one of Tiberius' leading opponents, demanded that the consul should intervene; but P. Mucius Scaevola, collaborator of Tiberius in the agrarian scheme, cautious and legally minded, in effect refused to act, contenting himself with a careful statement that 'if the people, under persuasion or compulsion from Tiberius, should vote anything that was unlawful, he would not regard this as binding'. It will be noticed that, if this wording is at all close to the original (which is not certain),[1] Scaevola not only declined to intervene but avoided expressing an opinion on whether or not Tiberius was acting illegally.[2] This was too much for the angry Nasica: certainly by implication and perhaps directly, he dramatically accused the consul of betraying the Res Publica, and he called on all who wished to save it to follow him. The majority of senators, joined by their attendants, streamed after him, no doubt in their own way as excited and angry as the crowd in the assembly. In so far as they had any clear idea at all of what they were going to do, their intention was surely to halt the proceedings and break up the assembly.

Such scenes as that which followed can scarcely ever be observed or reported with accuracy; yet it is not difficult to imagine how a rush intended to disperse a crowd and halt supposedly illegal proceedings

[1] Plutarch's story, Ti. Grac. 19. 3 f., that Scaevola refused to intervene is amply confirmed elsewhere: Val. Max. 3. 2. 17; Cic. De Domo, 91; Tusc. 4. 51; (Victor) De Vir. Ill. 64. 7. Nevertheless doubts arise about some features of Scaevola's statement as reported by Plutarch. Nasica is said to have demanded that he 'put down the tyrant' (cf. Additional Note Z, p. 353), to which Scaevola is said to have replied that he would use no violence and put no citizen to death without trial, 'but if the people . . .' (etc., as quoted). The references to tyranny and execution without trial look like post eventum intrusions. Granted that the former might derive from Nasica's emotive rhetoric, the latter would carry the improbable implication that there were calls for the death of Tiberius and that Nasica set out to kill him (cf. pp. 220 f.). The remainder of Scaevola's statement as reported by Plutarch is entirely plausible, but in view of the probability that there are intrusions in the passage the detailed wording cannot be relied upon as authentic.

[2] Presumably Scaevola believed that the disputed questions should be resolved by prosecution and judicial process—which would have presented the prospect of a fantastic tangle of litigation and political confusion.

could lead to bloodshed and killing. As one unorganized crowd attempted to disperse another, the assailants, in their efforts to hasten the process, seized broken chair legs and similar objects to use as truncheons, belabouring those who were in their path; side by side with the senators were their attendants, slaves and freedmen, suddenly presented with a unique opportunity to unleash their aggressive instincts, yet with little comprehension of the reasons for the violence; it is all too easy to understand how in the confused tumult and excitement the blows, encouraged by occasional resistance and counter-blows, became more savage—and in some cases lethal. Nor is it likely that all the casualties were the victims of direct assault. In the emotionally-charged crowd, suddenly faced with the onset of a mass of senators led by the Pontifex Maximus, excitement changed to fear, and those in front gave way, pushing back on those behind; and anyone who has been swept along in the tight press of even a cheerful and orderly crowd will understand how this could quickly turn into panic. It is not hard to imagine that as the panic spread numbers were trampled, crushed, or suffocated, or perhaps even pushed over the steep sides of the Capitoline hill.

How many died is uncertain: one source says two hundred, another more than three hundred,[1] but in such matters exaggeration is all too easy. In view of the lack of resistance and the primitive character of the weapons used it is hard to believe that as many as that were killed by blows, although many may have perished in the panic. But whatever the number of dead, the political implications were immense. Citizens had been killed without trial; killed moreover in an assault led by a private citizen, a *privatus*, with no magisterial authority; and among the dead was the central figure of the current political struggle, Tiberius Sempronius Gracchus, sacrosanct tribune of the plebs.

This interpretation has been unashamedly hypothetical. No one will ever know exactly what happened on the Capitol that day; few knew at the time and none can know now precisely how the violence began. The aim of the present discussion has been, first, to suggest that it is unlikely that anyone planned to be the first to use

---

[1] Oros. 5. 9. 3; Plut. *Ti. Grac.* 19. 10.

violence, let alone to kill a large number of political opponents, and, second, to try to show how violence could have developed readily but unintentionally out of the political tensions and struggles of the day, and out of the methods used in those struggles. Furthermore, those methods themselves are to be viewed in the perspective of current political attitudes. For there are other aspects of Tiberius' tribunate, besides his epoch-making death, to which revolutionary significance has sometimes been ascribed. The carrying of laws contrary to the wishes of the Senate, the reliance on an exploitation of the favour and sympathy of the masses, the deposition of a fellow tribune in order to remove the deadlock produced by the veto, the law dealing with money which under normal usage would have been handled by the Senate, the subordination of constitutional custom, if not of law, to an immediate political issue, or, it might fairly be said, to personal political interests: these have been regarded as exposing or re-exposing on the one hand the potentialities of the tribunate and of the popular assemblies and on the other the essential weakness of senatorial government. But by now it should be evident that Tiberius' use of the tribunate and the assembly was no sudden revival of powers long disused, that he did not surprise the Romans with the novelty of demagogic tactics. On the contrary, almost all his methods had been used in the recent past, in spirit if not in detail; and where there were innovations they were not in their essence revolutionary but accorded with current trends in political attitudes and methods. This is not to deprive Tiberius' tribunate of significance. To comprehend the urgency of the problems which he was attempting to resolve, to see how step after step in his actions had a close precedent, how they fit into the pattern of discernible attitudes, how reasonable they must have seemed to him, how often they are understandable reactions to the weapons used against him—none of this is to deny that the energy and determination with which he fought, using every available method and subordinating everything to the immediate issue, had profound consequences; that his very successes, and above all perhaps the impression created that in the end he was defeated only by a resort to force and massacre, contributed substantially to the gradual breakdown of the existing pattern of orderly government in Rome. Nevertheless, the conduct of Tiberius' tribunate marks an important stage in the development of a long process rather than the beginning of that process.

In that long process there is an evident affinity between the contributions of Tiberius Gracchus and Scipio Aemilianus. Scipio's career, like Tiberius', marks a stage of development, not the beginning; he too was a man of his time, using the methods of his predecessors but 'improving' upon them, using them more efficiently and more vigorously; nor was he the only politician of the age to make a contribution of this kind. Nevertheless, when the events of 133 are examined in relation to their political background the outstanding figure in that background is Scipio. By subordinating major constitutional obstacles to immediate issues, by using the veto as a means of political blackmail, by so extensively cultivating and exploiting popular favour as an instrument with which to defy the Senate, all in the interests of his personal ambition, not only had he done much to prepare the way for Tiberius, to develop the political attitudes underlying so many of Tiberius' actions, but he had created a situation of exceptional and extreme factional hostility in which popular appeal was a key factor.

The news of Tiberius' death reached Scipio while he was still at Numantia. Every allowance must be made for the probability that the account he received came from sources hostile to Tiberius, sources which would have put the most favourable interpretation possible upon the killing; yet in the broader perspective Scipio's comment, besides being politically unfortunate, cannot but seem to be tinged with unconscious irony. For he quoted a verse of Homer:[1]

ὣς ἀπόλοιτο καὶ ἄλλος ὅτις τοιαῦτά γε ῥέζοι.
'So perish likewise all who work such deeds!'

[1] Appendix II, no. 48.

XVII

THE LAST YEARS

THERE is a sense in which the death of Tiberius was both the climax and the termination of the immediate struggle; one faction had succeeded, the other had been routed; and the brief outburst of violence was ended. Yet both sides, probably equally stunned and shocked by the turn of events, must soon have realized that so far from being finished the underlying struggle was bound to continue, only with intensified bitterness and determination, over-shadowed by the menacing precedent of a resort to force. Indeed it was by no means self-evident that the bloodshed would not be followed by a riotous and violent reaction. Rome's escape from such an eventuality must be credited partly to the Gracchan leaders,[1] who chose to counter-attack through legal channels, and partly to a number of sensible measures designed to forestall such an explosion. Thus the bodies of the victims, including that of Tiberius, were not allowed normal burial but were thrown into the Tiber that same night—a source of offence but a wise precaution.[2] The obsequies of a popular tribune in 138 and of one of Tiberius' friends earlier in 133 had both occasioned popular demonstrations, for which a Roman funeral, especially of a man of Tiberius' lineage and standing, was all too well suited.[3] Then the Decemviri were instructed to consult the Sibylline oracles. On their instructions elaborate expiatory rites were performed—in the ancient shrines of distant Sicily, not in Rome, where the ceremonies might have been inflammatory.[4] Further, the

[1] The term 'Gracchan' is used in this chapter as a convenient label for one of the factions in the subsequent struggle, but no deeper connotation should be read into it than that most of the men concerned had been associated with Tiberius Gracchus.

[2] App. B.C. 1. 16; Plut. Ti. Grac. 20. 3 f.; Livy, Epit. 58; Oros. 5. 9. 3; Vell. 2. 6. 7; (Victor) De Vir. Ill. 64. 8; Val. Max. 6. 3. 1d.

[3] p. 130; Plut. Ti. Grac. 13. 4 f.; cf. 20. 4, where the reported offer of Gaius Gracchus to bury his brother's body at night implies a recognition of the danger of disturbances.

[4] Cic. Verr. 2. 4. 108; cf. Diod. 34/35. 10, usually associated with the slave rebellion but more probably referring to the episode mentioned by Cicero.

Senate itself, as a conciliatory gesture, seems to have called for the election of a new agrarian commissioner to take Tiberius' place, an appointment which was obtained by P. Licinius Crassus Mucianus, father-in-law of Gaius Gracchus and an adviser in the preparation of Tiberius' agrarian bill.[1]

The authors of these measures are not named, but it is a reasonable guess that a major part was played by the presiding consul, P. Mucius Scaevola. Cicero, in two passages, would have his audience understand that after Tiberius' death Scaevola actually defended Nasica's actions as legally justified.[2] That is not easily believed. Not only would it have conflicted in principle with Scaevola's earlier stand but Cicero himself in another passage shows that Nasica was exceedingly unwilling to have Scaevola sit in judgement on his action, going so far as to assert in the Senate that Scaevola was prejudiced; and in addition Cicero elsewhere names Scaevola as one of the Gracchan leaders in the following years.[3] On the other hand, the many decrees of the Senate through which Scaevola is alleged to have defended Nasica's action may very well have been in reality a series of sensible precautionary measures intended to forestall a renewal of violence, to reduce the tension, and to channel the coming struggle into legal paths.

It is noteworthy that from the point of view of Nasica and his followers these moves are all defensive in character. Fundamentally, the same is true of the main form of propaganda which they developed: that Tiberius had been aiming at a *regnum*, at a tyranny, and that for this reason it was entirely justifiable for even a private citizen to bring about his death; Tiberius was a new Spurius Maelius, Nasica a new Servilius Ahala. But though this argument persisted and is familiar from the works of Cicero, and though it succeeded in sidetracking some into disputes about such technicalities as whether Ahala had been a private citizen or in office as *magister equitum*, the resort to this extreme interpretation of Tiberius in order to exculpate Nasica reveals a basically defensive attitude.[4] However plausibly each

---

[1] Plut. *Ti. Grac.* 21. 1 f.; *MRR* i, p. 495.

[2] Cic. *De Domo,* 91; *Pro Planc.* 88.   [3] Cic. *De Orat.* 2. 285; *Rep.* 1. 31.

[4] Quint. *Inst.* 5. 13. 24; Sall. *Bell. Iug.* 31. 7; Cic. *Pro Mil.* 8; 72; *Brut.* 103; 212; *In Cat.* 1. 29; *Phil.* 8. 13; *De Amic.* 41; *De Off.* 1. 76, 109; Val. Max. 3. 2. 17; 5. 3. 2e; 6. 3. 1d; Plut. *Ti. Grac.* 19. 2 f., with Additional Note Z, p. 353; cf. Cic. *Rep.* 2. 49, where Tiberius' name is almost certainly to be restored.

side might accuse the other of having been the first to use force, only one side had killed.

Not surprisingly, therefore, in the ensuing months the first phase of the struggle centred around Nasica and found him on the defensive. It is said that he was subject to public abuse, and that the charge of tyranny was thrown back at him. He was accused of killing citizens without trial, of murdering a sacrosanct and inviolable tribune. In the Senate some sort of *quaestio*, or board of inquiry, was set up—in what form and with what precise function is unknown—and M. Fulvius Flaccus succeeded in having Scaevola nominated one of the members (*iudices*) despite many protests, especially from Nasica, who alleged that Scaevola was prejudiced. In addition there were threats of prosecution, threats which must soon have turned to reality.[1] Plainly, in a trial, especially a trial in the tribal assembly, Nasica would have been in grave danger of conviction—not to mention the possibility that such proceedings might have triggered off fresh disturbances. So he was sent off on an embassy to the newly acquired province of Asia. He was saved from prosecution, from formal condemnation, but politically he had suffered a major defeat. He had been driven into virtual exile; he must have known that politically he was a spent force and that he might never be able to return to Rome. In the event he died at Pergamum, very soon afterwards, probably within the year.[2]

Not everything, however, favoured the Gracchans; their opponents had certain assets. First, they had a majority in the Senate. Second, all those senators who had followed Nasica had every incentive to maintain close co-operation and unity. Third, if the bloodshed had created anger and bitterness, it had created also fear. In the immediate aftermath the 'anti-Gracchans' were well placed to exert pressure upon

---

[1] Plut. *Ti. Grac.* 21. 4 f.; Cic. *De Orat.* 2. 285.

[2] Plut. *Ti. Grac.* 21. 4 f.; Val. Max. 5. 3. 2e; (Victor) *De Vir. Ill.* 64. 9; Cic. *Rep.* 1. 6; *Pro Flacc.* 75; *ILS* 8886; cf. Cic. *De Amic.* 41; Plin. *Nat. Hist.* 7. 120. It is usually supposed that he was one of the five *legati* mentioned in Strabo, 14. 1. 38. It is uncertain whether he left Rome late in 133 or early in 132. Plut. *Ti. Grac.* 20. 6 indicates that he was still active in Rome early in 132, but in Cic. *De Amic.* 37 and Val. Max. 4. 7. 1 Nasica's role is assigned to Laelius. Cic. *De Orat.* 2. 285 also might suggest that he was in Rome after the end of Scaevola's consulship. Cf. Hansen, *The Attalids*, pp. 143 f.; Magie, *Roman Rule in Asia Minor*, ii, p. 1033 n. 1. He was dead in time to be replaced as Pontifex Maximus not later than early 131: *MRR* i, p. 499; cf. below, p. 234.

cowed and submissive clients. Hence their success at the consular elections, when the candidates elected for 132 were P. Popillius Laenas and P. Rupilius, the latter a *novus homo* of humble origin who owed his advancement to the patronage of Scipio Aemilianus. Popillius' connexions may have lain elsewhere—there is a hint of discord between his cousin Marcus and Scipio—but the present emergency counted for more than such divisions.[1]

When Popillius and Rupilius took office they sought to rebut the accusations of murder and to publicize the counter-charge of attempted tyranny by instituting a special *quaestio* directed against the supporters of Tiberius. Significantly, the consuls' chief adviser, and apparently the most influential figure involved in the proceedings, was C. Laelius. Tiberius' aristocratic associates were in no great danger. The consuls would scarcely have dared to attack men like Appius Claudius, Crassus Mucianus, P. Mucius Scaevola, or M. Fulvius Flaccus, and in any case most of the Gracchan senators will have been attending the Senate at the time of Tiberius' final assembly. The victims were men of humbler rank. Probably they were not very numerous, but some were executed and others driven into exile. Among the former were Diophanes of Mytilene and a certain C. Villius, while Blossius of Cumae, after a famous inquisition at the hands of Laelius, fled from Rome and joined the rebel Aristonicus in Asia. Presumably such methods were intended both to reinforce the claim that the killing of Tiberius was justified and to perpetuate the climate of fear. But they were dangerous methods, of questionable legality and liable to increase hostility as well as fear.[2]

It was perhaps shortly after this that Scipio Aemilianus arrived back in Rome. Admittedly it has been suggested that he had hastened back from Numantia in time to assist Rupilius at the consular elections.[3] If so, he played a very discreet role, for it is Laelius, not he, who appears as the active figure behind the *quaestio* of 132. His support for Rupilius was not necessarily in the form of personal canvas at this time, nor could it have been so in the fullest sense; for

[1] pp. 83 f. and 93.
[2] Cic. *De Amic.* 37; Val. Max. 4. 7. 1; Vell. 2. 7. 3 f.; Plut. *Ti. Grac.* 20. 4 f.; *C. Grac.* 4. 2; Sall. *Bell. Iug.* 31. 7. Plut. *Ti. Grac.* 20. 6 less plausibly names Nasica as the inquisitor of Blossius. For the possible relevance of *ILS* 23 see Additional Note ZA, p. 353.
[3] Simon, *Roms Kriege*, p. 190; Cic. *De Amic.* 73.

he did not hold his triumph, and therefore did not enter the city, until some time in 132.[1] More probably he did not arrive back from Spain until that year, perhaps in the spring or early summer.

Scipio celebrated his second triumph, and to 'Africanus' he added a new *cognomen*, 'Numantinus'. But, though it had been a great irritation to Rome, Numantia was not another Carthage, either in repute or in wealth; the booty was slight, the captives were few; the victorious troops received a bounty of only seven *denarii* each: later the elder Pliny was to marvel that they were satisfied with this meagre sum, but he probably inferred their contentment from the absence of mutiny.[2] In the second century B.C. soldiers expressed their discontent with their votes, not their swords; and Scipio will not have forgotten that in 167 one hundred *denarii* had been deemed insufficient by his father's troops.[3] If he himself did not pay more, it was because his resources were exhausted.

The most disappointing aspect of the triumph, however, was that the achievement of ending the Numantine war, which two years before had seemed to promise new glory and new influence, was irrelevant to the issues which now dominated the political scene. Not that the new pattern was wholly independent of the old: the Gracchan faction was essentially that which had been and still was centred around Ap. Claudius Pulcher; and possibly it was old enmities which led Metellus Macedonicus, though he had criticized Tiberius and had a marriage tie with Nasica, to take a leading part in the Gracchan attacks on Aemilianus.[4] Even so, the roles were strangely reversed. Now it was Appius Claudius and his associates who could hope to command sufficient popular favour to outweigh the ties and pressures of their opponents' *clientelae*; and Scipio found his closest supporters and himself inextricably committed to the other side, to allies who recently had been his opponents, to a group which indeed commanded a majority in the Senate, which no doubt was looking forward to availing itself of his popular appeal and saw in him the outstanding leader it required, but whose recent actions had made it exceedingly unpopular with the masses and heavily dependent on

[1] Cic. *Phil.* 11. 18; cf. Livy, *Epit.* 59; Eutrop. 4. 19. 2.

[2] Plin. *Nat. Hist.* 33. 141; cf. Oros. 5. 7. 18; Flor. 1. 34. 17. Numantinus: App. *Iber.* 98; (Victor) *De Vir. Ill.* 58. 6; Ampel. 18, 23, 24; Plin. *Ep.* 8. 6. 2. Other refs. to triumph collected in *MRR* i, p. 498.   [3] pp. 78 f.   [4] Cic. *Rep.* 1. 31; cf. pp. 312 f.

the machinery of *clientelae* for influence in the assemblies, especially the tribal assemblies. Thus the position in which he found himself was in direct contrast with one of the main political weapons, one of the chief sources of strength, which he had exploited in the past.

During 132 the political struggle began to go in favour of the Gracchans. It is not difficult to guess at plausible explanations for this. Benefits were probably beginning to flow from the work of the agrarian commission, which achieved much in 132 and 131.[1] The *quaestio* of Popillius and Rupilius may have proved a double-edged weapon; as immediate fears subsided, its legacy of anger and resentment may well have been more potent than the arguments that Tiberius had sought a *regnum*. Moreover the Gracchans harped on the theme that Tiberius had been within the law and that those who had killed him were guilty of a shocking crime,[2] arguments which were reinforced by the early death of Nasica, which many must have seen as divine retribution for his sacrilege.

This last event necessitated the appointment by a tribal assembly of a new Pontifex Maximus, and thereby provided the Gracchans with the occasion of an important electoral success. The candidate elected in place of Nasica was one of the leaders of the Gracchan faction, P. Licinius Crassus Mucianus,[3] agrarian commissioner and father-in-law of Gaius Gracchus. Other successes followed. Mucianus himself was elected to the consulship of 131, and although he was to quarrel with his colleague, L. Valerius Flaccus, about the military command in Asia, there is some reason to suspect that the latter too was associated with the Gracchan faction.[4] And among the tribunes of the plebs for 131 was C. Papirius Carbo, one of the ablest, most fluent, and most forceful orators of his day.

Carbo took the offensive, introducing a bill which reaffirmed the admissibility of re-election to the tribunate as often as was desired. The fate of this bill, which raised directly the issue central to the final

[1] The great majority of the surviving *termini* were set up by the commission when Claudius and Mucianus were still alive: Degrassi, *Inscr. Lat. Lib. R.P.* i, nos. 467–72, 474, with note on 472.

[2] Carbo's question to Scipio Aemilianus implies such contentions: p. 233. Cf. Cic. *De Orat.* 2. 170; Plut. *Ti. Grac.* 21. 5.   [3] *MRR* i, p. 499. Cf. Cic. *Rep.* 1. 31.

[4] p. 192 n. 3. The quarrel: p. 234. It was probably at this election or the next that L. Rupilius was defeated despite the support of Scipio: Cic. *De Amic.* 73; *Tusc.* 4. 40; Plin. *Nat. Hist.* 7. 122.

crisis of Tiberius' tribunate, was of prime concern to both sides; for if successful it might undermine seriously the plausibility of the opposition's claim to legal justification; on the other hand its defeat would greatly strengthen their position. Among those who spoke in support of the measure was Tiberius' brother, Gaius Gracchus, (Fulvius Flaccus was associated with Gracchus and Carbo but is not known to have spoken) while the opposing speakers, including Laelius, were headed by Scipio himself, who delivered a speech of great sternness.[1] The bill was rejected by the assembly, but, though Cicero would have his readers believe otherwise and though Carbo may have erred tactically in focusing attention on this particular issue, in all probability it was defeated not so much by Scipio's rhetoric or by the actual convictions of the voters as by determined and united efforts to make the maximum possible use of *clientelae* and social pressure. That, it seems, was the opinion of Carbo himself; for during his tribunate he introduced, and carried, a law which extended the ballot to voting in legislative assemblies.[2] Moreover, Scipio's speech was far from being an unambiguous success. It was interrupted by a famous altercation which certainly demonstrated and almost as certainly accelerated substantially the decline in his popularity.[3] 'What', Carbo demanded, 'was Scipio's opinion concerning the death of Tiberius Gracchus?' Carbo was no innocent seeker after knowledge; he knew where Scipio stood. Probably by personal conviction, certainly by the actions of his closest political adherents, Scipio was fully committed against Tiberius. It does look as if he had managed to avoid making any public declaration on the matter since his return from Numantia, but now he was faced with a direct question intended to compel him to express his opinion in public. He could not possibly say that the killing of Tiberius was

---

[1] Livy, *Epit.* 59; Cic. *De Amic.* 96; cf. Appendix II, no. 52. The date of Carbo's tribunate: Münzer, *RE*, s.v. *Papirius*, no. 33, cols. 1017 f. If Taylor, 'Tiberius Gracchus' Last Assembly', *Athenaeum* (1963), pp. 51 f., were correct in supposing that *continuatio* of the tribunate was already prohibited explicitly, Carbo's proposal would be understood best as a new attempt to enact a measure which had constituted the true business of Tiberius' last assembly; even so its defeat would have been an objective of great importance for the opposition. But see Additional Note X, p. 351. Fulvius' association is attested in connexion with the altercation discussed below: Plut. *Ti. Grac.* 21. 8 = Appendix II, no. 50a.

[2] Cic. *De Leg.* 3. 35; cf. *De Orat.* 2. 170.

[3] For this episode see Appendix II, nos. 50 and 51, and refs. cited there.

unjustified: that would be a betrayal of his friends and allies, and possibly of his own conscience; but the consequences of answering that it was justified were all too obvious. He seems to have tried a compromise: 'si is occupandae rei publicae animum habuisset, iure caesum videri.' 'If he intended to seize the state he was killed justly.' But the attempt at compromise was vain. At 'iure caesum videri' the crowd roared its disapproval, perhaps led by a claque of freedmen followers of the Gracchans. As the second Africanus, the conqueror of Carthage, faced the howling mob, his sharp tongue gave expression to his anger and his wounded pride: 'I who have not feared the clamour of hostile armies will not fear the din made by you to whom Italy is only a step-mother.' Much is in doubt: which of the surviving versions is closest to Scipio's actual words; whether this outburst silenced the crowd; whether Scipio intended to direct the remark at a claque of freedmen. But its significance is clear. On top of *iure caesum videri* Scipio had presented his opponents with a second and quite gratuitous weapon with which to assail his reputation. The outburst both signified and sealed his forfeiture of popular favour. The defeat of Carbo's bill was a serious reverse for the Gracchans, but for Scipio personally it was a costly victory.

This forfeiture of popular favour can be seen also in another event. The consuls of 131 quarrelled as to which of them should take charge of military operations in the newly acquired province of Asia, where a rebellion led by Aristonicus, a pretender to the Pergamene throne, had assumed considerable proportions. In the ordinary course of events sortition would have settled the matter, but in this instance L. Valerius Flaccus happened to be flamen Martialis, and Mucianus, in his capacity as Pontifex Maximus, threatened to impose a fine if Valerius abandoned his sacred duties. In consequence the dispute was referred to the tribal assembly, which gave opportunity for someone to propose that the task should be entrusted to neither of the consuls but to Scipio, who had recently celebrated his second triumph and was undeniably the greatest military leader in Rome. The contest was won by Mucianus; two tribes only voted for Scipio.[1]

---

[1] Cic. *Phil.* 11. 18. There is no indication whether this vote was before or after Scipio's altercation with Carbo. It may have been after if Carbo introduced his proposal very soon after taking office.

The political misfortunes of such a man as Scipio are unlikely to arouse much sympathy in the modern reader, but at least it is possible to glimpse something of what they meant to him. He had set out on his career anxious and determined to prove himself a worthy son of Paullus, a worthy heir to Africanus; he had struggled unscrupulously to that end, had earned for himself the name 'Africanus', and had added to it 'Numantinus'; he had destroyed Carthage, Rome's age-long enemy, and had defeated and destroyed Numantia, where so many others had failed; he had achieved the censorship; twice he had been elected consul, on both occasions contriving to appear specially summoned to office despite technical ineligibility; he had gloried in, had deliberately exploited the prestige and popularity which his exploits engendered, and had used these as major supports of his political eminence; he had been the great popular hero, immensely proud of his achievements. Now, less than fifteen years after the cheering crowds had acclaimed the triumph of the new Africanus, only three years after he had swept over constitutional obstacles to a second consulship and the command against Numantia, he was con-fronted by a hostile mob shouting and jeering its anger; his prestige had slumped to the point where only two of the thirty-five tribes were to vote to give him a new command. No wonder such a man, faced with the tumultuous and howling evidence of the transformation in his fortunes, gave way to his anger in an outburst so revealing of scorn and wounded arrogance.

Yet these public humiliations were not the full measure of Scipio's misfortunes. By this time his marriage had become acutely unsatis-factory. His wife was Sempronia, sister of the dead Tiberius and the actively hostile Gaius Gracchus; she is said to have been unattractive, unloved and unloving; and she was childless: there was no heir to the line of Africanus.[1] From such a situation the Roman aristocrat had two well-established avenues of escape: divorce followed by another marriage, or the adoption of a son. Scipio would seem to have had every incentive for the former, and there is no clear diffi-culty in the way of either of these alternatives. Yet he took no action. Plainly he felt debarred from both courses. At his reasons it is possible only to guess. Perhaps the divorce of Sempronia would have entailed

[1] App. B.C. 1. 20. Other refs. to the marriage: p. 13 n. 2.

the return of her dowry, which is likely to have been substantial. In view of his enormous expenditure since 134, and of the low bounty paid to the troops from Numantia, it is unlikely that he had much ready money available and he may have been unwilling to face the sale of substantial property or the return of valuable estates.[1] As for the failure to adopt, it may be relevant that his own experiences as an adopted son seem not to have been wholly satisfactory. His relations with his new family, at least some of whom had regarded him as an unworthy successor to Africanus, were somewhat uneasy;[2] and he clearly felt a strong link with his mother Papiria, although she must have been divorced by Paullus very soon after Scipio was born.[3] Thus the circumstances of his own youth might have created a prejudice against adoption. But there is a second possible reason. In his censorship Scipio had solemnly, and no doubt bitingly, attacked those who, to secure the privileges of fatherhood, used adoption instead of producing children of their own.[4] If Scipio had resorted to adoption without first trying a second marriage his words would have been remembered. His enemies would not have failed to ridicule him, and what can be discerned of his character suggests that he was the last man wittingly to expose himself to ridicule, let alone at this particular time.

But even if these explanations are entirely wide of the mark, it is evident that something inhibited Scipio from taking a step which was both natural and, prima facie, highly desirable from his own point of view. It is possible, of course, that he was not displeased at the prospect of his own career being seen by posterity as the final brilliance of the line of Africanus; much more probably he found in the situation a sense of frustration and failure.[5]

Both the marital problem and the popular antagonism were now constant factors in the situation, but there is reason to believe that the unhappy experiences of early 131 represent the nadir of Scipio's

[1] Note the very small quantities of gold and silver he is said to have possessed at the time of his death in 129: Plin. *Nat. Hist.* 33. 141; (Victor) *De Vir. Ill.* 58. 11; 'Plut.' *Apophth. Scip. Min.* 1.

[2] pp. 20 and 36.   [3] pp. 13 and 32.

[4] Appendix II, no. 16; cf. Appendix IX.

[5] Another source of personal distress for Scipio was the death of his brother, Fabius Maximus Aemilianus, some time between the Numantine campaign and Scipio's own death in 129, when Fabius' son was in charge of the obsequies: Cic. *Pro Mur.* 75; Val. Max. 7. 5. 1.

political fortunes. He accepted the challenge of the changed situation and, bringing a new issue to bear upon the struggle, in a strange reversal of fortune emerged as the dominating figure among the majority in the Senate, in opposition to a minority whose popularity enabled them to win disproportionate influence in the assemblies. This is certainly the situation reached by the beginning of 129, but the actual course of the struggle in 131 and 130 is obscure. Nothing further is known about Scipio's activities in these years, and the few events which are recorded permit only an uneven and disjointed sketch.

At the censorial elections held in 131 the successful candidates were for the first time both plebeians. The inevitable inference that they had been rival candidates is amply confirmed by their identity, for they were Metellus Macedonicus and Q. Pompeius. This result, though scarcely likely to have given much pleasure to Scipio, probably represents an even division of honours as between the Gracchans and their opponents; for Pompeius had been an extremely vigorous opponent of Tiberius, while Metellus is likely already to have gone over to the Gracchans. But it would be unwise, not to say implausible, to assume that this election was wholly dominated by the contest between the Gracchans and their opponents. About the conduct of the census itself remarkably little is known; it is not even known whether it was affected by the past antagonism of the censors towards each other. Nothing at all is recorded about Pompeius, and Metellus figures in only two episodes, though both were rather sensational. One of them was his famous speech urging that in order to maintain the safety of Rome it was the duty of all men to marry and to beget children,[1] a theme which came not inappropriately from Metellus in view of 'that numerous cohort which called him father',[2] but which is likely to have grated upon the ears of Scipio. The other incident, very different in kind, arose because Metellus excluded from the list of senators one of the tribunes of the plebs, C. Atinius Labeo. In retaliation Atinius arrested Metellus and prepared to have him

---

[1] Livy, *Epit.* 59; Gell. 1. 6. 1 f., 7 f. (erroneously 'Numidicus'); Suet. *Aug.* 89. 2; *ORF*², fgts. 4–7, pp. 107 f. The speech was evidently satirized by Lucilius, 676 f. M. Cf. Berger, 'A Note on Gellius, *N.A.*, I, 6', *AJPh* 67 (1946), pp. 320 f.

[2] Plin. *Nat. Hist.* 7. 143; cf. 7. 59.

hurled from the Tarpeian Rock. This untoward eventuality was prevented, as no doubt everyone concerned had anticipated, by the veto of other tribunes, but they did not intervene when Atinius went on to confiscate and consecrate Metellus' property. The fundamental issue in this dispute was probably whether or not the tribunate should automatically confer membership of the Senate; but whether it was in any way linked with the struggle between the Gracchans and their opponents it is impossible to say.[1]

The Gracchans enjoyed further successes. M. Perperna, almost certainly of their faction,[2] was one of the consuls elected for 130, and although his colleague, L. Cornelius Lentulus, probably did not share these associations (he is no more than a name, but no such name is ever linked with the Gracchans), when Lentulus died in office the suffect elected in his place was an Appius Claudius Pulcher, perhaps a cousin of the Princeps Senatus.[3] But the Gracchans also suffered serious loss in the deaths of two notable leaders. During 130 P. Crassus Mucianus, campaigning in Asia, was defeated in battle and killed; and at about this same time Appius Claudius himself, the Princeps Senatus, died. Mucianus' place as Pontifex Maximus was taken by his brother, P. Mucius Scaevola, and the two vacancies on the agrarian commission were filled by M. Fulvius Flaccus and C. Papirius Carbo, able and energetic men but not comparable to their predecessors in seniority and prestige.[4] The death of Claudius in particular is likely to have impaired the fortunes of the Gracchans. This may have been evident at the consular elections for 129, when they perhaps won neither place;[5] but in any case the weakening of the Gracchan leadership cannot but have facilitated the attack on the agrarian commission which Scipio was preparing for 129.

By the end of 130 the complaints of the Italian allies about the activities of the agrarian commission had reached considerable proportions. They came in part, no doubt, from wealthy Italians who

---

[1] Livy, *Epit.* 59; Plin. *Nat. Hist.* 7. 143 f.; Cic. *De Domo*, 123. Additional Note ZB, p. 354.

[2] p. 192.

[3] p. 192.

[4] Crassus: Cic. *Rep.* I. 31; Vell. 2. 4. I (*proconsul*); other refs. *MRR* i, p. 503. Claudius: Cic. *Rep.* I. 31; App. *B.C.* I. 18; he died early enough for the censors of 131–130 to name a successor as Princeps Senatus: *MRR* i, p. 500. For their successors see *MRR* i, p. 503.

[5] C. Sempronius Tuditanus was definitely not a Gracchan: App. *B.C.* I. 19. There is no significant information about the political associations of his colleague, M'. Aquillius.

forfeited Roman *ager publicus* on which they, like wealthy Romans, had encroached; and probably resentment could be aroused among the lower orders because the redistribution of land benefited Romans only. More important, however, were the disputed cases, where boundaries were in question, or where land alleged to be Roman *ager publicus* was claimed by the Italians to be rightfully theirs. The agrarian commissioners used their judicial powers to decide such cases and thereby created a great deal of resentment among the Italian aristocracies; more serious still, it could be asserted with much plausibility that this form of Roman judicial activity violated the treaty-rights of the allies.[1]

The complaints were seized upon by Scipio as a powerful weapon for use against the Gracchans. It does not follow that they were simply exploited cynically to that one end. Quite apart from obligations towards clients and questions of legal justice, there were powerful reasons for heeding the Italians, reasons with some appeal to the ordinary citizen as well as to the statesman. The allied states made a massive contribution to the Roman armies, and if through resentment they were, for example, lethargic in levying the contingents for which they were asked, this could prove an acute embarrassment, especially in view of the difficulties so frequently experienced in the Roman levy itself.

In the early months of 129 Scipio began his attack, which evidently was planned to minimize the opposition by proceeding step by step, instead of attacking the whole agrarian programme at once. Details are disputed, but events seem to have followed roughly the following course. Scipio first laid a proposal before the Senate. Presumably this was the occasion of his speech against the *lex iudiciaria* of Tiberius Gracchus (a speech of which the only surviving excerpt seems totally irrelevant to the declared subject).[2] The Senate accepted the proposal, which evidently drew attention to the infringement of the treaties, on that ground declared illegal the commissioners' exercise of judicial power in respect of citizens of the allied states, and declared that until Tiberius' law could be suitably amended such jurisdiction should be

[1] App. *B.C.* 1. 18–19; Cic. *Rep.* 1. 31; 3. 41; *Schol. Bob. Mil.*, p. 118 Stangl.

[2] Appendix II, no. 53. Fraccaro, 'Oratori', pp. 393 f., attempts to establish the relevance of the fragment.

exercised only by the consul C. Sempronius Tuditanus.[1] Whether or not it was known already that Tuditanus was to conduct a campaign in Illyria, his departure for the war effectively stopped judicial proceedings for the time being.

This alone would have been sufficient to arouse the wrath of the Gracchans; but Scipio prepared to take the attack a stage further, probably by attempting actually to amend or repeal Tiberius' *lex iudiciaria*, and thereby formally to curtail or annul the judicial powers of the commissioners.[2] The Gracchans, seeing in this a deliberate attempt to halt the redistribution of land, resisted vigorously. Tension rose, apparently to a pitch comparable to the climaxes of 133. At a *contio* Scipio faced a Gracchan mob shouting 'kill the tyrant'—thus adopting the polemic of their opponents. His reply reveals much, both about himself and about the bitterness of the dispute: 'Naturally those who are enemies of their own country wish to destroy me first; for Rome cannot fall while Scipio stands, nor Scipio live when Rome has fallen.'[3] It was on that same evening, it seems, that he was escorted

---

[1] App. *B.C.* 1. 19. The interpretation adopted here is essentially that offered by Hardy, *Six Roman Laws*, p. 39, Last, *CAH* ix, pp. 42 f., and Scullard in Marsh, *Hist. of the Roman World*, p. 408, all of whom emphasize the objections to the idea that the decree suspended entirely the judicial functions of the commissioners. Geer, 'Notes on the Land Law', *TAPhA* 70 (1939), pp. 32 f., suggests that because the decree of the Senate was intended only as the preliminary for a *rogatio* which in fact was never voted upon, it was ineffective; but this seems to conflict too sharply with Appian's account. Gabba, *Appiani B.C. Liber Primus*, pp. 60 f., holds that Scipio secured the passage through the assembly of an *obrogatio*, transferring the judicial powers of the commissioners to the consuls (similarly Bilz, *Die Politik*, pp. 74 f.); but there is no good reason for doubting that the decision was taken only in the Senate, and it is hard to believe that, as Gabba suggests, Appian's words mean that the δῆμος, not the Senate, was persuaded by Scipio. That the work of the commission did continue is indicated by Dio, fgt. 84. 2 and App. *B.C.* 1. 21; cf. Livy, *Epit.* 59.

[2] *Schol. Bob. Mil.*, p. 118 Stangl indicates that Scipio's defence of the allies was left incomplete by his death. App. *B.C.* 1. 19 and Cic. *Rep.* 1. 31 both suggest he had further plans. Cf. also the mutilated notice in Obsequ. 28a: . . . *dissensione in legibus ferendis.* . . . Since there was great public tension and *contiones* were being held (below) it is likely that Scipio was sponsoring legislation. Cic. *Rep.* 6. 12 implies a proposal to make Scipio dictator, which would indeed account for the tension, and for the outcry 'Kill the tyrant'; but in view of the total lack of other evidence this should be regarded as an anachronism which Cicero has allowed to slip into this highly coloured passage.

[3] Appendix II, no. 54. This probably happened on the last day of Scipio's life, being the same incident as that mentioned in Plut. *C. Grac.* 10. 5 (Fulvius . . . τὴν ἡμέραν ἐκείνην ἐπὶ τοῦ βήματος τῷ Σκιπίωνι λελοιδορημένον) and Oros. 5. 10. 9 (*Africanum pridie pro contione de periculo salutis suae contestatum, quod sibi pro patria laboranti ab improbis et ingratis denuntiari cognovisset*). Cf. also App. *B.C.* 1. 19, where his opponents are reported to have alleged that he intended to cause bloodshed in order to destroy the Gracchan law. Another indication of

home by a massive crowd of supporters.[1] He retired to his room, intending, it is said, to compose another important speech, which was to be delivered the next day. In the morning he was found dead.[2]

No inquiry was held into the cause of death,[3] and the funeral oration written by Laelius seems to have implied that it was natural; but whether he really believed this or was trying to avoid some scandal it is impossible to say.[4] Rumours of murder were rife: Cornelia, Sempronia, Gaius Gracchus, M. Fulvius Flaccus, and Carbo are all mentioned as suspects;[5] ten years later Carbo's prosecutor, the orator L. Licinius Crassus, was to state bluntly that Carbo had been an accomplice in procuring the death of Scipio.[6] A counter-charge is preserved: that Scipio committed suicide because he knew he could not achieve what he had promised.[7] The truth cannot now be recovered: possibly no one was certain even at the time.

extreme tension is Obsequ. 28a, which says of a prodigy of 129, *angues duo ... civilem caedem portenderunt.*

[1] Cic. *De Amic.* 12. Cicero says *senatu dimisso*; either this is incorrect or the Senate had met after the *contio*, which is entirely possible.

[2] Livy, *Epit.* 59; Oros. 5. 10. 9; Vell. 2. 4. 5; App. *B.C.* 1. 20; Plut. *C. Grac.* 10. 5; *Rom.* 27. 5; (Victor) *De Vir. Ill.* 58. 10; Cic. *Pro Mil.* 16; *Schol. Bob. Mil.*, p. 118 Stangl; Val. Max. 5. 3. 2d.

[3] Cic. *Pro Mil.* 16; Livy, *Epit.* 59; Plut. *C. Grac.* 10. 6; Vell. 2. 4. 6; Val. Max. 5. 3. 2d; Plin. *Nat. Hist.* 10. 123. Such a variety of comments upon this suggests that Plutarch, loc. cit., may be correct in reporting that an inquiry was sought but was prevented by popular opposition.

[4] *Schol. Bob. Mil.*, p. 118 Stangl = *ORF*², Laelius, fgt. 22, p. 121. Cf. Gabba, *Appiani B.C. Liber Primus*, pp. 63 f. The fragment is extremely corrupt but almost certainly contained the word *morbus*, which strongly suggests a reference to a natural death; for a plausible restoration see Badian, *JRS* 46 (1956), p. 220. Carcopino, *Autour des Gracques*, pp. 83 f., attempts not only to prove that death was natural but to identify a particular cause, but his arguments are inconclusive (Fraccaro, *Athenaeum* 9 (1931), pp. 311 f. = *Opusc.* ii, pp. 69 f.). Renard, 'L'Assassinat de Scipion', *RUB* 37 (1931–2), pp. 483 f., attempts to prove assassination.

[5] App. *B.C.* 1. 20 (Cornelia and Sempronia); Livy, *Epit.* 59; Oros. 5. 10. 10 (Sempronia); *Schol. Bob. Mil.*, p. 118 Stangl (Sempronia and Gracchus); Plut. *C. Grac.* 10. 5 f. (Fulvius and Gracchus); Cic. *Ad Quint. Frat.* 2. 3. 3; *Ad Fam.* 9. 21. 3 (Carbo); Cic. *Rep.* 6. 12 and 14 (relatives). Murder also mentioned or implied in Cic. *De Fat.* 18; *De Amic.* 12; *Pro Mil.* 16; *De Nat. Deor.* 3. 80; Val. Max. 4. 1. 12; 5. 3. 2d; 8. 15. 4; Vell. 2. 4. 5 f.; (Victor) *De Vir. Ill.* 58. 10; Plut. *Rom.* 27. 5; Plin. *Nat. Hist.* 10. 123.

[6] Cic. *De Orat.* 2. 170.

[7] App. *B.C.* 1. 20; Plut. *Rom.* 27. 5.

EPILOGUE

THE public career of Scipio Aemilianus, despite its dazzling brilliance, has a curiously negative quality. Some allowance, it is true, must be made for the inadequacy of the surviving sources: it is conceivable, for example, that for the solution of the urgent social and economic problems of the day Scipio devised and advocated plans of which we know nothing. Yet the fact remains that he made no positive contribution. Laelius' attempted reform, whatever its scope and purpose, was not pressed nor reintroduced; and at the end of his life Scipio was energetically leading the assault on Tiberius Gracchus' agrarian programme, the one great effort which had been made to resolve the domestic problems. Granted that there were potent political reasons for his attitude, and even that he may have judged the scheme unsatisfactory in itself, so far as is known he had no alternative to offer. It is unlikely that his influence on foreign policy was unusual or remarkable. In general it probably would have followed much the same lines without him, especially in the west; after the embassy of 140–139 he may have done more to determine policy towards the Hellenistic east, but little is known about this and there is certainly no sign of a novel or distinctive approach; and in two of the major decisions taken during the period of his pre-eminence, the renewal of the Viriatic war in 140 and the annexation of the kingdom of Pergamum in 133, he had no part at all. Even his military achievements, valuable though they were, may not have had very profound significance; for it is difficult to believe that either Carthage or Numantia could have held out indefinitely.

In so far as Scipio's career does have long-term significance, this lies in its relationship to the decline of the Roman Republic. That decline into the confusion and the civil wars from which the Principate was to emerge was a long and complex phenomenon, and it has engendered much controversy. None the less, among the multiplicity of factors which together constituted the causes there is no doubt that considerable importance is to be attached to the growth of *popularis* methods and to the increasing readiness to subordinate constitutional requirements and the rule of law to immediate and personal advantage. In this process Scipio played a very substantial role. It is one of the characteristics of his career that, with conspicuous success, he placed his own advancement above both usage and the law, that in the furtherance of his own ambitions he cultivated and exploited popular favour as an instrument with which to defy the Senate. In so doing he not only provided formal precedents but helped to break down psychological barriers, to create a political atmosphere in which such methods could be tolerated and, because of their evident success, imitated. Both in this way and by assisting in the creation of a situation of tense factional hostility, in which his own methods had made popular appeal a key factor, he did much to give the political crisis of 133 its particular shape and intensity; and thereby he is not without responsibility for its epoch-making eruption into violence and bloodshed. He himself was part of a process, advancing trends evident in the actions of others, both predecessors and contemporaries; but his own contribution was notable, and without it the development of these trends might have differed substantially in pace and in form.

As for Scipio's death, it can be viewed, as Appian says, as 'an incident in the sedition of Gracchus'.[1] Such an impression is indeed conveyed by the rumours and accusations which it provoked, reflecting the political confrontation of the Gracchans and their opponents.[2] Moreover the funeral of a Scipio, of the conqueror of Carthage and Numantia, could not but be a spectacle which might be exploited for political ends in the immediate struggle.[3] Laelius was perhaps taking advantage of this opportunity when at the conclusion of the funeral speech which he composed for delivery by Scipio's nephew, Q. Fabius Maximus, he wrote: 'Wherefore it is not possible to give sufficient thanks to the immortal gods for this above all, that he, endowed with that mind and with those talents, was born a citizen of this state; nor is it possible to feel sufficient distress and bitterness that . . . he has perished in that very season when both you, citizens of Rome, and all who desire the safety of this state had most need of

---

[1] App. *B.C.* 1. 20.   [2] p. 241.

[3] Scipio's nephew, Q. Fabius Maximus, gave a public funeral banquet. The parsimony of Q. Aelius Tubero in his preparation of a *triclinium*, admirable though it might seem to Seneca two centuries later (*Epist.* 95. 72; 98. 13), was plainly out of character with the rest of the arrangements. Cic. *Pro Mur.* 75 f.; Val. Max. 7. 5. 1.

him alive.'¹ But above all there is a sense in which the death of Scipio marks a decisive point in this immediate struggle, in that it made inevitable the failure of the attack on the agrarian commission—though it should not be assumed too readily that the attack would have succeeded even if Scipio had lived.

In reality, however, the passing of Scipio had greater significance in the pattern of Roman politics than as an incident and a source of propaganda in the Gracchan affair. For nearly twenty years Scipio had been the outstanding political figure in Rome. He could not be ignored or overlooked; for every Roman in public life one of the key questions had been whether he was for or against Scipio—or whether Scipio was for or against him. Despite changes in the patterns and issues of politics, despite fluctuations in fortune, this remained a dominant feature to the end. It was not so much superseded by the Gracchan dispute as merged with it; indeed the origins of that dispute itself were not wholly independent of this element. The disappearance of such a commanding personality opened the way, despite the pattern of the Gracchan dispute, for new alignments, new friendships, and new alliances, for others to seek and exercise enhanced influence. One of the first to appreciate the new situation was Metellus Macedonicus, who, though in recent years an active opponent of Scipio, yet instructed his sons to carry Scipio's bier.² Fourteen years later, when these same men carried Metellus himself, three of them had held the consulship and the fourth was a candidate for that office; one had celebrated a triumph and had been censor; a second was about to become censor; and their cousin, Macedonicus' nephew, had been consul and had triumphed. In one sense at least, as the four Metelli bore the second Africanus to his tomb³ they symbolized the end of one era of politics and the beginning of another.

¹ *Schol. Bob. Mil.*, p. 118 Stangl = *ORF*², Laelius, fgt. 22, p. 121. The passage contains a number of corruptions, for the most serious of which (here omitted) see p. 248 n. 4. Cf. also fgt. 23 = Cic. *Pro Mur.* 75. Elsewhere, *De Orat.* 2. 341, Cicero says that the speech was delivered by Q. Tubero, but in the light of the other passages this is generally regarded as an error: *ORF*², ad loc.

² 'Plut.' *Apophth. Caec. Met.* 3; Val. Max. 4. 1. 12; cf. Plin. *Nat. Hist.* 7. 144. Metellus' words to his sons are variously reported. The version of Val. Max. is plainly embellished and unreliable. The Plutarch version (cf. also *De Frat. Amore*, 14), which is not actually incompatible with that of Pliny, is suspiciously similar to one of the sentiments in Laelius' funeral oration (fgt. 22, quoted above).

³ The Cornelii were not cremated: Cic. *De Leg.* 2. 57; Plin. *Nat. Hist.* 7. 187.

APPENDIX I

The Dates of Scipio's Birth and Death

SCIPIO AEMILIANUS died sometime in the first half of 129, probably in spring or early summer. This is established by means of Cicero's *De Republica*, the dramatic date of which is the *feriae Latinae* of 129.[1] Elsewhere Cicero makes it clear that the dialogue is to be understood as having taken place a few days before Scipio's death.[2] The year 129 is attested also by Cicero, *De Nat. Deorum* 2. 14; Velleius 2. 4. 5; and Orosius 5. 10. 9. Other sources are compatible with this date but are not explicit.

The date of Scipio's birth is slightly more controversial. Two sources give a figure for his age at the time of the battle of Pydna in 168: Livy says he was in his seventeenth year, Diodorus 'about the seventeenth year'.[3] It is virtually certain that both passages were derived from Polybius, who should have been well informed. Since the date of the battle according to the Roman calendar was 4 September,[4] it follows that Scipio was born in the later part of 185 or in 184.

Polybius' account of his famous conversation with Scipio, in which he undertook to assist the latter, contains the statement that at that time Scipio was not more than eighteen years old: οὐ γὰρ εἶχε πλέον ἐτῶν ὀκτω-καίδεκα τότε.[5] The conversation took place not long after Polybius' arrival in Rome, which probably occurred very late in 167 or early in 166,[6] and

---

[1] *Rep.* 1. 14. The date of the Latin Festival was variable. Prior to 154, when consuls still entered office on 15 March, it was usually held in spring or early summer; normally consuls did not leave for their provinces until it was over. It is uncertain whether the old arrangements were retained after 153, when the beginning of the consular year was changed to 1 January (so Marquardt, *Röm. Staatsverwaltung*, iii², p. 298; Mommsen, *Röm. Forsch.* ii, p. 105), or whether the festival came to be held rather earlier in the year (so Samter, *RE*, s.v. *Feriae Latinae*, col. 2214; but the very limited evidence all concerns the years 56–44).

[2] *De Amic.* 14.   [3] Livy, 44. 44. 3; Diod. 30. 22.

[4] Livy, 44. 37. 8. As an eclipse was involved, the record of the date is likely to have been reliable. The Julian date was 22 June, but it is the Roman calendar that is relevant to the present problem.

[5] Polyb. 31. 24. 1. Diod. 31. 26. 5 is derived from this.

[6] The surviving Achaean exiles were released in the seventeenth year (Paus. 7. 10. 12) and while Scipio was in Rome (Plut. *Cato Mai.* 9. 2 f. = Polyb. 35. 6). This can only have been after Scipio's return from Spain, scarcely earlier than the late summer or autumn of 150; but by the spring of 149 Polybius was in Greece (Polyb. 36. 11). Nissen, 'Die Oek. der Gesch. des Polybios', *RhM* 26 (1871), p. 272.

this has led some to prefer 184 to 185 for the year of Scipio's birth;[1] but in reality there is nothing in the passage incompatible with Scipio's nineteenth birthday falling in the later part of 166. Thus the passage would be compatible with either 185 or 184.

A more precise passage is Cic. *Rep.* 6. 12: *Sed eius temporis ancipitem video quasi fatorum viam. Nam cum aetas tua septenos octiens solis anfractus reditusque converterit, duoque ii numeri, quorum uterque plenus alter altera de causa habetur, circuitu naturali summam tibi fatalem confecerint, in te unum atque in tuum nomen se tota convertet civitas, te senatus, te omnes boni, te socii, te Latini intuebuntur, tu eris unus, in quo nitatur civitatis salus, ac, ne multa, dictator rem publicam constituas oportet, si impias propinquorum manus effugeris.*

On this Macrobius comments, obviously correctly, *per septenos octiens solis anfractus reditusque quinquaginta et sex significat annos.*[2] It is clear that Cicero believed that at the time of his death, shortly after the *feriae Latinae* of 129, Scipio had either completed or had very nearly completed his fifty-sixth year. On the widest possible interpretation this must mean that Cicero placed his fifty-sixth birthday in 129, not 128; therefore he believed that Scipio was born in 185, not 184. Moreover, Cicero's figure is not only precise but, owing to his circumlocutory expression, cannot have suffered corruption.

If, as some have believed, Polybius was in conflict with Cicero, it would be necessary to reject the latter's testimony in favour of that of Scipio's contemporary and friend; but it has been seen that the Polybian evidence is compatible with a date in 185. There is, therefore, no reason to reject the opinion of Cicero, who is likely to have made some effort to discover the correct date.

None of the other evidence is satisfactory. *Schol. Bob. Mil.*, p. 118 Stangl says that Scipio *excessit vita sex et quinquaginta annos natus*, but this may have been deduced from the passage in the *De Republica* and therefore may not be independent evidence. Velleius, 2. 4. 6, says *decessit anno ferme LVI*, but figures in the text of Velleius, including this very section, have suffered considerable corruption,[3] so that this is not particularly strong support for Cicero's evidence. The statement of Gellius, 3. 4. 2, that Scipio was under forty when he was prosecuted by Ti. Claudius Asellus (i.e. in 140) is

---

[1] Lincke, *Scipio*, p. 3; Münzer, *RE*, s.v. *Cornelius*, no. 335, col. 1440. Bilz, *Die Politik*, p. 5, and De Sanctis, *Storia*, iv. 3, p. 58, are non-committal.

[2] *Comm. in Somn. Scip.* 1. 6. 83.

[3] The text states that Scipio was first elected consul *anno XXXVI*, which cannot be correct and does not agree with the figure for Scipio's age at death. It is usually emended to *XXXVIII*, but in theory it might be the later figure that has been corrupted, for example from *LIV*; cf. next note.

certainly an error, while 'Plutarch' and Aelian, who say that he lived for fifty-four years, just conceivably might be taken to support 184 as the year of birth but really suggest 183, which is definitely not correct.[1]

To sum up, though there cannot be absolute certainty, the balance of the evidence favours 185 rather than 184 as the date of Scipio's birth.

[1] 'Plut.' Apophth. Scip. Min. 1; Aelian, Var. Hist. 11. 9. 5. Even if Scipio was born in 184, at the least he must have nearly completed his fifty-fifth year at the time of his death. Münzer, RE, s.v. Cornelius, no. 335, col. 1440, plausibly suggests that the mistake in 'Plut.' and Aelian may have arisen from the confusion in the Latin sources of LVI and LIV.

APPENDIX II

Dicta Scipionis

THIS appendix contains all utterances attributed to Scipio Aemilianus, both *dicta* and fragments of speeches, with the following exceptions:

1. Straightforward military orders;
2. The long conversation recorded in Polyb. 31. 23. 9 f. (examined in Chapter II);
3. The words attributed to Scipio by Appian in his report of the negotiations with Phameas (*Lib.* 107);
4. The words attributed to Scipio by Polybius in his report of Hasdrubal's first attempt to negotiate (Polyb. 38. 8. 1 f.);
5. The advice Scipio is alleged to have given to Iugurtha (Sall. *Bell. Iug.* 8. 2).

The sayings have been numbered and as far as possible arranged chronologically; sub-headings indicate various periods in Scipio's career and also the *incerta*. The latter include items where the attribution to this Scipio is uncertain as well as those which cannot be associated with any definite date or period. The most important modern works are Fraccaro's 'Oratori ed orazioni', *Studi storici per l'ant. class.* 5 (1912), pp. 317 f., esp. pp. 362 f. (abbreviated 'Oratori'), and Malcovati's *ORF²*. References are given to both of these wherever appropriate. A comparative table identifies the passages common to *ORF²* and this collection.

BEFORE 147

1. App. *Lib.* 71

ὁ δὲ Σκιπίων ἐθεᾶτο τὴν μάχην ἀφ᾽ ὑψηλοῦ καθάπερ ἐκ θεάτρου. ἔλεγέν τε πολλάκις ὕστερον, ἀγῶσι συνενεχθεὶς ποικίλοις, οὔποτε ὧδε ἡσθῆναι· μόνον γὰρ ἔφη τόνδε τὸν πόνον ἄφροντις ἰδεῖν, μυριάδας ἀνδρῶν συνιούσας ἐς μάχην ἕνδεκα. ἔλεγέν τε σεμνύνων δύο πρὸ αὐτοῦ τὴν τοιάνδε θέαν ἰδεῖν ἐν τῷ Τρωϊκῷ, τὸν Δία ἀπὸ τῆς Ἴδης καὶ τὸν Ποσειδῶνα ἐκ Σαμοθράκης.

The battle mentioned in this passage is the one fought between Massinissa and the Carthaginians in the winter 151–150 (for the date see further Appendix III. 1, pp. 270 f.).

Despite πολλάκις ὕστερον the *dictum* is so closely associated with a particular event that it has been placed here rather than among the *incerta*.

2. Polyb. 35. 4. 8–12

Πόπλιος Κορνήλιος [Ἀφρικανός]. . . . (9) . . . ἀναστὰς εἶπεν εἴτε χιλίαρχον εἴτε πρεσβευτὴν πέμπειν αὐτὸν εἰς τὴν Ἰβηρίαν μετὰ τῶν ὑπάτων ἐξεῖναι· πρὸς ἀμφότερα γὰρ ἑτοίμως ἔχειν. (10) καίτοι γ᾽ ἔφη κατ᾽ ἰδίαν μὲν αὑτῷ τὴν εἰς Μακεδονίαν ἔξοδον ἅμα μὲν ἀσφαλεστέραν ⟨ἅμα δ᾽ οἰκειοτέραν⟩ εἶναι· . . . (12) ἀλλὰ τοὺς τῆς πατρίδος καιροὺς ἔφη κατεπείγειν μᾶλλον καὶ καλεῖν εἰς τὴν Ἰβηρίαν τοὺς ἀληθινῶς φιλοδοξοῦντας.

Date: early 151.
See pp. 42 and 45 f.

3. Polyb. 36. 8. 4–5

αἱ δὲ σημεῖαι τῶν Ῥωμαίων συνεπεφεύγεσαν εἰς βουνόν· καὶ πάντων δόντων γνώμας ὁ Σκιπίων ἔφη, (5) * * * ὅταν ἐξ ἀκεραίου βουλεύωνται, καὶ πλείω ποιεῖσθαι πρόνοιαν τοῦ μηδὲν παθεῖν ἢ τοῦ δρᾶσαι κακῶς τοὺς ἐχθρούς.

Date: autumn 149, when Scipio was a military tribune in the army of Manilius.

4. App. *Lib.* 103

(Four cohorts were cut off by Hasdrubal. The Romans) ἐπεὶ δ᾽ ἔμαθον, ἠπόρουν, καὶ τοῖς μὲν ἐδόκει φεύγειν καὶ μὴ κινδυνεύειν ἅπασι δι᾽ ὀλίγους, ὁ δὲ Σκιπίων ἐδίδασκεν ἀρχομένων μὲν ἔργων εὐβουλίᾳ χρῆσθαι, κινδυνευόντων δὲ ἀνδρῶν τοσῶνδε καὶ σημείων τόλμῃ παραβόλῳ. αὐτὸς δ᾽ ἐπιλεξάμενός τινας ἱππέων ἴλας, ἐπανοίσειν ἔφη ἐκείνους ἢ χαίρων αὐτοῖς συναπολεῖσθαι.

Date: autumn 149, when Scipio was a military tribune in the army of Manilius.

SCIPIO'S FIRST CONSULSHIP AND PROCONSULSHIP, 147–146

5. Cic. *Verr.* 2. 2. 28–29

Africani est hoc, hominis liberalissimi—verum tamen ea liberalitas est probanda quae sine periculo existimationis est, ut in illo fuit: (29) cum ab eo quidam vetus adsectator et ex numero amicorum non impetraret uti se praefectum in Africam duceret, et id ferret moleste, 'Noli', inquit, 'mirari si tu hoc a me non impetras. Ego iam pridem ab eo cui meam existima-tionem caram fore arbitror peto ut mecum praefectus proficiscatur, et adhuc impetrare non possum.'

Date: 147.

(It is conceivable, though not probable, that the subject is Africanus Maior, not Aemilianus.)

6. App. *Lib*. 116

Scipio's speech to the army in Africa demanding the re-establishment of discipline. Though it is certainly based upon an actual event, in its present form the speech is a construction by Appian. It is too long to be quoted here.

Date: 147.

7a. Polyb. 38. 19 = 'Plut.' *Apophth. Scip. Min.* 5

ἐπεὶ δὲ παρελθὼν εἰς τὸ τεῖχος, τῶν Καρχηδονίων ἐκ τῆς ἄκρας ἀμυνο-
μένων, εὗρε τὴν διὰ μέσου θάλασσαν οὐ πάνυ βαθεῖαν οὖσαν, τοῦ Πολυβίου
συμβουλεύοντος αὐτῷ κατασπεῖραι τριβόλους σιδηροῦς ἢ σανίδας ἐμ-
βαλεῖν κεντρωτάς, ὅπως μὴ διαβαίνοντες οἱ πολέμιοι προσμάχωνται τοῖς
χώμασιν, ἔφη γελοῖον εἶναι, κατειληφότας τὰ τείχη καὶ τῆς πόλεως ἐντὸς
ὄντας, εἶτα πράττειν ὅπως οὐ μαχοῦνται τοῖς πολεμίοις.

7b. Val. Max. 3. 7. 2

Aviti spiritus egregius successor Scipio Aemilianus, cum urbem prae-
validam obsideret, suadentibus quibusdam ut circa moenia eius ferreos
murices spargeret omniaque vada plumbatis tabulis consterneret habenti-
bus clavorum cacumina, ne subita eruptione hostes in praesidia nostra
impetum facere possent, respondit *non esse eiusdem et capere aliquos velle
et timere.*

Date: 147, at the time of the assault on the commercial quay; cf. App. *Lib.*
124. So Kahrstedt, *Gesch. der Karthager*, p. 658, preferable to Gsell, *Hist. anc.*
ii, p. 75 n. 4 and iii, p. 398 n. 1, who links the incident with the breaching of the
walls in 146. Cf. Baradez, 'Nouvelles recherches sur les ports antiques de Carthage', *Karthago* 9 (1958), pp. 45 f., esp. pp. 74 f.

8a. Polyb. 38. 20. 1–3

ὅτι τοῦ Ἀσδρούβου τοῦ τῶν Καρχηδονίων στρατηγοῦ ἱκέτου παραγενο-
μένου τοῖς τοῦ Σκιπίωνος γόνασιν, ὁ στρατηγὸς ἐμβλέψας εἰς τοὺς συνόν-
τας " Ὁρᾶτ' " ἔφη " τὴν τύχην, ὦ ἄνδρες, ὡς ἀγαθὴ παραδειγματίζειν
ἐστὶ τοὺς ἀλογίστους τῶν ἀνθρώπων. (2) οὗτός ἐστιν Ἀσδρούβας ὁ
νεωστὶ πολλῶν αὐτῷ καὶ φιλανθρώπων προτεινομένων ὑφ' ἡμῶν ἀπαξιῶν,
φάσκων δὲ κάλλιστον ἐντάφιον εἶναι τὴν πατρίδα καὶ τὸ ταύτης πῦρ, νῦν
πάρεστι μετὰ στεμμάτων δεόμενος ἡμῶν τυχεῖν τῆς ζωῆς καὶ πάσας τὰς
ἐλπίδας ἔχων ἐν ἡμῖν. (3) ἃ τίς οὐκ ἂν ὑπὸ τὴν ὄψιν θεασάμενος ἐν νῷ
λάβοι διότι δεῖ μηδέποτε λέγειν μηδὲ πράττειν μηδὲν ὑπερήφανον ἄνθρω-
πον ὄντα; "

8b. Diod. 32. 23

(Scipio) ὁ δὲ παρακαλέσας αὐτὸν θαρρεῖν καὶ πρὸς τοὺς συνεδρεύοντας φίλους εἰπών, "Οὗτός ἐστιν ὁ πρότερον μὴ βουλόμενος ἐπὶ πολλοῖς φιλανθρώποις σωθῆναι· τοιαύτην μεταβολὴν ἡ τύχη καὶ δύναμιν ἔχει, πᾶσαν ἀνθρωπίνην ὑπεροχὴν ἀνελπίστως σφάλλουσα."

Date: 146.

9a. Polyb. 38. 21. 1–3

ὅτι.................παρ....καὶ δι../............................
...............vι..... / το δικαιον.................ευ...ρων φησιν ο πολυβιοσ / εγων οτι και τιν......ραν επι................αν..... /
τούτου κάλλιον ουτ......και.......τουτ εἴρηται παρὰ /......καὶ ἐπιστρέψας ἐξ αὐτῆς καὶ λαβόμενός μου τῆς δεξιᾶς, " ὦ Πολύβιε " ἔφη " καλὸν μέν, ἀλλ' οὐκ οἶδ' ὅπως ἐγὼ δέδια καὶ προορῶμαι, μήποτέ τις ἄλλος τοῦτο τὸ παράγγελμα δώσει περὶ τῆς ἡμετέρας πατρίδος." ταύτης δε......πραγματικωτέραν / καὶ νουνεχεστέραν οὐ ῥάδιον εἰπεῖν. τὸ γὰρ ⟨ἐν⟩ τοῖς μεγίστοις κατορθώμασι καὶ ταῖς τῶν ἐχθρῶν συμφοραῖς ἔννοιαν λαμβάνειν τῶν οἰκείων πραγμάτων καὶ τῆς ἐναντίας περιστάσεως καὶ καθόλου πρόχειρον ἔχειν ἐν ταῖς ἐπιτυχίαις τὴν τῆς τύχης ἐπισφάλειαν ἀνδρός ἐστι μεγάλου καὶ τελείου καὶ συλλήβδην ἀξίου μνήμης.

(This text is taken from Boissevain, *Excerpta*, iv, pp. 219 f. The text in Büttner-Wobst's edition of Polybius is identical except for a plain τι in place of the opening ὅτι and for two conjectural restorations printed in brackets. Büttner-Wobst had available Boissevain's readings of the manuscript; Boissevain then had available Büttner-Wobst's published edition for his own publication of the *Excerpta*.)

9b. Diod. 32. 24

ὅτι τῆς Καρχηδόνος ἐμπρησθείσης καὶ τῆς φλογὸς ἅπασαν τὴν πόλιν καταπληκτικῶς λυμαινομένης, ὁ Σκιπίων ἀπροσποιήτως ἐδάκρυεν. ἐρωτηθεὶς δὲ ὑπὸ τοῦ Πολυβίου τοῦ ἐπιστάτου τίνος ἕνεκα τοῦτο πάσχει εἶπε, "Διότι τῆς κατὰ τὴν τύχην μεταβολῆς ἔννοιαν λαμβάνω· ἔσεσθαι γὰρ ἴσως ποτέ τινα καιρὸν ἐν ᾧ τὸ παραπλήσιον πάθος ὑπάρξει κατὰ τὴν Ῥώμην·" καὶ τούτους τοὺς στίχους παρὰ τοῦ ποιητοῦ προηνέγκατο,

"ἔσσεται ἦμαρ ὅταν ποτ' ὀλώλῃ Ἴλιος ἱρὴ
καὶ Πρίαμος καὶ λαός."

9c. App. *Lib.* 132 = Polyb. 38. 22

ὁ δὲ Σκιπίων πόλιν ὁρῶν . . . τότε ἄρδην τελευτῶσαν ἐς πανωλεθρίαν ἐσχάτην, λέγεται μὲν δακρῦσαι καὶ φανερὸς γενέσθαι κλαίων ὑπὲρ πολεμίων· ἐπὶ πολὺ δ' ἔννους ἐφ' ἑαυτοῦ γενόμενός τε καὶ συνιδὼν ὅτι καὶ πόλεις καὶ ἔθνη καὶ ἀρχὰς ἁπάσας δεῖ μεταβαλεῖν ὥσπερ ἀνθρώπους δαίμονα, καὶ τοῦτ' ἔπαθε μὲν "Ἴλιον, εὐτυχής ποτε πόλις, ἔπαθε δὲ ἡ Ἀσσυρίων καὶ Μήδων καὶ Περσῶν ἐπ' ἐκείνοις ἀρχὴ μεγίστη γενομένη καὶ ἡ μάλιστα ἔναγχος ἐκλάμψασα ἡ Μακεδόνων, εἰπεῖν, ἐς Πολύβιον τὸν λογοποιὸν ἀποβλέψαντα, εἴτε ἑκών, εἴτε προφυγόντος αὐτὸν τοῦδε τοῦ ἔπους·

" ἔσσεται ἦμαρ ὅταν ποτ' ὀλώλῃ "Ἴλιος ἱρὴ
καὶ Πρίαμος καὶ λαὸς ἐυμμελίω Πριάμοιο."

Πολυβίου δ' αὐτὸν ἐρομένου σὺν παρρησία (καὶ γὰρ ἦν αὐτοῦ καὶ διδάσκαλος) ὅ τι βούλοιτο ὁ λόγος, φασὶν οὐ φυλαξάμενον ὀνομάσαι τὴν πατρίδα σαφῶς, ὑπὲρ ἧς ἄρα, ἐς τἀνθρώπεια ἀφορῶν, ἐδεδίει. καὶ τάδε μὲν Πολύβιος αὐτὸς ἀκούσας συγγράφει.

Date: 146.

These passages are discussed in Appendix IV. The quotation is of *Iliad*, 6. 448 f.

10. Cic. *Verr.* 2. 4. 73

(In Carthage was found the notorious bull of Phalaris.) Quem taurum cum Scipio redderet Agrigentinis, dixisse dicitur *aequum esse illos cogitare utrum esset Agrigentinis utilius, suisne servire anne populo Romano obtemperare, cum idem monumentum et domesticae crudelitatis et nostrae mansuetudinis haberent.*

Date: 146.

BETWEEN THE THIRD PUNIC WAR AND SCIPIO'S CENSORSHIP,
146–142

11. Festus 312 L., s.v. *Quatenus*

Sed antiqui quatenoc dicebant, ut Scipio Africanus in ea oratione, quam scribsit post quam ex Africa rediit: 'uti negotium natum erat, quatenoc castra nostra ita munita erant, ut posses partem exercitus abducere.'

Date: 146.
Fraccaro, 'Oratori', pp. 364 f.; *ORF*[2], fgt. 12, p. 124.
The speech is almost certainly Scipio's triumphal oration.

12. Val. Max. 6. 4. 2

Idem (Scipio Aemilianus), cum Ser. Sulpicius Galba et Aurelius consules in senatu contenderent uter adversus Viriathum in Hispaniam mitteretur, ac magna inter patres conscriptos dissensio esset, omnibus quonam eius sententia inclinaretur expectantibus, 'neutrum,' inquit, 'mihi mitti placet, quia alter nihil habet, alteri nihil est satis.' . . . Quo dicto ut neuter in provinciam mitteretur obtinuit.

Date: 144.

13. 'Plut.' *Apophth. Scip. Min.* 9

Ἀππίου δὲ Κλαυδίου περὶ τῆς τιμητικῆς ἀρχῆς ἁμιλλωμένου πρὸς αὐτὸν καὶ λέγοντος, ὅτι πάντας ὀνομαστὶ Ῥωμαίους αὐτὸς ἀσπάζεται, Σκιπίωνος ὀλίγου δεῖν ἀγνοοῦντος ἅπαντας, " ἀληθῆ λέγεις " εἶπεν· " ἐμοὶ γὰρ οὐκ εἰδέναι πολλοὺς ἀλλ' ὑπὸ μηδενὸς ἀγνοεῖσθαι μεμέληκεν."

Date: 142.

14. 'Plut.' *Apophth. Scip. Min.* 10

ἐκέλευε δὲ τοὺς πολίτας, ἐπειδὴ ἐτύγχανον πολεμοῦντες Κελτίβηρσιν, ἀμφοτέρους ἐπὶ τὴν στρατείαν ἐκπέμψαντας ἢ πρεσβευτὰς ἢ χιλιάρχους μάρτυρας λαμβάνειν καὶ κριτὰς τῆς ἑκάστου ἀρετῆς τοὺς πολεμοῦντας.

It is virtually certain that this passage should be read as being continuous with the preceding one, that it concerns candidature for the censorship of 142, and that the rival is Appius Claudius. There are no grounds to support the improbable suggestion of Simon, *Roms Kriege*, pp. 43 and 98, that the person referred to is Q. Fabius Maximus Aemilianus.

SCIPIO'S CENSORSHIP, 142–141

15. Gell. 4. 20. 1–10

Inter censorum severitates tria haec exempla in litteris sunt castigatissimae disciplinae. (2) Unum est huiuscemodi. (3) *Censor agebat de uxoribus sollemne iusiurandum; verba erant ita concepta: 'ut tu ex animi tui sententia uxorem habes?' Qui iurabat, cavillator quidam et canicula et nimis ridicularius fuit.* (4) *Is locum esse sibi ioci dicundi ratus, cum ita, uti mos erat, censor dixisset: 'ut tu ex animi tui sententia uxorem habes?',* (5) *'habeo equidem', inquit, 'uxorem, sed non hercle ex animi mei sententia.'* (6) *Tum censor eum, quod intempestive lascivisset, in aerarios rettulit causamque hanc ioci scurrilis apud se dicti subscripsit.* (7) Altera severitas eiusdem sectae disciplinaeque est. (8) *Deliberatum est de nota eius, qui ad censores ab amico advocatus est et, in iure stans, clare nimis et sonore oscitavit, atque inibi ut plecteretur fuit, tamquam illud indicium esset vagi animi et alucinantis et fluxae atque apertae securitatis.* (9) *Sed cum ille deiurasset invitissimum sese ac repugnantem oscitatione victum tenerique eo vitio, quod oscedo appellatur, tum notae iam destinatae exemptus est.* Publius Scipio Africanus, Pauli filius, utramque historiam posuit in oratione, quam dixit in censura, cum ad maiorum mores populum hortaretur.

Date: 142.
Fraccaro, 'Oratori', pp. 365 f.; ORF², fgt. 13, pp. 124 f.
No. **16** = ORF², fgt. 14 belongs to the same speech. Fraccaro, 'Oratori', pp. 366 and 372, and Malcovati, *ORF²*, p. 126, also assign to this speech no. **56** = ORF², fgt. 15, which in this collection has been placed among the *incerta*.

16. Gell. 5. 19. 15–16

Animadvertimus in oratione P. Scipionis, quam censor habuit ad populum de moribus, inter ea quae reprehendebat, quod contra maiorum instituta fierent, id etiam eum culpavisse, quod filius adoptivos patri adoptatori inter praemia patrum prodesset. (16) Verba ex ea oratione haec sunt: *In alia tribu patrem, in alia filium suffragium ferre, filium adoptivum tam procedere, quam si se natum habeat; absentis censeri iubere, ut ad censum nemini necessus sit venire.*

Date: 142.

Fraccaro, 'Oratori', pp. 368 f.; *ORF²*, fgt. 14, p. 126.

This passage, which belongs to the same speech as no. **15**, is discussed in Appendix IX.

17a. Val. Max. 6. 4. 2.

Qui (Scipio Aemilianus) cum haberet consortem censurae Mummium, ut nobilem ita enervis vitae, pro rostris dixit *se ex maiestate rei publicae omnia gesturum, si sibi cives vel dedissent collegam vel non dedissent.*

17b. (Victor) *De Vir. Ill.* 58. 9

Censor (Scipio Aemilianus), Mummio collega segniore, in senatu ait, '*Utinam mihi collegam aut dedissetis, aut non dedissetis.*'

Date: 142–141.

Fraccaro, 'Oratori', p. 366 n. 2, and Malcovati, *ORF²*, pp. 124 f. agree that this is a *dictum* and reject earlier suggestions that it is a fragment of a speech. *Pro rostris* (Val. Max.) might be a more appropriate place than in the Senate (*De Vir. Ill.*), but neither source can be pressed on such a detail.

18. Festus, 362 L., s.v. *Requeapse*

Scipio Africanus, Paulli filius, cum pro aede Castoris dixit, hac compositione usus est: '*quibus de hominibus ego saepe atque in multis locis opera, factis consiliis, reque eapse [saepe] bene meritus siem*', id est et re ipsa.

Date: 142 or 141.

Fraccaro, 'Oratori', p. 373; *ORF²*, fgt. 16, p. 126.

Fraccaro shows that the speech was almost certainly associated with the *recognitio equitum*. It was probably delivered in 142 rather than in 141.

19. 'Plut.' *Apophth. Scip. Min.* 11

ἀποδειχθεὶς δὲ τιμητὴς νεανίσκου μὲν ἀφείλετο τὸν ἵππον, ὅτι δειπνῶν πολυτελῶς, ἐν ᾧ χρόνῳ Καρχηδὼν ἐπολεμεῖτο, μελίπηκτον εἰς σχῆμα τῆς πόλεως διαπλάσας καὶ τοῦτο Καρχηδόνα προσειπὼν προύθηκε διαρπάσαι τοῖς παροῦσι· καὶ πυνθανομένου τοῦ νεανίσκου τὴν αἰτίαν δι᾽ ἣν ἀφῄρηται τὸν ἵππον, " ἐμοῦ γάρ " ἔφη " πρότερος Καρχηδόνα διήρπασας."

Date: 142 or 141.

20. Gell. 6. 12. 4–5

(Tunics coming right down over the arms were at first considered unbecoming for men and suitable only for women.) Hac antiquitate indutus P. Africanus, Pauli filius, . . . P. Sulpicio Gallo, homini delicato, inter pleraque alia, quae obiectabat, id quoque probro dedit, quod tunicis uteretur manus totas operientibus.

(5) Verba sunt haec Scipionis: '*Nam qui cotidie unguentatus adversum speculum ornetur, cuius supercilia radantur, qui barba vulsa feminibusque subvulsis ambulet, qui in conviviis adulescentulus cum amatore, cum chiridota tunica interior accubuerit, qui non modo vinosus, sed virosus quoque sit, eumne quisquam dubitet, quin idem fecerit, quod cinaedi facere solent?*'

Date: probably 142 or 141.
Fraccaro, 'Oratori', pp. 374 f.; *ORF²*, fgt. 17, p. 127.
The occasion of this attack was probably the *recognitio equitum*.

21a. Cic. *Pro Cluent.* 134

Qui (P. Africanus) cum esset censor et in equitum censu C. Licinius Sacerdos prodisset, clara voce ut omnis contio audire posset dixit *se scire illum verbis conceptis peierasse; si qui contra vellet dicere, usurum esse eum suo testimonio.* Deinde cum nemo contra diceret, iussit *equum traducere.*

21b. Val. Max. 4. 1. 10

Centurias recognoscens equitum, postquam C. Licinium Sacerdotem citatum processisse animadvertit, dixit *se scire illum verbis conceptis peierasse: proinde, si quis eum accusare vellet, usurum testimonio suo.* Sed nullo ad id negotium accedente '*transduc equum*' inquit '*Sacerdos, et lucrifac censoriam notam, ne ego in tua persona ut accusatoris et iudicis partes egisse videar.*'

21c. 'Plut.' *Apophth. Scip. Min.* 12

Γάιον δὲ Λικίνιον ἰδὼν παρερχόμενον " οἶδα " ἔφη " τοῦτον ἐπιωρκηκότα τὸν ἄνδρα· μηδενὸς δὲ κατηγοροῦντος, οὐ δύναμαι κατήγορος αὐτὸς εἶναι καὶ δικαστής."

21d. Quint. *Inst.* 5. 11. 13

Quintilian relates the Licinius Sacerdos story but himself indicates that his version is a paraphrase of Cicero's in the *Pro Cluentio* (134, quoted above as **21a**).

Date: 142 or 141.

22. Cic. *De Orat.* 2. 258

In hoc genus coniciuntur etiam proverbia, ut illud Scipionis, cum Asellus omnis se provincias stipendia merentem peragrasse gloriaretur: '*agas asellum*' et cetera.

Date: probably 142 or 141, but possibly 140.

Fraccaro, 'Oratori', p. 382; *ORF²*, fgt. 21, p. 129; Wilkins, commentary on *De Orat.*, ad loc.; Hiltbrunner, 'Dicta Scipionis', *Thesaurismata: Festschrift für Ida Kapp*, pp. 49 f., esp. pp. 58 f.

The *dictum* has generally been associated with the prosecution of Scipio by Ti. Claudius Asellus in 140, but Hiltbrunner points out that this is not attested and that Asellus' recital of his services would have been appropriate at the *recognitio equitum*, when Scipio attempted to deprive him of his horse (p. 120). He suggests further that *agas asellum* plays not only on Asellus' name but on the phrases *vende equum* and *traduc equum*; that Scipio ordered Asellus to sell his horse, the latter replied with the recital of his services, and Scipio responded with the proverb. Less convincing is Hiltbrunner's suggestion that *et cetera* refers not to the rest of this proverb but to other examples of proverbs; but his suggestion about the circumstances does not depend on this. The complete proverb cannot be identified with certainty; see Wilkins and Hiltbrunner, locc. citt.

23. Cic. *De Orat.* 2. 272

Est huic finitimum dissimulationi, cum honesto verbo vitiosa res appellatur; ut cum Africanus censor tribu movebat eum centurionem, qui in Pauli pugna non adfuerat, cum ille se custodiae causa diceret in castris remansisse quaereretque, cur ab eo notaretur, '*non amo*' inquit '*nimium diligentis.*'

Date: 142 or 141.

24. Val. Max. 4. 1. 10 (Cf. Script. Hist. Aug., *Max. et Balb.* 17. 8)

Qui (Africanus posterior) censor cum lustrum conderet inque solitaurilium sacrificio scriba ex publicis tabulis sollemne ei precationis carmen praeiret, quo di immortales ut populi Romani res meliores amplioresque facerent rogabantur, '*satis*' inquit '*bonae et magnae sunt: ita precor ut eas perpetuo incolumis servent*', ac protinus in publicis tabulis ad hunc modum carmen emendari iussit. Qua votorum verecundia deinceps censores in condendis lustris usi sunt.

Date: 141.

The authenticity and significance of this *dictum* are discussed in Appendix X.

25. 'Plut.' *Apophth. Scip. Min.* 8

Γαΐῳ δὲ Λαιλίῳ τῷ φιλτάτῳ τῶν ἑταίρων ὑπατείαν μετιόντι συμπράττων ἐπηρώτησε Πομπήιον εἰ καὶ αὐτὸς ὑπατείαν μέτεισιν. ἐδόκει δὲ ὁ Πομπήιος υἱὸς αὐλητοῦ γεγονέναι· τοῦ δὲ φήσαντος μὴ μετιέναι, ἀλλὰ καὶ τὸν Λαίλιον ἐπαγγελλόμενος συμπεριάξειν καὶ συναρχαιρεσιάσειν, πιστεύσαντες καὶ περιμένοντες ἐκείνῳ ἐξηπατήθησαν· ἀπηγγέλλετο γὰρ αὐτὸς ἐν ἀγορᾷ περιιὼν καὶ δεξιούμενος τοὺς πολίτας. ἀγανακτούντων δὲ τῶν ἄλλων, ὁ Σκιπίων γελάσας " ἀβελτερίᾳ γε " εἶπεν " ἡμῶν, καθάπερ οὐκ ἀνθρώπους μέλλοντες ἀλλὰ θεοὺς παρακαλεῖν, πάλαι διατρίβομεν αὐλητὴν ἀναμένοντες."

Date: 141.

Hiltbrunner, 'Dicta Scipionis', *Thesaurismata: Festschrift für Ida Kapp*, pp. 49 f. See pp. 121 f. and 311 f.

BETWEEN SCIPIO'S CENSORSHIP AND HIS SECOND CONSULSHIP, 141–135

26. Gell. 6. 11. 9

P. Africanus pro se contra Tiberium Asellum de multa ad populum: '*Omnia mala, probra, flagitia, quae homines faciunt, in duabus rebus sunt, malitia atque nequitia. Utrum defendis, malitiam an nequitiam an utrumque simul? Si nequitiam defendere vis, licet; si tu in uno scorto maiorem pecuniam absumpsisti quam quanti omne instrumentum fundi Sabini in censum dedicavisti, si hoc ita est: qui spondet mille nummum? si tu plus tertia parte pecuniae paternae perdidisti atque absumpsisti in flagitiis, si hoc ita est: qui spondet mille nummum? Non vis nequitiam. Age malitiam saltem defende. Si tu verbis conceptis coniuravisti sciens sciente animo tuo, si hoc ita est: qui spondet mille nummum?*'

Date: 140.

Fraccaro, 'Oratori', pp. 375 f.; *ORF²*, fgt. 19, pp. 128 f.

See pp. 127 and 175 f. Nos. **27** and **28** = *ORF²*, fgts. 20 and 22 belong to the same occasion (the prosecution of Scipio by Asellus). No. **22** = *ORF²*, fgt. 21 has generally been thought to do so as well, but see discussion ad loc.

27. Gell. 2. 20. 5–6

Sed quod apud Scipionem . . . legimus 'roboraria' . . . . (6) Verba ex oratione eius contra Claudium Asellum quinta haec sunt: '*Ubi agros optime cultos atque villas expolitissimas vidisset, in his regionibus excelsissimo loco grumum statuere aiebat; inde corrigere viam, aliis per vineas medias, aliis per roborarium atque piscinam, aliis per villam.*'

Date: 140.

Fraccaro, 'Oratori', pp. 375 f.; *ORF²*, fgt. 20, p. 129.

See nos. **26** and **28**. Although all these fragments belong to the trial in 140, Fraccaro, 'Oratori', p. 379, suggests that not all Scipio's speeches against Asellus (at least five: cf. *ex oratione quinta*) need do so. One or two might have been delivered during the censorship.

28. Cic. *De Orat.* 2. 268

Arguta est etiam significatio, cum parva re et saepe verbo res obscura et latens inlustratur; . . . ut Asello Africanus obicienti lustrum illud infelix, '*noli*' inquit '*mirari; is enim, qui te ex aerariis exemit, lustrum condidit et taurum immolavit.*'

Date: 140.
Fraccaro, 'Oratori', p. 382; *ORF²*, fgt. 22, p. 129.
See nos. **26** and **27**. Certain aspects of this *dictum* are discussed in Appendix X.

29. 'Plut.' *Apophth. Scip. Min.* 13

(Scipio, on his embassy to the East, visited Alexandria.) τοῦ δὲ βασιλέως μόλις ἁμιλλωμένου βαδίζουσιν αὐτοῖς δι' ἀργίαν καὶ τρυφὴν τοῦ σώματος, ὁ Σκιπίων ἀτρέμα πρὸς τὸν Παναίτιον ψιθυρίσας εἶπεν " ἤδη τι τῆς ἐπιδημίας ἡμῶν Ἀλεξανδρεῖς ἀπολελαύκασι· δι' ἡμᾶς γὰρ ἑωράκασι τὸν βασιλέα περιπατοῦντα."

Date: 140 or 139, probably the former.
Cf. Athen. 12. 549 d–e = Poseid. fgt. 6 *FGrH*. See pp. 127 and 177. For the chronology see esp. Astin, 'Diodorus and the Date of the Embassy to the East of Scipio Aemilianus', *CPh* 54 (1959), pp. 221 f.

30. In 138 Scipio delivered a number of speeches in the course of his unsuccessful prosecution of L. Aurelius Cotta. No words are preserved. The date is established by Livy, *Ox. Epit.* 55. Other references: Cic. *Pro Mur.* 58; *Div. in Caec.* 69; *Brut.* 81; Ps.-Ascon., p. 204 Stangl; Val. Max. 8. 1, abs. 11; Tac. *Ann.* 3. 66; App. *B.C.* 1. 22.

Fraccaro, 'Oratori', pp. 383 f.; *ORF²*, fgts. 23–26, pp. 129 f.; Badian, 'Mam. Scaurus Cites Precedent', *CR* N.S. 8 (1958), pp. 216 f.

The prosecution was certainly *repetundarum*, but the scene and details of the alleged offences are unknown. Badian hazards a guess that they concerned Italian *socii*, but this rests on the doubtful opinion that campaigns in northern Italy or Macedonia of sufficient importance to require a consular commander would have been mentioned in the epitomes of Livy or other surviving works in the Livian tradition. It is questionable whether the writers of these works were so meticulous.

31. Festus 277 L., s.v. *Potestur*

'*Potestur*'. Scipio Africanus in ea quae est de imperio D. Bruti.

Date: between 138 and 134.

Fraccaro, 'Oratori', pp. 386 f.; *ORF²*, fgt. 27, p. 131; Münzer, *RE*, s.v. *Iunius*, no. 57, col. 1022; Simon, *Roms Kriege*, p. 166.

D. Iunius Brutus Callaicus was consul in 138 and enjoyed great military success in Further Spain. He may have had an unusually long period of command, but this is not certain. All the works cited above take it as probable that the speech is to be assigned to 136 (Fraccaro: 137 or 136) and that Scipio was supporting the further prorogation of Brutus' *imperium*; but the evidence seems insufficient for conjecture on either of these points.

SCIPIO'S SECOND CONSULSHIP AND THE NUMANTINE CAMPAIGN, 134–133

32. 'Plut.' *Apophth. Scip. Min.* 15

τῶν δὲ Νομαντίνων ἀμάχων εἶναι δοκούντων καὶ πολλοὺς νενικηκότων στρατηγούς, ὕπατον ἀπέδειξε Σκιπίωνα τὸ δεύτερον ὁ δῆμος ἐπὶ τὸν πόλεμον· ὡρμημένων δὲ πολλῶν ἐπὶ τὴν στρατείαν, καὶ τοῦτο διεκώλυσεν ἡ σύγκλητος, ὡς ἐρήμου τῆς Ἰταλίας ἐσομένης. καὶ χρήματα λαβεῖν τῶν ἑτοίμων οὐκ εἴασαν, ἀλλὰ τὰς τελωνικὰς προσόδους ἀπέταξαν οὔπω χρόνον ἐχούσας.

ὁ δὲ Σκιπίων χρημάτων μὲν οὐκ ἔφη δεῖσθαι, τὰ γὰρ ἑαυτοῦ καὶ τῶν φίλων ἐξαρκέσειν· περὶ δὲ τῶν στρατιωτῶν ἐμέμψατο, χαλεπὸν γὰρ εἶναι τὸν πόλεμον, εἰ μὲν δι' ἀνδρείαν τῶν πολεμίων ἥττηνται τοσαυτάκις, ὅτι πρὸς τοιούτους, εἰ δὲ δι' ἀνανδρίαν τῶν πολιτῶν, ὅτι μετὰ τοιούτων.

Date: 134.

33. App. *Iber.* 85

ἔλεγέν τε πολλάκις τοὺς μὲν αὐστηροὺς καὶ ἐννόμους τῶν στρατηγῶν τοῖς οἰκείοις, τοὺς δὲ εὐχερεῖς καὶ φιλοδώρους τοῖς πολεμίοις εἶναι χρησίμους· τὰ γὰρ στρατόπεδα τοῖς μὲν εἶναι κεχαρμένα τε καὶ καταφρονητικά, τοῖς δὲ σκυθρωπὰ μέν, εὐπειθῆ δὲ καὶ πᾶσιν ἕτοιμα.

Date: 134.

34a. 'Plut.' *Apophth. Scip. Min.* 16 (fin.)

αὐτὸς δὲ σάγον ἐμπεπορπημένος μέλανα περιήει, πενθεῖν τὴν τοῦ στρατεύματος αἰσχύνην λέγων.

34b. Polyaen. 8. 16. 2 (fin.)

καὶ πρῶτος ἐνεπορπήσατο σισύραν μέλαιναν, τοῖς δὲ στρατηγοῖς ἐπὶ στιβάδος ἀνακείμενος ἑωρᾶτο φάσκων πενθεῖν τὴν τοῦ στρατεύματος ἀσωτίαν καὶ μαλακίαν.

Date: 134.

35a. Livy, *Epit.* 57

(Scipio said) alii scutum parum habiliter ferenti, *amplius eum scutum iusto ferre, neque id se reprehendere, quando melius scuto quam gladio uteretur.*

35b. Frontin. *Strat.* 4. 1. 5

Scipio Africanus, cum ornatum scutum elegantius cuiusdam vidisset, dixit *non mirari se, quod tanta cura ornasset, in quo plus praesidii quam in gladio haberet.*

Date: 134.
Cf. no. **36**.

36a. 'Plut.' *Apophth. Scip. Min.* 18

ἑτέρου δὲ θυρεὸν ἐπιδείξαντος εὖ κεκοσμημένον "ὁ μὲν θυρεός, " εἶπεν, " ὦ νεανία, καλός, πρέπει δὲ Ῥωμαῖον ἄνδρα μᾶλλον ἐν τῇ δεξιᾷ τὰς ἐλπίδας ἔχειν ἢ τῇ ἀριστερᾷ."

36b. Aelian, *Var. Hist.* 11. 9. 5

ἀσπίδα δὲ αὐτῷ τινος ἐπιδείξαντος εὖ κεκοσμημένην εἶπεν " ἀλλὰ τόν γε Ῥωμαῖον ἄνδρα προσήκει ἐν τῇ δεξιᾷ τὰς ἐλπίδας ἔχειν, ἀλλ᾿ οὐκ ἐν τῇ ἀριστερᾷ."

36c. Polyaen. 8. 16. 4

Σκιπίων στρατιώτην ἰδὼν μέγα φρονοῦντα ἐπὶ θυρεῷ κεκοσμημένῳ " αἰσχρόν " ἔφη " Ῥωμαῖον ἄνδρα τῇ ἀριστερᾷ χειρὶ μᾶλλον ἢ τῇ δεξιᾷ πιστεύειν."

Date: 134.
Cf. no. **35**.

37a. App. *Iber.* 85

κἂν τοῖς ἀλείμμασι καὶ λουτροῖς ἑαυτοὺς ἤλειφον, ἐπισκώπτοντος τοῦ Σκιπίωνος, ὡς αἱ ἡμίονοι, χεῖρας οὐκ ἔχουσαι, χρήζουσι τριβόντων.

Date: 134.

37b. 'Plut.' *Apophth. Scip. Min.* 16

λούεσθαι δὲ ἀπεῖπε, τῶν δὲ ἀλειφομένων τρίβειν ἕκαστον ἑαυτόν· τὰ γὰρ ὑποζύγια χεῖρας μὴ ἔχοντα ἑτέρου τρίψοντος δεῖσθαι.

37c. Polyaen. 8. 16. 2

προσέταξε . . . τῶν δὲ ἀλειφομένων ἕκαστον τρίβειν ἑαυτόν, τὰ γὰρ ὑποζύγια δεῖσθαι τῶν τριβόντων.

Date: 134.

38a. 'Plut.' *Apophth. Scip. Min.* 17

Μεμμίου δέ τινος χιλιάρχου λαβὼν ὑποζύγια, ψυκτῆρας διαλίθους παρα-κομίζοντα καὶ Θηρικλείους, " ἐμοὶ μέν " εἶπεν " ἡμέρας τριάκοντα καὶ τῇ πατρίδι, σαυτῷ δὲ τὸν βίον ἅπαντα τοιοῦτος ὢν ἄχρηστον πεποίηκας σεαυτόν."

38b. Frontin. *Strat.* 4. 1. 1

Quod maxime notabiliter accidit C. Memmio tribuno, cui dixisse traditur Scipio: '*mihi paulisper, tibi et rei publicae semper nequam eris.*'

Date: 134.

C. Memmius is very possibly the famous tribune of 111. Thirty days was presumably the period of his disgrace and punishment, during which he was 'useless' to Scipio. So Babbit in the Loeb edition of Plutarch, ad loc., better than the view of Cichorius, *Untersuchungen zu Lucilius*, p. 305, that thirty days was the interval between the arrival of Memmius and that of his more slowly moving baggage.

39. App. *Iber.* 85

ἀπεῖπεν δὲ καὶ ὁδεύοντας ἡμιόνοις ἐπικαθέζεσθαι· τί γὰρ ἐν πολέμῳ προσδοκᾶν ἔφη παρ' ἀνδρὸς οὐδὲ βαδίζειν δυναμένου;

Date: 134.

40a. Veget. 3. 10

Scipio Africanus sub aliis imperatoribus Hispanienses exercitus frequenter victos accepit; hos, disciplinae regula custodita, omni opere fossisque faciendis ita diligenter exercuit, ut diceret *fodientes luto inquinari debere qui madere hostium sanguine noluissent.*

40b. Florus, 1. 34. 10

(The Roman soldiers under Scipio's command) *ferre plenius vallum, qui arma nescirent, luto inquinari, qui sanguine nollent,* iubebantur.

Date: 134.

41a. Livy, *Epit.* 57

(Scipio) aegre propter onus incedenti dicebat: '*cum gladio te vallare scieris, vallum ferre desinito.*'

41b. 'Plut.' *Apophth. Scip. Min.* 19

τοῦ δὲ τὸν χάρακα ἄραντος σφόδρα πιέζεσθαι φάσκοντος " εἰκότως " ἔφη· " τῷ γὰρ ξύλῳ τούτῳ μᾶλλον ἢ τῇ μαχαίρᾳ πιστεύεις."

41c. Polyaen. 8. 16. 3

Σκιπίων στρατιώτην ἰδὼν χάρακα κομίζοντα "θλίβεσθαί μοι δοκεῖς" εἶπεν "ὦ συστρατιῶτα." τοῦ δὲ "καὶ πάνυ" φήσαντος, "εἰκότως" ἔφη· "ἐν γὰρ τῷ ξύλῳ τὴν ἐλπίδα τῆς σωτηρίας ἔχεις, οὐκ ἐν τῇ μαχαίρᾳ."

Date: 134.

42a. App. *Iber.* 87

ὡς . . . ἐς τὸ πρόσθεν ἔδει βαδίζειν, ὁδὸς μὲν ἦν παρὰ τὴν Νομαντίαν ἐπὶ τὰ πεδία σύντομος, καὶ πολλοὶ συνεβούλευον ἐς αὐτὴν τραπέσθαι. ὁ δ' ἔφη τὴν ἐπάνοδον δεδιέναι, κούφων μὲν τότε τῶν πολεμίων ὄντων, καὶ ἐκ πόλεως ὁρμωμένων καὶ ἐς πόλιν ἀφορμώντων. "οἱ δ' ἡμέτεροι βαρεῖς ἐπανίασιν ὡς ἀπὸ σιτολογίας καὶ κατάκοποι καὶ κτήνη καὶ ἁμάξας καὶ φορτία ἄγουσιν. δυσχερής τε ὅλως καὶ ἀνόμοιος ὁ ἀγών· ἡσσωμένοις μὲν γὰρ πολὺς ὁ κίνδυνος, νικῶσι δὲ οὐ μέγα τὸ ἔργον οὐδὲ ἐπικερδές." εἶναι δ' ἄλογον κινδυνεύειν ἐπὶ ὀλίγοις καὶ στρατηγὸν ἀμελῆ τὸν ἀγωνιζόμενον πρὸ τῆς χρείας, ἀγαθὸν δὲ τὸν ἐν μόναις παρακινδυνεύοντα ταῖς ἀνάγκαις. συγκρίνων δ' ἔφη καὶ τοὺς ἰατροὺς μὴ χρῆσθαι τομαῖς μηδὲ καύσεσι πρὸ φαρμάκων.

42b. 'Plut.' *Apophth. Scip. Min.* 20

ὁρῶν δὲ τὴν ἀπόνοιαν τῶν πολεμίων ἔλεγεν "ὠνεῖσθαι τοῦ χρόνου τὴν ἀσφάλειαν· τὸν γὰρ ἀγαθὸν στρατηγὸν ὥσπερ ἰατρὸν ἐσχάτης δεῖσθαι τῆς διὰ τοῦ σιδήρου θεραπείας."

Date: 134.

43a. Gell. 13. 3. 6 = Sempronius Asellio, fgt. 5

(On the identity of *necessitas* and *necessitudo*.) Hoc ego scripsi de utriusque vocabuli indifferentia, admonitus forte verbi istius, cum legerem Sempronii Asellionis, veteris scriptoris, quartum ex historia librum, in quo de P. Africano, Pauli filio, ita scriptum est: *Nam se patrem suum audisse dicere L. Aemilium Paulum, nimis bonum imperatorem signis conlatis non decertare, nisi summa necessitudo aut summa occasio data esset.*

43b. Val. Max. 7. 2. 2

Idem (Scipio Africanus) negabat *aliter cum hoste confligi debere, quam aut si occasio obvenisset aut necessitas incidisset.*

Date: 134 or 133.

That this *dictum* belongs to the Numantine campaign is established beyond reasonable doubt by its position in Asellio's history. *HRR* i², pp. 180 f.

44. Frontin. *Strat.* 4. 7. 4

Scipio Africanus fertur dixisse, cum eum parum quidam pugnacem dicerent: '*imperatorem me mater, non bellatorem peperit.*'

Date: 134 or 133.

Strictly speaking *incertum*, but the similarity of the sentiment to nos. **42** and **43** leaves little doubt that the reference is to Aemilianus in the Numantine campaign.

45. Livy, *Epit.* 57

Scipio amplissima munera missa sibi ab Antiocho, rege Syriae, cum celare aliis imperatoribus regum munera mos esset, pro tribunali [ea] accepturum se esse dixit omniaque ea quaestorem referre in publicas tabulas iussit: *ex his se viris fortibus dona esse daturum.*

Date: 134 or 133.

46. Livy, *Epit.* 57

Cum undique Numantiam obsidione clusisset et obsessos fame videret urgeri, hostes qui pabulatum exierant, vetuit occidi, quia diceret *velocius eos absumpturos frumenti, quod haberent, si plures fuissent.*

Date: 134 or 133.

47. Cic. *De Orat.* 2. 267

Ex quo genere etiam illud est, quod Scipio apud Numantiam, cum stomacharetur cum C. Metello, dixisse dicitur: '*si quintum pareret mater eius, asinum fuisse parituram.*'

Date: 134 or 133.

C. Metellus was the fourth and youngest son of Q. Metellus Macedonicus. Cf. Wilkins, commentary on *De Orat.*, ad loc.: 'Scipio meant that the brothers fell off so rapidly in intellectual powers, that if there had been a fifth son, he would have been an ass.' In addition, however, Scipio was almost certainly playing on the idea of a personal *cognomen*: C. Metellus was called Caprarius; if there had been another brother he would have been known as Asinus. This interpretation is implied cautiously by Münzer, *RE*, s.v. *Caecilius*, no. 84.

48a. Plut. *Ti. Grac.* 21. 7

Σκιπίων ὁ Ἀφρικανός . . . παρὰ μικρὸν ἦλθεν ἐκπεσεῖν καὶ στέρεσθαι τῆς πρὸς τὸν δῆμον εὐνοίας, ὅτι πρῶτον μὲν ἐν Νομαντίᾳ τὴν τελευτὴν τοῦ Τιβερίου πυθόμενος, ἀνεφώνησεν ἐκ τῶν Ὁμηρικῶν·

"ὣς ἀπόλοιτο καὶ ἄλλος ὅτις τοιαῦτά γε ῥέζοι."

48b. Diod. 34/35. 7. 3 = Poseid. fgt. 110 f. *FGrH*

ὅτι προσέπεσε τοῖς περὶ τὸ στρατόπεδον ἡ τοῦ Γράκχου τελευτή, καὶ τὸν Ἀφρικανόν φασιν ἐπιβοῆσαι τοιαῦτα,

"ὣς ἀπόλοιτο καὶ ἄλλος ὅτις τοιαῦτά γε ῥέζοι."

Date: 133.
The quotation is of *Odyssey*, 1. 47.

49a. Val. Max. 8. 15. 7

Inhaerent illi voci posterioris Africani septem C. Marii consulatus ac duo amplissimi triumphi. Ad rogum enim usque gaudio exultavit, quod, cum apud Numantiam sub eo duce equestria stipendia mereret et forte inter cenam quidam Scipionem interrogasset, si quid ipsi accidisset, quemnam res publica aeque magnum habitura esset imperatorem, respiciens se supra ipsum cubantem *'vel hunc'* dixerit.

49b. Plut. *Marius* 3. 4

καί ποτε λόγου μετὰ δεῖπνον ἐμπεσόντος ὑπὲρ στρατηγῶν, καὶ τῶν παρόντων ἑνὸς εἴτ' ἀληθῶς διαπορήσαντος εἴτε πρὸς ἡδονὴν ἐρομένου τὸν Σκιπίωνα, τίνα δὴ τοιοῦτον ἕξει μετ' ἐκεῖνον ἡγεμόνα καὶ προστάτην ὁ Ῥωμαίων δῆμος, ὑπερκατακειμένου τοῦ Μαρίου τῇ χειρὶ τὸν ὦμον ἠρέμα πατάξας ὁ Σκιπίων " τάχα δὲ τοῦτον " εἶπεν.

Date: 134 or 133.

THE LAST YEARS, 132–129

50a. Plut. *Ti. Grac.* 21. 8

ἔπειτα τῶν περὶ Γάιον καὶ Φούλβιον αὐτοῦ (Scipio) δι' ἐκκλησίας πυνθανομένων, τί φρονοίη περὶ τῆς Τιβερίου τελευτῆς, οὐκ ἀρεσκομένην τοῖς ὑπ' ἐκείνου πεπολιτευμένοις ἀπόκρισιν ἔδωκεν. ἐκ τούτου γὰρ ὁ μὲν δῆμος ἀντέκρουσεν αὐτῷ λέγοντι, μηδέπω τοῦτο ποιήσας πρότερον, αὐτὸς δὲ τὸν δῆμον εἰπεῖν κακῶς προήχθη.

Date: 131.

This passage, which follows directly on no. **48**, contains no words of Scipio but is included because of its importance for the understanding of nos. **50** and **51**. For this group of *dicta* and the occasion see pp. 233 f.; Astin, 'Dicta Scipionis of 131 B.C.', *CQ* N.S. 10 (1960), pp. 135 f.; Fraccaro, 'Oratori', pp. 387 f.; *ORF²*, pp. 131 f. The occasion was a speech by Scipio, but Livy, *Epit.* 59 (= no. **50d**) errs in making the *dictum* a quotation from the speech: see no. **52**.

50b. Cic. *De Orat.* 2. 106

Carboni tribuno plebis . . . P. Africanus de Ti. Graccho interroganti responderat *iure caesum videri.*

50c. Cic. *Pro Mil.* 8

An est quisquam qui hoc ignoret, cum de homine occiso quaeratur, aut negari solere omnino esse factum aut recte et iure factum esse defendi? Nisi vero existimatis dementem P. Africanum fuisse, qui cum a C. Carbone tribuno plebis seditiose in contione interrogaretur quid de Ti. Gracchi morte sentiret, responderit *iure caesum videri*.

50d (= 52). Livy, *Epit.* 59

Cum Carbo tribunus plebis rogationem tulisset, ut eundem tribunum plebis, quotiens vellet, creare liceret, rogationem eius P. Africanus gravissima oratione dissuasit; in qua dixit *Ti. Gracchum iure caesum videri*.

50e. Grillius, *Comm. in de Invent. Cic.*, p. 598 (Halm, *Rhet. Lat. Min.*)

Et Scipio, tantus vir, qui productus a tribuno pl. eos (the two Gracchi) dixit *iure caesos videri*.

50f and **51a.** Val. Max. 6. 2. 3

Cn. Carbo tribunus pl. . . . P. Africanum a Numantiae ruinis . . . venientem, ab ipsa paene porta in rostra perductum quid de Ti. Gracchi morte . . . sentiret interrogavit. . . . At is *iure eum caesum videri* respondit. Cui dicto cum contio tribunicio furore instincta violenter succlamasset, '*Taceant,*' inquit, '*quibus Italia noverca est.*' Orto deinde murmure '*Non efficietis*' ait '*ut solutos verear quos adligatos adduxi.*' Universus populus ab uno iterum contumeliose correptus erat—quantus est honos virtutis—et tacuit.

50g and **51b.** Vell. 2. 4. 4

Hic (Scipio), eum interrogante tribuno Carbone, quid de Ti. Gracchi caede sentiret, respondit, *si is occupandae rei publicae animum habuisset, iure caesum.* Et cum omnis contio acclamasset, '*hostium*', inquit, '*armatorum totiens clamore non territus, qui possum vestro moveri, quorum noverca est Italia?*'

50h and **51c.** (Victor) *De Vir. Ill.* 58. 8

Ob res gestas superbus, *Gracchum iure caesum videri* respondit: obstrepente populo, '*Taceant,*' inquit, '*quibus Italia noverca, non mater est*'; et addidit, '*Quos ego sub corona vendidi*'.

51d. 'Plut.' *Apophth. Scip. Min.* 22

ἐπεὶ δὲ τὴν Νομαντίαν ἑλὼν καὶ θριαμβεύσας τὸ δεύτερον πρὸς Γάιον Γράκχον ὑπέρ τε τῆς βουλῆς καὶ τῶν συμμάχων κατέστη διαφορά, καὶ λυπούμενος ὁ δῆμος ἐθορύβησεν αὐτὸν ἐπὶ τοῦ βήματος, "ἐμέ" εἶπεν "οὐδέποτε στρατοπέδων ἀλαλαγμὸς ἐθορύβησεν, οὔτι γε συγκλύδων ἀνθρώπων, ὧν οὐ μητέρα τὴν Ἰταλίαν ἀλλὰ μητρυιὰν οὖσαν ἐπίσταμαι."

51e. Polyaen. 8. 16. 5

Σκιπίων ὑπὸ τοῦ δήμου θορυβούμενος "ἐμέ" ἔφη "οὐδὲ στρατιωτῶν ἐνόπλων ἀλαλαγμὸς ἐξέπληξεν, οὔτι γε συγκλύδων ἀνθρώπων θόρυβος, ὧν οἶδά γε τὴν Ἰταλίαν μητρυιάν, οὐ μητέρα." τούτῳ τῷ λόγῳ συνεστάλησαν καὶ τοῦ θορυβεῖν ἐπαύσαντο.

52. In 131 Scipio delivered a speech in opposition to the proposal of C. Carbo that repeated tenure of the tribunate should be permitted. Cic. *De Amic.* 96; Livy, *Epit.* 59 (= no. **50d**). No words are preserved from it, though Livy, *Epit.* wrongly treats as a quotation from it the phrase *iure caesum videri.*

ORF², fgts. 28 and 29, pp. 131 f. See no. **50a** and references there.

53. Macrob. *Sat.* 3. 14. 6–7

Nobilium vero filios et, quod dictu nefas est, filias quoque virgines inter studiosa numerasse saltandi meditationem testis est Scipio Africanus Aemilianus, qui in oratione contra legem iudiciariam Ti. Gracchi sic ait: '*docentur praestigias inhonestas, cum cinaedulis et sambuca psalterioque eunt in ludum histrionum, discunt cantare, quae maiores nostri ingenuis probro ducier voluerunt: eunt, inquam, in ludum saltatorium inter cinaedos virgines puerique ingenui. Haec cum mihi quisquam narrabat, non poteram animum inducere, ea liberos suos homines nobiles docere, sed cum ductus sum in ludum saltatorium, plus medius fidius in eo ludo vidi pueris virginibusque quingentis, in his unum (quod me rei publicae maxime miseritum est) puerum bullatum, petitoris filium non minorem annis duodecim, cum crotalis saltare, quam saltationem impudicus servulus honeste saltare non posset.*'

Date: probably 129.
Fraccaro, 'Oratori', pp. 393 f.; ORF², fgt. 30, p. 133.

54. 'Plut.' *Apophth. Scip. Min.* 23

τῶν δὲ περὶ τὸν Γάιον βοώντων κτεῖναι τὸν τύραννον "εἰκότως" εἶπεν "οἱ τῇ πατρίδι πολεμοῦντες ἐμὲ βούλονται προανελεῖν· οὐ γὰρ οἷόν τε τὴν Ῥώμην πεσεῖν Σκιπίωνος ἑστῶτος οὐδὲ ζῆν Σκιπίωνα τῆς Ῥώμης πεσούσης."

Date: probably 129.
Fraccaro, 'Oratori', p. 391; cf. Astin, *CQ* N.S. 10 (1960), p. 139 n. 3.
See p. 240.

INCERTA

55. Cic. *De Orat.* 2. 253 = Lucil. 1280 M.

Ambigua . . . ut illud Africani, quod est apud Lucilium
  'Quid Decius? Nuculam an confixum vis facere?' inquit.

Badian, 'P. Decius P. f. Subulo', *JRS* 46 (1956), p. 91.

56. Festus, 137 L.

Scipio Aemilianus ad populum: 'vobis', inquit, 'rei publicae praesidio erit
is, quasi millus cani.'

  Fraccaro, 'Oratori', pp. 366 and 372; *ORF²*, fgt. 15, p. 126.
  Both Fraccaro and Malcovati assign this fragment to Scipio's speech concerning *mores maiorum*, delivered in his censorship (nos. **15** and **16** = *ORF²*, fgts.
13 and 14), but this must remain uncertain. The subject might, for example, be
an individual.

57. Isid. *Etym.* 2. 21. 4 (Halm, *Rhet. Lat. Min.*, p. 517)

Climax est gradatio . . . ut est illud Africani: 'ex innocentia nascitur dignitas,
ex dignitate honor, ex honore imperium, ex imperio libertas.'

  Fraccaro, 'Oratori', pp. 399 f.; *ORF²*, fgt. 32, p. 134.

58. Isid. *Etym.* 2. 21. 4 (Halm, *Rhet. Lat. Min.*, p. 517)

Fit autem hoc schema (climax) non solum in singulis verbis, sed etiam in
contexione verborum, ut apud Gracchum . . . sic et apud Scipionem: 'vi
atque ingratis coactus cum illo sponsionem feci, facta sponsione ad iudicem
adduxi, adductum primo coetu damnavi, damnatum ex voluntate dimisi.'

  Fraccaro, 'Oratori', p. 400; *ORF²*, fgt. 33, p. 134.

59. Festus, 334 L. = Lucil. 963 f. M.

'Redarguisse' per e litteram Scipio Africanus Pauli filius dicitur enuntiasse,
ut idem etiam 'pertisum'. Cuius meminit Lucilius, cum ait 'Quo facetior
videare, et scire plus quam caeteri, pertisum hominem, non pertaesum
dicere; ferum nam genus.'

  Fraccaro, 'Oratori', pp. 400 f.; *ORF²*, fgt. 34, p. 134.

60. Quint. *Inst.* 1. 7. 25

Quid dicam 'vortices' et 'vorsus' ceteraque ad eundem modum, quae
primus Scipio Africanus in e litteram secundam vertisse dicitur?

  ORF², fgt. 35, p. 134.

61. Cic. *De Off.* 1. 90

Panaetius quidem Africanum auditorem et familiarem suum solitum ait dicere, *ut equos propter crebras contentiones proeliorum ferocitate exultantis domitoribus tradere soleant, ut iis facilioribus possint uti, sic homines secundis rebus ecfrenatos sibique praefidentis tamquam in gyrum rationis et doctrinae duci oportere, ut perspicerent rerum humanarum imbecillitatem varietatemque fortunae.*

62. Cic. *Tusc.* 2. 62

Itaque semper Africanus Socraticum Xenophontem in manibus habebat, cuius in primis laudabat illud, *quod diceret eosdem labores non aeque gravis esse imperatori et militi, quod ipse honos laborem leviorem faceret imperatorium.*

The reference is to Xen. *Cyropaed.* 1. 6. 25. Cf. Cic. *Ad Quint. Frat.* 1. 1. 23.

63. Script. Hist. Aug.; *Antoninus Pius* 9. 10

(Antoninus) . . . cum semper amaverit pacem eo usque ut Scipionis sententiam frequentarit, qua ille dicebat *malle se unum civem servare quam mille hostes occidere.*

64. Val. Max. 7. 2. 2

Scipio vero Africanus *turpe esse* aiebat *in re militari dicere 'non putaram'*, videlicet quia explorato et excusso consilio quae ferro aguntur administrari oportere arbitrabatur.

65a. Frontin. *Strat.* 4. 7. 16

Scipio Africanus dicere solitus est *hosti non solum dandam esse viam ad fugiendum, sed etiam muniendam.*

65b. Veget. 3. 21

Ideoque Scipionis laudata sententia est, qui dixit *viam hostibus, qua fugerent, muniendam.*

66. Cic. *De Orat.* 2. 249

'*Quid hoc Navio ignavius?*' severe Scipio.

MSS. *Naevio*; cf. Wilkins, commentary on *De Orat.*, ad loc. There is no indication which Scipio is the speaker.

67. Cic. *De Amic.* 62

Sed . . . (Scipio) querebatur *quod omnibus in rebus homines diligentiores essent; capras et oves quot quisque haberet, dicere posse, amicos quot haberet, non posse dicere, et in illis quidem parandis adhibere curam, in amicis eligendis neglegentis esse nec habere quasi signa quaedam et notas, quibus eos qui ad amicitias essent idonei, iudicarent.*

It is possible that this is a genuine utterance of Scipio's, but it is at least as likely that it is attributed to him fictitiously by Cicero. Falconer, Loeb edition, ad loc., notes the resemblance to Xen. *Mem.* 2. 4. 1 and 4.

68. Cic. *De Amic.* 59–60

(A view which Scipio used to condemn in the strongest terms.) Negabat *ullam vocem inimiciorem amicitiae potuisse reperiri quam eius qui dixisset ita amare oportere, ut si aliquando esset osurus; nec vero se adduci posse ut hoc, quem ad modum putaretur, a Biante esse dictum crederet, qui sapiens habitus esset unus e septem; impuri cuiusdam aut ambitiosi aut omnia ad suam potentiam revocantis esse sententiam.* . . .

60. (We ought to have care in forming friendships so that we never begin a friendship with someone whom we might sometime hate.) Quin etiam, *si minus felices in diligendo fuissemus, ferendum id* Scipio *potius quam inimicitiarum tempus cogitandum* putabat.

See comment on no. 67; this is even less likely to be a genuine utterance. Falconer, Loeb edition, ad loc., notes Arist. *Rhet.* 2. 13 with regard to the mention of Bias.

COMPARATIVE TABLE

ORF²	*This collection*	ORF²	*This collection*
12	11	22	28
13	15	23–26	30
14	16	27	31
15	56	28–29	52
16	18	30	53
17	20	32	57
19	26	33	58
20	27	34	59
21	22	35	60

APPENDIX III

Preliminaries to the Third Punic War

1. *Chronology*

RECONSTRUCTIONS of the chronology of the events leading up to the Third Punic War have differed on several points.[1] Since the problem does not affect seriously the main theses of this book all that is offered here is a summary of the chronology adopted in Chapter V and some notes to clarify the principles underlying that reconstruction, which agrees most nearly with the views of Kienast, *Cato*, pp. 127 f.

153: Dispute between Carthage and Massinissa leads to a Roman embassy. (App. *Lib.* 68 = second embassy of Livy, *Epit.* 47, which must belong to this year.)

152: New dispute; embassy of Cato and Nasica; Carthaginians refuse arbitration. (First embassy of Livy, *Epit.* 48 = App. *Lib.* 69 = Zon. 9. 26.)

Late 152 or 151: Gulussa's complaints about Carthage; new embassy. (Second embassy of Livy, *Epit.* 48.)

151: Return of embassy; resolution to refrain from war if Carthage disarms, otherwise next consuls to put the question of war. (Livy, *Epit.* 48.)

Winter 151–150: War between Carthage and Massinissa; Carthage defeated.

(i) The scheme accepts the obvious inference that 153 is the date of the dispute linked by App. *Lib.* 68 with Roman involvement in Celtiberia. Moreover, Appian also links the dispute with fighting between Massinissa's son and other Spanish forces, evidently in Africa. This is very probably identical with the siege of Oecile, which occurred in the praetorship of Mummius, in 153 (App. *Iber.* 57; Simon, *Roms Kriege*, pp. 23 f.). There is no force in the argument of Gsell, *Hist. anc.* iii, p. 320, that this dispute must have been earlier, on the ground that 153 would leave insufficient time for the subsequent events narrated by Appian.

[1] See esp. Kahrstedt, *Gesch. der Karthager*, pp. 614 f., 620 f.; Gsell, *Hist. anc.* iii, pp. 320 f.; Gelzer, 'Nasicas Widerspruch', *Philologus* 86 (1931), pp. 261 f.; Kienast, *Cato*, pp. 127 f.; Rossetti, 'La Numidia e Cartagine fra la II e la III guerra punica', *PP* 15 (1960), pp. 336 f.

(ii) Kahrstedt's opinion (*Gesch. der Karthager*, pp. 622 f.) that the account of the first senatorial embassy in Livy, *Epit.* 48 is a distorted doublet of the second has been accepted widely; but Kienast, *Cato*, p. 155 n. 150, rightly considers it unnecessary. There is distortion arising from pro-Roman propaganda—which is obviously present—but none of the difficulties requires the assumption of a doublet.

(iii) Gelzer, 'Nasicas Widerspruch', *Philologus* 86 (1931), pp. 262 f., and Kienast, *Cato*, pp. 127 f. and n. 150, correctly deduce that the first embassy mentioned in Livy, *Epit.* 48, Cato's embassy in App. *Lib.* 69, and Nasica's in Zon. 9. 26 are in all probability identical. There are important correspondences between Appian and Livy and between Livy and Zonaras. It should be remembered that all three sources are in effect epitomes.

(iv) Kienast, *Cato*, p. 128, suggests that the second embassy of Livy, *Epit.* 48 did not appear before the Senate until early 150. This is apparently because the consequent decree laid down that if Carthage did not disarm the next consuls were to put the question of a Punic war; and war was actually declared under the consuls of 149. But the next entry in the *Epitome* records Nasica's action against the permanent theatre, which might conceivably be placed in 150 but much more probably belongs to 151 (Oros. 4. 21. 4). Moreover, the departure of the embassy is recorded before the dispute about the levy of 151. In fact, it is quite possible that the consuls of 150 did put the question of war to the Senate, even though the open declaration of war did not come until 149.

(v) Simon, *Roms Kriege*, pp. 48 f., has tried to establish that when Scipio Aemilianus was sent to procure from Massinissa reinforcements for Lucullus' Spanish campaigns, he went to Africa direct from Rome, in 151, before he went to Spain.[1] This would imply that the war between Carthage and Massinissa, and the great battle which he watched, occurred much earlier in 151 than is usually supposed. But the wording of App. *Lib.* 72 (ἐς 'Ιβηρίαν ... ἐπανῆει) and Val. Max. 2. 10. 4 (*ex Hispania in Africam*) is against Simon's suggestion. His chronological arguments have no real force, particularly as he argues for 151 as against 150 (cf. *MRR* i, p. 457 n. 2 for the same antithesis), whereas the obvious time is the autumn and winter of 151. Nor is it a satisfactory argument that Lucullus could not have anticipated prorogation for 150 and therefore would not have sent for elephants after the campaign of 151. Simon himself (op. cit., p. 59) recognizes that, especially in southern Spain, commanders often had opportunity to campaign in the spring before the arrival of their successor, and Lucullus' decision to winter in Turdetania strongly suggests that his

[1] pp. 47 and 51.

campaign in 150 was already planned. Simon's real difficulty seems to be his belief that Lucullus could not have attacked the Vaccaei or massacred the inhabitants of Cauca if Scipio had been present. The argument is that since Scipio had in effect provided Lucullus with his staff, he, Scipio, must have been very influential in the *consilium*; further, that Scipio would not have approved of these actions. The latter may well be true, at least as regards Cauca, but the former is very dubious. It is at least as likely that the more truth there is in the story that Scipio's example shamed Lucullus' officers into serving in a war which they were anxious to avoid, the less willingly will they have supported Scipio's views in the *consilium*. The present reconstruction therefore retains the traditional date for the mission, the war, and the battle.

2. Roman Motives for the Destruction of Carthage

Cato agitated not merely for war against Carthage and its further subjection but for the physical destruction of the existing city, the site of which offered very considerable commercial and strategic advantages. The Roman demands in 149 confirm that the majority of senators ultimately gave their support to this extreme policy. The debate among scholars about the motives underlying this decision[1] has its principal origin in the belief that not only was Carthage too weak to be a menace to Rome but that hard-headed Roman politicians cannot have feared her or seen in her a genuine threat.

One explanation, put forward by Mommsen,[2] is that the rising commercial and mercantile interests at Rome pressed for the removal of a flourishing rival; but this has found little support and at best is admitted only as a secondary element.[3] Fatal to it is the silence of the sources,

---

[1] Mommsen, *Hist. of Rome*, iii, p. 239; Kahrstedt, *Gesch. der Karthager*, pp. 613 f.; Gsell, *Hist. anc.* iii, pp. 312 f., esp. pp. 329 f.; Schur, *RE*, s.v. *Massinissa*, col. 2163; Saumagne, 'Les Prétextes juridiques', *RH* 167 (1931), pp. 225 f., and 168 (1931), pp. 1 f.; Gelzer, 'Nasicas Widerspruch', *Philologus* 86 (1931), pp. 261 f., esp. pp. 295 f.; Zancan, 'Le cause della terza guerra punica', *AIV* 95, pt. 2 (1935–6), pp. 529 f.; Bilz, *Die Politik*, pp. 15 f. and 28 f.; Adcock, 'Delenda est Carthago', *CHJ* 8 (1946), pp. 117 f.; Scullard, *Roman Politics*, pp. 240 f.; Kienast, *Cato*, pp. 125 f.; Badian, *Foreign Clientelae*, pp. 125 f.; Hoffmann, 'Die römische Politik', *Historia* 9 (1960), pp. 309 f.; De Sanctis, *Storia*, iv. 3, pp. 1 f., esp. pp. 17 f.; Walsh, 'Massinissa', *JRS* 55 (1965), pp. 149 f. The sources for many of the events discussed in this section are noted in Chapter V, esp. pp. 49 f. In the remainder of this section articles listed in this note are cited by title only.

[2] Loc. cit.

[3] e.g. Romanelli, *Storia delle province romane dell'Africa*, pp. 31 f., esp. p. 34; De Sanctis, *Storia*, iv. 3, 21 f. For arguments against this theory see esp. Adcock, 'Delenda est Carthago', pp. 117 f.

especially Polybius at 36. 9. To this may be added the Roman failure to occupy or to utilize the site and facilities of Carthage until many years later, and our total ignorance as to whether Carthaginian rivalry really was a serious irritant to Roman traders. It is at least as likely that the main commercial gains of the war accrued to Utica and other African towns which had sided with Rome.

Some have pointed to the place of the Third Punic War in the broad pattern of change in Roman foreign policy.[1] The policy of paternalist predominance, once advocated by Scipio Africanus and Flamininus, had proved a failure. In Greece and the Hellenistic east it had failed to maintain order and stability and had generated resentment. The Third Macedonian War signalled a trend towards more direct domination and harsher treatment, a trend carried further in the Fourth Macedonian and Achaean Wars, at the very time of the final Punic war. Similarly in Africa the policy had failed; Massinissa's repeated claims to Carthaginian territory produced recurring crises. Each side was increasingly inclined to act on its own initiative; if Rome was to retain her predominance she must dominate more directly.[2] All this is true, but even this is not enough to explain the extremism of Rome's attitude towards Carthage. A firm and definitive decision on the boundary question would quickly have restored stability. The destruction of the city was not necessary for that end, or indeed in order to disarm Carthage, as events showed. Something more was involved.

Of the theories arising from the presupposition that Rome could not really have feared Carthage, the most important is that of Kahrstedt,[3] who argued that Roman policy had created a situation in which Massinissa might easily have gained control of Carthage and thus become a formidable power without any African rival to keep him in check: fear of Numidia led Rome to destroy Carthage and occupy its territory before Massinissa himself could do so. Although several distinguished scholars have accepted this suggestion, the sum of the arguments advanced by the considerable opposition group tells overwhelmingly against it.[4] It has

---

[1] Hoffmann, 'Die römische Politik', pp. 330 f.; De Sanctis, *Storia*, iv. 3, pp. 20 f.; cf. Badian, *Foreign Clientelae*, ch. iv.

[2] This is especially the viewpoint of De Sanctis, loc. cit.

[3] *Gesch. der Karthager*, pp. 615 f.

[4] Gelzer, 'Nasicas Widerspruch', pp. 295 f.; Zancan, 'Le cause', pp. 575 f.; Bilz, *Die Politik*, pp. 20 f. and 28 f.; Adcock, 'Delenda est Carthago', pp. 118 f.; Kienast, *Cato*, p. 130; Badian, *Foreign Clientelae*, pp. 134 f.; Hoffmann, 'Die römische Politik', *passim*; De Sanctis, *Storia*, iv. 3, pp. 18 f. The discussion which follows is a synthesis, drawing heavily upon points made by all these writers, and probably owing most to the arguments of Badian, Kienast, and Hoffmann.

been pointed out that there is remarkably little positive evidence for the theory, that serious fear of Massinissa is most improbable (far more improbable than fear of Carthage), that Roman senators would have found little moral or practical difficulty in altering policy in order to stop the Numidian encroachments, and that it is by no means necessarily the case that Roman motives were entirely rational and calculating. It has been plausibly argued that Rome's experiences in the east had induced a mistrust of every indication of unrest and an inclination to see a potential danger to her own position in all states which had once played a leading role.[1] With this may be linked the growth of a belief in harsh punishment and terrorism as a necessary method of maintaining Roman supremacy, a belief evident in practice and probably formulated in literature at this time.[2] Moreover, the theory depends upon the assumption that the Roman intention was to take over the territory of Carthage, but there is no evidence and no justification for supposing that the demand for the transfer of the city inland was not genuinely the last demand, or that it was deliberately intended to drive the Carthaginians to resistance, or that the Senate did not mean what it said when it promised that if the Carthaginians obeyed instructions they would retain not only their lands but their freedom and autonomy.[3] Lastly, Roman fears of Carthage were not entirely baseless. It is not merely that despite total disarmament Carthage was able to maintain a fierce resistance for three whole years. Although the disaster inflicted by Massinissa temporarily swung majority support behind leaders who believed any resistance to Rome to be useless, for most of the crisis period the Carthaginians seem to have followed men who believed that military self-assertion was both practicable and desirable. The stocks of arms surrendered to the Romans, as well as the ability to field a large army against Massinissa, testify to lengthy preparations for war. The raiding of Numidian territory in 153 is symptomatic of the attitude which in the next year led to the refusal of Roman arbitration—a refusal which clearly implied a readiness to resist Massinissa by force and carried an obvious risk of offending Rome.[4] The same implications are involved even more clearly in the actual war with Massinissa: the likelihood of Roman intervention must have been obvious and must have been thought

[1] Hoffmann, 'Die römische Politik', pp. 330 f.

[2] Diod. 32. 2 and 4; both passages were associated with the account of the Third Punic War and both were probably taken from Polybius.

[3] Polyb. 36. 4. 4; Diod. 32. 6. 1; App. *Lib.* 76. Cf. Polyb. 3. 5. 5.

[4] Badian, *Foreign Clientelae*, p. 129, suggests that the intention of the ambassadors to arbitrate περὶ ἁπάντων implies that they at last offered to fix a frontier. If this is so the Carthaginian refusal is especially significant.

of, though perhaps not rationally estimated, when it was decided to pursue the Numidians beyond the borders. The anti-Roman leaders must have believed that if they could smash Numidia, their position would be sufficiently strong at least to make a good bargain with Rome, if not to strike at her directly. At least as far as Numidia was concerned they may well have had good grounds for their hopes, for there are plenty of signs that disaffection was possible within the kingdom. In 153 it had been possible to incite rural Africans against Massinissa; in 152 there were probably Numidians serving under Carthage; just before the battle of 151/150 two Numidian chieftains with a large force of cavalry deserted the king; another such desertion occurred as late as 148, and at that time the Carthaginians clearly had hopes of winning over Micipsa and Mastanabal and thus exploiting the recent division of Massinissa's powers among his sons;[1] indeed the ambitions of Massinissa's numerous sons, legitimate and illegitimate, must have offered a most promising field of intrigue. Had the Carthaginians beaten Massinissa in battle his kingdom might easily have disintegrated. And even the defeat, disastrous though it was, might have been redeemed if fortune had been kinder. Throughout the crisis Romans and Carthaginians alike must have been conscious that Massinissa was nearly ninety: death must come soon—and incapacity perhaps very soon. What would happen then? Rome must have feared, and Carthage hoped, that a self-assertive Carthage would win control before Roman arms could intervene. The king's death—or a stroke— might reverse in an instant the result of the battle; and in the meanwhile, if the Carthaginians in panic had executed some of the anti-Roman party and given their support to those who advocated abject apology and submission, Hasdrubal had escaped and had collected a large rebel army. Clearly there were those in Carthage who put their trust in the sword— backed by a flourishing economy—and at times the people were willing to follow them. In the event they miscalculated, and perhaps it was always hopeless; but the ease with which such miscalculations could be made was shown clearly enough a few years later by the fiasco and tragedy of Achaea. Cato and his supporters may or may not have feared that a resurgent Carthage with a strong anti-Roman party might have found an opportunity of striking a really damaging blow at Rome herself; at least they will have feared, and not without good reason, that if nothing were done, intervention to compel Carthage to disarm would be possible only at a fearful cost in blood and suffering, the even more fearful alternative being to leave Carthage alone to rearm and strengthen her power as she

[1] App. Lib. 68; 70; 111; Livy, Epit. 48.

wished. Given such a fear and such grounds for fear, given the new, more suspicious, harsher outlook in foreign policy, it is not too difficult to understand the decision to deprive Carthage not merely of her armaments but of the strategic site which was the ultimate source of her strength.

3. Nasica's Opposition[1]

The sources record several different arguments with which Scipio Nasica is said to have opposed Cato's policy towards Carthage. The *Epitome* of Livy, referring to discussions which occurred before the open war between Carthage and Massinissa in 151, reports first the exhortation that nothing should be done rashly (*nihil temere faciundum*), and a little later the contention that there was not yet a *iusta causa* for war against Carthage. Both of these sentiments are evidently reflected in a brief fragment of Diodorus which, though it does not mention Nasica, beyond reasonable doubt has reference to this same dispute, and which is very likely to have been derived from Polybius.[2] There is some affinity between the *iusta causa* idea and the statement of Polybius that disagreement about the effect on foreign opinion very nearly led the Romans to refrain from war, though the two are not identical.[3] Other arguments attributed to Nasica emphasize the need for a 'counterweight of fear'. This is found in three forms. The first is that an external source of fear was necessary in order to maintain Rome's warlike qualities and military efficiency; the second, that without such a fear to check her Rome would suffer from faction and civil discord at home; the third, closely associated with the second, is that without this fear Rome would commit excesses in her dealings with foreign and subject peoples.[4]

It is impossible to be absolutely sure that Nasica did not use other important arguments or have other considerations in mind, but conjectures

---

[1] See esp. Gelzer, 'Nasicas Widerspruch', *Philologus* 86 (1931), pp. 261 f.; Bilz, *Die Politik*, pp. 22 f.; Kienast, *Cato*, pp. 130 f.; Hoffmann, 'Die römische Politik', *Historia* 9 (1960), pp. 309 f., esp. pp. 340 f. In the remainder of this section the articles by Gelzer and Hoffmann are cited by title only.

[2] Livy, *Epit.* 48; Diod. 32. 5.   [3] Polyb. 36. 2; cf. fgt. 99 B-W.

[4] The first version: Oros. 4. 23. 9; Zon. 9. 30. The second: Plut. *Cato Mai.* 27. 2 f.; Diod. 34/35. 33. 5 f. (which refers back from the context of 111 B.C.); Aug. *De Civ. Dei*, 1. 30. The third: Diod. loc. cit.; Aug. loc. cit. Thus the third version is mentioned only in conjunction with the second. Flor. 1. 31. 5 (*ne metu ablato . . . luxuriari felicitas inciperet*) seems closest to the first version. The version in App. *Lib.* 69 is imprecise, saying that Nasica desired the source of fear 'because the Romans were already changing their way of life'. Livy, *Epit.* 49, Zon. 9. 26, and Ampel. 19. 11 mention only the fact of opposition, not the grounds for it. Diod. 34/35. 33. 4 mentions also the assertion that 'Rome's strength should be measured not by the weakness of others but by being seen to be greater than the great'.

about such possibilities, though not without interest, produce only hypothetical results which cannot be properly tested.[1] The present discussion concentrates upon another problem, also difficult but more amenable to positive conclusions, namely whether Nasica did use all the arguments recorded or whether some of them are *post eventum* constructions by later writers. Gelzer accepts all of them as genuine and endeavours to show that they had clear antecedents, even though he thinks that Nasica's policy in itself was something new.[2] Others have expressed doubts in varying degrees, the extreme position being taken by Hoffmann, who holds that the 'counterweight' arguments are entirely *post eventum* constructions by a later generation which linked the end of Carthage with the beginning of the Roman revolution; that Nasica's real concern, springing chiefly from religious considerations, was that there should be a technically valid *iusta causa*; and that once the Carthaginians had provided this by sending their army across the Numidian border in the winter 151–150, Nasica acquiesced in Cato's policy, to which he was not opposed in principle.[3]

Hoffmann has perhaps gone too far. To start with, although religious considerations may have been involved in the *iusta causa* argument, that is scarcely the full picture. Since Polybius, at 36. 2, says explicitly that the Romans were looking for a pretext which would appeal to foreign opinion, and furthermore emphasizes that this was a major consideration in the dispute, it is hard to believe that Nasica did not have the wider meaning very much in mind when he insisted upon a *iusta causa*; and continued opposition on this score is conceivable even after the Carthaginian invasion of Numidia had provided Rome with a *iusta causa* in the sense of a pretext which was adequate in religious and legal terms. In fact there is positive evidence that Nasica did continue his opposition beyond that point, for this is attested not only by Zonaras (i.e. Dio) but also by Livy.[4] Although Livy admittedly worked from the later annalists, his evidence on a particular event such as this cannot easily be dismissed.

Hoffmann advances other arguments in support of his contention that Nasica was not opposed to Cato's policy in principle, but they are not especially weighty. It is true that in 155 Nasica had been the commander

---

[1] This is a feature of the discussion by De Sanctis, *Storia*, iv. 3, pp. 23 f.

[2] 'Nasicas Widerspruch', pp. 261 f. He includes a discussion of App. *Lib.* 65, where, according to the received text, Cato in 167 is said to have quoted Africanus for a similar idea of a 'counterweight of fear'. Bilz, *Die Politik*, pp. 24 f., points to its inappropriateness in the time of Africanus, and Hoffmann, 'Die römische Politik', pp. 318 f., goes further, showing that there is a real possibility that the text is at fault.

[3] 'Die römische Politik', pp. 337 f. and 340 f.

[4] Zon. 9. 26; Livy, *Epit.* 49.

who destroyed the Dalmatian capital, Delminium; but the decision to do this was not necessarily entirely his, and in any case it is far from certain that this action could have been regarded as comparable to the destruction of Carthage; they may well have seemed quite different issues. Again, there is no contradiction between Nasica's subsequent appointment in 147 as Princeps Senatus and his opposition to the policy which had triumphed. Not only was the selection of a Princeps Senatus much influenced by traditional factors, but one of the censors who made the choice, L. Cornelius Lentulus Lupus, is known to have opposed Cato on the Carthaginian issue.[1] Finally, the presence of Nasica's son in the expeditionary force of 149 and his employment on the mission to receive the surrendered Punic armaments[2] is not a safe guide to the father's policy, first because the son, under military orders, may have had little say in the matter, but also because it is quite conceivable that the policy then being pursued (allowing the Carthaginians to build a new city ten miles inland and promising them freedom and autonomy) was not Cato's but a compromise.[3]

But if all this undermines Hoffmann's suggestion that from 150 Nasica acquiesced in Cato's policy, it does not necessarily mean that Nasica used the 'counterweight of fear' argument: that is a separate question. For, though it may be admitted that the Carthaginian attack on Massinissa gave Rome a *iusta causa* for war, it would still have been possible throughout the crisis to argue that the destruction of Carthage would seem to others an outrage and would have a most undesirable effect on foreign opinion—all the more so if Cato did press for something more drastic than the policy actually adopted in 149.

Hoffmann points out that the 'counterweight' idea does not appear in the surviving passages of Polybius. Polybius, 36. 2 shows that the major argument which nearly stopped the Romans going to war concerned the effect on foreign opinion, and Hoffmann sees in the previous excerpt, 36. 1, a strong hint that Polybius did not consider any other arguments to have been important. Hence he concludes that there is no link between Polybius and the later writers who give prominence to the 'counterweight' concept; and since these writers were not working from Nasica's authentic speeches, which were not preserved, it is particularly easy to envisage the

[1] Lentulus: p. 53. The Princeps Senatus was always a patrician ex-censor, or occasionally the patrician censor himself; frequently the senior surviving member of this category was chosen: Mommsen, *Röm. Staats.* iii, p. 970. In 147 Nasica was certainly the senior, and the only other patrician ex-censor who could still have been alive was M. Valerius Messala, censor 154, who began the theatre which in 151 (or 150) Nasica persuaded the Senate to destroy (p. 48).

[2] App. *Lib.* 80.   [3] pp. 52 f.

idea as a *post eventum* construction. Unfortunately Hoffmann has not quite proved that Polybius did not include or did not know of the idea. In 36. 1 he is explaining why he is reporting only arguments actually used in the dispute, and of them only the most opportune and effective (τὰ καιριώτατα καὶ πραγματικώτατα). It remains open either that the 'counterweight' idea may have been mentioned in a lost passage (for what survives is only a series of disconnected excerpts), or that Polybius regarded it as ineffective (in which case it might have been recorded by some Roman contemporary and taken up by later writers). On the other hand, the explicit statement in 36. 2 that disagreements about the possible effect on foreign opinion very nearly led the Romans to refrain from war, does make it very difficult to believe that the 'counterweight' idea was an important and effective element in the discussion.

The second form of the 'counterweight' argument (concerned with civil discord) is found only in Plutarch, in Augustine, and in a passage of Diodorus (probably derived from Poseidonius) which is concerned primarily with the death of Nasica's grandson in 111. The third form (external excesses) is found only in the latter two passages, and of these Augustine would carry little weight on his own account. Gelzer and Bilz feel that the Plutarch passage is Polybian in origin, on account of an apparent affinity with Polybius' theory of the decline of Rome's mixed constitution.[1] But this is an uncertain argument, and Hoffmann rightly notes that Plutarch's account of Nasica's arguments is introduced with a hint of hypothesis, ὡς ἔοικεν. The more elaborate Diodorus passage, and with it the third form of the 'counterweight' argument, was suspected, before Hoffmann attacked it, by Bilz and Kienast,[2] on the ground that Nasica could not possibly have prophesied so clearly the future course of events; and again Hoffmann notes that in this Diodorus passage the arguments are all attributed to Nasica's supporters, not to Nasica himself, thus hinting at the absence of an authentic source. And indeed the possibility of Nasica's argument having been perverted in the light of later events is only too obvious.

On the other hand, the 'counterweight' argument in some form is undeniably very widely spread in the sources.[3] If Nasica used it at all, it must surely have been in the first form, that Carthage was needed as a stimulant to military efficiency. This would have been reasonably in harmony with recent events: the Dalmatian war, said to have been

---

[1] Gelzer, 'Nasicas Widerspruch', p. 273; Bilz, *Die Politik*, pp. 22 and 24 f.
[2] Bilz, *Die Politik*, pp. 22 f.; Kienast, *Cato*, pp. 131 f.
[3] p. 276 n. 4.

undertaken principally to keep the army in training; Nasica's resolution prohibiting seating at *ludi*, lest it undermine Roman hardiness;[1] and the recent troubles in Spain. Admittedly this form of the argument is found only in Orosius and Zonaras, but Orosius is likely to have taken it from Livy; and it is worth remembering that the *Epitome* of Livy, mentioning the *iusta causa* argument, is the closest to what survives of Polybius.[2] Even so, an argument which presupposed that Carthage, if not vigorously controlled, could again become a menace, patently would have been two-edged. It is hard to believe that such a skilled and successful politician as Nasica would have made too much play with it; and this coincides with the impression given by Polybius. Thus if Nasica used the idea at all, Kienast is probably right in supposing that he employed it merely as a rhetorical 'topos', which was elaborated by writers of a later generation in the light of Rome's subsequent misfortunes.[3]

4. *Scipio, Cato, and the Third Punic War*

This section is a summary, with a few additional points and modifications, of the arguments which the author put forward in 'Scipio Aemilianus and Cato Censorius', *Latomus* 15 (1956), pp. 159 f. The main conclusion, that Scipio supported Cato rather than Nasica, is rejected by Badian, *Foreign Clientelae*, p. 132 n. 1 (evidently with particular reference to the negotiations after the battle between Massinissa and the Carthaginians), with the comment that it presupposes an interrelation between internal politics and foreign policy for which he sees no evidence.

The main contentions underlying the conclusion accepted in this book can be summarized as follows:[4]

(i) The tendency to presuppose that Scipio Aemilianus would naturally have supported 'the Scipios' against Cato is unjustified. His background links with Cato, as well as with Nasica, were strong.

(ii) There is no trace of any sort of opposition between Scipio and Cato, even in sources such as Polybius which in one way or another would be especially likely to reflect such opposition if it had existed. Here may be

[1] Dalmatia: Polyb. 32. 13; the seating: p. 47.
[2] Especially if Diod. 32. 5 is derived from Polybius.
[3] *Cato*, p. 132. Walbank, 'Political Morality and the Friends of Scipio', *JRS* 55 (1965), pp. 6 f., rejects Hoffmann's interpretation and offers a brief defence of the theory that the 'counterweight' argument, with particular reference to internal stability, was the essence of Nasica's opposition.
[4] Full evidence is cited in the article in *Latomus* 15 (1956), pp. 159 f. Cf. also Additional Note ZC, p. 355.

added the particular argument that although there are a large number of anecdotes about each of them, many preserving witty and biting sayings directed against other people, there is none indicating any trace of hostility between these two.

(iii) On the other hand, there is strong and reliable evidence for a friendly and co-operative relationship at the very time when the Carthaginian crisis was at its climax. This is quite improbable if Scipio had sided with Nasica in a dispute of such length and importance. It is particularly hard to believe that under such circumstances he would have even approached Cato about the Achaean exiles, let alone secured his support.

(iv) It is not credible that Scipio would have been elected to the consulship of 147 in the face of tremendous resistance if his opponents had been able to play upon earlier opposition to the destruction of Carthage.

(v) Scipio thought the firing of Carthage καλόν: Polyb. 38. 21. 1; cf. Appendix II, no. 9a.

(vi) Polybius, Scipio's friend and admirer, gives much prominence to the arguments justifying Rome's action against Carthage: 36. 9. 2 f.; cf. Walbank, 'Political Morality and the Friends of Scipio', *JRS* 55 (1965), pp. 1 f., esp. pp. 8 f.

(vii) The account of Scipio's part in the negotiations between Carthage and Massinissa (App. *Lib.* 72) contains nothing to suggest that he supported Nasica's policy rather than Cato's. He could scarcely have refused to act, and neither the extent of the Carthaginian concessions nor the issue on which the negotiations broke down encourages the belief that he was especially favourably disposed to the Carthaginians.

(viii) The discussion in *Latomus* laid excessive stress on the common enmities of Cato and Scipio as an indication of political alliance. This presupposed too clear a division of Roman politicians into two large semi-permanent factions, a view which is not followed in this book (cf. esp. pp. 95 f.).

(ix) The discussion in *Latomus* also overestimated the effect that Scipio's support is likely to have had on the ultimate decision.

APPENDIX IV

Scipio's Tears at Carthage

1. *The Three Versions*

THREE accounts survive of the occasion when Scipio shed tears and quoted Homer over the ruins of Carthage: Appian, *Lib*. 132 (included in the text of Polybius at 38. 22); Diodorus, 32. 24; Polybius, 38. 21. The latter two are fragments, both from the Byzantine compilation of *Excerpta de Sententiis*, and thus are not in precise context. All three are quoted in full in Appendix II, no. 9.

The Polybian fragment, besides being divorced from its context, is badly mutilated. While the later and larger part of the excerpt is more or less complete, only a few isolated words can be distinguished in the opening lines. Although it is unmistakably concerned with the same incident as the passages in Appian and Diodorus, as it stands it has no reference to tears and does not contain the quotation from Homer. The tears could easily have been mentioned in the first few lines, and since the incident is the same as that described by Appian and Diodorus it is probable that they were. But the quotation was almost certainly not copied by the excerptor; for it does not follow the words of Scipio, which are almost the first coherent surviving words of the excerpt, and the few surviving letters from the opening lines are sufficient virtually to exclude the possibility that it was in the mutilated portion.[1] This is a point of some interest. Despite verbal differences, the words of Scipio reflect the same utterance as is reported in Appian and Diodorus; these authors show that this utterance was an answer to a question put by Polybius; and there is no difficulty about interpreting the Polybius fragment itself in this way. But since the excerptor evidently found it possible to record Polybius' question without first giving the Homeric quotation, it seems virtually certain that the question did not concern the quotation. Furthermore, it is very likely that the καλὸν μέν with which Scipio's answer begins picks up the τούτου καλλίον towards the end of the broken passage: Polybius'

---

[1] A reference to Homer is sometimes restored at the end of the fragmentary section, immediately before the text becomes continuous. If this is correct, it would seem that at the scene Polybius may have mentioned Homer, which in turn may have prompted Scipio's quotation. See the hypothetical restoration of Boissevain, *Excerpta*, iv, p. 219.

question probably included something to the effect 'What could be finer than this?'

Although the accounts given by Appian and Diodorus both have their ultimate origin in Polybius, there are differences of emphasis between them and one important difference concerning the order of events. In Appian the Homeric quotation, uttered by Scipio as he shed tears and meditated, comes before Polybius' question, and that question is about the quotation, not about the tears; whereas in Diodorus the sequence is that Scipio shed tears, Polybius asked why, Scipio gave his answer and added the quotation.

It seems clear that Diodorus is to be preferred to Appian. In the first place, he was using Polybius directly, whereas Appian, though he refers to Polybius' history, probably got his information through an intermediate source. Second, Diodorus' version of Scipio's reply is closer than Appian's to the Polybian original. Third, it has just been seen that like Diodorus, and unlike Appian, the Polybian fragment implies that Polybius' question was not about the Homeric quotation.

2. *Occasion*

In one important discussion the assumption is made that the incident occurred as Scipio watched the final scenes of the capture of Carthage, at the climax of six days and nights of ferocious fighting.[1] This is certainly implied by Appian, who in his continuous narrative relates it immediately after the suicide of Hasdrubal's wife and before such matters as the arrangements made by Scipio for plundering the captured city. At first sight the excerpts from Polybius and Diodorus might seem to confirm this, since both follow excerpts concerned with Hasdrubal's wife. On closer examination, however, they are found to contradict rather than to support.

Both excerpts are separate excerpts, not continuous with the preceding fragments about Hasdrubal's wife.[2] There is no necessity, therefore, for them to have been closely linked in substance or in time with the preceding excerpts; the very fact that they are separate suggests that there was no especially close link and that in the original something intervened; and the intervening section could have been considerable. With this in mind, it is possible to look again at the internal evidence of the excerpts

[1] Scullard, 'Scipio Aemilianus', *JRS* 50 (1960), p. 61.
[2] The Loeb edition of Polybius obscures this point. Boissevain, *Excerpta*, iv, p. 219 line 9, clearly distinguishes a new excerpt beginning with Ὅτι. Büttner-Wobst, in a note on p. 500 of his edition of Polybius, also recognizes the division, though he does not make it clear in the text, printing an isolated τι.

themselves. The words attributed to Scipio in the Polybian, and therefore the most reliable, version show that Scipio had just issued a crucial order concerning the city, an order in some sense dramatically final. The nature of that order is indicated by the opening words of the Diodorus fragment: 'When Carthage had been set on fire and the flames were destroying the entire city . . . .' The order seems to have been for the firing of such of the city as still stood, part of the work of total destruction. If this is corrrect, there must have been an interval since the end of the fighting of at least several days, and probably longer, to allow for the systematic plundering of the city.[1] Since Appian's version of the incident seems in any case to be the least precise, the sequence of his narrative cannot be regarded as a serious objection to this conclusion.

3. Interpretations

It is not surprising that such a dramatic incident has been subjected to varying interpretations, some very imprecise, others tending to treat it as a key to the understanding of Scipio's political outlook. Mommsen, for example, saw in Scipio's reaction horror and a presentiment of the retribution that would inevitably follow such a misdeed.[2] On this there is no need to linger: the only hint of remorse is Appian's κλαίων ὑπὲρ πολεμίων, which is surely his own expression; the general tone of all three passages is contrary, dwelling upon the inconstancy of Fortune; and the καλὸν μέν of the original Polybian version in itself as good as disproves remorse. Another opinion is that Scipio recognized that his action was a fatal step in removing the external sources of fear which helped to prevent social decay, an interpretation which takes on dramatic irony when combined with the view that Scipio believed the destruction of Carthage to be necessary. In this way Gelzer is led to speak of Scipio's 'hopeless pessimism'.[3] This interpretation has rightly been rejected by Aymard, followed by Brink and Walbank.[4] 'Hopeless pessimism' is far too strong an expression for anything in the records of the incident and seems to conflict with Polybius' praise of Scipio, whom, he says, the episode showed to be 'a great and perfect man, a man in short worthy to be remembered'.

---

[1] Cf. App. Lib. 133: 'for a certain number of days he permitted the army to plunder.'
[2] Hist. of Rome, iii, p. 258.
[3] 'Nasicas Widerspruch', Philologus 86 (1931), p. 294. Bilz, Die Politik, p. 34, offers a less dramatic version of the same explanation. Cf. also De Sanctis, Storia, iv. 3, p. 74.
[4] Aymard, 'Deux anecdotes', pp. 101 f., esp. pp. 109 f.; Brink and Walbank, 'The Construction of the Sixth Book of Polybius', CQ N.S. 4 (1954), esp. pp. 104 f.; Walbank, 'Polybius and the Roman State', GRBS 5 (1964), pp. 252 f.

Scipio's words contain no hint of any sense of any personal responsibility for the fate which he fears Rome will one day suffer, nor indeed do they imply a conviction that decline has already set in.[1] Instead the whole emphasis is upon the mutability and inconstancy of Fortune, linked with the belief that all earthly things must perish eventually.

A rather different assessment of the episode is offered by Scullard. He holds that the degree and importance of Scipio's emotional experience is unreasonably minimized in the statement of Brink and Walbank that 'the famous scene beside the burning city of Carthage is no more than a recognition of the instability of human fortune, and the certain doom of all mortal things. Scipio here revealed a proper Hellenistic sensibility.'[2] Scullard's opinion is that for Scipio the incident, coming at the end of six days of continuous toil and horror, when he was 'in a state of physical exhaustion and mental exaltation', was a profound emotional and psychological crisis, which is the key to the interpretation of his subsequent policies. Henceforth he was guided by a determination to maintain the stability of the mixed constitution, the breakdown of which had brought destruction upon Carthage and would do the like for Rome.

Two questions arise here. The first is to what extent or whether at all other evidence supports the suggestion that the idea of preserving the mixed constitution played a major part in Scipio's political thinking. Obviously Scullard's combination of this idea with the experience at Carthage is a matter of hypothesis; for, although the idea of eventual inevitable decline was clearly present in the Carthage incident, the accounts of that incident in no way present this in terms of the mixed constitution. Consequently this problem is reserved for a separate discussion.[3]

The second and more immediate question concerns the intensity of the emotional experience: was it a decisive crisis? That Scipio's tears, his explanation, and his quotation from Homer are unlikely to have been mere charlatanism may be conceded readily, for the occasion was one which was bound to generate genuine emotions, probably of a very mixed character and not easily put into words. Nevertheless, the accounts of the incident surely need not imply an intense emotional outburst. By ἐδάκρυεν Diodorus (Polybius) need not necessarily mean that Scipio shed a flood of tears, that he truly wept. It is also possible to envisage moist eyes, with a tear or two trickling down either cheek; and this would be much more

---

[1] On this theme cf. also Additional Note ZC, p. 355.
[2] Scullard, 'Scipio Aemilianus', *JRS* 50 (1960), esp. pp. 61 f.; Brink and Walbank, 'The Construction of the Sixth Book of Polybius', *CQ* N.S. 4 (1954), p. 104.
[3] Appendix V.

consistent with Polybius' praise of Scipio's attitude as that of 'a great and perfect man, a man in short worthy to be remembered'. Moreover, the incentive to imagine a more intense outburst, with copious tears, is much reduced if, as is highly probable, the incident occurred not as the climax of a week of unceasing toil but at least several days later, at the firing of the ruins.

Scullard's interpretation does not rest on the tears alone. He says that 'what obviously made the most profound impression on Polybius was Scipio's fear for Rome. . . . Surely Polybius' vivid and emphatic record of the scene was inspired less by the fact that Scipio reacted as would be expected of him than by the fact that his fears for Rome were sincere and may have crystallized at this tragic moment against the background of the smoking city.' There is a sense in which these statements are true, in that Polybius certainly implies that Scipio was sincere, that the episode should not be treated as 'nothing more than a Hellenistic gesture to Tyche'— if the word 'gesture' is taken to imply little more than outward formality.[1] Nevertheless, these remarks carry overtones which seem to suggest to the reader that Polybius was impressed by the depth and extent of Scipio's fears. This is not so. What really impressed him—and doubtless aroused in him much satisfaction as well as approval—was that Scipio was not completely carried away by exultant pride, that at the pinnacle of success he was able to preserve sufficient detachment to remember and reflect upon the mutability of Fortune—this it is that stamps Scipio as 'a great and perfect man, a man in short worthy to be remembered'.

Furthermore, of Scipio's feelings at this moment and in this period of triumph the only surviving record is of this presentiment of the ultimate fate of Rome. Consequently there is a temptation to assume that this was the dominating feature of his thoughts. It is perhaps just conceivable, though in view of our fragmentary evidence entirely unproven, that he attempted to put into words no other emotion, but other powerful emotions there must have been, and it is highly questionable whether the meagre evidence available gives any justification whatsoever for assigning dominance to this one.

That Scipio was genuinely moved may be agreed without hesitation, as also that, doubtless amid a welter of emotions, of pride and triumph, of relief and joy, he felt sadness at the reminder that sooner or later all earthly things must pass, one day the greatness of Rome no less than the greatness of Carthage, perhaps in the same manner as Carthage. What

---

[1] But this is not what Walbank intended; see his further explanation of 'Hellenistic sensibility' in 'Polybius and the Roman State', *GRBS* 5 (1964), p. 254.

cannot be agreed is that Scipio's emotion was so profound, his fears for the future so intense, that they are likely to have conditioned his outlook from that time on. It is theoretically possible that examination of the rest of Scipio's career might suggest just such a dominating idea; but in practice it does not, and the claim to have found it is made only in terms of an urgent anxiety to maintain the balance of the mixed constitution—which merits separate treatment. The point being made here is that what is known of the incident at Carthage gives no grounds for starting with the hypothesis that Scipio's subsequent policies were motivated substantially by fears for the future of Rome.

APPENDIX V

Scipio and Polybius' Theory of the Mixed Constitution

In the sixth book of his history Polybius discussed the reasons for the phenomenal success of Rome in achieving, within a short space of time, the domination of virtually the whole Mediterranean world. It is well known that he considered the fundamental basis of this success to have been the Roman constitution, which he saw as an excellent example of a 'mixed constitution', compounded of elements of monarchy, aristocracy, and democracy. He believed that such a constitution, though not exempt from the natural law that all things must perish, would have quite exceptional stability and permanence, enjoying considerable freedom from the operation of the 'natural cycle' of constitutions from monarchy through to ochlocracy; the excessive growth and corruption of any one of the three elements would be checked by the other two, so that the balance would be maintained or automatically restored. To round off his extended exposition of this theory and of its exemplification in Rome, Polybius discussed briefly the manner in which the mixed constitution would perish —for, however stable it might be, it must eventually perish under the natural law which decreed ultimate doom for everything.[1] His explanation was that when a state had achieved dominance long-established prosperity would breed extravagance and undue ambition; this would lead to both flattery and exploitation of the *demos*, with the result that eventually the *demos* would reject the authority of the principal men and itself take almost complete control; hence there would emerge democracy and ochlocracy, the later stages of decline in the 'natural cycle'.

This explanation of Rome's success and of how she would decline was put forward, in writing, by a close friend and confidant of Scipio Aemilianus. Although publication probably occurred at a time when circumstances

---

[1] 6. 57. Both this appendix and the interpretations principally under discussion accept that the exposition in the sixth book of Polybius was composed as a unity, substantially as it stands. The hypothesis of extensive and ill-fitting revisions in the light of later events rests too much on an unwillingness to accept that Polybius could have been guilty of inconsistencies, and the case for unitary composition seems overwhelming. See esp. Brink and Walbank, 'The Construction of the Sixth Book of Polybius', *CQ* N.S. 4 (1954), pp. 97 f.

were beginning to separate the two men for long periods,[1] it is scarcely conceivable that Scipio was completely unaware of his friend's theory. This being so, it must inevitably be asked whether Scipio himself accepted the theory, whether he took it seriously, and whether it influenced his own political activity.

There is a certain fascination about the *a priori* assumption that there was a link between the Greek's theory and the Roman's policies, that Scipio must have shared and taken seriously Polybius' views. Consequently there have been attempts to discern the influence of the theory in certain events. Scipio's tears at Carthage, for example, have been interpreted as a recognition that he had removed the last external source of fear and thus was the agent who set Rome on the inevitable path of decline prophesied by Polybius. This interpretation is rejected in Appendix IV; it is entirely unsupported by the sources, which contain no hint of any sense of personal responsibility for the fate which one day must overtake Rome. Much more important than this is the suggestion that the urgent necessity of maintaining the stability of the existing (mixed) constitution was a major element in Scipio's political thinking. This interpretation is urged by Bilz and, with more detailed application to Scipio's career, by Scullard.[2]

There is perhaps no need to discuss at length Bilz's picture of a man whose belief in the excellence of the existing constitution blinded him to its actual serious inadequacy for the direction of large-scale wars—an inadequacy demonstrated by his own extra-constitutional command against Numantia—and to the need for reform in the direction of autocracy.[3] Quite apart from the serious doubt as to whether anyone could be expected to have recognized inadequacy of this kind at this date,[4] it is wildly improbable that any Roman of this period would have thought of autocracy as a solution. To say the least, there is no need for a special explanation of Scipio's failure to do so. Nevertheless, there remains the underlying notion that the idea of maintaining the existing mixed constitution became a major factor in Scipio's outlook, and it is this which Scullard has worked out in detail as a serious hypothesis.

Scullard traces the idea from the incident of Scipio's tears at Carthage, where he suggests that thoughts of the uncertainty of Rome's future may well have stabbed Scipio's mind with peculiar intensity and dramatic

---

[1] Walbank, *Commentary on Polybius*, pp. 292 f. and 636.

[2] Bilz, *Die Politik*, pp. 6 f., esp. p. 14; cf. p. 70. Scullard, 'Scipio Aemilianus', *JRS* 50 (1960), pp. 59 f.   [3] *Die Politik*, esp. pp. 78 f.; cf. pp. 64 f.

[4] In the sources military reverses are almost invariably attributed to the personal failings of commanders. There is no suggestion that the causes were to be found in weaknesses in the constitutional or administrative machinery.

force, fusing with knowledge of moral decline at Rome to give a flash of illumination to misgivings about Rome's future well-being. Since Scipio's thoughts are likely to have 'moved on similar lines' to those of Polybius, he may have returned to Rome 'profoundly disquieted at the thought of any threat to Rome's internal stability. The policy therefore that he might be expected to follow would not be that of radical reform but an effort to maintain and, where necessary, to re-establish the traditional balance of the mixed constitution by restraining any who threatened to disturb it, be they Commons or Nobles.' Scullard goes on to examine Scipio's subsequent career, suggesting that this policy is to be seen as the motive, or at least an important motive, behind many of his actions.

Scullard's interpretation of the scene at Carthage is questioned in Appendix IV: it is by no means certain that Scipio's tears represent so intense an outburst as he suggests; although the eventual decline of Rome certainly entered into Scipio's thoughts, it is unsafe to assume that it was the dominating idea in his mind, at any rate for more than a few moments; and the accounts of the incident give no good reason for believing that Scipio felt Rome to be in danger of early decline. It may be added that these accounts neither make nor imply any reference to the mixed constitution, and that it is purely a modern hypothesis that when Scipio thought of decline he necessarily thought in terms of the breakdown of the mixed constitution. All this casts doubt on Scullard's suggestion about the origin of what he believes to have been Scipio's policy; and certainly the incident at Carthage does not in itself justify *a priori* belief in such a policy. But rejection of this starting-point does not necessarily invalidate Scullard's general hypothesis.

It is difficult either to prove or to disprove a hypothesis such as Scullard puts forward. Direct statements of Scipio's views on such matters are lacking, which is neither surprising nor significant. Recourse must be had to examining the known events of Scipio's career in the light of the hypothesis; and Scullard's view is that the hypothesis provides an intelligible motive for Scipio's actions. When the actions he discusses are examined one by one, in each case it is perfectly easy to conceive of an alternative motive, at least as plausible and in keeping with what is known of Scipio's character and circumstances; yet in each case it is impossible to prove such a hypothesis to the exclusion of Scullard's. This is true also of Scipio's concern about moral decline, for which other explanations are possible[1] but which could conceivably have been linked with a fear that

---

[1] See pp. 292 f. and esp. pp. 117 f. Another topic which has been brought into the discussion is Scipio's supposed anti-expansionist foreign policy after 146. Even if he did advocate

moral decay would lead to constitutional decline. In other words, examination of the individual episodes is not going to provide proof either way; nor, of course, does Scullard attempt to establish his case by proof in particular instances. Leaving aside the incident at Carthage, his case really rests upon, first, the attractiveness of the assumption that Scipio cannot have been uninfluenced by Polybius' theory, and second, the fact that a considerable number of events are susceptible of explanation in terms of the one dominant motive. It is a case for which it is perhaps unreasonable to demand positive proof; but it is legitimate to ask whether the hypothesis fits quite well enough.

It is not being contested that Scipio knew Polybius' theory that Rome had a mixed constitution; nor that he may have given general intellectual consent to that theory; nor that he may well have agreed that this mixed constitution was a source of strength, certainly in so far as he understood it to mean government by the senatorial aristocracy, which is what it often meant to Polybius when it came to specific instances.[1] The question at issue is whether Scipio had these ideas at the forefront of his mind in the course of his ordinary activities; and there are a number of events which make it difficult to believe that he did. Even if, to meet Scullard strictly on his own ground, no account is taken of the election in 148 and other of Scipio's activities before 146, there remains a striking similarity between his behaviour and the kind of behaviour which Polybius thought would undermine the mixed constitution. It is hard to credit that in seeking the censorship he would have made use of men who 'frequented the Forum and were able to gather a crowd and to force all issues by shouting and inciting passions', if he had been acutely conscious that stability might be threatened by excessive rivalry for office, by love of office, and by flattery of the people for the sake of ambition for office, and by the people being swayed by passion.[2] If he had been thinking of these dangers, and of the possibility that one day the people might refuse to obey the aristocracy, it is scarcely credible that in 135–134 he would again have used popular pressure to have himself not merely exempted from the law and elected consul but appointed to an important military command, manifestly in defiance of the will of the Senate. Polybius had stressed the importance of the Senate's financial powers for keeping in check the 'monarchical' army commanders, yet Scipio in 134 flaunted his ability to

---

such a policy, there is no necessity to conclude that he was motivated by concern about the mixed constitution; and in fact it is doubtful if he did formulate an anti-expansionist policy. See Appendix X.

[1] 6. 51. 6 f., 56. 6 f., 57. 8.   [2] Plut. Aem. 38. 4; Polyb. 6. 57.

defy the Senate's refusal of funds by raising cash from his own fortune and from his friends and clients. Similarly, when the Senate refused permission for a normal levy, he raised what was virtually a private army.[1] In short, if Scipio had had as a dominant motive in his mind the need to preserve the mixed constitution in accordance with the theories of Polybius, it is very unlikely that he would have acted as he did in these instances. This does not necessarily mean that he did not give intellectual assent to those theories; it does mean that in practice he saw no relationship between them and these actions of his. And if he failed to see a relationship in these particular instances, it is hard to believe that at any time concern about the mixed constitution played a substantial part in his practical thinking or political motives.

It is not surprising that this should have been so. It is not merely that there are inconsistencies inherent in Polybius' theory and distortions in applying it to Rome, distortions to which a Roman noble can scarcely have been blind; nor yet that the idea of decline plays a very minor part in Polybius' exposition, which is much more concerned with emphasizing the longevity and the self-correcting tendencies of the mixed constitution.[2] The whole underlying attitude of mind, which regarded as real and practical political issues the questions of the form of the constitution and which section of the community should govern, simply did not correspond to the day-to-day experiences and problems of the Roman politician. However clever and attractive the philhellene Roman may have found such theorizing, for him these were not immediate issues. However fascinated he was by sophisticated expositions of the excellence of the existing order, the aristocratic predominance was something he took for granted, accepted by all whom he met, and received from the *mores maiorum*. When Scipio, like others, exploited popular feeling and the popular machinery in order to defy the will of the majority in the Senate, he saw this as a political tactic within the accepted general framework, not as a threat to government by the aristocracy.

Polybius shared his countrymen's enjoyment of theoretical speculation, but he was also a practical and experienced man of affairs. His theory that Rome's success was attributable to her mixed constitution was matched by a recognition of the excellence and the significance of her military practices. More than a third of what survives of his sixth book consists of a detailed treatment of this topic. Here he was surely much closer to the thinking of the Roman aristocracy. For it was a military aristocracy, in which military and political advancement were intimately interlinked

---

[1] For these events see esp. pp. 135 f. and 182 f.   [2] Additional Note ZC, p. 355.

and military service was a prerequisite for public office. Rome had become supreme by winning wars, and if in the years after 146 Scipio and others felt concern about the welfare of the state their attention is more likely to have been focused on problems of military efficiency than on the preservation of a constitutional balance.[1]

[1] See further pp. 117 f. and 171 f.

APPENDIX VI

The 'Scipionic Circle' and the Influence of Panaetius

1. The 'Scipionic Circle'

THE phrase 'the Scipionic Circle', current since the middle of the nineteenth century, recurs constantly in studies of Roman civilization and
especially of Roman literature and Graeco-Roman philosophy. Customarily it is used to designate a group of philhellene *litterati* centred
around Scipio Aemilianus who were mainly responsible for the modification of traditional Roman ideas through a certain synthesis with Greek
thought, producing a kind of Graeco-Roman intellectualism; a group
which in its interests and influence was quite distinctive in Roman society.
The term 'Scipionic Circle' is essentially an invention of modern scholarship.[1] The only ancient authority underlying it is a phrase in Cicero's *De
Amicitia*, where Laelius is made to speak of *amicitia* between superior and
inferior: *saepe enim excellentiae quaedam sunt, qualis erat Scipionis in nostro,
ut ita dicam, grege.*[2] In its content the phrase is vague, and it is by no means
certain that it has reference to community of cultural interests. That does
not mean that 'Scipionic Circle' may not be employed in a valid and
meaningful way; but there is a clear danger of imprecision, as a result of
which it seems often to have acquired a number of misleading overtones.
One of these is exaggeration of the uniqueness of these cultural and intellectual interests; and from that there seems to have developed a tendency
to think of the 'circle' as a kind of club to which all Roman *litterati* or
philhellenes would naturally belong. A further development is then to
identify this supposedly highly distinctive cultural group as a distinctive
political group whose outlook and policies were conditioned by these
cultural interests. There have even been attempts to portray the 'circle'
as owing its existence as a political group primarily to its common cultural
and intellectual interests—though these extreme interpretations have
commanded little support.[3]

---

[1] Brown, *Scipionic Circle*, pp. 16 f., traces it to German scholars of the middle of the
nineteenth century, ultimately to Bernhardy, *Grundriß der römischen Litteratur*[2] (Halle,
1850), pp. 191 f. [2] Cic. *De Amic.* 69.

[3] Brown, *Scipionic Circle*; Schur, *Das Zeitalter des Marius und Sulla*. The latter called forth
a vigorous and effective protest from Syme, *JRS* 34 (1944), pp. 105 f.; cf. also some pertinent
remarks by Earl, 'Terence and Roman Politics', *Historia* 11 (1962), p. 477.

Any outstanding personality can be said to have around him a 'circle' of
friends and acquaintances with whom he shares common interests of one
kind or another—though he does not necessarily share the same interests
with all of them. It is equally true that among those associated with Scipio
were a number of men who are known to have been interested in literature and in Greek thought;[1] but he also had political associates for whom
no such interest is attested,[2] so that it cannot be assumed without question
that such interests were a *sine qua non* of association with him (which in
any case would be an improbable assumption to make about a leading
politician). That still leaves open, however, the question of whether these
interests were wholly or largely peculiar to Scipio's 'circle', whether they
were a characteristic (not necessarily the basic characteristic) which distinguished it from other groups.

It would not be easy to credit that this was the case even in the light of
what is known about the growing influence of Greek culture in Rome
earlier in the second century,[3] and there is sufficient particular evidence
from Scipio's own time to disprove it outright. Despite the severe limitations in our knowledge of the literature and the personalities of the period
we do know of several men with similar interests who were not associated
with Scipio and some of whom were certainly at odds with him. Thus
A. Postumius Albinus, cos. 151, emerges even from the hostile account
of Polybius as an enthusiastic and knowledgeable philhellene with strong
literary interests;[4] M. Aemilius Lepidus Porcina was the first Roman
orator in whose speeches Cicero found certain characteristics of Greek
rhetoric;[5] M. Fulvius Flaccus was *studiosus litterarum*;[6] L. Calpurnius Piso
Frugi, writer of an important history, was certainly a *litteratus*;[7] P. Licinius
Crassus Dives Mucianus could speak fluently in five Greek dialects;[8] and
if we know of the contacts with Scipio enjoyed by Terence, Lucilius, and
Panaetius because later generations judged them the great figures of the
age, it is as well to remember that there were other writers at work, and

---

[1] The persons chiefly associated with the 'circle' are usually taken to be those used by
Cicero as the *dramatis personae* of his *De Republica*.

[2] e.g. the Servilii brothers, and P. and L. Rupilius.

[3] Cf. Polybius' reference, 31. 24. 6 f., to teachers of Greek learning flocking to Rome
c. 167.

[4] Polyb. 39. 1. 1 f. For Polybius' prejudice see Münzer, *RE*, s.v. *Postumius*, no. 31, esp.
col. 906 f. Cf. Cic. *Brut.* 81, *litteratus*; *Acad. Pr.* 2. 137, *doctum sane hominem*. The anecdote in
the latter passage demonstrates a familiarity with Greek philosophy.

[5] Cic. *Brut.* 95 f.   [6] Cic. *Brut.* 108.

[7] Cf. Cichorius, *RE*, s.v. *Calpurnius*, no. 96; Cicero's judgement on his *annales* is *sane
exiliter scriptos*: *Brut.* 106.

[8] Val. Max. 8. 7. 6; Quint. *Inst.* 11. 2. 50.

especially that there was one other of enduring fame, Accius, whose work also showed a blending of Greek and Roman elements and whose patron was not Scipio but D. Iunius Brutus Callaicus.[1]

Intellectual and cultural interests with a philhellenic bias were not, therefore, confined to the 'circle' of Scipio Aemilianus. It may well be that the particular *litterati* associated with Scipio exercised exceptional influence upon later generations, and that in this respect the term 'Scipionic Circle', defined with suitable caution, may have a valuable application. It seems more doubtful if it is possible to go further and find a common cultural thread among three such diverse writers as Terence, Lucilius, and Panaetius, the works of two of whom survive only in fragments, or, even further, to trace that same thread in the brief fragments of the Roman historical writers known to have had contacts with Scipio—let alone to establish that it was peculiar to this group and was not to be found in other literature of the time which is now almost entirely lost. But such matters as these do not fall within either the scope of this book or the competence of its author.[2] What is of immediate concern, however, is whether Scipio's cultural pursuits had any discernible effect on his political activities. Theoretically this could have been so even though those pursuits were not unique in their general character. This is a complex question, having special but not exclusive reference to the possible influence of Panaetius; and it calls for extended treatment.

2. *Panaetius and Scipio*

Panaetius of Rhodes, the Stoic philosopher, had contacts with several eminent Romans. Attested are C. Laelius, C. Fannius and Q. Mucius Scaevola (the sons-in-law of Laelius), Q. Aelius Tubero, P. Rutilius Rufus, and especially Scipio Aemilianus.[3] Since Scipio had connexions with all the others, and all of them except Laelius were much younger than he, it is virtually certain that Panaetius' contacts with the others were derivatives of an initial relationship with Scipio himself. The apparent intimacy of that relationship has encouraged a tendency to assume that Panaetius exercised a significant influence upon the political outlook of Scipio. Out of this there have arisen several theories about the manner

---

[1] Cic. *Brut.* 107; *De Leg.* 2. 54; *Pro Arch.* 27; *Schol. Bob. Arch.*, p. 179 Stangl; Val. Max. 8. 14. 2. For Brutus' philhellenism see Münzer, *RE*, s.v. *Iunius*, no. 57, col. 1024.

[2] See esp. Büchner, *Röm. Literaturgesch.*, pp. 142 f.

[3] e.g. Cic. *De Fin.* 4. 23; *Brut.* 101, 113 f.; *De Orat.* 1. 75; *Rep.* 1. 34; *Pro Mur.* 66. Numerous other refs. collected by van Straaten, *Pan. Fragmenta*[3], nos. 2, 8–25, 137–47.

in which Scipio may have been influenced, two of which will be discussed in sections 3 and 4;[1] but first it is necessary to consider briefly the general character of the relationship between the two men.[2]

Only one event in this relationship is dated securely. In 140–139 Panaetius accepted an invitation by Scipio to accompany him on his embassy to the countries of the eastern Mediterranean.[3] They were together, therefore, for a year or more at this time. It is likely, and it is usually assumed, that Scipio had met Panaetius before he issued the invitation, although there is no evidence whatsoever about any previous contacts. It is entirely possible that prior to 140 these had been brief and not very intimate (assuming that they had occurred at all), but in any case a close relationship probably developed only after 146. Prior to 151 Panaetius is unlikely to have acquired sufficient eminence as a philosopher or teacher in his own right, and in the period 151–146 Scipio was fully occupied in Spain and Africa.[4]

Panaetius is known to have lived in Scipio's house for a considerable time, probably during several separate visits to Rome, and Cicero clearly believed the relationship to have been intimate and friendly.[5] That on occasion, and especially during the embassy, Panaetius was expected to discuss and to discourse upon philosophical matters seems plain enough, and in this respect he could be termed an instructor. But it is rash to assume that he was an instructor or an adviser in any wider sense. Admittedly certain writers in late antiquity use words such as *praeceptor* to describe the relationship, but, quite apart from the possible imprecision

---

[1] The two are chosen because they appear to have had the most extensive influence; it is not possible to examine every theory of the relationship between Panaetius and Scipio. For other studies see esp. Kaerst, 'Scipio Aemilianus, die Stoa und der Prinzipat,' *NJP* 5 (1929), pp. 653 f.; Hammond, 'Ancient Imperialism', *HSPh* 58 (1948), pp. 105 f., esp. pp. 147 f.; Pohlenz, *Ant. Führ.*, pp. 113 f., esp. pp. 143 f., *Die Stoa*, pp. 203 f., pp. 205 f. and 259 f., *RE*, s.v. *Panaitios*, no. 5, cols. 423 f. and 437. Cf. also Reitzenstein, 'Die Idee des Principats bei Cicero und Augustus', *NGG* for 1917, pp. 399 f. and 481 f.

[2] Much of the rest of this section follows van Straaten, *Panétius*, pp. 3 f., esp. pp. 10 f., who rightly sounds a note of caution.

[3] Cic. *Acad. Pr.* 2. 5; Plut. *Cum Princ. Phil.* 1 = Poseid. fgt. 30 *FGrH*; 'Plut.' *Apophth. Scip. Min.* 13; 14; Athen. 12. 549 d = Poseid. fgt. 6 *FGrH* (with 'Poseidonius' in error for 'Panaetius').

[4] Cichorius, 'Panaitios und die attische Stoikerinschrift', *RhM* 63 (1908), pp. 220 f., arguing from *Index Stoic. Hercul.* col. 56, Vell. 1. 13. 3, and Plin. *Nat. Hist.* 5. 9, holds that Panaetius was with Scipio at Carthage in 147, but the argument is fallacious: Tatakis, *Panétius*, pp. 26 f.; Pohlenz, *RE*, s.v. *Panaitios*, no. 5, col. 422, cf. 440; van Straaten, *Panétius*, pp. 12 f. Traversa, ed. of *Index Stoic. Hercul.* p. 79, also holds that there is a reference to a military expedition in the company of Scipio, but it seems improbable that the passage concerns Scipio at all.

[5] Cic. *Pro Mur.* 66; *Tusc.* 1. 81; 4. 23; *De Off.* 1. 90; *Ad Att.* 9. 12. 2.

arising from both the date and the character of these writings, they need refer to no more than general philosophical instruction.[1] There is no evidence at all that Panaetius' opinions were sought on matters of practical politics, or that any great weight was given to his opinions by the Roman statesman; there is certainly nothing to justify a description of Panaetius as Scipio's 'maître de conscience'.[2]

It will be objected that direct political consultation is not disproved by these arguments but only shown to be unattested, and that in any case Panaetius is likely to have influenced Scipio in a less direct and specific manner; that he will have discussed with Scipio problems of ethics and probably also of constitutional theory, and that it is ideas on these matters which will have influenced Scipio's approach to political problems. There can be little doubt that there were such discussions, but it cannot be taken for granted that the philosopher's arguments actually led Scipio to form or modify policies, or even that they conditioned his general outlook. The actions of statesmen are not necessarily moulded by all or any of the opinions of the speculative thinkers with whom they associate—Socrates and Alcibiades, Aristotle and Alexander come readily to mind; nor—for excellent reasons—do scholars attempt to attribute the public actions of Cicero to the influence of the Stoic Diodotus, who lived in his house as Panaetius lived in Scipio's.[3] Moreover, by the earliest time a close relationship is likely to have developed Scipio was far from being an impressionable youth; he was almost forty, a mature, experienced, and highly successful political and military figure. Again, however real the friendship between the two men, however much instruction Panaetius gave, Scipio cannot but have seen the relationship as that of patron and client; in a very real sense he must have remained conscious of his own greatly superior status. Finally the need for caution is suggested also by the fact that among all the numerous references to Scipio and his learning he is nowhere said to have been a Stoic;[4] and in one passage Cicero shows that he at least

---

[1] Pomp. Porph. *Comm. in Hor. Carm.* 1. 29. 13; Themist. *Or.* 34. 8; *Epigram. Bob.* 37. 45 f.; Suidas, s.vv. Παναίτιος and Πολύβιος. Cic. *Pro Mur.* 66 says that the discourse and precepts of Panaetius made Scipio not *asperior* but *lenissimus*. In view of its context this is not reliable evidence about the extent of Panaetius' influence, but in any case it has no reference to political matters.

[2] Tatakis, *Panétius*, p. 19. Cic. *De Off.* 1. 90 = Appendix II, no. 61 contains a *dictum*, reported by Panaetius, in which Scipio spoke of the desirability of successful men disciplining themselves by study, but the reason he gave was not that they should acquire knowledge or understanding but that this would forestall overconfidence.

[3] Cic. *Brut.* 309; *Ad Fam.* 13. 16. 4.

[4] Cic. *Brut.* 118 f., when taken with 82 f., is virtual proof that Cicero knew of no suggestion that Scipio and Laelius were adherents of Stoicism.

had no reason to believe that Scipio followed the political theories of any Greek.[1]

The conclusion of all this is plain. It cannot be assumed *a priori* that Scipio's political activities were influenced by the opinions of Panaetius; the burden of proof lies rather on the other side. To discover Panaetius' views tells us nothing about Scipio's views, unless detailed examination of the known words and actions of the latter reveals a close correspondence not readily explicable by coincidence with traditional Roman attitudes and practices.

3. *The Justification of Imperialism*

One of the most important and best known theories about the influence of Panaetius upon Scipio is that formulated by Capelle.[2] This starts from the famous lectures on justice and injustice which Carneades delivered at Rome in 155. In the course of these he argued that Rome's empire was based upon injustice and could not be retained without injustice. He was not saying that the empire was immoral, but that it was amoral, without a moral basis; and he was not attacking Roman rule over others but the concept of 'natural justice'. There was nothing new in the general conception of this argument; but it was a novelty to apply it to the Roman empire. This, Capelle believes, posed the serious problem of whether an ethical basis could be found for the Roman empire; and he holds that Panaetius responded to this challenge and formulated a justification for empire. This justification, clearly in the same line of thought as Aristotle's theory of the natural slave, contended that some men are by nature fitted for servitude, so that it is positively to their advantage to be ruled by others; therefore it is morally justifiable that they should be conquered and subjected to alien rule. But this justification is applicable only if alien rule actually does benefit them, so that it presupposes a positive duty on the part of the rulers to promote the material and moral welfare of their subjects. These ideas, Capelle believes, were taken up by Scipio and his circle and thereby achieved a significant place in the development of Roman thought.

This theory cannot actually be proved to be wrong; there simply is not sufficient evidence to do this. On the other hand there is no strong reason

---

[1] Cic. *Rep.* 1. 36, where the views expressed are Cicero's own; but it is plain that he did not know of any obvious conflict between them and the policies of Scipio. Earl, 'Terence and Roman Politics', *Historia* 11 (1962), pp. 477 f., esp. pp. 480 f., comments upon the 'dichotomy between Greek theories and Roman practice'. Cf. also Strasburger, 'Poseidonios on Problems of the Roman Empire', *JRS* 55 (1965), p. 45, n. 52.

[2] 'Griech. Ethik und röm. Imperialismus', *Klio* 25 (1932), pp. 86 f.

for supposing it to be correct; it has too many uncertainties to be admissible in any assessment of Scipio, or indeed of Panaetius. The main points may be summarized as follows:

(i) There is no evidence that Carneades' lectures were felt at the time to have posed a serious or an urgent problem about the basis of Roman rule;[1] nor is it an obvious hypothesis that this was so, since it is by no means certain that the basis of Roman rule was an element of great importance in the lectures. Carneades was arguing against the concept of 'justice' as something founded in nature, and his remarks about rule over others were intended to illustrate this. They are known through the version of his disputation which Cicero put into the mouth of Furius in the third book of his *De Republica*, and even there it appears from the surviving fragments (supplemented by references in Lactantius and elsewhere) that there were many other examples and other aspects of the argument.[2] Even in Cicero's version the amorality of the Roman empire does not seem to have been the dominating feature.

(ii) There is no good evidence that Panaetius ever expounded the justification attributed to him in Capelle's theory. This justification is found in the third book of Cicero's *De Republica*, in the fragments of Laelius' defence of justice in reply to the arguments of Furius/Carneades, and Capelle accepted Schmekel's conclusion that Cicero's source for this argument was a work by Panaetius.[3] But Schmekel's arguments, of which the chief is a supposed parallelism between *Rep.* 3 and *De Leg.* 1, complemented by an inference from *De Leg.* 3. 14 that Panaetius was the source for *De Leg.* 1, have been challenged very convincingly by van Straaten.[4] Van Straaten has not so much refuted them as shown them to be without adequate foundation. Although the definition of 'true law' in *Rep.* 3. 33 (part of Laelius' speech) may well have had a Stoic origin, there is no special reason for supposing that it came from Panaetius rather than from any other Stoic writer, or indeed that the whole of Laelius' defence of justice came *en bloc* from a single source: both suppositions could be true, neither need be. If Cicero did take the justification from a single Stoic source, that source might just as well have been Poseidonius, in whose

---

[1] It is noteworthy that although Cato's dislike of the embassy of philosophers was inspired especially by Carneades, among the reasons given for this there is no mention of Carneades' references to the injustice of empire: Plut. *Cato Mai.* 22. 5 f.; 23. 1; Plin. *Nat. Hist.* 7. 112.   [2] *Rep.* 3. 8 f.

[3] Cic. *Rep.* 3. 32 f.; Schmekel, *Die Philosophie der mittleren Stoa*, pp. 55 f.

[4] *Panétius*, pp. 308 f. Strasburger, 'Poseidonios on Problems of the Roman Empire', *JRS* 55 (1965), pp. 44 f., also considers that there is no good reason to attribute this justification of empire to Panaetius.

writings the general idea was certainly to be found,[1] or Diogenes, the contemporary and adversary of Carneades.[2] Yet it is such an obvious notion, particularly to a class familiar with the works of Aristotle, that it must surely have been almost a stock answer whenever the question of justification was raised. There seems to be no good reason why Cicero should have depended very closely on any particular source for his justification of empire, but if he did so we can scarcely hope to identify that source with any degree of confidence.

(iii) Even if it be supposed that Panaetius did formulate this justification of rule over others, there is no evidence at all to determine at what stage in his career he did so. The widely accepted conservative estimates place his death nearly twenty years after that of Scipio.[3]

(iv) Even if Panaetius did formulate this justification, the theory would not necessarily have been felt to imply any more positive obligation towards the welfare of subject peoples than protection from foreign enemies, the maintenance of law and order by strict control, and the avoidance of corruption or extortion on the part of governors. In so far as it would have had implications of this kind it would have been offering nothing new. Such obligations had long been recognized in Rome. If the establishment in 149 of the standing procedure to try cases of extortion is an indication that misgovernment was not a rarity, it is also a sign that disapproval was strong and fairly widespread—at a date long before Panaetius can have exercised any significant influence.[4]

(v) Even if Panaetius did formulate this justification, there is no evidence in Scipio's known words or actions that it had any influence upon him, or that he showed any remarkable concern for the welfare of the subject peoples. It is true that in 138 he prosecuted Aurelius Cotta for extortion and that earlier, in 144, the essence of the witticism with which he opposed sending either Cotta or Ser. Galba to Spain was that both were likely to prove corrupt.[5] But Scipio himself is known to have had high moral standards, characterized by integrity and *fides*,[6] and disapproval of

---

[1] Capelle, 'Griech. Ethik und röm. Imperialismus', *Klio* 25 (1932), pp. 99 f.; but Strasburger, op. cit., pp. 46 f., does not believe that this conception played such a central role in Poseidonius' thought as Capelle suggests.

[2] Cic. *De Leg.* 3. 13 f. shows that Diogenes did touch upon practical political matters; but the topic need not have been considered only in a work devoted to political philosophy.

[3] Tatakis, *Panétius*, p. 33; van Straaten, *Panétius*, pp. 23 f., with refs. cited there. Philippson, 'Panaetiana', *RhM* 78 (1929), pp. 338 f., and Pohlenz, *Antikes Führertum*, pp. 125 f., cf. *RE*, s.v. *Panaitios*, no. 5, col. 425, argue for a date about a decade later, which is possible but not probable.

[4] pp. 58 f.   [5] pp. 105 and 129; Appendix II, no. 12.

[6] pp. 16 f.

extortion was no novel idea. No doubt Scipio quite genuinely disapproved of extortion and misgovernment, but these two items do not constitute evidence for unusual concern about the matter. There is nothing here which cannot be accounted for in full by established Roman practice, nothing which requires or suggests the special explanation of Panaetius' influence, which in any case is unlikely to have affected Scipio's public actions as early as 144. Also it is to be remembered that in both these instances, and especially in 144, there is a strong suspicion that considerations of political advantage were involved. There is just one other *dictum* which in a sense reflects the same basic idea as the justification of empire which Panaetius is alleged to have advanced, though it has never been brought into the discussion. When Scipio in 146 handed back to Agrigentum the notorious bull of Phalaris, which was among the spoils found in Carthage, he is reported to have said that the Agrigentines could with propriety reflect upon whether it was more expedient to serve their own rulers or to submit to the Roman people, since they had one and the same object as a monument both of native cruelty and of Roman mildness.[1] But it would be absurd to elevate this rather obvious witticism into a serious statement of policy, a manifestation of a philosophical theory, or even an indication of an underlying preoccupation with the justification of imperialism. Moreover, it is very unlikely that before 146 there had been any significant contact between Scipio and Panaetius and most improbable that Scipio's actions at this date would have been influenced in any way at all by Panaetius.

4. Humanitas

The words *humanitas* and *humanus* are of unmistakable importance in the writings of Cicero, where they are often used not only to indicate a contrast with what is divine, immortal, animal, or inanimate, but to embrace many or even all of the qualities proper to the ideal civilized man, to man fully developed as man, irrespective of race or nation. Opinions have differed widely (not the least reason being that Cicero himself does not by any means use the word with a consistent meaning) about the precise content of the concept, as also about the extent of its similarity to and derivation from the Greek concepts of παιδεία and φιλανθρωπία, about its relationship to Stoic 'anthropology', and about the part which Panaetius may or may not have played in its development; but there is a considerable measure of agreement that a vital element in it was awareness of

[1] Appendix II, no. 10.

common humanity, of the fundamental nature common to all men, as a positive and valuable thing in itself; and the belief that this awareness should lead to a sympathetic understanding of all the actions and passions of men.[1] In short, *humanitas* embraced humanitarianism. This humane attitude to one's fellow men seems to have been understood as in part the product of intellectual culture and learning, which, as achievements peculiar to man and to the developed nature of man, were also important elements in *humanitas*. But it is chiefly in its humanitarian aspect that the concept could be related to political life, since a consistent *humanitas* would imply a humane attitude to political and public problems.

There are two ways in which this concept may enter into discussions of Scipio Aemilianus. The first is the common opinion that it originated and was adopted as an ideal in the so-called 'Scipionic Circle', with the general implication that the spirit of *humanitas* informed the actions and policies of Scipio and his associates. The second is the possibility that these actions and policies were informed by a spirit which was in fact that of *humanitas* even though Scipio and his friends had not consciously formulated the concept itself. In either case many scholars would be inclined to see some relationship between such an outlook and the teachings of Panaetius,who showed a greater readiness than did other Stoic philosophers to take into account the nature and circumstances of the individual as well as human nature in general, and to recognize other aspects of human nature besides the capacity for knowledge and understanding.[2] If it were established that Scipio and his friends did manifest the spirit of *humanitas* this possibility would have to be examined very seriously; but it would be quite illegitimate to argue the other way round, to infer that because Panaetius developed these philosophical views Scipio and his friends must have manifested the spirit of *humanitas*.

The first and most important question, therefore, is whether the spirit of *humanitas* was so manifested. Cicero and Valerius Maximus both speak of Scipio's *humanitas*, and the former's obvious general enthusiasm for him suggests that he did regard him as an embodiment of this idea. But this is not such strong evidence as it sounds, partly because Cicero's admiration of Scipio has undoubtedly led to some idealization, but also because his thoughts are so often centred upon Scipio's culture and learning. It is this

---

[1] For the voluminous literature see esp. Büchner, *Lat. Lit. und Sprache*, pp. 186 f., and 'Humanum und humanitas', *Studium Generale* 14 (1961), pp. 636 f. Much of the impetus has come from Reitzenstein's notable study *Werden und Wesen der Humanität im Altertum*. Cf. also Heinemann, *RE*, Suppl.-Bd. V, s.v. *Humanitas*; Clarke, *The Roman Mind*, pp. 135 f.; Moritz, *Humanitas*.

[2] Cf. van Straaten, *Panétius*, pp. 219 f.

aspect of *humanitas* which he has in mind in two of the only three passages in which he explicitly applies the term to Scipio;[1] and in the third passage *humanitas* refers to the restoration to Thermae of statues from Carthage and is contrasted with the rapacity of Verres—scarcely an instance which throws penetrating light on to Scipio's character.[2] Even less helpful is the evidence of Valerius Maximus. Among his examples of *humanitas* he offers two illustrations of this quality in Scipio: the first concerns the return to Sicily of statues found at Carthage; the second is an anecdote which really concerns the elder Africanus but which Valerius has mistakenly associated with Aemilianus.[3] Of course there are many passages, in Cicero and elsewhere, ascribing various virtues to Scipio; and if sometimes such an ascription seems to be a generalization from a single event, nevertheless it is clear that many of them reflect genuine features of his character, notably his *fides* and his interest in culture and learning. Few will doubt that the latter is comprehended in the Ciceronian concept of *humanitas*, and in this respect the use of this term with reference to Scipio is entirely reasonable. But whether *humanitas* in the Ciceronian sense manifested itself in Scipio's public and political activities is another question, concerning which the essential evidence is Scipio's known actions and words. Something relevant to this was said about certain of these actions and words in the preceding section of this Appendix;[4] and beyond that it is possible to say only that in the opinion of the author there is nothing which suggests a distinctively sympathetic or humanitarian understanding of other men, of man valued as man, and that there are some indications of a harshness which is not easily reconciled with such an outlook.[5]

There remains the widespread opinion that *humanitas* was an ideal formulated in Scipio's 'circle'. No ancient source states that this was so, and modern opinion seems to rest in great measure upon an exaggerated picture of the uniqueness of the 'Scipionic Circle', which is assumed to be the only likely source of such a concept; and frequently this is fortified by the conviction that Panaetius' views must have played some part. No doubt there is also an assumption that Scipio and his friends must have formulated the ideal which Cicero saw in them, though plainly this need not have been so. Very little literature survives either from Scipio's generation or from the immediately succeeding generations, with the result that there is insufficient material for tracing with any confidence the inception of the idea, how widely and when it was accepted, and how

---

[1] Cic. *De Orat.* 2. 154; *Verr.* 2. 4. 98.　　　　　　　　[2] Cic. *Verr.* 2. 2. 86.
[3] Val. Max. 5. 1. 6 and 7.　　　　[4] pp. 301 f.　　　　[5] pp. 17 and 331.

much was contributed by the Ciceronian age itself. In so far as modern
attributions of the full concept to the 'Scipionic Circle' rest on anything
more than *a priori* assumption, their basis is the belief that it is to be found
in the plays of Terence—with which is associated the further assumption
that Terence was reflecting the attitudes and ideals of his patrons.

In the surviving plays of Terence there are several instances of the use
of *inhumanus* to mean 'cruel' or 'harsh', and correspondingly of *humanus*
to mean something of the order of 'kind'.[1] Thus in addition to the purely
generic meaning of *humanus*, indicating 'that which is human' or 'that
which is customarily associated with human beings', there is a development towards the notion of the specially good qualities of the human
being. Probably this usage developed from the contrast between the
human and the beast, but whatever its origin it still falls far short of the
Ciceronian ideal of *humanitas*; furthermore it is not even a usage original
to Terence, for there is an instance in Plautus.[2] All this is widely recognized, and Terence's usage, as so far discussed, has not been claimed to be
more than a suggestive indication of a trend in thought. There is, however, one famous line—and one only—which seems to show a further
development: *homo sum: humani nil a me alienum puto*.[3] This is the reason
given by one character for attempting to intervene in and remedy the
apparent unhappiness of his neighbour, so that it does seem to represent
an attitude of sympathy and humane concern derived from a consciousness
of common humanity; it is a harbinger of a vital element in Ciceronian
humanitas.

Nevertheless there is a need for caution. In the first place it has been
argued seriously, though perhaps not decisively, that the line was not
an original idea but was derived from Menander.[4] Secondly, there simply
is not enough literature surviving to determine whether or not this use of
humanus was to be found in any other writings of the second century. And
thirdly this line does come from a comedy, where it is a neat response to
Chreme, tantumne ab re tuast oti tibi aliena ut cures ea quae nil ad te attinent?[5]
It is a clever piece of repartee. It is by no means self-evident that this
solitary line should be regarded as the expression of a deeply felt social

---

[1] e.g. *And.* 113; 236; 278; *Hec.* 499; *Phorm.* 509; *Eun.* 880; *Heaut.* 99; 1046; cf. *Adelph.* 934.
[2] *Most.* 814.   [3] *Heaut.* 77.
[4] Bickel, ''Ανθρωπον ὄντα', *RhM* 90 (1941), p. 352; 'Menanders Urwort der Humanität',
RhM 91 (1942), pp. 186 f.; A. Körte, 'Zu Terenz Haut. 77', *Hermes* 77 (1942), pp. 101 f.;
Dornseiff, 'Nichts Menschliches ist mir fremd', *Hermes* 78 (1943), pp. 110 f. But cf. De
Sanctis, *Storia*, iv. 2. 1, p. 36 n. 80; Büchner, 'Humanum und humanitas', *Studium Generale*
14 (1961), p. 638.
[5] *Heaut.* 75 f.

attitude, of a consciously formulated ideal of human character and human behaviour. It is even more dubious if it is sufficient evidence for the belief that this ideal was consciously formulated or adopted by Terence's aristocratic patrons, that its humanitarian implications were thought out and applied with earnest conviction to political policies. This one line has to be set not only against a lack of distinctive indications of humanitarianism in Scipio's public life but also against the positive signs that he was capable of cruelty and harshness.

APPENDIX VII

Laelius' Proposal for Reform

Later the neighbouring rich men used fictitious personages to transfer the rentals to themselves, and in the end they held most of them openly in their own names. Then the poor, who had been driven away, no longer offered themselves readily for military service and neglected the rearing of children, with the result that soon the whole of Italy was aware of a shortage of freemen and was full of barbarian prisoners through whom the rich farmed the land when they had driven away the citizens. Therefore Gaius Laelius, the friend of Scipio, attempted to remedy this situation, but when the rich opposed him he was alarmed by the clamour and desisted, and on that account was nicknamed 'Wise' or 'Prudent' (for the word *Sapiens* seems to have either meaning).[1]

Laelius' proposal is mentioned nowhere else than in this one passage of Plutarch's account of Tiberius Gracchus. Consequently there has been ample room for speculation about date, content, motive, and general significance.

Tibiletti implies that the scheme, which Plutarch links with the population problem, was not necessarily concerned with the redistribution of *ager publicus*, even though it probably was agrarian in character, but may have been along the traditional lines of colonial or viritane settlement, particularly in the north.[2] But, as Scullard observes,[3] it is not easy to envisage why such a traditional scheme should have aroused opposition on this scale; and although Plutarch's words may not require us in strict logic to understand a scheme concerned with *ager publicus*, the general character of his context undoubtedly suggests such a connexion. The balance of probability inclines, therefore, towards the customary view

---

[1] Plut. *Ti. Grac.* 8. 4 f. It is widely accepted that the episode is not the true origin of the name 'Sapiens': Scullard, 'Scipio Aemilianus', *JRS* 50 (1960), p. 62; Münzer, *RE*, s.v. *Laelius*, no. 3, cols. 406 f.

[2] 'Ricerche di storia agraria', *Athenaeum* 28 (1950), pp. 183 f., esp. pp. 234 f. The main (and entirely justified) burden of Tibiletti's discussion is the inadequacy of the evidence to support the bold constructions put upon it. He does not suggest explicitly that the proposal was for colonial or viritane settlement in distant areas, but that this may have been so is implied in his discussion and particularly by his views that these traditional methods persisted longer than is often supposed (pp. 232 f.) and that Tiberius Gracchus' systematic attack on *latifundia* was a new conception (p. 239).

[3] 'Scipio Aemilianus', *JRS* 50 (1960), pp. 62 f.

that the scheme would have involved some redistribution of *ager publicus*; but on the available evidence it is quite unsafe to assume that it was anything like a full-blown anticipation of Tiberius Gracchus' scheme, either in scope or in purpose.

Three dates have been suggested for the proposal: Laelius' praetorship in 145;[1] his consulship in 140;[2] or an entirely unattested tribunate around 151.[3] This last is so hypothetical that it is virtually impossible to comment. The total lack of evidence, and especially of any mention of a tribunate by Cicero, must count against it. Moreover, if this date were correct, Laelius' failure to renew his proposal later when he and Scipio enjoyed greatly increased prestige and influence would suggest that his concern about it was not very deep and that the episode was of no great importance. Scullard inclines towards 145 on the ground that in that year at any rate there was a known need: the numerous veterans of the recent wars, especially from Africa and Macedonia, would have posed a major problem of resettlement, which Laelius' plan may have been designed to facilitate. On the other hand, these wars had been relatively short and, moreover, profitable. Booty will have cushioned many against immediate distress and there may have been no immediate concern about the effects of demobilization. Thus if this motive was present at all it might just as easily have prompted an attempt in 140, about which time, moreover, groups of veterans were probably returning from six years of unprofitable campaigning in Spain.[4] In short, this kind of hypothesis about the needs of the moment does little to resolve the problem of date. There is, however, one further considera-tion. Although praetors had the right to initiate legislation, remarkably few praetorian laws are known, and for the most part those that are known are of minor importance.[5] This suggests that Laelius is more likely to have made his attempt when he was consul than when he was praetor.

---

[1] e.g. Greenidge, *Hist. of Rome*, p. 102 n. 1; Scullard, 'Scipio Aemilianus', *JRS* 50 (1960), pp. 63 f., who in n. 19 disposes of the objection advanced by Cardinali, *Studi Graccani*, pp. 113 f.

[2] Münzer, *RE*, s.v. *Laelius*, no. 3, col. 406; Bilz, *Die Politik*, p. 47; Carcopino, *Hist. rom.* ii, p. 175; Broughton, *MRR* i, p. 479; McDonald, 'Rome and Italy', *CHJ* 6 (1939), p. 144; De Sanctis, *Storia*, iv. 3, p. 259.

[3] Heitland, *The Roman Republic*, ii, p. 254; Cardinali, *Studi Graccani*, p. 115; Fraccaro, *Studi*, i, p. 76; Tibiletti, 'Ricerche di storia agraria', *Athenaeum* 28 (1950), p. 235 n. 1; Cary, *Hist. of Rome*[2], p. 283; Taylor, 'Forerunners of the Gracchi', *JRS* 52 (1962), p. 24.

[4] Scullard himself, 'Scipio Aemilianus', *JRS* 50 (1960), p. 64, admits 140 as a possibility. For six years as the normal period in Spain see p. 169 n. 3. Many troops had been sent to Ulterior in 147–145 (App. *Iber.* 61, 64, 65); the survivors should have returned *c.* 141–139. Veterans from Celtiberia in 140: App. *Iber.* 78.

[5] Mommsen, *Röm. Staats.* ii[3], p. 127, with examples in n. 3. The *lex Aurelia iudiciaria* of 70 is of quite exceptional importance for a praetorian law.

Some discussions of this episode imply that the reason why Laelius did not persevere in the face of strong opposition was that he did not wish to split the state or to start a revolution[1] (a view especially attractive to those who think that the purpose of his proposal was precisely to forestall a revolution). In so far as this is based on the evidence it reads too much into Plutarch's phrase φοβηθεὶς τὸν θόρυβον,[2] which surely refers to Laelius' reaction to the outcry among the wealthy, probably an actual clamour in the Senate, which his proposal provoked. It is most unlikely that he envisaged the outbreak of violence or revolution as the alternative to desisting. Even in 133, when the economic and social pressures were much greater than in 140, let alone 145 or 151,[3] Tiberius Gracchus did not attempt to carry his reform by force and his opponents did not attempt to prevent it by force. The fact is that once the strength of the opposition to Laelius' plan became apparent, presumably in the Senate, he probably saw no point in pressing it further. It would have been useless to put it before an assembly without the support of the Senate, or in the face of the Senate's disapproval, since a tribune certainly would have been found to veto it; and at this stage no one had yet found a way to do what Tiberius Gracchus succeeded in doing in 133—nullifying a veto under such circumstances. Therefore defeat was certain.[4]

Some of the discussions which imply that Laelius withdrew his plan in order to avoid splitting the state also suggest that he introduced it in the first place in order to forestall a potentially revolutionary situation. With some justification the historian writing after the event may see in Laelius' failure the defeat of a proposal which might have halted, or at least retarded, the accumulation of those social and economic pressures which were to play an important part in the critical events of 133; but it is a very different matter to assert that Laelius himself was thinking in similar terms, that he believed himself to be trying to avert a serious threat to order and stability.[5] There are several reasons for doubting such an

---

[1] Mommsen, *Hist. of Rome*, iii, p. 317; Heitland, *The Roman Republic*, ii, pp. 254 f.; Bilz, *Die Politik*, p. 48. In a modified form, McDonald, 'Rome and Italy', *CHJ* 6 (1939), p. 145; Scullard, 'Scipio Aemilianus', *JRS* 50 (1960), p. 65.

[2] Plut. *Ti. Grac.* 8. 5.

[3] On the development of these problems see Ch. XIII, esp. pp. 165 f.

[4] In view of the probability that there was constitutional deadlock there is no necessity to seek other hypotheses to explain the withdrawal, such as the suggestions that Laelius and Scipio's coterie in general were easy-going and ineffective in political matters: Last, *CAH* ix, p. 20; Greenidge, *Hist. of Rome*, p. 102, developed by Fraccaro, *Studi*, i, p. 77.

[5] Mommsen, *Hist. of Rome*, iii, p. 317; Last, *CAH* ix, pp. 19 f., though he thought Laelius' effort feeble; McDonald, 'Rome and Italy', *CHJ* 6 (1939), pp. 144 f. Bilz, *Die Politik*, p. 47, though not explicit, seems to share this attitude.

interpretation. In the first place, even as late as 140 not only were the economic and social problems much less severe than in 133 but the extent of
their growth can scarcely have been foreseen; for the distress and discontent must have been increased greatly by the unexpected duration of the
Spanish wars, by the famine of 138, and by the Sicilian slave rebellion, none
of which can have been anticipated.[1] Secondly, the interpretation assumes
that Laelius' main concern was the relief of distress and discontent, whereas
Plutarch indicates that it was with the problem of man-power available
for military service. It may be objected that Plutarch's version of the
motive is not decisive evidence, but it is not on that account necessarily
false and it is better than no evidence at all; furthermore there is a good
deal of other evidence that this man-power problem was attracting
attention.[2]

The third reason for doubting whether Laelius' chief concern was to
prevent a revolution exploding from distress and discontent is that this
would carry a strong implication that in 133 those associated with Scipio
should have been ready to bow to the necessity of Tiberius Gracchus'
proposals and were antagonized only by his methods; whereas, though
absolute proof is impossible, it is highly probable that Laelius and the
nexus around Scipio were, and were expected to be, opposed to the
agrarian proposals from the start.[3] The fourth and last objection to this
'anti-revolutionary' hypothesis is that it rests upon the misconception that
economic pressure from the distressed masses was the direct and only
important cause of the crisis of 133, and especially of its 'revolutionary'
aspects. If this were so, it would be possible to conceive that it was pre-
dictable and that Laelius recognized that it might happen; but in reality this
is far too simplified a view both of the course of events and of the factors
at work; in particular there were other powerful issues involved in the
situation which led to the outbreak of violence.[4] That is not to deny that
the economic and social troubles did play a major part, or that they had
constituted a growing political problem; but, to say the least, it is questionable whether anyone in 145 or 140 foresaw the nature or the gravity
of the crisis which was to arise from them, let alone whether Laelius
should be portrayed as struggling to stave off an incipient revolution.[5]

---

[1] Ch. XIII, esp. pp. 166 f.   [2] pp. 171 f.
[3] pp. 198 f.   [4] Ch. XV and esp. Ch. XVI, *passim*.
[5] It is obviously profitless to speculate about the significance of the episode in terms of
factional politics when neither the date nor the nature of the proposal can be determined
with confidence.

APPENDIX VIII

Prosopographia

IN respect of several individuals and families the interpretation of personal political relationships adopted in Chapter VIII differs from conclusions which have been put forward in other studies. The most important instances concern Münzer's examination of the aristocratic factions in the age of Scipio Aemilianus. Valuable though this discussion is, it is at fault both in certain particulars and in a general tendency to consider the political scene in terms of only two factions.[1] The latter notion is rejected elsewhere;[2] some mistaken particulars, in which the error is often linked with the 'two party' interpretation, are considered in this appendix, the primary purpose of which is to establish a positive interpretation rather than to refute the views of Münzer and others.

1. Q. Pompeius

In *De Amicitia* 77, Cicero puts into Laelius' mouth the following words: *Ab amicitia Q. Pompei meo nomine se removerat, ut scitis, Scipio; propter dissensionem autem, quae erat in re publica, alienatus est a collega nostro Metello; utrumque egit graviter ac moderate* (MSS. *graviter auctoritate*) *et offensione animi non acerba.*

'Scipio, as you know, had withdrawn from the friendship of Q. Pompeius on my account; moreover, on account of a dispute which occurred in the state he was alienated from our colleague Metellus; in each case he acted seriously and with moderation, with no bitter resentment.'

The occasion of the breach with Pompeius is certainly the incident in 142 when Pompeius was supposed to be assisting Laelius in his candidature for the consulship but instead canvassed on his own behalf while Scipio and Laelius were waiting for him. 'Plutarch', who reports this in the *Apophthegmata*, continues, 'The rest were indignant, but Scipio laughed and said, "It is because of our own stupidity; for, just as if we were

---

[1] *Röm. Adels.*, pp. 225 f. The same general comment applies to the discussion by Carcopino, *Hist. rom.* ii, pp. 171 f., whose conclusions, except as regards the Servilii, largely follow those of Münzer.

[2] Ch. VIII, esp. pp. 95 f.

intending to call not upon men but upon gods, we have been wasting any amount of time waiting for a flute-player." [1]

Münzer inferred from these passages that the breach between Scipio and Pompeius was not serious: there was no bitter resentment, and Scipio passed the matter off with a joke; and Münzer goes on to suppose that friendly relations were soon restored.[2] This is mistaken. In the first place it is very improbable that Scipio treated lightly an act of deliberate defiance and deception by a client, a *novus homo*, who not only offered himself as a candidate in opposition to his patron's most intimate friend but actually brought about Laelius' defeat and a year's delay before his consulship.[3] In the second place the evidence really indicates a serious quarrel. Whatever Cicero had in mind when he spoke of Scipio's moderation, the simultaneous reference to Metellus Macedonicus suggests that it was nothing incompatible with serious political hostility; and in the context of Roman public life the phrase *ab amicitia . . . se removerat* can only indicate the formal severance of all political association and alliance. As for the alleged absence of bitter resentment, grave doubts must be felt about this in the light of the joke reported in the *Apophthegmata*. The essence of Scipio's joke is clear. He punned on Pompeius' filiation, *Auli filius* (cf. the Graecism *Aulides*), calling him *auletes*, a flute-player.[4] This was very witty, but it was no mere light-hearted pleasantry. In a society which was exceptionally conscious of social status it was a sharp, deliberate, and scornful insult, an insult which carried the direct implication that Pompeius was unsuitable for public office, and which seems remarkably like a manifestation of *offensio animi acerba*. For a subsequent *rapprochement* between the two men, surely *a priori* improbable, there is no evidence whatsoever; on the contrary, it is explicitly attested that in 136 Pompeius was an *inimicus* of another of Scipio's intimate friends, L. Furius Philus.[5]

2. Q. Caecilius Metellus Macedonicus

In *De Amicitia* 77 (quoted in section 1, above, with reference to Q. Pompeius) Cicero reveals that Metellus Macedonicus was at one time among

---

[1] 'Plut.' *Apophth. Scip. Min.* 8 = Appendix II, no. 25; cf. Cic. *Tusc.* 5. 54. See pp. 121 f.

[2] *Röm. Adels.*, pp. 248 f.

[3] This point and certain of those which follow are noted also by Earl, *Tiberius Gracchus*, pp. 99 f.

[4] Filiation: *Fasti Cap. Cons.*; Val. Max. 8. 5. 1. It is fortunate that although 'Plutarch' or his source took the reference to a flute-player literally he has preserved the joke quite clearly. It is discussed at length by Hiltbrunner, 'Dicta Scipionis', in *Thesaurismata: Festchrift für Ida Kapp*, pp. 49 f. There is no justification for Bilz's rejection of the story as an invention to excuse the defeat of Laelius (*Die Politik*, p. 59 n. 153).

[5] Dio, fgt. 82; Val. Max. 3. 7. 5.

Scipio's *amici* but that the two became estranged over some public dissension. The further implication that the dispute was conducted with moderation is echoed, indeed is put more strongly, in *De Officiis*, 1. 87: *fuit inter P. Africanum et Q. Metellum sine acerbitate dissensio*. But this assertion is hard to reconcile even with references to Metellus as an *inimicus*, and especially with Cicero's own description of him as an *auctor* behind the *obtrectatores et invidi Scipionis* in 129.[1] Moreover Lucilius attacked him, it is said to please Scipio.[2] Perhaps Cicero's milder statements were influenced by Metellus' reaction to Scipio's death, or perhaps the *dissensio* was originally without bitterness and only in the course of time led on to 'serious and well attested *inimicitiae*'.[3]

Antagonism can be discerned through a considerable period. The first definite implication belongs to the year 138, when Metellus defended L. Aurelius Cotta against the prosecution brought by Scipio himself.[4] Then in 136 he, like Pompeius, is mentioned as an *inimicus* of Furius Philus;[5] in 134 or 133 his youngest son was the object of one of Scipio's insulting witticisms;[6] it was probably in 131 or 130 that he was attacked in one of the first of Lucilius' satires;[7] and in the early part of 129 he is attested as a leader of a senatorial group opposed to Scipio—the *obtrectatores et invidi Scipionis*.[8] Contrast came in 129 with the news of Scipio's death, which he stated to have been a national misfortune, instructing his sons to carry Scipio's bier.[9] Whatever the reasons for this remarkable volte-face, the important point is that it clearly was a volte-face. The evidence leaves virtually no room for doubt that from 138 or earlier until his death Scipio numbered Metellus Macedonicus among his political opponents.

It has been necessary to argue this case at some length because Münzer took a very different view, believing that Metellus was an opponent of Scipio from the earliest stages but moved towards alliance with him from about 135.[10] It will be observed that this interpretation involves the outright rejection of several of the items of evidence mentioned above, a rejection which cannot be justified, since there is no good evidence for the

---

[1] Cic. *Rep.* 1. 31; Val. Max. 4. 1. 12; Plin. *Nat. Hist.* 7. 144; 'Plut.' *Apophth. Caec. Met.* 3.

[2] Hor. *Sat.* 2. 1. 62 f., and the Scholiast on 72: *Lucilius eum in gratiam Scipionis carpsit*.

[3] Val. Max. 4. 1. 12.   [4] Cic. *Brut.* 81; cf. Livy, *Ox. Epit.* 55.

[5] Dio, fgt. 82; Val. Max. 3. 7. 5.   [6] Appendix II, no. 47.

[7] Lucil. 676–87 M. seem to be a parody of Metellus' speech on marriage, delivered in 131 or 130 (p. 237); this was in Book 26, the first book of the Satires to be published: Marx, C. Lucil. *Carm. Reliquiae*, i, pp. xxvi f., esp. xxx f. Other discussions of the chronology of the Satires: Cichorius, *Untersuch. zu Lucil.*, pp. 63 f.; Kappelmacher, *RE*, s.v. *Lucilius*, no. 4, cols. 1624 f.; Warmington, *Remains of Old Latin* (Loeb Class. Library), iii, pp. xii f.

[8] Cic. *Rep.* 1. 31.   [9] p. 244.

[10] *Röm. Adels.*, pp. 246 f.; pp. 252 f.

alleged move towards alliance in the later years. Münzer may have been influenced by Metellus' outspoken attack on Tiberius Gracchus in 133,[1] but this is not evidence of alliance with Scipio and his friends in any other respect; in theory it might have provided a basis for a *rapprochement* but Cicero's explicit statement that in 129 Metellus was among the *obtrectatores et invidi Scipionis* proves that it did not do so. It is true that one of Metellus' daughters was married to the son of Scipio Nasica Serapio and that Münzer dates this marriage to *c.* 135, about three years after Metellus' defence of Cotta.[2] But in fact there is no reason why the marriage should not have taken place a few years earlier than 135. The son of the marriage was probably praetor *c.* 94,[3] giving a *terminus ante quem* of *c.* 135 for the marriage itself, but this is only a *terminus*. It is possible that the son was praetor at the minimum age, that he was the first-born child and that he was born within a year or so of the marriage itself; but it is equally possible that none of these things was so. He might have been a little late achieving his praetorship; there may have been elder daughters of whom nothing is known, or children who did not reach maturity, or still-born children, or simply delayed conception. The marriage cannot be pushed back too far, but there is no difficulty at all in supposing that it took place no later than 139 or 138, in which case it may have antedated Metellus' estrangement from Scipio Aemilianus.

There remains the question of the date of the breach between Metellus and Scipio. The consuls in office in 144, when Metellus was elected consul for 143, were Ser. Sulpicius Galba and L. Aurelius Cotta, both of whom were at odds with Scipio.[4] Hence it has been suggested that Metellus' defence of Cotta in 138 was a requital for assistance in obtaining the consulship,[5] in which case the breach with Scipio probably would have occurred in or before 144, before Metellus himself became consul. But this is a weak argument, for various reasons. First, there is no doubt that certain modern scholars have greatly overestimated the influence of the presiding consul on the outcome of elections; it was in no way unusual for men to be elected who were opposed politically to the presiding magistrate. Second, in this instance there is nothing at all to indicate whether Galba or Cotta presided. Lastly it is known that Metellus offered himself for the consulships of 145 and 144,[6] so that his second humiliating

---

[1] Plut. *Ti. Grac.* 14. 4; cf. Cic. *Brut.* 81.

[2] Cic. *Brut.* 212, *Post Red. in Sen.* 37; *Ad Quir.* 6; *De Domo*, 123; Münzer, *Röm. Adels.*, pp. 252 f.

[3] Obsequ. 51; *MRR* ii, p. 14.   [4] p. 90.

[5] Münzer, *Röm. Adels.*, pp. 247 f.; Badian, 'Caepio and Norbanus', *Historia* 6 (1957), p. 321.   [6] pp. 100 and 104.

defeat was inflicted by Cotta himself, which makes an early *rapprochement* seem rather unlikely.

None of this disproves the suggestion that the breach occurred in 144; it merely shows that the arguments for that date are not very strong. There are some slightly stronger, though not decisive, arguments for a date in or not long before 138. A certain Q. Occius who in 140 was serving in Further Spain as an officer under one of Scipio's political allies, Q. Fabius Maximus Servilianus, had been one of Metellus' *legati* in Hither Spain in 143–142.[1] This choice of a man of obscure family who subsequently served under Servilianus, very possibly in the same capacity, suggests that Metellus' breach with Scipio was after rather than before his consulship. Secondly, if the marriage between Metellus' daughter and Nasica Serapio's son can be put without difficulty as early as 138, it is clearly less plausible to push it back a further six years, both on account of the known son of the marriage and because at the time when Macedonicus achieved election in 144 Serapio was only thirty-seven or thirty-eight years of age,[2] which is uncomfortably, though not impossibly, early for his son's marriage. It is more probable therefore that the breach between Metellus and Scipio Aemilianus took place after the former's consulship and proconsulship, and perhaps not long before its first known manifestation in 138.

3. Q. Fabius Maximus Servilianus, Cn. Servilius Caepio, and Q. Servilius Caepio

Münzer held that these men were enemies of Scipio. The key incident for his view is that Cn. and Q. Servilius Caepio were among the leading witnesses against Q. Pompeius when he was prosecuted *c.* 138.[3] Since Münzer believed that Pompeius was still one of Scipio's associates he naturally inferred that the Servilii were hostile to both men. But since there is good reason to believe that there had been no *rapprochement* between Scipio and Pompeius (section 1, above), the hostility of the Servilii towards the latter in fact proves nothing about their relationship with Scipio, and other evidence can be given more weight than Münzer allows it.[4]

---

[1] Val. Max. 3. 2. 21; Livy, *Ox. Epit.* 53 and 54. The order of events in *Ox. Epit.* 54 just admits the possibility that in 140 Occius was serving under Servilianus' brother, Q. Servilius Caepio, but the usual opinion that he was under Servilianus himself is more probable.

[2] p. 101 n. 1.

[3] *Röm. Adels.*, pp. 245 f.; pp. 249 f.; Cic. *Pro Font.* 23; 27; Val. Max. 8. 5. 1.

[4] Münzer also refers to the story in Val. Max. 2. 2. 1 of a Q. Fabius Maximus who, just before the Third Punic War, discussed secret proceedings of the Senate with a P. Crassus, in

It so happens that all the positive evidence concerns Servilianus. There is first the significant fact that he was the adoptive brother of Scipio's natural brother, Q. Fabius Maximus Aemilianus.[1] These adoptions point to a political association in the previous generation and it would be surprising if the adoptive brothers themselves were not linked politically. Contemporary evidence is found in the presence of Fannius, the son-in-law of Laelius, in Servilianus' army in Spain,[2] and especially in the marriage of Servilianus' son to the daughter of Scipio's protégé, P. Rupilius, a man of obscure background and a very unlikely choice unless there had been close political links.[3]

There is no positive evidence about the political associations of the other two brothers, but when three brothers reached the consulship three years in succession there is a very strong presumption that politically they stood very close to one another; and nothing is known about Cn. and Q. Servilius to contradict this.

4. *Calpurnii*

It has been argued by Earl that L. Calpurnius Piso Frugi, cos. 133, would naturally have found a place in the group which promoted Tiberius Gracchus' agrarian bill, and that his attitude towards Tiberius 'at first may have been, if not active support, at least benevolent neutrality'.[4] This conclusion derives from two main considerations: that Frugi himself was a serious-minded reformer and as such was likely to have looked favourably upon a sensible scheme for reform; and that the past political associations of the Calpurnii, whose rise to consular rank was comparatively recent, were with the Fulvii and Claudii.

The first of these considerations carries little weight, and indeed Earl himself does not seem to attach a great deal to it. The fact that Frugi had set up a new procedure for dealing with extortion by provincial governors gives no clue to his attitude to land reform or to Tiberius' specific proposals; nor is it so certain that it was impossible to believe honestly that those proposals were unsatisfactory, even though intelligent men like Appius Claudius, P. Scaevola, and P. Crassus Mucianus thought them

the mistaken belief that he was already a member of the Senate (*Röm. Adels.*, pp. 264 f.; *RE*, s.v. *Fabius*, no. 115; s.v. *Licinius*, no. 72). He holds that the Fabius was Servilianus, that the Crassus was Mucianus, and that the story reveals Crassus as an established friend of Fabius. In fact neither of the identifications is at all certain, and the story can equally well be taken to show that this Fabius was far from familiar with Crassus.

[1] App. *Iber.* 67. [2] App. *Iber.* 67. [3] p. 82.

[4] 'Calpurnii Pisones', *Athenaeum* 38 (1960), pp. 283 f., esp. p. 296. Forrest and Stinton, 'The First Sicilian Slave War', *P & P* 22 (1962), pp. 88 f., also remark on this possibility.

sensible. It may be granted that nothing known about Frugi's character conflicts with the suggestion that he supported the bill, but equally nothing conflicts with the possibility that he opposed it.

The ancestral connexions of the Calpurnii are a more serious matter. Undoubtedly Earl has pointed to a significant event in 210, when Q. Fulvius Flaccus, returning to Rome to hold elections, summoned the propraetor C. Calpurnius Piso from Etruria to take his place as commander of the army at Capua.[1] Since this is the first Calpurnius known to have reached such a rank, and nearly the first known at all, the incident is very suggestive. It is also possible that in 184 this Piso's son, C. Calpurnius Piso cos. 180, and his fellow propraetor L. Quinctius Crispinus were supported in a dispute by the consul P. Claudius Pulcher, though this is by no means proved.[2] But another episode, apparently taken by Earl to indicate political ties between the Calpurnii and the Fulvii Flacci, rather suggests the contrary.

C. Piso died in office as consul in 180, perhaps from the plague which in that year was claiming many victims. His wife, Quarta Hostilia, had a son by a previous marriage, Q. Fulvius Flaccus, who was elected suffect consul in Piso's place. A rumour went round that Hostilia had poisoned Piso in order to secure the consulship for her son, who already had suffered three defeats: it was said that after Fulvius' third defeat she had told told him to prepare to canvass again and that he would be consul within two months. In fact she was tried and convicted for the alleged crime.[3] Now it is true that this story shows that a Calpurnius had married the widow of a Fulvius, and that he had a stepson who was a Fulvius. But, besides describing an episode which could easily have embittered relationships between the two families, it leaves no doubt at all that relations between Piso and his stepson were extremely bad; in fact it is absolutely clear that they had been rival candidates for the plebeian consulship of 180, and that Fulvius' third defeat was inflicted by his stepfather. Since this episode is the last significant information which survives about relations between the two families until after 133, it is patently hazardous to assume that there was a close association in the intervening years.[4] As it happens

---

[1] Livy, 27. 6. 1; Earl, 'Calpurnii Pisones', *Athenaeum* 38 (1960), pp. 285 f. The other matters in which this Calpurnius is linked with Fulvii are not significant because, as Earl rightly observes, they were formal procedures concerning which he was acting as an agent with little discretion.

[2] Livy, 39. 38. 8 f.   [3] Livy, 40. 37. 1, 4 f.

[4] Earl, 'Calpurnii Pisones', *Athenaeum* 38 (1960), pp. 291 and 293, mentions that the colleague of the Calpurnius who was consul in 135 was a Fulvius Flaccus, and that another member of that family presided when Frugi was elected to the consulship of 133; but these

there are a number of hints that the primary connexions of the Calpurnii
now lay elsewhere, and that Frugi was not associated with the Gracchans.
These are no more than hints, but taken as a whole they are suggestive.

The first point is that Frugi was a leading opponent of Gaius Gracchus,
who attacked him in a speech unusually full of abuse;[1] and Gaius' chief
ally was, of course, a Fulvius Flaccus. It is true that the only specific issue
mentioned is Gaius' proposal for corn subsidies; and, as Earl suggests, it is
conceivable that Frugi became hostile only when Tiberius' methods became 'revolutionary'. But if he did not follow Fulvius the whole way in
his support of the Gracchans, how far can he be supposed to have gone?
The burden of proof lies rather with those who suggest that he followed
Fulvius at all, especially in view of the implications of the episode in 180.

The second hint concerns the removal from office of one of Rome's
first two consuls, L. Tarquinius Collatinus, cos. 509. The surviving
accounts disagree as to whether his *imperium* was abrogated or he abdicated
under pressure. This divergence may very well have originated with the
search for precedents for or against the deposition of Octavius by Tiberius
Gracchus. The earliest surviving account of the deposition of Collatinus
is that which Piso Frugi gave in his *Annales*. Unfortunately the fragment
is insufficient to establish which version he gave, but the balance of probability is slightly inclined towards abdication under pressure—the version
unfavourable to Tiberius.[2]

A further and stronger hint from Frugi's *Annales* is his version of the
killing of Sp. Maelius by Servilius Ahala. This is known to have become
a source of argument after the death of Tiberius Gracchus. Those who
defended Scipio Nasica's action compared him to Servilius Ahala, the
tyrannicide; the Gracchans rejoined that Ahala was dictator or *magister
equitum* and acted with the authority of his office, but the defenders of
Nasica denied that Ahala held either office and insisted that he was a
private citizen at the time. Frugi gave this latter version.[3]

Piso Frugi is best remembered for the *lex Calpurnia* of 149 which established the standing *quaestio de repetundis* to handle charges of extortion by

---

facts are not significant. The consul of 135 was the fourth Calpurnius to hold the office but
the first to have a Fulvius as his colleague, and colleagues who were not political allies were
quite common. Similarly the influence of presiding magistrates on the outcome of elections
is sometimes overestimated; e.g. a Fulvius presided in 135 when Scipio Aemilianus was
elected to his second consulship.

[1] Cic. *Pro Font.* 39; *Tusc.* 3. 48; *Schol. Bob. Flacc.*, p. 96 Stangl; *ORF²*, fgts. 39 f., pp.
186 f.

[2] Additional Note R, p. 348.

[3] Piso, fgt. 24; Quint. *Inst.* 5. 13. 24; p. 228; *MRR* i, p. 56.

provincial governors. As Earl recognizes, this law was almost certainly occasioned by the outcry concerning the behaviour of Ser. Sulpicius Galba. This suggests that Frugi was no friend or ally of Galba; but when in that same year an attempt was made to prosecute Galba he was defended by a Fulvius, a Fulvius Nobilior.[1] Moreover, Galba had close connexions with P. Licinius Crassus Mucianus, with whom he formed a marriage alliance.[2] Here are further hints that Piso may not have been on good terms with the faction which promoted the agrarian bill of 133.

Finally there is the singular fact that the first two Calpurnii to achieve the consulship, in 180 and 148, had Postumii as colleagues. Conceivably this may have been sheer coincidence, but it would have been a very singular coincidence, and it is much more likely that the Calpurnii achieved high office as protégés of the Postumii.

The conclusion to be drawn from all this is that in the period under discussion the primary associations of the Calpurnii were probably not with the Fulvii and Claudii but with the Postumii. That is not to say that there was no co-operation at all with the Fulvii and Claudii; the Postumii and Calpurnii were certainly among the opponents of Scipio Aemilianus and it is a reasonable assumption that at various times many of Scipio's opponents acted in concert against him. But it cannot be taken for granted that the electoral successes of the Calpurnii in 139, 135, and 133 are to be reckoned as successes for the Claudian–Fulvian faction. And, if anything, the evidence suggests that in 133 Frugi is distinctly more likely to have opposed Tiberius Gracchus' plans than to have supported them or to have been benevolently neutral.

5. *The Marriage of Tiberius Gracchus*

The marriage of Tiberius Gracchus, the tribune of 133, to the daughter of Ap. Claudius Pulcher is usually believed to have taken place c. 143. This belief derives from the arguments of Fraccaro and Münzer,[3] in which there are two main elements. (1) C. Gracchus is reported to have said, in the period 123–121, '*Si vellem aput vos verba facere et a vobis postulare, cum genere summo ortus essem et cum fratrem propter vos amisissem, nec quisquam de P. Africani et Tiberi Gracchi familia nisi ego et puer restaremus, ut pateremini hoc tempore me quiescere, ne a stirpe genus nostrum interiret et uti aliqua propago generis nostri reliqua esset: haud scio an lubentibus a vobis impetrassem.*'[4]

---

[1] p. 58.   [2] p. 92.

[3] Fraccaro, *Studi*, i, p. 42 n. 4; Münzer, *Röm. Adels.*, pp. 268 f.

[4] *Schol. Bob. Sull.*, p. 81 Stangl = *ORF*[2], fgt. 47, p. 190; on this cf. also Münzer, *RE*, s.v. *Sempronius*, no. 40.

From this it is inferred that all the sons of Tiberius Gracchus were dead
before 121. (2) In 102 Metellus Numidicus affirmed that *tres tantummodo
filios Graccho fuisse, e quibus unum in Sardinia stipendia merentem, alterum infan-
tem Praeneste, tertium post patris mortem natum Romae decessisse.*[1] It is assumed
that the son who died in Sardinia will have been serving there with his
uncle, Gaius, in 126; hence he must have been born no later than 142. It
may be added that even if he did not go until later in this war (which lasted
till late 123 or early 122) his birth could not be placed later than 139.

Earl attempts to show that there is no substance in these arguments, and
that the marriage could have been in or soon after 137.[2] It would then
reflect the quarrel between Gracchus and Scipio Aemilianus over the
foedus Mancinum. Earl suggests that the youth who died in Sardinia could
equally well have been serving there under M. Metellus, between 115
and 111; and he argues that the *puer* mentioned by C. Gracchus could not
have been the latter's own son, since in 121 Gaius had only one child
alive,[3] and that was a daughter. Instead the *puer* should be understood to
be a son of Tiberius Gracchus, in fact to be the youth who died in Sardinia.
Furthermore, the fact that Gaius spoke of him as a *puer* suggests, though
it does not prove, that he was born no earlier than 137. Earl does not
claim to have proved a date for the marriage, only that there is no good
reason to put it earlier than 137.

Earl's reconstruction is undeniably possible; he does show that the
arguments of Fraccaro and Münzer do not constitute irrefutable proof.
Nevertheless, not all his points are as strong as they may at first appear,
and the balance of probability still favours the earlier date. In the first
place it will be observed that even if the *puer* was a son of Tiberius, it
could still be correct that the son who died in Sardinia went there in 126;
the *puer* could be the third son, who died at Rome. Secondly, there is no
evidence that Gaius had a daughter; this is only an unproven, not to say
far-fetched, conjecture by Münzer.[4] This being so, there is no good reason
why Gaius' one child should not have been a boy, and it is natural, though
not inevitable, to infer that the *puer* mentioned by Gaius was his own son;[5]
and that interpretation would imply, as Fraccaro and Münzer saw, that
the sons of Tiberius were all dead by 121.

---

[1] Val. Max. 9. 7. 2; the context establishes that Tiberius is meant.
[2] *Tiberius Gracchus*, pp. 67 f.   [3] Plut. *C. Grac.* 15. 2: τὸ παιδίον.
[4] *Röm. Adels.*, pp. 272 f.
[5] Earl takes the Tiberius Gracchus mentioned by Gaius in this passage to be the tribune of
133. Even so his identification of the *puer* would not be established. In fact it is at least as
likely that the elder Tiberius is meant, just as the P. Africanus, as Earl notes, is probably the
elder Africanus (compare Plut. *Ti. Grac.* 17. 5).

A further point may be added. Sempronius Asellio wrote of Tiberius Gracchus, of whom he was a contemporary, *orare coepit id quidem, ut se defenderent liberosque suos, eum, quem virile secus tum in eo tempore habebat, produci iussit populoque commendavit prope flens.* This passage, referring to an incident at the end of Tiberius' life, is quoted by Gellius as an example of an archaic usage by which the plural *liberos* might be used even where only one child was meant.[1] Whether or not Gellius is correct in asserting that there was such a usage, the distinct emphasis of *virile secus* leaves little doubt that he is wrong in this instance. The natural interpretation is that Tiberius had two or more children alive but that only one was a boy; in other words, there was at least one daughter alive. Furthermore, if Tiberius had only one son alive immediately before his own death, it follows that the one who died in infancy at Praeneste was already dead. Therefore at least three children had been born to Tiberius before his own death. If there were only three, the date which Earl suggests for the marriage is just possible, but only just; if there was more than one daughter, the marriage preceded the affair of the *foedus Mancinum*.

[1] Semp. Asell. fgt. 7; Gell. 2. 13. 1 f.

APPENDIX IX

Scipio on Adopted Sons: Gellius 5. 19. 15–16

THE following is a translation of an extract from Scipio's speech *De Moribus* and of the remarks with which Gellius introduces the extract. The whole passage will be found at Appendix II, no. 16.

I have noticed in the speech *De Moribus* which P. Scipio as censor delivered to the people that among the practices with which he found fault because they were contrary to the usage of our forefathers he condemned this also, that an adoptive son was of profit to his adoptive father in respect of the rewards of fathers (*inter praemia patrum*). The words from the speech are as follows: 'The father votes in one tribe, the son in another, the adoptive son brings as much advantage as if he (the adoptive father) had a son of his own flesh; orders are given to register those not present, so that there is no need for anyone to come to the census.'

This fragment is discussed at length by Fraccaro,[1] but his interpretation is vitiated by the assumption that the first and third clauses of the fragment have nothing at all to do with adoption, let alone with the particular point of Gellius' introductory comment, to which he allows only the second clause to be relevant; in fact he takes the three clauses to refer to three disparate ideas, linked by little more than the theme *contra maiorum instituta*. But since Gellius quotes all three clauses to illustrate his comment it is a reasonable assumption that he understood all three to be relevant to his explicit interpretation of Scipio's words.[2] Also, three clauses which grammatically are so closely knit must surely be associated closely in thought, must revolve around a single idea.[3]

The whole fragment can and should be interpreted as a coherent unity, the purport of which is summed up in Gellius' statement that Scipio found

[1] 'Oratori', pp. 368 f.

[2] All the more so if the passage was taken from the legal writings of Masurius Sabinus, as Fraccaro conjectures. The conjecture is plausible but cannot be proved or disproved.

[3] Mommsen, *Röm. Staats.* ii³, p. 365 n. 1 and iii, p. 183 n. 2, also seems to regard the first clause as unconnected with adoption. Taylor, *Voting Districts*, pp. 280 f., attempts to remedy this but still fails to connect the third clause. Also this discussion suffers both from a questionable translation of *quam si se natum habeat* (cf. Badian, *JRS* 52 (1962), p. 209) and from an unconvincing association of the words *praemia patrum* with the *praemia legis*, the rewards given to successful prosecutors in certain kinds of cases; these rewards included transfer to a more desirable tribe.

fault with the practice by which an adoptive son was of profit to his adoptive father in respect of the 'rewards of fathers'. The central point is that the state conferred certain benefits for paternity, as a stimulus to the birth-rate. Scipio's complaint is that some men were obtaining these benefits on the strength of having adopted children, and thereby were thwarting the purpose of the rewards.

The evidence for intervention in this field by the state, and especially by the censors, is quite considerable; the Augustan *ius liberorum* and Caesar's πολυπαιδίας ἆθλα,[1] though perhaps novel in detail, were only developments of a principle which had a long Republican history. Cicero, explaining the duties of censors, includes the curt instruction *caelibes esse prohibento*;[2] the censors are known to have required the citizen to declare on oath that he had a wife *liberum quaerundum gratia*;[3] and the same kind of intervention is implied in several anecdotes and passing remarks.[4] But although the existence of the system is certain there is very little evidence for the details of its operation—which in any case must have varied from period to period. There is some evidence for the imposition of monetary penalties on bachelors,[5] and one passage suggests the possibility, otherwise unattested but *a priori* attractive, that men with a certain number of sons, or perhaps adult sons, had some claim to exemption from the levy.[6]

Thus there is no difficulty in the notion of rewards given by the state for paternity, or in Scipio being concerned with them in his capacity as censor. The real problem lies in determining the relevance to this of the first clause of Scipio's fragment: *in alia tribu patrem, in alia filium suffragium ferre*. This has been taken to mean that by having the father enrolled in one tribe and the son in another a family is securing influence in two tribes.[7] This could indeed be a consequence of adoption, the adopted son remaining in his old tribe; and it might be argued that in this way the father was

---

[1] Dio, 43. 25. 2.   [2] Cic. *De Leg.* 3. 7.

[3] Gell. 4. 3. 2; 17. 21. 44; Dion. Hal. 2. 25. 7; Cic. *De Orat.* 2. 260; Gell. 4. 20. 3 f.: the latter two without the reference to children, the formula for which recurs, however, in Suet. *Iul.* 52. 3.

[4] Dio, 56. 6. 4; Dion. Hal. 9. 22. 2; Plut. *Cato Mai.* 16. 2; *Camill.* 2. 4; Val. Max. 2. 9. 1; Festus, 519 L., s.v. *uxorium*. Cf. also Metellus Macedonicus' speech *de prole augenda* in 131: p. 237.

[5] Plut. *Camill.* 2. 4; Val. Max. 2. 9. 1; Festus, 519 L., s.v. *uxorium*. Mommsen, *Röm. Staats.* ii³, p. 395, esp. n. 6, suggests a multiple census for bachelors, but after 167, when *tributum* ceased to be collected, this would have been ineffective.

[6] Livy, 42. 34. 12 f., in the speech of Sp. Ligustinus. For an incentive for freedmen cf. Livy, 45. 15. 1 f.: at some census prior to 168 a son five years of age had exempted freedmen from compulsory transfer to one of the four urban tribes.

[7] Fraccaro, 'Oratori', pp. 368 f.; Taylor, *Voting Districts*, pp. 280 f.; cf. Scullard, 'Scipio Aemilianus', *JRS* 50 (1960), p. 68 n. 36.

profiting from having an adopted son. But although this could happen it is not the subject of Scipio's complaint. Such an interpretation of the first clause forces a divorce in thought between it and both Gellius' comment and the second clause; for an advantage of this kind brought by an adopted son cannot be held to be among the *praemia patrum*, which in the context must mean at the least the advantages accruing to fathers who have begotten their own sons; and similarly the adopted son could not be said in this respect to be as advantageous as a son by birth: the point would be that he was more advantageous.[1]

The difficulty seems to arise from too positive an interpretation of the first clause of the fragment, from the assumption that in itself it describes something about which Scipio was complaining. In the context a more satisfactory interpretation is that Scipio draws attention to registration in different tribes not in order to criticize the advantages arising from this but as a rhetorical device to point the contrast between the adopted son and the son by birth, to stress the artificial status of the former, the fact that the adoptive father is not really a father; the purpose is to emphasize the enormity of the situation complained of in the second clause—that the 'father' profits as much from the adopted son as if he had a son by birth. The third clause drives home the point: since sons can be registered in absence, there is no need for them to come to the census; the adoptive father gets his privileges without even having to show a son in person.

---

[1] It might be suggested that the first clause was a complaint about the (profitable) practice of father and son being enrolled in different tribes and that the second clause means that for this purpose an adoptive son is as useful as a son by birth. But this would accentuate the divorce from Gellius' comment. Furthermore, since an adopted son is much more likely to be enrolled in a different tribe from his adoptive father than a son by birth from his real father, we should expect the second clause to be reversed: for this purpose a son by birth is as useful as an adopted son. Cf. Badian, *JRS* 52 (1962), pp. 209 f.

Satis Bonae et Magnae: Valerius Maximus 4. 1. 10 and Expansion of the Empire

VALERIUS MAXIMUS retails an anecdote according to which Scipio as censor, when performing the closing sacrifice of the censorship, changed the customary prayer from a request that the *populi Romani res* be made *meliores amplioresque* to one that they be kept perpetually safe, on the ground that they were '*satis bonae et magnae*'. The new wording, Valerius adds, was retained by subsequent censors. The full text will be found at Appendix II, no. 24.

The authenticity of this anecdote, which some have interpreted as an important indication of Scipio's policies, was denied first by Marx.[1] Rejection or acceptance of his arguments has sometimes been brief or even tacit, but there are three important re-examinations of the problem, by Bilz, Aymard, and Scullard.[2] Aymard rejects the anecdote, Bilz rejects the details but thinks that the prayer was altered in the sense indicated, and Scullard holds it possible that the anecdote is authentic and thinks that even if it is a fiction it is an indication of Scipio's policy.

Some of the subsidiary arguments advanced by Marx carry little or no weight and may be left out of account. His case really rests on three major contentions:

(i) That Cic. *De Orat.* 2. 268 proves that the ceremony of the *suovetaurilia* and *lustratio* was performed not by Scipio but by his colleague Mummius; therefore Scipio did not recite the prayer and the whole story is fiction.

(ii) That to have changed the solemn and sacred prayer in this way would have been a most grave offence.

(iii) That the circumstances of the time and Scipio's own attitude to current problems render it incredible that he should ever have said that the *populi Romani res* were *satis bonae*.

These points, and certain others, will now be discussed one by one.

---

[1] 'Animadversiones criticae', *RhM* 39 (1884), pp. 65 f.

[2] Bilz, *Die Politik*, pp. 42 f.; Aymard, 'Deux anecdotes', pp. 101 f.; Scullard, 'Scipio Aemilianus', *JRS* 50 (1960), p. 68 with n. 38.

Cicero, *De Orat.* 2. 268 (= Appendix II, no. 28) reads: *ut Asello Africanus obicienti lustrum illud infelix, 'noli', inquit, 'mirari; is enim, qui te ex aerariis exemit, lustrum condidit et taurum immolavit.'* [*Tacita suspicio est, ut religione civitatem obstrinxisse videatur Mummius, quod Asellum ignominia levavit.*]

The bracketed sentence is usually regarded as a gloss, on account of its superfluity as well as of the un-Ciceronian *ut*.

A passage of Gellius attests that in his censorship Scipio had wished to deprive Ti. Claudius Asellus of his horse and a passage of Dio attests that Mummius thwarted some of Scipio's disciplinary actions.[1] Therefore the customary and natural interpretation of the *dictum* reported by Cicero is that Mummius, the very man who had rescued Asellus from *ignominia*, had performed the final ceremonies: no wonder the *lustrum* was *infelix*! This interpretation produces a direct conflict between Cicero and Valerius Maximus. If Mummius performed the ceremony, Scipio did not;[2] and if he did not, Valerius' anecdote is false. In such a conflict between Cicero and Valerius Maximus there could be little doubt which should be preferred even if there were no other reasons for questioning Valerius' story.[3] (In fact, as will appear shortly, there are other grounds.)

It was this argument especially which persuaded Aymard;[4] and any attempt to defend Valerius' story has to circumvent it. Scullard has cautiously put forward a re-interpretation of the Cicero passage which would resolve the conflict.[5] Perhaps, he suggests, the censor whose wish to remove someone from the list was vetoed by his colleague was obliged to restore the name himself; Scipio was saying, 'No wonder the *lustrum* was *infelix*, for I who performed it had restored your name to the list.' There would then be a strong tinge of irony in '*qui te ex aerariis exemit*', since the real responsibility lay elsewhere. Scullard admits that this

---

[1] Gell. 3. 4. 1; Dio, fgt. 76. 1.

[2] Only one censor, selected by lot, performed the ceremony: Varro, *De Ling. Lat.* 6. 87; Mommsen, *Röm. Staats.* i³, p. 40 n. 3 and p. 42 n. 4.

[3] Cf. Lucil. 394 f. M. (from Gell. 4. 17. 1):

> Scipiadae magno improbus obiciebat Asellus
> lustrum illo censore malum infelixque fuisse.

Marx, 'Animadversiones criticae', *RhM* 39 (1884), pp. 65 f., thought Lucilius the probable source of Scipio's anecdote, but this is by no means necessarily the case. Bilz, *Die Politik*, pp. 42 f., judged Cicero's anecdote inherently self-contradictory, on the grounds that the taunt of the *infelix lustrum*, confirmed by this fragment of the contemporary Lucilius, shows that Scipio did perform the ceremony. This is not so. *Lustrum* is used not only of the ceremony but of the period initiated by the ceremony (e.g. Suet. *Aug.* 97); therefore Asellus' taunt could refer to misfortunes which occurred subsequent to the ceremony and which he was attributing to Scipio's maladministration of the censorship.

[4] 'Deux anecdotes', pp. 113 f.

[5] 'Scipio Aemilianus', *JRS* 50 (1960), p. 68 n. 38.

hypothesis may seem rather strained and that it might be ruled out if we knew more about censorial procedure; but it would reconcile Cicero and Valerius Maximus.

There are difficulties about this hypothesis. It does seem rather strained, and it is not the natural interpretation of the Latin; for if this were the intended meaning we should expect the first person rather than the third (*ego . . . qui . . . exemi . . . condidi et . . . immolavi*).[1] Moreover, as Aymard had already observed, if it is accepted that the bracketed sentence is a gloss, it still remains evident that some reader knowledgeable enough to know the name of Scipio's colleague understood the *dictum* in the sense which is customarily given to it.[2] In general, therefore, Scullard's tentative suggestion seems an unlikely explanation. In all probability it is correct to see a conflict between the two passages, and the fact that there are other grounds for disbelieving Valerius leaves little reason for accepting such an uncertain interpretation of Cicero.

Marx's second argument, judged decisive by Bilz,[3] seems to Aymard the least satisfactory. Really it is composed of two arguments. The first, which Marx had particularly in mind, is that Scipio's action would have been a violation of required ritual, a breach of religious rules; and there is plenty of evidence for Roman insistence on exactitude in the performance of ritual.[4] Against this view Aymard argues that it is essential to distinguish between the inviolable formulary parts of the prayer (especially the invocations) and the actual requests made in the prayer. While the former might never be varied, the latter might well be—though he agrees that Valerius' story does presuppose that Scipio's action was at least unusual, not to say shocking.[5] In cold logic, of course, such a distinction can be drawn, and the texts which mention invariability of wording are not sufficiently precise to determine the issue—after all, they were written for readers entirely familiar with this concept of invariability. On the other hand, Aymard does not dispose effectively of the example of the Salii, preserving unchanged *carmina* whose meaning was scarcely understood by the priests themselves;[6] the fault necessitating the repetition of the

---

[1] Admittedly Mommsen took Scipio to be the subject of the sentence: *Röm. Staats.* ii³, p. 412 n. 3.   [2] 'Deux anecdotes', p. 115.

[3] *Die Politik*, pp. 43 f.; decisive, that is, against the authenticity of the setting and details; Bilz would still accept Scipio's responsibility for the change in the prayer: see below, p. 329 n. 7.

[4] e.g. Cic. *De Har. Resp.* 23; Plin. *Nat. Hist.* 28. 11; Aymard, 'Deux anecdotes', p. 111 n. 7.

[5] 'Deux anecdotes', pp. 110 f.

[6] Quint. *Inst.* 1. 6. 40; Aymard, 'Deux anecdotes', pp. 111 f. In this respect the farmer's *lustratio agri* of Cato *De Agr. Cult.* 141 does not offer an apt comparison with the state and public ceremonies of the priestly colleges and the magistrates.

Latin festival in 176 was the omission of a request;[1] and in general one may doubt if the logically valid distinction was firmly recognized in practice. Since the whole *carmen* was recited from a prepared text, a procedure the point of which was to achieve verbal exactitude,[2] it is a reasonable conclusion that such exactitude was required throughout and that it was at the least highly questionable whether it was permissible to alter the wording of such an important public prayer without the authority of the Senate or, more probably, of the pontifices. In other words, though not absolutely decisive, this particular argument advanced by Marx carries very great weight.

But closely related to it, and not clearly distinguished in Marx's original article, is a second argument, which has been expanded by Aymard:[3] in effect that, whatever the technicality, public feeling would have made such an action impossible. Scipio was a controversial political figure, and to tamper on his own initiative with the established wording of a public prayer of such importance would have been to present his enemies with a magnificent weapon to use against him. It is scarcely credible that he would have taken such a risk or indeed that, if the *lustrum* was alleged to have been *infelix* for this reason, subsequent censors should have followed his example.[4] Furthermore, the nature of the alleged change would have added enormously to the political risk: what could not his enemies have made of an assertion that the *populi Romani res* were *satis bonae*, that they did not need to be improved?

This merges into Marx's third line of argument, which has not received the attention it deserves. Possibly this neglect is due to Valerius Maximus' interpretation of the story only in terms of the territorial extent of Roman rule; but in themselves the words reported in the anecdote are not necessarily confined to this, and certainly would not have been allowed to remain so by political opponents. Marx did not base his case on the alleged change from *ampliores* and the use of *satis magnae*, since he recognized that the wars of the time were not necessarily regarded as wars of conquest. Even here it may be wondered if *ampliores* and *magnae* could have been interpreted only in this territorial sense; but the heart of the matter is the alleged dismissal of *meliores* and the assertion that the *populi Romani res* were *satis bonae*. Probably the military campaign in Hither Spain was going well at this time, but the latest news from Further Spain

---

[1] Livy, 41. 16. 1 f.   [2] Plin. *Nat. Hist.* 28. 11.
[3] 'Deux anecdotes', p. 118.
[4] Cf. the religious apprehension generated by the slight *vitium* in the Latin Festival of 176: Livy, 41. 16. 1 f.

is likely to have been of defeat and retreat, and in any case both rebellions remained alive;[1] in 142 a plague had been raging;[2] as censor Scipio had exhorted the people to return to the *mores maiorum*, and it is scarcely likely that he thought that this had been achieved, especially as he had complained angrily about his colleague who had thwarted his attempts to carry out a stern censorship;[3] and he knew, as Laelius' abortive proposal demonstrates, that there was a need for some kind of social or agrarian reform.[4] In the face of all this it would have been hard indeed to deny the appropriateness of *meliores*, and even if Scipio had been thinking in territorial terms he must have seen what damaging interpretations could be put upon such a change and such a *dictum*.

There is a further point. Aymard observes that it might be expected that the censor would always have prayed for the preservation of the existing state of things: *ut eas perpetuo incolumes servent*.[5] Was this an innovation at all? Did the *carmen* ever include the request to the immortal gods *ut populi Romani res meliores amplioresque facerent*? If it was included and was, as Valerius implies, a legacy from earlier times, it is unlikely to have been understood primarily in a territorial sense; for in such a sense it would have stood in conflict, at least in spirit, with the fetial law, an institution which establishes 'that the Roman *mos maiorum* did not recognize the right of aggression or a desire for more territory as just causes for war'.[6] And if the phrase was not understood primarily in a territorial sense Marx's third line of argument can scarcely be challenged.[7]

The cumulative effect of these arguments, all weighty in themselves, leaves no real choice but to regard Valerius' anecdote as fiction. Yet there

---

[1] p. 123. [2] Oros. 5. 4. 8 f.; Obsequ. 22.
[3] Ch. X, esp. pp. 119 and 121. [4] Appendix VII.
[5] 'Deux anecdotes', p. 119.

[6] Frank, *Roman Imperialism*, pp. 8 f.; cf. Heuss, *Die völkerrechtlichen Grundlagen*, pp. 18 f. That is not to say that the Romans were not guilty of aggression or that desire for territorial expansion was never an actual motive for war; but it was not acceptable as the official, formal motive. Cf. Diod. 32. 5; Polyb. 36. 2 and fgt. 99 B–W.

[7] Bilz, *Die Politik*, pp. 42 f., regards Marx's argument from the immutability of religious formulae as decisive against the details of Valerius' story, though he rejects the evidence of Cic. *De Orat.* 2. 268 (above, p. 326 n. 3). He holds that underlying Valerius' story is the reality that Scipio did bring about, though by more orthodox means, some change in the *carmen*, and that this change was not concerned with internal affairs but, as Valerius indicates, only with the restriction of the empire to the boundaries at that time established. But, as Aymard notes, 'Deux anecdotes', p. 110, it is extremely difficult to separate the details from the essence of the anecdote; and if the actual changes given by Valerius are rejected there is very little left. As for the supposed exclusively territorial reference of the change, it is highly unorthodox, to say the least, to place more reliance on Valerius' comments than upon the anecdote itself.

remains a problem: why should anyone have invented the story? Aymard's answer, surely the only one possible, is that it is propaganda for a policy of containment within existing borders and against further expansion; and he notes that this was government policy in the reign of Tiberius, when Valerius Maximus was writing.[1] The inventor of the story would not have to worry about such matters as the political consequences which would have followed for Scipio or whether the change and the *dictum* were appropriate to the particular circumstances of 141 B.C. But why choose Scipio as the vehicle of this propaganda? Scullard suggests that 'even if the anecdote is to be rejected, the words ascribed to Scipio may still represent his policy: otherwise their attribution to him is somewhat pointless'.[2] Yet not necessarily so. Scipio was one of the conquering heroes of the Republic, the destroyer of Carthage and Numantia; in the words of an intimate contemporary, '*necesse enim fuisse ibi esse terrarum imperium ubi ille esset*';[3] in the words of Cicero: '*Erat in eo . . . auctoritas tanta quanta in imperio populi Romani quod illius opera tenebatur.*'[4] The *auctoritas* of such a man would be a powerful support to the anti-expansionist case: Scipio may have been chosen as the subject of the anecdote precisely *because* he was famed as a conqueror. In other words, while it is conceivable that Scipio was chosen because he was anti-expansionist, it is equally possible that he was chosen because he was very nearly the opposite, because the idea of anti-expansionism was not normally associated with his name.

When, however, it comes to choosing between these two possibilities there is a singular lack of direct evidence (which is probably why the anecdote has bulked so large in discussions of Scipio). Not that this period was without expansionist developments. The annexation of Africa and Macedonia, Brutus Callaicus' penetration into north-west Spain, and the formation of the province of Asia could all be placed in this category. But Scipio was not even in Rome when Attalus' legacy was accepted, and there is no hint of his attitude on two of the other topics.[5] It is argued elsewhere that he favoured Cato's policy towards Carthage and that there is no reason to believe that he regretted what was done;[6] but that is not relevant for those who believe that he became anti-expansionist after the Punic war. Nevertheless, the balance of probability inclines against an

---

[1] 'Deux anecdotes', pp. 119 f.

[2] 'Scipio Aemilianus', *JRS* 50 (1960), p. 68.

[3] From the *laudatio* written by Laelius but spoken by Q. Fabius Maximus: *ORF*², pp. 121 f. and 199, from Cic. *Pro Mur.* 75.

[4] *Pro Mur.* 58.

[5] On Brutus' campaigns and Scipio's speech about his *imperium* see pp. 146 f.

[6] Appendix III. 4 and IV.

anti-expansionist interpretation of Scipio's policy. The only positive evidence for it is Valerius Maximus' anecdote; the present writer holds firmly to the view that Scipio had no qualms about the Third Punic War; and if then or later he had set his face against extension of the empire it may well be wondered if Laelius would have written *necesse enim fuisse ibi esse terrarum imperium ubi ille esset*.[1]

In addition another aspect of Scipio's outlook may be noticed: his belief in the severe punishment of recalcitrant peoples, as a means of securing Rome's rule by examples of terrorism. For this there is plenty of evidence: Scipio's attitude to the Celtiberians in 152–151;[2] his attitude to Carthage; his treatment of the deserters;[3] his terrorism at Lutia;[4] the annihilation of Numantia and the reasons suggested by Appian for this action;[5] finally the direct expression of such a principle of security through terrorism in two passages of Diodorus which were almost certainly taken from Polybius and which very possibly reflect Scipio's sentiments.[6] All this is not, of course, positively incompatible with an anti-expansionist policy, but it does suggest an attitude of mind which it would be surprising to find in combination with such a policy.

Two brief points remain. First, if by any chance it should be the case that Scipio favoured an end to or a halt in the extension of Rome's empire, it does not need a concern for the preservation of the 'mixed constitution' to account for this. Indeed it is argued elsewhere that there are grounds for doubting whether Scipio did have such a concern;[7] and the policy could be explained quite satisfactorily by such considerations as the inadequacy of military resources, or the incomplete pacification of areas already annexed, or a belief that new conquests would bring insufficient advantage to compensate for the trouble and expense involved. Finally, if, as seems much more probable, the anti-expansionist policy is a myth, it does not necessarily follow that the exact opposite is true, that Scipio was positively in favour of an extension of the empire; it need mean no more than that he was prepared to judge each case on its merits.

[1] Above, p. 330 n. 3.   [2] p. 41.   [3] p. 76.
[4] App. *Iber.* 94.   [5] App. *Iber.* 98; cf. p. 154.
[6] Diod. 32. 2 and 4.   [7] Appendix V.

Appian and Plutarch on Tiberius Gracchus

THERE survive two moderately full narratives of the tribunate of Tiberius Gracchus, written by Appian and Plutarch.[1] A great deal of attention has been given to two important problems which they present: whether or in what degree they are derived from a common source; and, in view of the differences between them, which is to be preferred. The present note is concerned with the latter question,[2] on which majority opinion has long favoured Appian. This opinion finds its extreme form in the work of Carcopino,[3] who holds that there is no common source, that the two accounts are incompatible at many points, that Appian's is vastly superior, and that at virtually every point where Plutarch differs from Appian he is wrong. Naturally much of Carcopino's argument is devoted to establishing Appian's correctness and Plutarch's unreliability in respect of particular details, the culmination being the denial of the story of Tiberius' interference with the legacy of Attalus, which is not mentioned by Appian. Upon this last matter there has been a general rejection of Carcopino's views, and many of his other arguments have been sufficiently refuted in reviews by Gelzer and Fraccaro or in an important study by Geer, all of whom are inclined to accept as genuine much of the material found in Plutarch but omitted by Appian.[4] In addition certain scholars have expressed some unwillingness to accept the general superiority of Appian.[5]

---

[1] App. *B.C.* 1. 7–17; Plut. *Ti. Grac.*

[2] Concerning the former question, the case for supposing that Appian's principal (or only) source was among the sources used by Plutarch rests primarily upon a number of alleged parallels. These are listed by Meyer, *Untersuch. zur Gesch. der Gracchen*, p. 379 n. 2, and Fraccaro, *Studi*, i, p. 26 n. 1, but only in one instance does the verbal similarity seem at all remarkable (Plut. *Ti. Grac.* 19. 5 and App. *B.C.* 1. 16: καὶ τὸ κράσπεδον τοῦ ἱματίου, κτλ.), and this happens to concern the final catastrophe, where the two accounts are most strikingly at variance. In fact they are irreconcilable on many important points concerning the last two days of Tiberius' life, and this makes it difficult, though not actually impossible, to believe that Plutarch made direct use of Appian's source. Whether a common source lay further back in the complex lineage of their immediate sources it is impossible to decide.

[3] *Autour des Gracques*, ch. 1. For earlier and less extreme assertions of Appian's superiority see esp. Meyer, *Untersuch. zur Gesch. der Gracchen*, esp. pp. 384 f., and Fraccaro, *Studi*, i.

[4] Gelzer, *Gnomon* 5 (1929), pp. 648 f.; Fraccaro, *Athenaeum* 9 (1931), pp. 291 f., esp. pp. 302 f. = *Opusc.* ii, pp. 53 f., esp. pp. 62 f.; Geer, 'Plutarch and Appian', *Studies in Honor of E. K. Rand*, pp. 105 f.; cf. Additional Note O, p. 346.

[5] Gelzer, loc. cit.; cf. his review of Taeger, *Tiberius Gracchus*, in *Gnomon* 5 (1929), pp. 296 f.; Badian, *Foreign Clientelae*, pp. 172 and 296 n. Q; Earl, *Tiberius Gracchus*, pp. 84 f.

This more cautious attitude is entirely justifiable. In the first place, until the last stages of the story the two sources are not seriously in conflict. With a few minor exceptions the differences consist of material supplied by Plutarch but not by Appian. This is scarcely surprising, since Appian's account is much shorter than Plutarch's and passes rapidly from one key meeting of the assembly to another with virtually no reference to events in between; indeed it is likely that he has epitomized his source, and in consequence has some awkward transitions from one scene to another. There is no *a priori* reason why many of the extra details given by Plutarch should not be authentic, even though certain of them are the product of later propaganda and others may have been coloured by dramatic writing;[1] and on two major points there is external evidence to support Plutarch.[2] Where the two authors do disagree fundamentally and irreconcilably is precisely where this is to be expected most, in the account of the last two days of Tiberius' life. For it is here that partisan distortion is likely to be at its greatest, though certainly not confined to this section alone.

It is highly improbable that there was ever a strictly accurate or impartial account of Tiberius' tribunate, particularly in view of its cata-strophic conclusion. The records of eye-witnesses are almost certain to have been tinged with prejudice for or against Tiberius, quite apart from the difficulty of observing or recalling exactly what did happen; and an accurate *post eventum* reconstruction of such a series of episodes, pieced together from evidence collected from eye-witnesses, would be a gigantic task even for a person equipped with all the techniques and resources of a modern journalist or historian. Any narrative ever written is virtually certain to have contained inaccuracies, arising from careless reporting, from rumour, from partisan fictions, from distortions, and from sup-pression of inconvenient facts. There is therefore an *a priori* implausibility in supposing any one surviving version to be consistently reliable and always superior to another, and all the more so when both must be several stages removed from the original versions of participants and eye-witnesses.

This *a priori* judgement is reinforced by the faults which can be dis-cerned in both the surviving versions. Badian and Earl have pointed to a number of weaknesses in Appian's narrative, especially in his account of the episode in which Tiberius referred the agrarian dispute to the Senate;[3] and to these must be added his omission of the appropriation of the Pergamene treasure and above all the famous 'Italian element' in his

[1] Additional Notes N, O, P, S, pp. 346 f.; cf. p. 209 n. 3 and p. 212 n. 3.

[2] Legacy of Attalus: p. 212, with Additional Note V, p. 350. The controversy with Annius: p. 213.   [3] p. 332 n. 5.

version, which in truth is a gross distortion of the facts.[1] On the other hand Plutarch does have a tendency to dramatize his narrative, does incorporate some *post eventum* fabrications, and gives an account of the proceedings on the penultimate day of Tiberius' life which is almost certainly more tendentious than Appian's.[2] In fact both incorporate tendentious material, and neither is consistently favourable to one side in the struggle, though in the final stages Plutarch's narrative tends rather to favour the Gracchans and Appian's their opponents. With regard to the outbreak of violence on the final day neither version is easily credited exactly as it stands.[3]

The general conclusion must be, then, that neither version is to be trusted exclusively at the expense of the other; that details found in one but not the other must be weighed on their individual merits; and that where the two accounts contradict each other the only possible method, unsatisfactory as it may be, is to consider their relative plausibility on the particular point at issue.

[1] Badian, *Foreign Clientelae*, pp. 169 f. for a definitive refutation of the view that the agrarian proposals were to benefit Italians as well as Romans.

[2] p. 333 n. 1; Additional Note Y, p. 352.

[3] pp. 221 f.; on Appian cf. also Additional Note P, p. 347.

The Interpretation of the Census Statistics

VARIOUS sources, chiefly Livy and the *Epitome* of Livy, have preserved the totals of *civium capita* registered at many of the censuses of the Roman Republic. Although there is no doubt that some of the figures have been corrupted in transmission and that the efficiency and completeness of the census was not always uniform, these statistics and the trends they reveal are extremely valuable evidence. They would be more valuable still if it were possible to establish with certainty precisely what section of the population is designated by *civium capita*. As it is, this topic has been the subject of voluminous controversy, which is unlikely to be finally resolved without fresh evidence. Four principal solutions have been proposed, but there are serious objections to two of these.[1] Since a dogmatic choice between the remaining two would be hazardous, it is desirable to examine the significance of the figures in the light of each of them in turn.

The figures pertinent to the present study are as follows:

174	269,015	147	322,000
169	312,805	142	328,442
164	337,452	136	317,933
159	328,316	131	318,823
154	324,000	125	394,736

It is possible that the *civium capita* are the *adsidui*, i.e. all those male citizens, except freedmen, who had sufficient property to be registered in the five classes of the *comitia centuriata* and who were therefore liable for conscription at the levy.[2] If this is so, there are two conceivable explanations for the enormous rise, of almost 76,000, which apparently occurred between 131 and 125. The increase may reflect the work of the Gracchan

---

[1] The first is that the *civium capita* are the *iuniores* only: Mommsen, *Röm. Forsch.* ii, pp. 401 f.; *Röm. Staats.* ii³, pp. 410 f.; Nissen, *Italische Landeskunde*, ii, pp. 112 f. Against this see Beloch, *Die Bevölkerung*, pp. 312 f.; 'Die Bevölkerung Italiens', *Klio* 3 (1903), pp. 471 f. The second, revived by Bourne, 'The Roman Republican Census', *CW* 45 (1952), pp. 129 f., is that they are citizens *sui iuris*, against which see Beloch, *Die Bevölkerung*, pp. 312 f.; Gabba, 'Ancora sulle cifre', *Athenaeum* 30 (1952), pp. 161 f.

[2] Herzog, 'Die Bürgerzahlen', in *Comm. Phil. in Hon. Th. Mommseni*, pp. 124 f.; Gabba, 'Le origini dell'esercito professionale', *Athenaeum* 27 (1949), pp. 187 f.; 'Ancora sulle cifre', *Athenaeum* 30 (1952), pp. 161 f.; cf. Earl, *Tiberius Gracchus*, pp. 35 f.

agrarian commission: thousands of *proletarii* had been given land and thereby had become *adsidui*. Or it may have been in these years that the property qualification for the fifth class was reduced from 4,000 to 1,500 asses; and this too would have transformed numerous *proletarii* into *adsidui*.[1] In favour of the first explanation is the reasonable expectation that the reforms would have produced an increase in the number of registered *adsidui*.[2] On the other hand the increase is very large. Admittedly the net gain in 131 over 136 is only 900, but without the Gracchan reforms there would probably have been a substantial decrease, so that the true increase effected by the reforms would have been significantly greater than 900, probably several thousands. By 125, therefore, the net increase was at least 77,000 and probably 80,000 or more. This would imply a remarkable degree of success on the part of the land-commissioners: the resettlement over only seven years of an average of more than 11,000 men per year, or more than a quarter of a million people in all. There is therefore something to be said for the alternative explanation, or for the combination of both of them together. But both of them depend upon two premises: that the *civium capita* are the *adsidui*, and that the census figures for 131 and especially for 125 have been accurately transmitted; and neither of these premises is beyond questioning.

This increase between 131 and 125 is the most powerful of the arguments for the view that the *civium capita* are the *adsidui*. The alternative explanation, which is in many ways preferable, is that the term designates all adult male citizens, irrespective of property or status;[3] but it is extremely difficult to envisage how this total citizen class can have increased by almost 25 per cent. in six years. There cannot possibly have been such a startling improvement in the efficiency of registration, nor can slaves have been formally manumitted in such enormous numbers. The only recourse is to

---

[1] This is the view of Gabba (see previous note).

[2] Fraccaro, 'Assegnazione agrarie', *Scr. in on. di Contardo Ferrini*, i, pp. 262 f. = *Opusc.* ii, pp. 87 f., argues that the recipients of the Gracchan holdings would not have become *adsidui*, but his objections cannot stand against the evidence that Tiberius' reforms did envisage an improvement in the man-power problem: App. *B.C.* 1. 7 f., esp. 11; Plut. *Ti. Grac.* 8. 4.

[3] Beloch, *Die Bevölkerung*, pp. 312 f., who has been widely followed. *Prima facie* this is what the expression would be expected to mean, and the exception *praeter orbos orbasque*, upon which Gabba relies heavily, 'Le origini dell'esercito professionale', *Athenaeum* 27 (1949), pp. 187 f., does not seem incompatible with this. It is significant that even during the Third Macedonian War, when there were exceptional efforts to raise troops, the number of legionaries evidently did not rise above 65,000, which is only just over 20 per cent. of the census figure for 169. In 191–188 the legionaries were about 25 per cent. of the census total, and that was probably the highest percentage reached after the Second Punic War. For the military totals see Afzelius, *Die römische Kriegsmacht*, esp. p. 47.

suppose the figure corrupt, which, as Fraccaro shows, is not such a desperate expedient as it might at first seem, for the census statistics have been poorly transmitted in the manuscripts of the epitome of Livy, which alone records the figure for 125.[1]

The recorded census figures of the second century show a general rise up to 164, and thereafter a perceptible, though not a uniform, decline until 136. Though some of the individual figures could be incorrect, the general pattern is clear and must be accepted at its face value. It shows a decline of nearly 6 per cent. over 18 years. If this is the decline in the numbers of the class available for the levy, while it does not represent a catastrophic collapse, it is quite sufficient to have caused serious concern, especially as all that we know about the circumstances would suggest, both to us and to the Romans, that it was likely to continue. But if, as seems more probable (despite the difficulty of the increase in 125), this is a decline in the total male citizen population, the position was even more alarming. For it is unlikely that the numbers of the *proletarii* were declining, so the reduction would have been almost entirely among the *adsidui*, and their numbers would have fallen by well over 6 per cent., probably by 8 per cent. or more;[2] and if the numbers of the *proletarii* were actually increasing, as is entirely possible, those of the *adsidui* were falling at an even greater rate.

Two further points may be made briefly. The first is that if the *civium capita* are the entire male citizen population, the declining total shown by the census figures indicates a low birth-rate, and this corresponds to the evidence of Appian and Plutarch, who both state that the poor were neglecting the rearing of children, and to the implications of the speech of Metellus Macedonicus in which he urged the people to marry in order to beget children.[3] Finally, whatever category the figures represent, the largest single drop was evidently revealed by the census of 136; the difference since 142 was 10,509, more than half the total decline since 164. Since any one figure may have suffered corruption in the manuscript tradition, it would be unwise to accept this point without reservations;

[1] Fraccaro, op. cit., pp. 265 f. = *Opusc.* ii, pp. 91 f.; note also that for the census of 174 the epitome not only gives a different figure from Livy, 42. 10. 2 but also has manuscript variations.

[2] Eight per cent. assumes a total of about 80,000 *proletarii* and freedmen, which is purely a guess but scarcely excessive for this period. The argument that the *proletarii* are unlikely to have been declining refers to their net numbers, i.e. including dispossessed *adsidui* who had become *proletarii*.

[3] App. *B.C.* 1. 10; cf. 1. 27; Plut. *Ti. Grac.* 8. 4; for Metellus see p. 237 and *ORF²*, pp. 107 f.

but if the figure is correct, it is likely to have come as a shock, especially as the previous census had shown the only rise since 164.[1]

[1] It is possible that the rise in 142 really reflects greater efficiency in the organization and conduct of the census. This would accord well with the character and talents of Scipio Aemilianus and was an aspect of the work where Mummius' attitude (p. 115) would not have interfered. But a decline in efficiency could not account for the whole difference in 136, especially as Ap. Claudius must have wished to emulate his rival.

ADDITIONAL NOTES

A. Very little is known of the kind of assistance which Polybius gave to Scipio, apart from the implication that in general he encouraged him to conduct himself in the ways described in 31. 25–29. Friedländer, 'Socrates enters Rome', *AJPh* 66 (1945), pp. 337 f., is virtually alone in holding that it consisted essentially of philosophical training. Admittedly Diod. 31. 26. 5 does say this, but the mention of philosophy is clearly an intrusion into a passage derived directly from Polyb. 31. 23–29, where it does not appear. It is much more probable that the common view is correct, that the assistance was more in the nature of practical advice and encouragement. Polybius himself was not especially well versed in either literature or philosophy (Ziegler, *RE*, s.v. *Polybios*, no. 1, cols. 1465 f.; Walbank, *Commentary on Polybius*, i, p. 2), and he clearly implies that this was not what he was offering (31. 24. 6). The one item of specific advice which happens to have been preserved is certainly not philosophical (p. 31).

B. Mommsen, *Röm. Staats.* i³, p. 532, notes that even in the last years of the Hannibalic War the public games staged by the aediles were having a marked effect on the elections. In 189 M'. Acilius Glabrio was considered a strong candidate in the censorial elections because of the extensive *congiaria* he had distributed (Livy, 37. 57. 10 f.). There is little doubt that there was a political purpose behind the games which L. Scipio Asiaticus gave for ten days in 186, announcing that he had vowed them when fighting Antiochus, four years before (Livy, 39. 22. 8 f.). Similarly the steep rise in donatives to victorious armies in this period is only partly accounted for by increased booty. In 179 a campaign against the Ligurians is said to have yielded almost no money, only a great quantity of arms, yet the troops received a donative of no less than 300 asses each, with the usual bonuses for centurions and cavalry (Livy, 40. 59. 2). In 167 the votes of troops discontented with their donative (in fact it was probably exceptionally large) came close to depriving Aemilius Paullus of his triumph over Perseus (Livy, 45. 35. 5 f.; Plut. *Aem.* 30. 4 f.). Other signs of growing extravagance in such matters are the gilded statue of his father set up by M'. Acilius Glabrio in 181 (Livy, 40. 34. 5); the two occasions on which the Senate saw fit to specify the maximum amount to be spent on games (Livy, 39. 5. 10, cf. 39. 22. 1 f., 40. 44. 10); the decree prohibiting the exaction of contributions for games from Italians or provincials (Livy, 40. 44. 11 f.); the increasing ostentation of funeral ceremonies, which might now last three or four days and include theatrical performances, the public distribution of meat, elaborate public banquets, and above all increasingly lavish gladiatorial games (e.g. Livy, 39. 46. 2 f., 41. 28. 11).

C. In the period 200–150 there are only two *plebiscita* known which are likely to have been carried contrary to the will of the Senate. They were close to each other in date and possibly in other respects. One was a law carried in 189 or 188 by the tribune Q. Terentius Culleo which was concerned with the enrolment of freedmen's children in the census lists (Plut. *Flam.* 18. 1). It is not mentioned by Livy and nothing is known of the methods used by Terentius to secure its passage. The second law was proposed in 188 by the tribune C. Valerius Tappo. It extended full franchise to three *civitates sine suffragio*, naming the tribes in which they were to be enrolled (Livy, 38. 36. 7 f.). At first it was vetoed by four tribunes, on the ground that it was not proposed on the authority of the Senate; 'but when they were informed that it was the right of the people, not the Senate, to bestow the franchise on whoever they wished, they desisted from their course'. Livy has almost certainly abbreviated the dispute. It is hard to believe that four tribunes who had taken up their stand on such a point could have been persuaded to withdraw unless there was some compromise acceptable to the Senate and saving its face, at least in form (e.g. some such solution as a decree of the Senate instructing the *populus* to decide the matter). But the close proximity of the two laws suggests some special political circumstances and Bleicken, *Volkstribunat*, pp. 68 f., and Taylor, *Voting Districts*, pp. 138 and 306 f., plausibly suggest that involved in both measures were attempts by politicians, notably Scipio Africanus, to influence tribal registration in such a way as to facilitate the extension of their own *clientelae*.

D. The sources disagree about the capacity in which Scipio went to Spain. Livy, *Epit.* 48 says explicitly *tribunus militum*, but App. *Iber.* 49 (πρεσβευτής), (Victor) *De Vir. Ill.* 58. 2, and Ampel. 22 equally explicitly assert that he was a *legatus*. Broughton, *MRR* i, p. 456 n. 1, draws attention to Oros. 4. 21. 1, which states that Macedonia had been assigned to Scipio by lot; he suggests that this may mean that Scipio had been elected *tribunus militum*. But on this point Orosius is almost certainly wrong, since Polybius, 35. 4. 11, says that the Macedonians had asked for Scipio by name. Polybius himself, in the surviving passage, says only that Scipio volunteered to serve either as tribune or as *legatus* (35. 4. 9). It is possible that he was never more precise about the point and that the cause of the variations is that he left open the way for inferences by those who used him as a source. Simon, *Roms Kriege*, p. 44, follows Münzer, *RE*, s.v. *Cornelius*, no. 335, col. 1442, and Schulten, *Numantia*, i, p. 347 n. 10, in the compromise suggestion that Scipio held both appointments. The fact remains that our best source says *tribunus militum*.

E. The naval commander at Carthage in 148 was L. Hostilius Mancinus. Livy, *Epit.* 51 refers to him as a *legatus* (sc. of Piso), but this has been doubted. Münzer, *RE*, s.v. *Hostilius*, no. 20, considers that he was probably praetor or propraetor, while *MRR* i, p. 462 n. 3 is very cautious. However, there is nothing in App.

Lib. 110 f. which is necessarily in conflict with Livy. Mancinus' status is very likely to have been the same as that of his successor, Serranus, and the indications are that he was a *legatus*. Scipio's direct control of the fleet is suggested not only by the course of the operations and by the tenor of Appian's narrative (cf. esp. *Lib.* 123, the ships of the Sidetae, which were present out of friendship for Scipio), but also by the fact that he entrusted some ships to Polybius to undertake a voyage of exploration: Plin. *Nat. Hist.* 5. 9 = Polyb. 34. 15. 7. It is true that in the Third Macedonian War the fleet had operated under a praetor, but there is no reason why there should not have been a return to the system of a *legatus* serving under the main military commander; in the Third Punic War the intimate link between naval and land operations in a very limited area suggests that the latter would have been preferable. In favour of praetorian status is only the fact that Mancinus was consul in 145, and therefore 148 was the last year in which he could have been praetor. This is a coincidence, but he could have been praetor a little earlier, and legates were often of praetorian status; the coincidence cannot outweigh the direct evidence of Livy. Thus, after the departure of Censorinus in 149, the fleet was almost certainly commanded by *legati*.

F. The most important consequence of Scipio's assault on Megara was that Hasdrubal and the Carthaginian field army abandoned their camp on the isthmus in order to reinforce the defenders of the city. Kromayer, *Schlachten-Atlas*, col. 53, holds that the attack itself was a feint, intended to produce precisely this result. De Sanctis, *Storia*, iv. 3, p. 62 n. 91, doubts this, on the grounds that the sources, depending heavily on Polybius, could be expected to have recorded such a plan, and that Hasdrubal would not have abandoned the camp unless the city was seriously threatened. On the other hand Scipio's gain was invaluable, in that without it he could not have undertaken his blockade by land. Moreover, it was one thing to break in with a small force at night, quite another to expect to exploit the foothold and to feed in reinforcements and supplies during the following day with the enemy's field army close in the rear. The question affects the standing of Scipio as a general. If De Sanctis is right he undertook an extremely hazardous operation and met with a well-deserved defeat which might have been even more serious. If Kromayer is right, as it is tempting to believe, Scipio successfully carried through a skilful and very profitable manœuvre. Zon. 9. 29 makes the assault sound more elaborate than does App. *Lib.* 117, but also gives the impression that it resulted in the capture of Megara, which is certainly an error, perhaps produced by epitomizing an already abbreviated account.

G. Scipio's sacrifice of the captured Carthaginian equipment to Mars and Minerva, mentioned in App. *Lib.* 133 in connexion with the disposal of spoils, is likely to have been linked with the games referred to in 135 (Paullus' sacrifice seems to have come at the end of his festival at Amphipolis: Livy, 45. 33.

1 f.). There was nothing unorthodox about the sacrifice itself. The custom was certainly ancient and established, and had recently been followed by Mummius in Spain (App. *Iber.* 57). But it is possible that Scipio's choice of deities is a significant echo of Paullus' dedication, which was to Mars, Minerva, Lua mater, and other appropriate deities (Livy, 45. 33. 2). Mars and Minerva do not seem to be specified in the other (admittedly few) known instances of the practice. The usual deity was evidently Volcanus: Livy, 1. 37. 5; 30. 6. 9; 41. 12. 6; Serv. *Aen.* 8. 562. Lua occurs in Livy, 8. 1. 6. On the other hand, Mummius' dedication (and also Sulla's in 86: App. *Mith.* 45) was τοῖς θεοῖς τοῖς ἐνυαλίοις, which could include Mars and Minerva: App. *Iber.* 57.

H. Plin. *Nat. Hist.* 33. 141 contains the statement that Scipio took home from Carthage only 4,370 pounds of silver. The context shows that Pliny was referring to a relatively small amount, so there is no question of the figure being seriously corrupt (though there is always the possibility, but scarcely the probability, that he used a figure already corrupt). Perhaps the Carthaginians traded out much of their silver during the war. On the other hand, App. *Lib.* 135 gives a glowing picture of Scipio's triumph, calling it πολύχρυσος, and an enormous amount of gold had certainly been seized in the temple of Apollo: App. *Lib.* 127. Moreover Polybius, 18. 35. 9, says that Carthage seemed to be the richest city in the world, and 'Plutarch', *Apophth. Scip. Min.* 1, states that of all generals Scipio especially enriched his troops; although both are primarily emphasizing Scipio's abstention from the spoils and thus may have exaggerated the wealth available, it seems obvious that the spoils must have been very considerable and certainly not notoriously meagre.

I. Münzer, *Röm. Adels.*, pp. 212 f., and Scullard, *Roman Politics*, p. 190, believe that in the 180's and 170's the Postumii occupied an independent position in factional politics and were in opposition to the 'Claudian–Fulvian' group which achieved great successes in the early 170's; they see the Postumian consulships of 174 and 173 as a Postumian revival at the expense of the 'Fulvian' group. Against this, however, Briscoe, 'Q. Marcius Philippus', *JRS* 54 (1964), pp. 73 f., argues that the distinction is invalid. His positive evidence for a link between Postumii and Fulvii is not strong. It has three main elements. 1. Both Q. Fulvius Flaccus cos. 237 and Sp. Postumius Albinus cos. 186 had Sulpiciae as their wives, but Briscoe himself admits that this sort of evidence is not decisive. 2. A Fulvius and a L. Postumius were consuls together in 229; the two censors of 174 were a Postumius and a Fulvius, who had been consuls in 180 and 179 respectively, and another Fulvius had been suffect consul in 180; but Briscoe himself, p. 76 and esp. n. 108, emphasizes that this kind of argument is dangerous. 3. Briscoe thinks that there is a link in the pattern of behaviour, in the sense of the '*nova sapientia*', the unprincipled conduct of public affairs, which he believes characterized this group; but it is very doubtful if he is correct in positing this '*nova sapientia*' as the major divisive issue in Roman politics in these years.

Briscoe does draw attention to certain anomalies in the detailed interpretations of Münzer and Scullard, and he rightly rejects one argument which has been used; but it is difficult to agree with his rejection of the most important argument. This is the long period between praetorship and consulship in the careers of the Postumii who were consuls in 174 and 173, having had to wait since 183 and 180 respectively; it looks as if they had been kept out of office by the 'Fulvian' group, which secured five of the six intervening patrician consulships. Briscoe attempts to show that if the Postumii were linked with this group they were not delayed unduly in comparison with other members. In asserting this he suggests that there were special circumstances governing three of the five cases, and he notes that the remaining two had themselves had to wait for a long period: the Manlius who was consul in 179 had been praetor in 188, and the one who was consul in 178 had probably been praetor in 189. But in fact this rather supports the Münzer–Scullard interpretation, since it looks as if the Manlii themselves had been kept out by the successes of others in the 180's, when two of the successful patrician consuls were Postumii, in 186 and 180, who had been praetors in 189 and 185 and who therefore achieved the consulship much more rapidly than the Manlii.

Finally some note should be taken of the position of the Postumii during the war against Perseus, for which short period there are a great many indications of factional alignments and hostilities. The remarkable thing is that the Postumii do not appear at all until 168, not even in 171 when the consul Licinius Crassus chose (Livy, 42. 31. 5) a group of officers who were mostly 'Fulvian'. But in 168 we find three Postumii, two under Paullus, one under Octavius, in positions of responsibility. (Paullus certainly chose his own officers: Livy, 44. 21. 1 f.) The obvious interpretation is that the Postumii were a powerful group in their own right who came to a temporary understanding with Paullus, probably helped him to the consulship, and helped to officer his army. This does not imply a permanent or enduring alliance—such was plainly not the case; but it is very difficult to reconcile with a supposed close association between the Postumii and the 'Fulvian' group.

J. The first two Roman commanders known in the Viriatic war are Vetilius and Plautius. It is now generally accepted that Vetilius was praetor in Ulterior in 147 and Plautius in 146. Simon, *Roms Kriege*, p. 77, would date the outbreak of the actual fighting to 148, a possible but by no means necessary inference from the report that Vetilius took a fresh army to Spain (App. *Iber.* 61). Vetilius' initial success was certainly in 147 (Livy, *Ox Epit.* 51), but Livy recorded his defeat under 146 (*Epit.* 52; Oros. 5. 4. 1 f.), which suggests that it occurred in the early months of the latter year: so Kornemann, *Livius-Epitome*, pp. 96 f. Both Gundel, *RE*, s.v. *Viriatus*, col. 210, and Simon, *Roms Kriege*, pp. 76 f., date the defeat to 147, the former because he finds it difficult to believe that the winter intervened between the success and the defeat, the latter because he believes that in 146 the new praetor Plautius would not have been given fresh troops unless news of the disaster had been received at Rome. But the Livian evidence is hard to explain away, and Simon's attempt to do so, by suggesting that Livy postponed his discussion of Viriatus until he had completed his account of the fall of Carthage, is not convincing; it is contrary to Livy's normal methods, and he did record fighting against the Lusitanians under 147 (*Ox. Epit.* 51).

K. The only indication of the date when Claudius Unimanus was in Spain is in Orosius, 5. 4. 3 f., who places his defeat after that of Plautius. The only indication of rank is that (Victor) *De Vir. Ill.* 71. 1 terms him *imperator*. There is general agreement that the defeat preceded the campaign of the consul of 145, Fabius Maximus Aemilianus, but several suggestions have been put forward as to the post he held. Kornemann, *Livius-Epitome*, p. 98, prefers to assign him to Ulterior in 145, as the immediate predecessor of Fabius, supposing that the consul was sent out only later in the year when news was received of the praetor's defeat. Simon, *Roms Kriege*, pp. 77 f., would place him in Citerior in 145 and similarly supposes that the praetor Laelius was a substitute sent after Claudius' defeat. But much the most attractive hypothesis is that of Mommsen, *Hist. of Rome*, iii, p. 223, that Claudius was praetor in Citerior in 146; this is followed by Schulten, 'Viriatus', *NJA* 39 (1917), p. 220, and De Sanctis, *Storia*, iv. 3, p. 224. (An alternative possibility, which would deny all weight to *imperator* in (Victor) *De Vir. Ill.* 71. 1, is that Claudius was the commander of the 4,000 men sent out by Plautius and virtually wiped out: App. *Iber.* 64.) There is even greater uncertainty about C. Nigidius, mentioned only in (Victor) *De Vir. Ill.* 71. 1 as defeated after Claudius. Mommsen, loc. cit., places him in Citerior in 145, and Simon, op. cit., pp. 78 f., also there but in 144. A better guess is probably that of Kornemann, op. cit., pp. 98 f., that he was the subordinate of Fabius Maximus Aemilianus in 145 (App. *Iber.* 65).

L. There can be little doubt that military affairs in 143 must have had some influence on the election of consuls for 142, but lack of information prevents any rational estimate of that influence.

(i) Since one of the candidates was L. Caecilius Metellus Calvus, the performance of his brother, Metellus Macedonicus, in Hither Spain must have been relevant, but it is difficult to assess how that performance must have seemed in Rome. He had achieved successes, notably the capture of Nertobriga, and also of Centobriga if that was a different town; but Contrebia, still in eastern Celtiberia, did not fall until 142, and only then could he safely commence the wide-ranging operations which brought most of Celtiberia under his control. See esp. Val. Max. 7. 4. 5 (Contrebia, *proconsule*); Livy, *Epit.* 53; Schulten, *Gesch. von Numantia*, pp. 66 f.; Simon, *Roms Kreige*, pp. 103 f.

(ii) In 143 the command in Further Spain was held by a praetor, probably a Quinctius, who won an early victory against Viriatus but subsequently suffered severe reverses and apparently lost the initiative altogether (App. *Iber.* 66, where, however, the imputation of cowardice suggests that there may be hostile distortion. On the chronological problems see Simon, *Roms Kriege*, pp. 80 f., and Astin, 'The Roman Commander', *Historia* 13 (1964), pp. 245 f., and references there). If news of these reverses reached Rome in time they are likely to have influenced the election, but in the absence of more information about the praetor himself and about the candidates in the election further speculation is useless.

(iii) A new Macedonian uprising was quelled by L. Tremellius Scrofa, quaestor under a Licinius Nerva; but its political impact is entirely unknown, and it is not even possible to determine whether it occurred in 143 or 142 (Livy, *Epit.* 53; Varro, *De Re Rust.* 2. 4. 1 f.; Eutrop. 4. 15. Obsequ. 22 may hint at 142).

M. Brunt, 'The Army and the Land', *JRS* 52 (1962), p. 72, holds that Tiberius Gracchus' agrarian scheme appealed mainly to the rural poor and that it was from these rather than from the urban proletariat that he drew most of his support; so also Gabba, *Appiani B.C. Liber Primus*, p. 41. The strongest evidence for Brunt's view is found in two passages of Appian. In *B.C.* 1. 13 Appian says that after the enactment of Tiberius' law the victors returned to the countryside (and that the disgruntled losers remained, making threats against Tiberius; but presumably these are the rich). In *B.C.* 1. 14 Appian states that when the elections approached in 133 Tiberius summoned 'those from the countryside' (τοὺς ἐκ τῶν ἀγρῶν); but since these were occupied with the harvest and could not come, he had recourse to the masses in the city (ἐπὶ τὸν ἐν τῷ ἄστει δῆμον κατέφευγε).

But Appian is not unambiguous on the point. 'Those in the fields' could easily include many city-dwellers who took advantage of the need for much casual labour in the countryside at harvest-time (and the demand could be very great: Cato, *De Agr. Cult.* 144 f.; Frank, *Economic Survey*, i, p. 170); the immense enthusiasm shown for Tiberius at the elections, especially on the last day (pp. 218 and 221), does not suggest a last-minute appeal to a new and hitherto largely indifferent source of support; and, more specifically, in *B.C.* 1. 14 Appian himself indicates that in his canvass Tiberius asserted that it was for the sake of the urban proletariat that he had endangered himself (continuing from κατέφευγε, quoted above: καὶ περιιὼν κατὰ μέρος ἑκάστων ἐδεῖτο δήμαρχον αὐτὸν ἐς τὸ μέλλον ἑλέσθαι, κινδυνεύοντα δι' ἐκείνους). Above all, in *B.C.* 1. 10, where Appian describes the attitudes of the two sides to Tiberius' proposed scheme, the complaints of the rich and the grievances of the poor, he says that while these groups were indulging in mutual recriminations, many other interested persons came in from the countryside and joined each group: in other words, this passage describes what we might reasonably expect, that the urban population was divided on the issue and that each side was supported by large numbers of rural voters.

A fragment of Diodorus, 34/35. 6. 1, which Brunt cites also, describes a great influx of rural voters for the vote on the bill and is important evidence against any suggestion that Tiberius' supporters were mainly urban and not rural, but it is no impediment to believing that they included both the urban and the rural poor. It is not safe to assume that even city-dwellers with no agrarian background would not have been attracted by Tiberius' scheme; in a time of great economic distress, as there is good reason to suppose this was (pp. 166 f.), many of the urban poor may have seen in the prospect of a plot of land their one hope of escape from desperation, and they could all too easily have failed to comprehend or have irrationally minimized the difficulties which would confront them. In any event, at least with respect to the Gracchan period, Brunt probably draws too sharp a distinction between the urban and the rural poor (he does mention, loc. cit., the possibility of rural labourers seeking shelter in Rome and other towns during the winter). With this distinction are associated his doubts about the generally accepted hypothesis of a substantial drift of rural poor into Rome, on which see pp. 165 f., esp. p. 165 n. 4.

N. There is some uncertainty about whether M. Octavius was eager or rather reluctant to exercise his veto against the agrarian bill. Plutarch, *Ti. Grac.* 10. 1 f., reports that he was a friend and companion of Tiberius and that only with difficulty was he persuaded to act, whereas Dio, fgt. 83. 4, says that he intervened willingly διὰ φιλονεικίαν συγγενικήν (almost certainly 'hereditary' and not implying kinship: Earl, 'M. Octavius', *Latomus* 19 (1960), pp. 662 f.). Both passages are somewhat suspect, in that Plutarch is clearly making the most of a dramatic and moralizing account (Octavius putting duty before friendship) which may have been worked up from some very slight association; while Dio's picture of the subsequent struggle manifestly exaggerates the degree of violence and reflects the disorders of a later period. On the whole, inherited *inimicitia* seems the more probable of the two. If there had been anything approaching *amicitia*, it is very hard to believe that Cicero would not have mentioned it in his *De Amicitia*, esp. 37 f. Octavius' inherited links were probably with Scipio Aemilianus (p. 87). A possible occasion for a feud may have arisen out of the murder of Octavius' father when he was in Syria on an embassy in 162, or rather out of the failure of the next embassy, headed by the elder Gracchus, to recommend drastic punitive action (*MRR* i, p. 443). Other refs. to Octavius' veto and to his opposition to Tiberius: App. *B.C.* 1. 12; Cic. *De Leg.* 3. 24; (Victor) *De Vir. Ill.* 64. 4; Flor. 2. 2. 5; Livy, *Epit.* 58; Oros. 5. 8. 3; Vell. 2. 2. 3.

O. Plutarch, *Ti. Grac.* 10. 4 f., reports a number of events between the first and the second assemblies at which Octavius vetoed the agrarian bill. These are omitted by Appian, *B.C.* 1. 12, who passes straight from the first to the second assembly (unless there was some mention of them in the *lacuna* which editors have suspected at this point), but there is no good reason for doubting the occurrence of the main items. Carcopino, *Autour des Gracques*, pp. 16 f., objects especially to the alleged *iustitium* (Plut. *Ti. Grac.* 10. 8; cf. Dio, fgt. 83. 6), but most subsequent writers accept it: cf. esp. Gelzer, *Gnomon* 5 (1929), pp. 649 f.; Last, *JRS* 18 (1928), p. 228; Fraccaro, *Athenaeum* 9 (1931), pp. 304 f. = *Opusc.* ii, pp. 63 f.; Geer, 'Plutarch and Appian', *Studies in Honor of E. K. Rand*, pp. 107 f.; Gabba, *Appiani B.C. Liber Primus*, p. 34. Thomsen, 'Erliess Tiberius Gracchus ein Iustitium?', *C & M* 6 (1944), pp. 60 f., rightly doubting whether a tribune was empowered to proclaim a *iustitium* as such (*contra* Mommsen, *Röm. Staats.* i³, p. 263), suggests that the proclamation was actually made by the consul P. Mucius Scaevola; but it is much more probable that Tiberius used his veto to achieve the same effect: Geer, loc. cit.; Nicolini, *Il Tribunato della Plebe*, pp. 111 f.

Two minor items in this section of Plutarch are very questionable and are generally rejected. The first (10. 4, with ref. back to 9. 2) is that Tiberius abandoned an initial intention to pay compensation to those who surrendered *ager publicus* under the bill. This notion of compensation may have resulted from a misunderstanding of the kind of argument found in App. *B.C.* 1. 11 or of the offer of compensation to Octavius, or from subsequent pro-Gracchan propaganda. It is beyond reasonable doubt that the second item, the story that there was a secret plot to kill Tiberius and that in consequence he carried a weapon hidden beneath his clothing (10. 9), is the product of recrimination and propaganda after the catastrophe.

P. Both App. *B.C.* 1. 12 and Plut. *Ti. Grac.* 11. 2 contain suggestions that at the second assembly at which Octavius vetoed the agrarian bill the Gracchans threatened or contemplated the use of force. The former states that when the proceedings opened Tiberius stationed at hand 'an adequate guard, as though he was about to force Octavius against his will', and the latter that, apparently after the veto had been imposed, Tiberius and his followers could force the issue by means of their superior numbers and were massing together for that purpose. Both versions are allegations of unfulfilled intentions and are highly improbable. In practice Tiberius did not use rioting or violence to secure the passage of his law; moreover such methods would have been in stark contradiction to the legalistic devices which he actually employed. Like the supposed secret plot to assassinate Tiberius (Additional Note O), these allegations are the product of recriminations and propaganda after the catastrophe.

Also patently untrue is Plutarch's assertion (*Ti. Grac.* 11. 1) that on this same occasion the opponents of the bill stole the voting-urns. Voting by ballot was not introduced for legislation until two years later; nor is it convincing to suppose that a later writer has transformed into voting-urns the *sitella* which was certainly used in the procedure (Leonard, *RE*, s.v. *Situlus*, col. 416; cf. esp. Cic. *De Nat. Deor.* 1. 106), for there was no need of such methods so long as Octavius was willing to maintain his veto. The story is an anachronism from the confusion of the last years of the Republic.

Q. App. *B.C.* 1. 12 states that the request that the dispute between Tiberius and Octavius should be referred to the Senate came from οἱ δυνατοί, presumably *principes*, but Plut. *Ti. Grac.* 11. 2 says with more precision that it was made by Μάλλιος καὶ Φούλβιος ἄνδρες ὑπατικοί. The Fulvius is usually thought to be one of the Flacci who were consuls in 135 and 134, but he could have been one of the Nobiliores who were consuls in 159 and 153 (the latter censor as recently as 136). Fraccaro, *Studi*, i, p. 104 n. 4, and Münzer, *RE*, s.v. *Manilius*, no. 12, col. 1138, believe that Μάλλιος is M'. Manilius, cos. 149. They are perhaps influenced by the fact that no Manlius had been consul since T. Torquatus in 165 and A. Torquatus in 164; but it is by no means impossible that one of these was still alive and able to appear as a senior statesman in 133 (T. Torquatus was certainly alive and active in 140: Livy, *Epit.* 54, *Ox. Epit.* 54). Although the consul of 149 is a possibility (cf. Dion. Hal. 11. 44. 2; Münzer, *RE*, s.v. *Manilius*, no. 15), 'Manilius' is usually given correctly or recognizably in the manuscripts of Greek works (e.g. Polyb. 36. 11. 1; App. *Iber.* 56, *Lib.* 75, 97 f. regularly Μανήλιος); and Μάλλιος is a very common Greek version of 'Manlius' (cf. Taylor, *Voting Districts*, p. 228). If 'Manlius' is correct, the way is open for the possibility, surely to be taken seriously, that the appeal was pre-arranged with Tiberius and contrived in order to enable him to demonstrate that before taking really drastic action he had left no conventional method untried.

R. There seems to be only one reported instance of the abrogation of a magistracy prior to 133 (Livy, 22. 25. 10 has no value as evidence; in Livy, 21. 63. 2 *abrogabatur* is inaccurate: Plut. *Marc.* 4. 2 f. and 6. 1; Zon. 8. 20). This is the deposition of L. Tarquinius Collatinus, cos. 509, concerning which the sources differ. It is conceivable, though undemonstrable, that the disagreement is a product of the search for precedents in 133. Cic. *Brut.* 53, *De Off.* 3. 40, and Obsequ. 70 explicitly speak of *abrogatio*, but Livy, 2. 2. 7 f., 4. 15. 4, Dion. Hal. 5. 10. 7–5. 12. 1, Plut. *Pop.* 7. 6, and Zon. 7. 12 all speak of abdication under pressure, although Dion. Hal. states that abrogation was proposed but impeded by Collatinus' veto. The earliest surviving evidence, fgt. 19 of Piso, who wrote in the Gracchan period, is unhelpful. The fragment itself is too brief to show which version Piso gave, and while slight verbal similarities with Livy, 2. 2. 7 suggest the possibility that Livy's version is derived from Piso, Dionysius, whose version differs from Livy's in many respects, is known to have made considerable use of Piso's work. It would be interesting evidence about Piso if it could be shown that his version was *abrogatio* or implied the possibility of *abrogatio*, but (*contra* Broughton, *MRR* i, p. 1) the indecisive evidence points, if at all, the other way.

S. Plutarch, *Ti. Grac.* 11. 4, says unequivocally that the deposition of Octavius from the tribunate was illegal, οὐ νόμιμον οὐδ' ἐπιεικές, but there seems to be no other surviving mention of an explicit prohibition of *abrogatio*. There seems little doubt that Plutarch's statement has a partisan origin and that in reality the legal position was not clear and explicit but sufficiently uncertain to be debatable, so that each side claimed that the law favoured its own position. According to Plutarch himself, *Ti. Grac.* 15, Tiberius delivered a speech in which he argued that the deposition was legally permissible. Fragment 5 of T. Annius Luscus, *ORF*², p. 106, from his speech against Tiberius, seems to be from an argument about *abrogatio*. Octavius himself disputed the validity of his deposition (pp. 208 f.; but an additional complication here is the possibility that he might have tried to use his veto). On the other side, Gaius Gracchus certainly accepted the legality of his brother's action, since he proposed a law concerning persons whose office had been abrogated (Plut. *C. Grac.* 4. 1 f.; cf. Diod. 34/35. 25. 2 = Poseid. fgt. 111 c *FGrH*); and subsequent examples of abrogation show that the precedent of 133 was followed (Mommsen, *Röm. Staats.* i³, p. 630).

T. Although it is often said that Tiberius Gracchus' aristocratic associates began to desert him when he resorted to extreme measures, there is little evidence to support this view and some positive reason to reject it.

(*a*) Appius Claudius did not refuse to serve as one of the agrarian commissioners immediately appointed under Tiberius' law, which it had been possible to enact only by deposing Octavius. Moreover, Dio, fgt. 83. 8 states that Tiberius was planning to have him elected cos. II for 132, which could be a later invention but is quite plausible and in any case suggests that Claudius supported Tiberius to the end (p. 351).

(*b*) In the last hours of Tiberius' life a Fulvius Flaccus, probably Marcus, warned Tiberius of the trend of the arguments in the Senate (p. 221); and it is a near certainty that Marcus was associated with the subsequent attempt of Papirius Carbo and Gaius Gracchus to establish the legitimacy of Tiberius' candidature for a second tribunate (p. 233); cf. also his attack on Nasica (p. 229, but this in itself would not necessarily imply approval of Tiberius' actions).

(*c*) P. Licinius Crassus Mucianus was elected agrarian commissioner in place of Tiberius, which shows that he retained the confidence of the masses and therefore had probably not deserted Tiberius.

(*d*) Cicero, *De Amic.* 37, arguing that friendship does not justify participation in immoral or unpatriotic activities, says that when Tiberius was 'troubling the state' he was abandoned by Q. Tubero and other *amici* of his own age. But Cicero does not specify at what point this occurred; it may refer to the whole of Tiberius' tribunate, including the agrarian bill, since there is no evidence at all that Tubero supported this. Cicero goes on to say (39) that, nevertheless, Tiberius did have followers in C. Carbo, C. Cato, and C. Gracchus, which at first sight might be taken to mean that others deserted him; and since others are known to have supported the agrarian bill, such desertion should have occurred later. But this is an unsafe inference from Cicero, who is hostile to Tiberius and in this context has a special interest in minimizing the support which he enjoyed; it cannot be allowed to outweigh the near certainty that Fulvius supported him even at the end or the probability that Claudius did so. Cicero, with no great precision, has concentrated attention upon a few close friends of Tiberius who were of his own generation.

(e) Cicero twice says, De Domo 91, Pro Planc. 88, that after Tiberius' death P. Mucius Scaevola defended the legality of Nasica's action; but it is very doubtful indeed if this is true (p. 228). Although Mucius did adopt a cautious ambiguity about the legality of what Tiberius was doing on the last day of his life, it is far from certain that this refers to the candidature for a second tribunate rather than to the rumours of disorder which were reaching the Senate (p. 223).

U. There is no mention of an attempt by Octavius to veto the *plebiscitum* which deposed him from the tribunate. Either he made no such attempt, which would imply a general recognition that the veto would not have been valid in this instance, or Tiberius overrode his veto on the basis of some plausible but unrecorded argument that it was not valid. The latter eventuality could have been important for Octavius' refusal to admit that he had been deposed legally. Mommsen, *Röm. Staats.* i³, pp. 286 f. with p. 287 n. 1, suggests that the veto could not be used against tribunician elections (tribunes were required by law to ensure that their successors were appointed: Livy, 3. 55. 14; cf. Bleicken, *Volkstribunat*, p. 76 with n. 2) and that Tiberius argued that the same principle should apply to the deposition. One difficulty in the way of this hypothesis was Fraccaro's contention, 'La procedura del voto', *AAT* 49 (1913–14), pp. 600 f. = *Opusc.* ii, pp. 235 f., that, while the tribes voted successively for legislative and judicial decisions, they voted simultaneously in the electoral procedure. The natural inference from both Appian and Plutarch is that the voting concerning Octavius was successive, though Geer, 'Plutarch and Appian', *Studies in Honor of E. K. Rand*, p. 109, rightly observes that this is not certain and that the references might be to successive reporting of votes which had been cast simultaneously. However, Hall, 'Voting Procedure', *Historia* 13 (1964), pp. 288 f., esp. pp. 292 f., has made a very plausible case for the hypothesis that successive voting was the original practice in elections as well and that this was still the case in 133. But if this removes one objection to Mommsen's explanation, there remains the fact that both Plutarch (*Ti. Grac.* 12. 1, 5: νόμος) and the *Epitome* of Livy, (58: *potestatem lege lata abrogavit*) speak of the proposal as a law. Cf. Fraccaro, *Studi*, i, p. 112 n. 2 and pp. 113 f.

V. Tiberius Gracchus' law concerning the legacy of Attalus is omitted by Appian but reported by Plutarch with an entirely reasonable explanation of its purpose. Livy, *Epit.* 58 patently reflects a hostile distortion when it indicates that, because there proved (already!) to be insufficient land to carry out the resettlement programme, the money was to be distributed to pacify those who had been disappointed in their avaricious hopes. This becomes even more hostile in the abbreviated versions of Oros. 5. 8. 4 and (Victor) *De Vir. Ill.* 64. 5, who speak of a distribution of the money to the people with no reference at all to the agrarian scheme; cf. also Val. Max. 3. 2. 17: *profusissimis largitionibus favore populi occupato.* The attempt of Carcopino, *Autour des Gracques*, pp. 33 f., to disprove the story of the law on chronological grounds has been rejected almost universally: see esp. Fraccaro, *Athenaeum* 9 (1931), p. 306 = *Opusc.* ii, p. 65.

W. The additional legislation which Tiberius Gracchus is alleged to have proposed during his canvass for a second tribunate is mentioned in Plut. *Ti. Grac.* 16. 1 and Dio, fgt. 83. 7 f. The details, though sometimes accepted, are suspect and often rejected as largely inappropriate and an anticipation of the proposals of Gaius Gracchus: Gabba, *Appiani B.C. Liber Primus*, p. 44; cf. Taylor, 'Tiberius Gracchus' Last Assembly', *Athenaeum* 41 (1963), p. 55 n. 8; Earl, *Tiberius Gracchus*, pp. 113 f.; but Scullard, in Marsh, *Hist. of the Roman World*[2], p. 407, rightly notes the plausibility of the general point that Tiberius announced new proposals. Of those reported, much the most convincing is the suggested curtailment of military service. Dio adds that Tiberius also planned a tribunate for his brother Gaius and a second consulship for Appius Claudius. Since these are unfulfilled intentions, recorded in only this source, which seems to reflect a tradition especially hostile to Tiberius, they cannot be treated as unquestionably reliable. This is particularly the case with regard to Gaius, who was still very young (though he seems to have been back in Rome by the time the elections were held: Plut. *Ti. Grac.* 20. 4). On the other hand, Dio could have preserved an authentic detail, especially in respect of Claudius. It is uncertain whether the prohibition on second consulships had been restored after Scipio's election in 135, but in any event what had been done then for Scipio might be done again for Claudius. A second consulship in 132 would observe the ten-year rule, and was an ambition which would be entirely intelligible in view of Scipio's achievement. Cf. Earl, *Tiberius Gracchus*, pp. 112 f., though he perhaps accepts the conclusion too confidently.

X. There is some disagreement about the legal conditions relating to *continuatio* of the tribunate in 133. Earl, *Tiberius Gracchus*, pp. 103 f., cf. p. 119 n. 1, contends that Tiberius' attempt to secure re-election, though gravely in conflict with the *mos maiorum*, was unambiguously legal. His main argument is that if there had been a law against it, this would have left some trace in our tradition. But Appian, *B.C.* 1. 14, explicitly says that Tiberius' opponents did object that it was illegal, and it is impossible to account for Carbo's *rogatio* of 131, *ut eundem tribunum pleb., quotiens vellet, creare liceret* (pp. 232 f.), unless the legal position was at least ambiguous. (Also Cic. *In Cat.* 4. 4 strongly suggests that in Cicero's view re-election would have been illegal.) On the other side, Taylor, 'Tiberius

Gracchus' Last Assembly', *Athenaeum* 41 (1963), pp. 51 f., argues that *continuatio* of the tribunate was prohibited explicitly by law (so also Mommsen, *Röm. Staats.* i³, p. 523, who further contends that this had always been the case; but Dio, fgt. 22 is not good evidence), and that Tiberius' last assembly was not electoral but legislative, to vote upon a *rogatio* which would legalize his candidature. If this were the case, Chapter XVI of this study would require modification on a few points but its general interpretation of events would not be affected substantially. (With regard to its contention that Tiberius' thought was not fundamentally revolutionary, Taylor's theory implies a very close parallel indeed between Tiberius' plan and the means by which Scipio Aemilianus had achieved his two consulships.) However, the arguments adduced by Taylor do not seem sufficient to refute Appian's clear indications that the assembly was electoral (*B.C.* 1. 14). The strongest of these arguments, based on the site of the assembly and the procedure adopted at it, lose much of their force in the light of Hall's plausible case that in 133 the tribes may still have been voting successively in elections: 'Voting Procedure', *Historia* 13 (1964), pp. 288 f., esp. pp. 292 f. The statements of App. *B.C.* 1. 2, Obsequ. 27a, and Ampel. 26. 1, cf. 19. 3, that Tiberius was killed while carrying laws are to be understood as brief general references to the whole tribunate, as Ampelius' references to agrarian legislation illustrate. The most probable interpretation of the situation in 133 remains that of Meyer, *Untersuch. zur Gesch. der Gracchen*, p. 392 with n. 3, that the legal position was controversial and is likely to have turned upon the question of whether the tribunate came within the terms of the rule applied to magistracies. Fraccaro, *Studi*, i, p. 148 n. 4, admits the possibility of this but surprisingly thinks that Tiberius would have shunned the argument that the tribunate was not a magistracy, on the ground that this would have debased the tribunate. Instead he suggests that Tiberius relied upon the argument of popular sovereignty used to support Scipio's election to the consulship of 147 (App. *Lib.* 112; p. 67); but if this were the case we should expect a *rogatio*, precisely as Taylor suggests.

Y. The proceedings at the assembly on the penultimate day of Tiberius Gracchus' life are described by Plutarch, *Ti. Grac.* 16. 2, as follows: 'When, as the vote was being taken, they (the Gracchans) saw that their opponents were winning, they resorted to abuse of their fellow-tribunes, and so protracted the time; then they dissolved the assembly, instructing it to meet on the following day. Then Tiberius went to the Forum. . . .' The fundamental differences between this and Appian's account, *B.C.* 1. 14, are (*a*) that the one implies that the initial voting was going against Tiberius, the other that it favoured him, and (*b*) that in Plutarch the direct motive for the adjournment is the adverse popular vote, whereas in Appian it is the adverse legal tangle which developed. For several reasons Appian's version seems likely to be nearer the truth, even though it contains some obscurities.

(1) The circumstantial detail in Appian's account seems both plausible and insufficiently dramatic to be the product of fiction.

(2) Appian's version is not positively pro-Gracchan: it portrays Tiberius' opponents as getting the best of the legal arguments and in no way represents them as acting improperly or illegally. Nevertheless it is much less obviously anti-Gracchan than Plutarch's account, which therefore seems to embody more extreme tendentiousness.

(3) Plutarch does not give a clear account of the dispute among the tribunes or of how this delayed the proceedings; since abuse (βλασφημία) in itself would scarcely have had this result, the dispute must have involved legal technicalities. Appian, on the other hand, gives an intelligible explanation involving just such technicalities.

(4) Appian's account of Mucius (Appian names him Mummius; see p. 211 n. 1) attempting to take over the presidency from Rubrius finds some confirmation in Plutarch's statement (18. 1) that it was Mucius who attempted to conduct the resumed assembly on the next day. Fraccaro, Studi I pp. 164 f., considering it too remarkable a coincidence that sortition should have given the presidency to this friend of Tiberius, suggests that Mucius took over the presidency only after the hostile tribunes had been driven from the assembly. But there is no reason why he should not have attempted to resume it from the beginning, thus taking up the dispute precisely where, according to Appian, it had been left on the previous day.

Z. According to Plutarch, *Ti. Grac.* 19. 2 f., Nasica's demand that the consul should take action against Tiberius Gracchus was prompted by reports that the latter was asking that he should be given a diadem, reports which arose from a misunderstanding of his gesture of putting his hand to his head. It is just possible that in the heat of the moment this was used, as a deliberate lie, to stir up passions in the Senate, but if so it is clear that even at the time the consul Scaevola did not believe it and it is not likely that many others would have done so. The notion that Tiberius might actually have desired the regalia of monarchy was evidently regarded as too far-fetched even to find an enduring place in the spate of propaganda which followed his death (p. 228), for although Plutarch's story is repeated in (Victor) *De Vir. Ill.* 64. 6 f. and Flor. 2. 2. 7, it is always in the form that the gesture was misinterpreted; no source alleges that Tiberius actually made such a request. All the sources quoted above state that the gesture was really an attempt by Tiberius to indicate that his safety was endangered; there is little doubt that it is this same gesture which in App. *B.C.* 1. 15 is interpreted as a pre-arranged signal to unleash violence.

ZA. The inscription *ILS* 23 reads as follows:

Viam fecei ab Regio ad Capuam, et in ea via ponteis omneis, miliarios, tabelarios- que poseivei. (A list of distances intervenes.) *Et eidem praetor in Sicilia fugiteivos*

Italicorum conquaeisivi, redideique homines DCCCCXVII. Eidemque primus fecei, ut de agro poplico aratoribus cederent paastores. Forum aedisque poplicas heic fecei.

The author of this inscription was for long believed to be P. Popillius Laenas, cos. 132 (Mommsen, *CIL* i². 2, pp. 509 f.), and the penultimate sentence has often been linked with the Gracchan agrarian programme. If this were correct, presumably it should be interpreted as an attempt to project a favourable image of concern about agrarian problems in order to palliate unfavourable reaction to the attacks on the Gracchans themselves. But even if the author is the consul of 132, such an interpretation meets with several difficulties, not the least the word *primus*, which even in a tendentious claim seems extraordinary in the context of 132. More probably the sentence refers either to local actions to assist the inhabitants of the Forum which this official established, or, like the preceding sentence, to the same man's activities in Sicily (cf. esp. Fraccaro, *Athenaeum* 9 (1931), pp. 294 f. = *Opusc.* ii, pp. 55 f.; Burdese, *Studi sull'ager publicus*, pp. 99 f.). In either case his chief concern may have been the reduction of brigandage. Furthermore, in recent years it has been argued that the road mentioned in the inscription was a Via Annia, not a Via Popillia, and hence that the author of the inscription was an Annius, not a Popillius (Bracco, 'L'*elogium* di Polla', *RAAN* 29 (1954), pp. 5 f.; Wiseman, '*Viae Anniae*', *PBSR* 32 (1964), pp. 21 f., esp. pp. 30 f., and bibliography cited there). These arguments are weighty, even though some uncertainties persist. In consequence, whether the road-builder was T. Annius Luscus cos. 153 (so Bracco), or T. Annius Rufus cos. 128, or the latter in 131, active in Italy while praetor in Sicily (so Wiseman, but he recognizes that there are serious difficulties about this, op. cit., esp. p. 33 n. 57), there is even less reason to suppose that his activity has any direct connexion with the Gracchan episode.

ZB. Tribunes were admitted to the Senate automatically as the result of a *lex Atinia*: Gell. 14. 8. 2, *Nam et tribunis, inquit* (sc. Ateius Capito), *plebis senatus habendi ius erat, quamquam senatores non essent ante Atinium plebiscitum.* There is no other reference to this plebiscite, which cannot be dated securely. There has been much support for the opinion of Mommsen, *Röm. Staats.* iii, pp. 858 and 862, that a date after 123 is required by the wording of the *Lex Acilia Repetundarum, CIL* i². 2. 583, esp. xiii, xvi, and xxii, cf. the *Lex Latina Tabulae Bantinae, CIL* i². 2. 582. 7 f.; but an attractive alternative explanation of these passages by Tibiletti, 'Le Leggi *de iudiciis repetundarum*', *Athenaeum* 31 (1953), pp. 68 f., based on para. 4 (lines 23 f.) of the *Lex Latina*, would remove this *terminus post quem*: Gabba, 'Note appianee', *Athenaeum* 33 (1955), pp. 220 f. Rossbach attempts to restore a reference to the *lex Atinia* under the year 149 in Livy, *Ox. Epit.* 50, line 109, but this is very tenuous. It is a remarkable coincidence that Atinius is the name of the tribune who in 131 went to extraordinary lengths when excluded from the Senate by Metellus Macedonicus, and it is hard to believe that there is no connexion at all between the law and these events. It is possible that

Metellus was refusing to recognize the validity of the *lex Atinia*, initiated by this tribune or by an earlier member of the family. Alternatively Atinius may have been attempting to assert the principle that tribunes should become members of the Senate, and the *lex Atinia* itself, whether introduced by this man or by a later member of his family, may have been introduced in consequence of Metellus' opposition.

ZC. One of the apparent attractions of interpretations of Scipio as an unwilling tool in the destruction of Carthage is that Polybius, in 6. 57, is often thought to take a most funereal view of the inevitable consequences of overcoming all external enemies: the mixed constitution would decline and collapse. But it should be noticed not only that 6. 57 itself envisages a long period of prosperity for the mixed constitution before the decline sets in, but that in an earlier chapter, 6. 18, Polybius actually claims as one of the great merits of the mixed constitution that it is self-correcting in respect of the corrupting tendencies consequent upon freedom from external menace (noted by Walbank, 'Polybius and the Roman State', *GRBS* 5 (1964), p. 254). In other words, even when there is no external menace, he positively envisages a long period of success and stability. He believes that this must end eventually, but only because he believes that all things must inevitably perish. It is because of this belief that all things must perish that in 6. 57 he rounds off his exposition with an explanation of how this exceptional stability will eventually break down; but the true emphasis of his thought seems to be not on this ultimate breakdown but on the strength and potential longevity of the mixed constitution.

The positive emphasis of Book 6 has been recognized by Brink and Walbank in their article entitled 'The Construction of the Sixth Book of Polybius', *CQ*, N.S. 4 (1954), esp. pp. 104 f.; cf. also Walbank, 'Polybius and the Roman State', *GRBS* 5 (1964), pp. 239 f., esp. pp. 252 f. But one statement in the first of these articles is perhaps overcautious: 'Although it is clear that at the time when he wrote Book 6 Polybius believed the μικτή to be endangered, there are no grounds for assuming that he also believed that the process of disintegration had already begun.' The query concerns the use of the word 'endangered'. This is acceptable in so far as it means that, since Polybius recognized that Rome had reached the epoch of the δυναστεία ἀδήριτος, he necessarily thought that the next change would be the beginning of disintegration; but 'endangered' is unfortunate in so far as it seems to suggest that he thought disintegration was liable to begin at any moment, that it could be seen to be threatening. It is at best uncertain whether he thought this when he subsequently wrote in 31. 25 of growing extravagance and immorality after the conquest of Macedon: it is a mistake to overrate the consistency of his thinking or to underrate his immediate interest in 31. 25, which is to emphasize the virtues of Scipio Aemilianus. What is clear is that when Polybius wrote Book 6, so far from hinting at imminent decline, he envisaged a long period of prosperity during which the mechanics of the μικτή, while certainly not guaranteeing permanence in the sense of eternity, would not merely 'ensure political success so long as the μικτή lasts' (so Brink and Walbank), but would ensure the lengthy preservation of the μικτή itself. Therefore it cannot easily be supposed that Polybius is likely to have focused Scipio's thoughts on the process of decline; if his theorizing had any influence at all on Scipio's outlook, it is more likely to have encouraged complacency about the merits and longevity of the existing order of things.

STEMMA I. THE FAMILY OF AEMILIUS PAULLUS

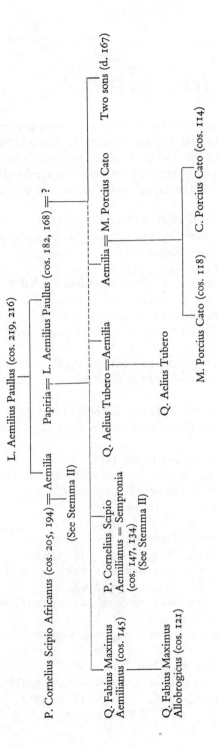

STEMMA II. THE FAMILY OF SCIPIO AFRICANUS

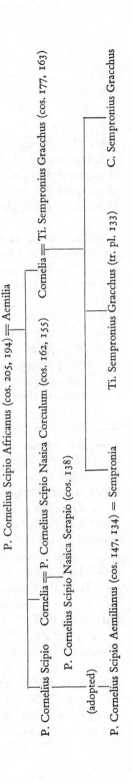

BIBLIOGRAPHY

THIS bibliography includes some works which are not cited directly in the text or notes although they have been consulted and are directly relevant; but also, in an attempt to preserve the usefulness of the bibliography against the threat of excessive size, it omits a number of items which have been cited only once or twice, as well as the works of reference listed under 'Abbreviations' (p. xiii).

ADCOCK, F. E. 'Delenda est Carthago', *CHJ* 8 (1944–6), pp. 117 f.

AFZELIUS, A. *Die römische Kriegsmacht während der Auseinandersetzung mit den hellenistischen Großmächten.* Copenhagen, 1944.

ARNOLD, E. V. *Roman Stoicism.* Cambridge, 1911.

ASTIN, A. E. *The Lex Annalis Before Sulla.* Collection Latomus XXXII. Brussels, 1958 (= *Latomus* 16 (1957), pp. 588 f., and 17 (1958), pp. 49 f.).

—— 'Scipio Aemilianus and Cato Censorius', *Latomus* 15 (1956), pp. 159 f.

—— 'Diodorus and the Date of the Embassy to the East of Scipio Aemilianus', *CPh* 54 (1959), pp. 221 f.

—— '*Dicta Scipionis* of 131 B.C.', *CQ*, N.S. 10 (1960), pp. 135 f.

—— 'Water to the Capitol: a Note on Frontinus *De Aquis* I. 7. 5', *Latomus* 20 (1961), pp. 541 f.

—— '*Professio* in the Abortive Election of 184 B.C.', *Historia* 11 (1962), pp. 252 f.

—— 'The Roman Commander in *Hispania Ulterior* in 142 B.C.', *Historia* 13 (1964), pp. 245 f.

—— 'Leges Aelia et Fufia', *Latomus* 23 (1964), pp. 421 f.

AYMARD, A. 'Deux anecdotes sur Scipion Émilien', *Mélanges de la société toulousaine d'études classiques*, ii, Toulouse, 1946, pp. 101 f.

BADIAN, E. *Foreign Clientelae (264–70 B.C.).* Oxford, 1958.

—— *Studies in Greek and Roman History.* Oxford, 1964.

—— 'Caepio and Norbanus', *Historia* 6 (1957), pp. 318 f.

—— 'Mam. Scaurus Cites Precedent', *CR*, N.S. 8 (1958), pp. 216 f.

—— 'From the Gracchi to Sulla (1940–59)', *Historia* 11 (1962), pp. 197 f.

—— Review of Malcovati, *ORF²*, *JRS* 46 (1956), pp. 218 f.

BALSDON, J. P. V. D. 'Some Questions about Historical Writing in the Second Century B.C.', *CQ*, N.S. 3 (1953), pp. 158 f.

BARADEZ, J. 'Nouvelles Recherches sur les ports antiques de Carthage', *Karthago* 9 (1958), pp. 45 f.

BARDON, H. *La Littérature latine inconnue*, i. Paris, 1952.

BELOCH, K. J. *Die Bevölkerung der griechisch-römischen Welt.* Leipzig, 1886.

—— 'Die Bevölkerung Italiens im Altertum', *Klio* 3 (1903), pp. 471 f.

BERGER, A. 'Note on Gellius, *N.A.*, I, 6', *AJPh* 67 (1946), pp. 320 f.

BEVAN, E. R. *The House of Seleucus*, 2 vols. London, 1902.

BILIŃSKI, B. 'De Capitolii loco, quo Tiberius Gracchus occisus est, observationes topographicae', *Meander* 15 (1960), pp. 417 f. (in Polish, résumé in Latin, p. 496).

BILZ, K. *Die Politik des P. Cornelius Scipio Aemilianus.* Stuttgart, 1935.

BLÁZQUEZ, J. M. 'El Impacto de la Conquista de Hispania en Roma (154–83 a.C.)', *Klio* 41 (1963), pp. 168 f.

BLEICKEN, J. *Das Volkstribunat der klassischen Republik.* Munich, 1955.

BOREN, H. C. 'Numismatic Light on the Gracchan Crisis', *AJPh* 79 (1958), pp. 140 f.

—— 'The Urban Side of the Gracchan Economic Crisis', *AHR* 63 (1958), pp. 890 f.

—— 'Tiberius Gracchus: The Opposition View', *AJPh* 82 (1961), pp. 358 f.

BOUCHÉ-LECLERCQ, A. *Histoire des Séleucides*, 2 vols. Paris, 1913–14.

BOURNE, F. C. 'The Roman Republican Census and Census Statistics', *CW* 45 (1952), pp. 129 f.

BRINK, C. O. and WALBANK, F. W. 'The Construction of the Sixth Book of Polybius', *CQ*, n.s. 4 (1954), pp. 97 f.

BRISCOE, J. 'Q. Marcius Philippus and *Nova Sapientia*', *JRS* 54 (1964), pp. 66 f.

BROWN, R. M. *A Study of the Scipionic Circle.* Iowa, 1934.

BROWN, T. S. 'Greek Influence on Tiberius Gracchus', *CJ* 42 (1946–7), pp. 471 f.

BRUNT, P. A. 'The Army and the Land in the Roman Revolution', *JRS* 52 (1962), pp. 69 f.

VAN DEN BRUWAENE, M. *L'Influence culturelle du cercle de Scipion Émilien.* Schaerbeck, 1938.

—— 'L'Opposition à Scipion Émilien après la mort de Tiberius Gracchus', *Phoibos* 5 (1950–1), pp. 229 f.

BÜCHNER, K. *Römische Literaturgeschichte.* Stuttgart, 1957.

—— 'Humanum und humanitas in der römischen Welt', *Studium Generale* 14 (1961), pp. 636 f.

—— and HOFMANN, J. B. *Lateinische Literatur und Sprache in der Forschung seit 1937. Wissenschaftliche Forschungsberichte*, 6. Bern, 1951.

BÜTTNER, R. *Der jüngere Scipio.* Gütersloh, 1897.

BURDESE, A. *Studi sull'ager publicus.* Turin, 1952.

CALVERT, R. L. 'M. Claudius Marcellus cos. II 155 B.C.', *Athenaeum* 39 (1961), pp. 11 f.

CAPELLE, W. 'Griechische Ethik und römischer Imperialismus', *Klio* 25 (1932), pp. 86 f.

CAPOZZA, M. 'Le Rivolte servili di Sicilia nel quadro della politica agraria romana', *AIV* 95 (1957), pp. 79 f.

CARCOPINO, J. *Autour des Gracques.* Paris, 1928.

—— and BLOCH, G. *Histoire romaine*, ii, pt. 1: *Des Gracques à Sulla.* Paris, 1935.

CARDINALI, G. *Studi graccani.* Genoa, 1912.

CARNEY, T. F. 'Rome in the Gracchan Age', *Theoria* 15 (1960), pp. 38 f.

CAVAIGNAC, E. 'A propos des monnaies de Tryphon. L'ambassade de Scipion Émilien', *RN* 13 (1951), pp. 131 f.

CIACERI, E. *Processi politici e relazioni internazionali*. Rome, 1918.

CICHORIUS, C. *Untersuchungen zu Lucilius*. Berlin, 1908.

—— 'Panaitios und die attische Stoikerinschrift', *RhM* 63 (1908), pp. 197 f.

CLARKE, M. L. *The Roman Mind*. London, 1956.

CRAMER, F. H. *Astrology in Roman Law and Politics*. Philadelphia, 1954.

—— 'Expulsion of Astrologers from Ancient Rome', *C & M* 12 (1951), pp. 9 f.

DEGRASSI, A. *Inscriptiones Italiae*, xiii. 1: *Fasti Consulares et Triumphales*; xiii. 3: *Elogia*. Rome, 1947 and 1937.

—— *Inscriptiones Latinae Liberae Rei Publicae*, i. Florence, 1957.

DE SANCTIS, G. *Storia dei Romani*, 4 vols. Turin and Florence, 1907–64.

DUDLEY, D. R. 'Blossius of Cumae', *JRS* 31 (1941), pp. 94 f.

EARL, D. C. *Tiberius Gracchus. A Study in Politics*. Collection Latomus LXVI. Brussels, 1963.

—— 'Calpurnii Pisones in the Second Century B.C.', *Athenaeum* 38 (1960), pp. 283 f.

—— 'M. Octavius, trib. pleb. 133 B.C., and his successor', *Latomus* 19 (1960), pp. 657 f.

—— 'Terence and Roman Politics', *Historia* 11 (1962), pp. 469 f.

EHRHARDT, A. A. T. 'Imperium und Humanitas. Grundlagen des römischen Imperialismus', *Studium Generale* 14 (1961), pp. 646 f.

FERGUSON, W. S. 'The Lex Calpurnia of 149 B.C.', *JRS* 11 (1921), pp. 86 f.

FORREST, W. G. G. and STINTON, T. C. W. 'The First Sicilian Slave War', *P & P* 22 (1962), pp. 87 f.

FRACCARO, P. *Studi sull'età dei Gracchi*, i: *La tradizione storica sulla rivoluzione graccana*. Città di Castello, 1914.

—— *Opuscula*, 3 vols. Pavia, 1956–7.

—— 'Sui Fannii dell'età graccana', *RAL* 19 (1910), pp. 656 f. (= *Opusc.* ii, pp. 103 f.).

—— 'Oratori ed orazioni dell'età dei Gracchi' (also with the general heading 'Studi sull'età dei Gracchi', i), *Studi storici per l'Antichità classica* 5 (1912), pp. 317 f. and 6 (1913), pp. 42 f.

—— 'La procedura del voto nei comizi tributi romani', *AAT* 49 (1913–14), pp. 600 f. (= *Opusc.* ii, pp. 235 f.).

—— 'Ancora sulla questione dei Fannii', *Athenaeum* 4 (1926), pp. 153 f. (= *Opusc.* ii, pp. 119 f.).

—— 'Due recenti libri sui Gracchi' (reviews of Taeger, *Tiberius Gracchus*, and Carcopino, *Autour des Gracques*), *Athenaeum* 9 (1931), pp. 291 f. (= *Opusc.* ii, pp. 53 f.).

—— 'Assegnazioni agrarie e censimenti romani', *Scritti in onore di Contardo Ferrini* (Milan, 1947), i, pp. 262 f. (= *Opusc.* ii, pp. 87 f.).

FRANK, T. *Roman Imperialism*. New York, 1914.
—— *An Economic Survey of Ancient Rome*, i: *Rome and Italy of the Republic*. Baltimore, 1933.
FRIEDLÄNDER, P. 'Socrates Enters Rome', *AJPh* 66 (1945), pp. 337 f.
VON FRITZ, K. *The Theory of the Mixed Constitution in Antiquity*. New York, 1954.
GABBA, E. *Appiani Bellorum Civilium Liber Primus*. Florence, 1958.
—— 'Le origini dell'esercito professionale in Roma: i proletari e la riforma di Mario', *Athenaeum* 27 (1949), pp. 173 f.
—— 'Ancora sulle cifre dei censimenti', *Athenaeum* 30 (1952), pp. 161 f.
—— 'Note appianee', *Athenaeum* 33 (1955), pp. 218 f.
GEER, R. M. 'Plutarch and Appian on Tiberius Gracchus', *Classical and Mediaeval Studies in Honor of E. K. Rand* (New York, 1938; ed. L. W. Jones), pp. 105 f.
—— 'Notes on the Land Law of Tiberius Gracchus', *TAPhA* 70 (1939), pp. 30 f.
GELZER, M. *Die Nobilität der römischen Republik*. Leipzig–Berlin, 1912 (= *Kleine Schriften*, i, pp. 17 f.).
—— *Vom Römischen Staat*, 2 vols. Leipzig, 1943.
—— *Über die Arbeitsweise des Polybios*. Heidelberg, 1956 (= *Kleine Schriften*, iii, pp. 161 f.).
—— *Kleine Schriften*, 3 vols. Wiesbaden, 1962–4.
—— 'Nasicas Widerspruch gegen die Zerstörung Karthagos', *Philologus* 86 (1931), pp. 261 f. (= *Vom Röm. Staat*, i, pp. 78 f. = *Kleine Schriften*, ii, pp. 39 f.).
—— 'Der Rassengegensatz als geschichtlicher Faktor beim Ausbruch der römisch-karthagischen Kriege', *Rom und Karthago* (Leipzig, 1943; ed. J. Vogt), pp. 178 f. (= *Vom Röm. Staat*, i, pp. 49 f.).
—— Review of Taeger, *Tiberius Gracchus*, *Gnomon* 5 (1929), pp. 296 f. (= *Kleine Schriften*, ii, pp. 73 f.).
—— Review of Carcopino, *Autour des Gracques*, *Gnomon* 5 (1929), pp. 648 f.
GREEN, P. 'The First Sicilian Slave War', *P & P* 20 (1961), pp. 10 f. Cf. additional note in *P & P* 22 (1962), pp. 92 f.
GREENIDGE, A. H. J. *History of Rome*, i. London, 1904.
—— and CLAY, A. M. *Sources for Roman History, 133–70 B.C.²*, revised by E. W. Gray. Oxford, 1960.
GRENFELL, B. P. and HUNT, A. S. *Oxyrhynchus Papyri*, iv (contains no. 668, Livy, *Ox. Epit.*, with commentary). London, 1904.
GSELL, S. *Histoire ancienne de l'Afrique du Nord*, iii and vii. Paris, 1918 and 1928.
HALL, U. 'Voting Procedure in Roman Assemblies', *Historia* 13 (1964), pp. 267 f.
HAMMOND, M. 'Ancient Imperialism: Contemporary Justifications', *HSPh* 58–59 (1948), pp. 105 f.
HANSEN, E. V. *The Attalids of Pergamon*. New York, 1947.
HARDY, E. G. *Six Roman Laws*. Oxford, 1911.
HEITLAND, W. E. *The Roman Republic*, 3 vols. Cambridge, 1909.
HERBERT, K. 'The Identity of Plutarch's Lost *Scipio*', *AJPh* 78 (1957), pp. 83 f.

HERZOG, E. 'Die Bürgerzahlen im römischen Census vom Jahr d. St. 415 bis zum Jahr 640', *Commentationes Philologae in Hon. Th. Mommseni*, Berlin, 1877, pp. 124 f.

HEUSS, A. *Die völkerrechtlichen Grundlagen der römischen Außenpolitik in republikanischer Zeit*. *Klio*, Beiheft 31. Leipzig, 1933.

HILTBRUNNER, O. 'Dicta Scipionis', *Thesaurismata: Festschrift für Ida Kapp*, Munich, 1954, pp. 49 f.

HOFFMANN, W. 'Die römische Politik des 2. Jahrhunderts und das Ende Karthagos', *Historia* 9 (1960), pp. 309 f.

JONES, A. H. M. 'De Tribunis Plebis Reficiendis', *PCPhS*, N.S. 6 (1960), pp. 35 f.

KAERST, J. 'Scipio Aemilianus, die Stoa und der Prinzipat', *NJP* 5 (1929), pp. 653 f.

KAHRSTEDT, U. *Geschichte der Karthager von 218–146* (vol. iii of O. Meltzer, *Geschichte der Karthager*). Berlin, 1913.

KATZ, S. 'The Gracchi: an Essay in Interpretation', *CJ* 38 (1942), pp. 65 f.

KIENAST, D. *Cato der Zensor*. Heidelberg, 1954.

KNIBBE, D. 'Die Gesandtschaftsreise des jüngeren Scipio Africanus im Jahre 140 v. Chr.: ein Höhepunkt der Weltreichspolitik Roms im 2. Jahrhundert', *JÖAI* 45 (1960), pp. 35 f.

KONTCHALOVSKY, D. 'Recherches sur l'histoire du mouvement agraire des Gracques', *RH* 153 (1926), pp. 161 f.

KORNEMANN, E. *Die neue Livius-Epitome aus Oxyrhynchus*. *Klio*, Beiheft 2. Leipzig, 1904.

KROMAYER, J. and VEITH, G. *Antike Schlachtfelder*, iii. Berlin, 1912.

—— *Schlachten-Atlas zur antiken Kriegsgeschichte*. Leipzig, 1922–9.

LINCKE, E. *P. Cornelius Scipio Aemilianus*. Dresden, 1898.

McDONALD, A. H. 'The History of Rome and Italy in the Second Century B.C.', *CHJ* 6 (1939), pp. 124 f.

McSHANE, R. B. *The Foreign Policy of the Attalids of Pergamum*. Illinois, 1964.

MAGIE, D. *Roman Rule in Asia Minor*, 2 vols. Princeton, 1950.

MARQUARDT, J. *Römische Staatsverwaltung*, iii². Leipzig, 1885.

MARSH, F. B. *A History of the Roman World, 146–30 B.C.²*, revised by H. H. Scullard. London, 1953.

MARX, F. *C. Lucilii Carminum Reliquiae*, 2 vols. Leipzig, 1904–5.

—— 'Animadversiones criticae in Scipionis Aemiliani historiam et C. Gracchi orationem adversus Scipionem', *RhM* 39 (1884), pp. 65 f.

MEYER, E. 'Untersuchungen zur Geschichte der Gracchen', *Kleine Schriften*, i² (Halle, 1924), pp. 363 f. (= pp. 381 f. of the first edition, Halle, 1910).

MOMMSEN, T. *Römische Forschungen*, 2 vols. Berlin, 1864–79.

—— *Römisches Staatsrecht*, 3 vols. Leipzig, 1887–8.

—— *The History of Rome*, English translation by W. P. Dickson². London, 1913.

MORITZ, L. A. *Humanitas*. Cardiff, 1962.

Münzer, F. *Römische Adelsparteien und Adelsfamilien*. Stuttgart, 1920.
—— 'Anmerkungen zur neuen Livius-epitome', *Klio* 5 (1905), pp. 135 f.
—— 'Die Fanniusfrage', *Hermes* 55 (1920), pp. 427 f.
—— 'Das Konsulpaar von 139 v. Chr.', *Klio* 24 (1931), pp. 333 f.
Niccolini, G. *I fasti dei tribuni della plebe*. Milan, 1934.
Nissen, H. *Italische Landeskunde*, 2 vols. Berlin, 1883–1902.
—— 'Der caudinische Friede', *RhM* 25 (1870), pp. 1 f.
Pascal, C. *Studi romani*. Fasc. 4: 'Il partito dei Gracchi e Scipione Emiliano'. Turin, 1896.
Philippson, R. 'Panaetiana', *RhM* 78 (1929), pp. 337 f.
Pohlenz, M. *Antikes Führertum. Cicero De Officiis und das Lebensideal des Panaitios*. Leipzig–Berlin, 1934.
—— *Die Stoa*, 2 vols. Göttingen, 1948–9.
Rambaud, M. *Cicéron et l'histoire romaine*. Paris, 1953.
Rathke, G. *De Romanorum Bellis Servilibus*. Berlin, 1904.
Reitzenstein, R. 'Scipio Aemilianus und die stoische Rhetorik', *Straßburger Festschrift zur XLVI. Versammlung deutscher Philologen* (Strasbourg, 1901), pp. 143 f.
—— *Werden und Wesen der Humanität im Altertum*. Strasbourg, 1907.
—— 'Die Idee des Principats bei Cicero und Augustus', *NGG* for 1917, pp. 399 f. and 481 f.
Renard, M. 'L'Assassinat de Scipion Émilien', *RUB* 37 (1931–2), pp. 483 f.
Romanelli, P. *Storia delle province romane dell'Africa*. Rome, 1959.
Rossetti, S. 'La Numidia e Cartagine fra la II e la III guerra punica', *PP* 15 (1960), pp. 336 f.
Saumagne, C. 'Les Prétextes juridiques de la IIIᵉ guerre punique', *RH* 167 (1931), pp. 225 f., and 168 (1931), pp. 1 f.
Schmekel, A. *Die Philosophie der mittleren Stoa*. Berlin, 1892.
Schulten, A. *Numantia*, i and iii. Munich, 1914 and 1927.
—— *Geschichte von Numantia*. Munich, 1933.
—— 'Viriatus', *NJA* 39 (1917), pp. 209 f.
Scullard, H. H. *Roman Politics, 220–150 B.C.* Oxford, 1951.
—— 'Roman Politics', *BICS* 2 (1955), pp. 15 f.
—— 'Scipio Aemilianus and Roman Politics', *JRS* 50 (1960), pp. 59 f.
—— *See also* F. B. Marsh.
Seyrig, H. *Notes on Syrian Coins*. American Numismatic Society Notes and Monographs, no. 119. New York, 1950.
Simon, H. *Roms Kriege in Spanien, 154—133 v. Chr.* Frankfurt am Main, 1962.
Sinclair, T. A. *A History of Greek Political Thought*. London, 1951.
Smith, R. E. *The Failure of the Roman Republic*. Cambridge, 1955.
—— *Service in the Post-Marian Roman Army*. Manchester, 1958.
van Straaten, M. *Panétius*. Amsterdam, 1946.
—— *Panaetii Rhodii Fragmenta³*. Leiden, 1962.

STRASBURGER, H. 'Poseidonios on Problems of the Roman Empire', *JRS* 55 (1965), pp. 40 f.

STUART, M. 'Pliny, *Historia Naturalis*, xxxi, 41', *AJPh* 64 (1943), pp. 440 f.

—— 'P. Oxyrhynchus 668. 188–90', *CPh* 39 (1944), pp. 40 f.

—— 'The Denarius of M'. Aemilius Lepidus and the Aqua Marcia', *AJA* 49 (1945), pp. 226 f.

TAEGER, F. *Tiberius Gracchus*. Stuttgart, 1928.

TATAKIS, B. N. *Panétius de Rhodes*. Paris, 1931.

TAYLOR, L. R. *The Voting Districts of the Roman Republic*. Rome, 1960.

—— 'Forerunners of the Gracchi', *JRS* 52 (1962), pp. 19 f.

—— 'Was Tiberius Gracchus' Last Assembly Electoral or Legislative?', *Athenaeum* 41 (1963), pp. 51 f.

THOMSEN, R. 'Erließ Tiberius Gracchus ein Iustitium?', *C & M* 6 (1944), pp. 60 f.

TIBILETTI, G. 'Il possesso dell'*ager publicus* e le norme *de modo agrorum* sino ai Gracchi', *Athenaeum* 26 (1948), pp. 173 f., and 27 (1949), pp. 3 f.

—— 'Ricerche di storia agraria romana', *Athenaeum* 28 (1950), pp. 183 f.

—— 'Le leggi *de iudiciis repetundarum* fino alla guerra sociale', *Athenaeum* 31 (1953), pp. 5 f.

TRAVERSA, A. *Index Stoicorum Herculanensis*. Genoa, 1952.

VALGIGLIO, E. *Plutarco. Vita dei Gracchi*. Rome, 1957.

DE VISSCHER, F. 'La Deditio internationale et l'affaire des Fourches Caudines', *CRAI* for 1946, pp. 82 f.

VOGT, J. *Struktur der antiken Sklavenkriege*. Mainz, 1957.

WALBANK, F. W. *A Historical Commentary on Polybius*, i. Oxford, 1957.

—— 'Polybius and the Roman State', *GRBS* 5 (1964), pp. 239 f.

—— 'Political Morality and the Friends of Scipio', *JRS* 55 (1965), pp. 1 f.

—— *See also* C. O. Brink.

WALSH, P. G. *Livy. His Historical Aims and Methods*. Cambridge, 1961.

—— 'Massinissa', *JRS* 55 (1965), pp. 149 f.

WILKINS, A. S. *M. Tulli Ciceronis De Oratore Libri Tres*. Oxford, 1892.

WIRSZUBSKI, C. *Libertas as a Political Idea at Rome during the Late Republic and Early Principate*. Cambridge, 1950.

ZANCAN, L. 'Le cause della terza guerra punica', *AIV* 95, Pt. 2 (1935–6), pp. 529 f.

INDEX

THIS index is intended to provide a reasonably full and useful guide, principally to proper names, but of necessity the entries are to some extent selective. Men of consular rank are designated by the date of the first consulship only.

ISBN 0–19–	Author	Title
8264011	ALEXANDER Paul J.	The Patriarch Nicephorus of Constantinople
8143567	ALFÖLDI A.	The Conversion of Constantine and Pagan Rome
9241775	ALLEN T.W	Homeri Ilias (3 volumes)
6286409	ANDERSON George K.	The Literature of the Anglo-Saxons
8219601	ARNOLD Benjamin	German Knighthood
8208618	ARNOLD T.W.	The Caliphate
8142579	ASTIN A.E.	Scipio Aemilianus
8144059	BAILEY Cyril	Lucretius: De Rerum Natura (3 volumes)
814167X	BARRETT W.S.	Euripides: Hippolytos
8228813	BARTLETT & MacKAY	Medieval Frontier Societies
8219733	BARTLETT Robert	Trial by Fire and Water
8118856	BENTLEY G.E.	William Blake's Writings (2 volumes)
8111010	BETHURUM Dorothy	Homilies of Wulfstan
8142765	BOLLING G. M.	External Evidence for Interpolation in Homer
814332X	BOLTON J.D.P.	Aristeas of Proconnesus
9240132	BOYLAN Patrick	Thoth, the Hermes of Egypt
8114222	BROOKS Kenneth R.	Andreas and the Fates of the Apostles
8214715	BUCKLER Georgina	Anna Comnena
8203543	BULL Marcus	Knightly Piety & Lay Response to the First Crusade
8216785	BUTLER Alfred J.	Arab Conquest of Egypt
8148046	CAMERON Alan	Circus Factions
8143516	CAMERON Alan	Claudian
8148054	CAMERON Alan	Porphyrius the Charioteer
8148348	CAMPBELL J.B.	The Emperor and the Roman Army 31 BC to 235
826643X	CHADWICK Henry	Priscillian of Avila
826447X	CHADWICK Henry	Boethius
8222025	COLGRAVE B. & MYNORS R.A.B.	Bede's Ecclesiastical History of the English People
8131658	COOK J.M.	The Troad
8219393	COWDREY H.E.J.	The Age of Abbot Desiderius
8241895	CROMBIE A.C.	Robert Grosseteste and the Origins of Experimental Science 1100–1700
8644043	CRUM W.E.	Coptic Dictionary
8148992	DAVIES M.	Sophocles: Trachiniae
814153X	DODDS E.R.	Plato: Gorgias
825301X	DOWNER L.	Leges Henrici Primi
814346X	DRONKE Peter	Medieval Latin and the Rise of European Love-Lyric
8142749	DUNBABIN T.J.	The Western Greeks
8154372	FAULKNER R.O.	The Ancient Egyptian Pyramid Texts
8221541	FLANAGAN Marie Therese	Irish Society, Anglo-Norman Settlers, Angevin Kingship
8143109	FRAENKEL Edward	Horace
8142781	FRASER P.M.	Ptolemaic Alexandria (3 volumes)
8201540	GOLDBERG P.J.P.	Women, Work and Life Cycle in a Medieval Economy
8140215	GOTTSCHALK H.B.	Heraclides of Pontus
8266162	HANSON R.P.C.	Saint Patrick
8581351	HARRIS C.R.S	The Heart and Vascular System in Ancient Greek Medicine
8224354	HARRISS G.L.	King, Parliament and Public Finance in Medieval England to 1369
8581114	HEATH Sir Thomas	Aristarchus of Samos
8140444	HOLLIS A.S.	Callimachus: Hecale
8212968	HOLLISTER C. Warren	Anglo-Saxon Military Institutions
9244944	HOPKIN-JAMES L.J.	The Celtic Gospels
8226470	HOULDING J.A.	Fit for Service
2115480	HENRY Blanche	British Botanical and Horticultural Literature before 1800
8219523	HOUSLEY Norman	The Italian Crusades
8223129	HURNARD Naomi	The King's Pardon for Homicide – before AD 1307
9241783	HURRY Jamieson B.	Imhotep
8140401	HUTCHINSON G.O.	Hellenistic Poetry
9240140	JOACHIM H.H.	Aristotle: On Coming-to-be and Passing-away
9240094	JONES A.H.M	Cities of the Eastern Roman Provinces
8142560	JONES A.H.M.	The Greek City
8218354	JONES Michael	Ducal Brittany 1364–1399
8271484	KNOX & PELCZYNSKI	Hegel's Political Writings
8212755	LAWRENCE C.H.	St Edmund of Abingdon
8225253	LE PATOUREL John	The Norman Empire
8212720	LENNARD Reginald	Rural England 1086–1135
8212321	LEVISON W.	England and the Continent in the 8th century
8148224	LIEBESCHUETZ J.H.W.G.	Continuity and Change in Roman Religion
8143486	LINDSAY W.M.	Early Latin Verse
8141378	LOBEL Edgar & PAGE Sir Denys	Poetarum Lesbiorum Fragmenta
9240159	LOEW E.A.	The Beneventan Script
8115881	LOOMIS Roger Sherman	Arthurian Literature in the Middle Ages
8241445	LUKASIEWICZ Jan	Aristotle's Syllogistic
8152442	MAAS P. & TRYPANIS C.A .	Sancti Romani Melodi Cantica
8113692	MANDEVILLE Bernard	The Fable of the Bees (2 volumes)
8142684	MARSDEN E.W.	Greek and Roman Artillery—Historical
8142692	MARSDEN E.W.	Greek and Roman Artillery—Technical
8148178	MATTHEWS John	Western Aristocracies and Imperial Court AD 364–425
9240205	MAVROGORDATO John	Digenes Akrites
8223447	McFARLANE K.B.	Lancastrian Kings and Lollard Knights
8226578	McFARLANE K.B.	The Nobility of Later Medieval England
814296X	MEIGGS Russell	The Athenian Empire
8148100	MEIGGS Russell	Roman Ostia
8148402	MEIGGS Russell	Trees and Timber in the Ancient Mediterranean World
8141718	MERKELBACH R. & WEST M.L.	Fragmenta Hesiodea
8143362	MILLAR F.G.B.	Cassius Dio
8142641	MILLER J. Innes	The Spice Trade of the Roman Empire